Learn Beginner and Intermediate Spanish for Adults

Speak Spanish In 30 Days!

5 Books in 1

Explore to Win

THIS COLLECTION INCLUDES THE FOLLOWING BOOKS:

Complete Spanish Workbook For Adult Beginners:
Essential Spanish Words And Phrases You Must Know

Learn Spanish for Adult Beginners Handbook:
Your Proven Guide to Speaking Spanish in 30 Days!

Learn Spanish with Short Stories for Adult Beginners:
Shortcut Your Spanish Fluency! (Fun & Easy Reads)

Learn Intermediate Spanish for Adults Workbook:
Go from Spanish Beginner to Intermediate in 30 Days!

Learn Intermediate Spanish with Short Stories for Adults
Shortcut Your Spanish Fluency! (Fun & Easy Reads)

Table of Contents

BOOK 1

Complete Spanish Workbook
for Adult Beginners

Essentials Spanish Words and Phrases You Need to Know

Explore to Win

Book 1 Description

How amazing would it feel if learning conversational Spanish came naturally to you?

Learning a brand new language, especially Spanish, can seem extremely daunting for students. Unfortunately, 80% of students give up before ever becoming conversationally fluent in Spanish... which means they'll never be able to unlock and experience all the amazing social treasures the language provides.

It's not the students who are to blame though, in actuality, it is the majority of Spanish language products on the market today. Most learning guides and workbooks will carelessly dispense a dizzyingly disorganized list of Spanish words in front of you like lottery numbers and expect that to be enough to sow the seeds of conversational fluency.

This is why we teamed up with a world-class Spanish coach—who is responsible for teaching celebrities, politicians, and over 1,000+ students Spanish quickly, acing their assessments and surpassing all their goals—to bring you this ultimate Spanish workbook - consciously curated to make you conversational, fast!

In order to transform your Spanish speaking capabilities, this workbook includes very specific elements inside, such as:

- A comprehensive, organized guide of essential words you'll use in EVERYDAY conversation. This isn't just a random list of scattered words—these carefully selected words will be the bread & butter of the vocabulary you'll use in 80% of your conversations. Accompanied by a brief definition, contextual example, and a phonetic pronunciation aid for each word, so you can employ them in action immediately.

- Punch-packing phrases that you can quickly whip out to convey your message and be understood by others quickly and clearly... every single time. Your days of being misunderstood by Spanish speakers, and not being considered 'one of them' will be over once and for all when you begin to include these practical phrases in your Spanish arsenal.

- Exclusive activities and carefully crafted quizzes thoughtfully plugged in by a world-class language coach to help you RETAIN the plethora of Spanish secrets held inside this guide. What separates successful students from unsuccessful students is their ability to retain what they have learned. This workbook will guarantee your place in the first group... even with no prior Spanish education.

- A vast array of categories are conveniently arranged for your ease of access, ranging from 'Restaurants & Bars' to 'Business & Work'. Learn to wield your Spanish skills effectively in all contexts; double down and master one area or both. The choice is entirely yours and with the freedom within this workbook, you can't make any mistakes.

The benefits of learning Spanish are truly mind-blowing; it gives you the tools you need to boost your happiness exponentially, keep your brain sharp with your memory intact, and enrich all aspects of your life—especially socializing! The good news is you can get started now, and enjoy all these benefits simply by cracking open the covers of this book.

Never again will you have to worry about being one of those students that have a difficult time comprehending Spanish and eventually just give up. Instead, do yourself a favor by opening your mind to all the amazing benefits Spanish will have on your life, by purchasing your copy of this, the ultimate Spanish workbook, today!

Introduction

Imagine you're on a vacation with your family in a native Spanish-speaking country. You're all enjoying a beautiful beach when a waiter approaches you to take your order. His English isn't the best, so there's bound to be issues ordering the food and beverages without mistakes. Are you able to take control of the conversation in Spanish to communicate exactly what you want? Can you provide the meal your family desires without problems or miscommunication?

Spanish is easily one of the most important languages in the modern era. With more than 500 million Spanish speakers around the world, it's no wonder that so many people are interested and willing to learn this beautiful language. It's relevant for business conversations, traveling, and often even small talk in your hometown. There are plenty of cultural products in Spanish such as books, movies, and music that can only be truly enjoyed with a good understanding of the Spanish language. This means that there's a good portion of the world that you're missing just by being unable to have a conversation in Spanish, which is what brought you to this book in the first place. You need a fast and reliable way to learn Spanish, and this book has been designed for you.

By going through the following chapters, you'll learn everything that you need to have casual conversations, be productive in a professional environment, understand written Spanish texts, and handle yourself while visiting a Spanish-speaking country. The knowledge in these pages has been structured and reinforced with examples and exercises in order to make sure it's cemented in your brain. You'll know how to speak Spanish for the rest of your life; and if you happen to forget minor details, its simple design will help you navigate the book with ease and revise whatever knowledge you need to refresh.

Without a doubt, learning a new language is one of the best things we can do, since it will not only help us to expand our knowledge more and more, but it will also be very helpful for any occasion that we have it. Similarly, in terms of work, learning such a popular language is one of the best things we can do for our career, as it will help us further expand our resume, and thus be able to have many new job opportunities. It is confirmed that bilingual people have many more opportunities in today's world of work, especially considering that we live in a world that has gone through a process of globalization, which means that the vast majority of companies need proactive people who are able to communicate in other languages. Many people believe that learning a language is only for when we go on vacation or something, but the truth is that this has countless short-term and long-term benefits for us, apart from the fact that learning a language is also a lot of fun.

Every day that you spend without learning Spanish is a day further away from your goal. Tomorrow you could find yourself in a situation where a couple of Spanish phrases will be the difference between making a good or a bad impression. This book promises to prepare you for these sorts of situations. All you need to do is go through the chapters in order, pay attention, and do the activities. You already know why you should do it, and you have the way to do it in front of you, all that's left for you now is to take the first step with the following chapter.

Chapter 1: Learning a New Language

Most people around the world are constantly looking for a way to be a more complete person, and of course, more intelligent. Learning a new language is one of the easiest and most wonderful ways we have to strengthen our personal growth, as well as to add much more knowledge to our minds. However, when we take care of learning to speak a language as popular and wonderful as Spanish, this becomes even more interesting, since it is not only a language that will serve us for the two things that we mentioned above but also will serve us in many other aspects of our lives since this is one of the most widely spoken languages in the world. Of course, we all know that English is the universal language, and therefore the most important of all.

However, there are more than 460 million native speakers of Spanish in the world, which tells us about the enormous importance of learning a language as popular as this one. In fact, Spanish is the most learned language throughout the universities in the United States, since numerous statistics show that more than 50% of American students choose to learn to speak Spanish every year, a figure that is undoubtedly enormous. There are many people who believe that Spanish is only spoken in South American countries, but the truth is that it is spoken in many other countries around the world.

Of course, South America is the continent where Spanish is spoken the most since all of its countries (with the exception of Brazil and Guyana) have Spanish as their official language. In addition, in some other countries such as Mexico, the Dominican Republic, Puerto Rico, Cuba, and Spain, Spanish is also spoken as the official language. Each of these countries has a different way of adapting Spanish since even in many of those countries, such as Spain, there are other unofficial alternative languages that are spoken in certain provinces. The point is that Spanish is a language spoken in many countries, so learning this wonderful language will bring us numerous advantages, regardless of the main reason why we are learning it.

For example, there are many people who want to speak Spanish for work reasons, since this would allow them to expand their resume and access many more opportunities in the business world, especially if we take into account that today we live in a world so globalized and dynamic where all business is done globally. In the same way, there are many other people who only want to learn to speak Spanish as a form of self-improvement, since they know that in this way they will expand their knowledge even more, just as they will be able to exercise their brain in various cognitive areas. like memory, multitasking, and many other things. The point is that no matter the reason why we are learning Spanish since this is going to be very useful to us in many aspects of our lives, therefore, the main objective of this book is that we can learn everything necessary to develop an excellent level of Spanish, on par with that of a native speaker.

The pace of learning of people is not the same, it depends on the capabilities of each one, our dedication, and our motivations. Learning Spanish, like any other language, can be simple and fun if we adapt the method to the way each of us learns. To speak a language well it is necessary to invest a certain amount of time. Once the base is acquired and the fear of ridicule is overcome, everything will go much faster. Set yourself small challenges, reward yourself for achievements, and above all, enjoy your progress. This means that we cannot pretend to learn to speak a language perfectly in a matter of a few days, since it requires a lot of effort, motivation, and dedication.

A Little Bit of History

Like most of the languages we know today, Spanish is a language that was born from Common Latin (also known as Vulgar Latin). This language was born thousands of years ago in the Iberian Peninsula, which today is a region that is part of Spain and Portugal. However, it was not until the year 1200 that this language began to become popular in Spain and, basically, little by little it became the official language of that country, which was the first to make it its official language.

In fact, different versions of the language began to be formed in that country, since not only was Castilian spoken (which is the most common way of speaking Spanish) but Andalusian and Catalan were also formed.

Hundreds of years later, at the time of colonization, Spain was the country that was in charge of discovering and conquering most of the countries of America. That is why from the year 1600, this language began to be quite popular in countries such as Venezuela, Colombia, Ecuador, Argentina, Bolivia, Peru, Chile, Uruguay, and many other countries on the continent. Little by little this language was mixed among the natives until it became the official language a few years after each of those countries.

However, despite being the country where this language originated and being the country that made it popular throughout the world, today Spain has less than 10% of all Spanish-speaking people, which undoubtedly speaks of the extensive growth and expansion that this language has had throughout the world.

Tips to Learn a New Language

There are many methods and ways that will help us speed up this entire learning process and make it much more comfortable. In this way, we will be able to feel much more satisfied throughout this process, so that in this way we make sure to learn each of these topics perfectly. One of those methods that we can use is to read books or articles in Spanish. When we read, we not only expand our knowledge, but we will also become aware of many grammatical structures and new words that will help us carry out this learning process in the best possible way. That is why it is always recommended to read in Spanish so that we can learn to pronounce each of the words that we see, just as we learn each of the grammatical structures that we are going to see throughout this book.

Another way in which we can accelerate this learning process is by listening to music in Spanish. This is not only a good learning method, but we are also going to be able to have a lot of fun and be able to learn some of the slang and popular words that are said daily in Spanish.

The good thing is that today music in Spanish is quite popular around the world, as well as some podcasts that we can listen to, enjoy and take advantage of to learn some of the most important things about this incredible language. Finally, we can also practice watching movies entirely in Spanish, and putting the subtitles in English. In this way, we are going to make sure that we understand everything that they are saying in the film and that we can understand the way in which people commonly speak to you in Spanish.

However, the method that has been proven throughout history as the most effective when it comes to consolidating ourselves speaking a new language is to practice with another person who also knows how to speak Spanish or is learning. If it is a person who already knows how to speak perfect Spanish, it will be excellent since we are going to have a person who can correct our mistakes when pronouncing or writing something, as well as tell us some of the easiest ways in which we can learn certain grammatical structures. Similarly, when we talk to a person who already knows how to speak Spanish perfectly, we are going to be practicing various factors such as listening and speaking, which are often the most difficult to master.

If we practice with a person who, like us, is just learning the language, then we will also have the advantage that we will not feel sorry if we make a mistake or make a mistake, since we know that this is likely to happen to them as well. to the other person. Through this method, we can also encourage each other to continue learning all the wonders of this language that undoubtedly has a lot to offer us, and that has shown that if we put all our efforts we can achieve incredible things in a very short time. The important thing is that we are not afraid of making mistakes because although none of us is perfect, we can all learn the wonders of this language much easier than we imagine.

Never Stop Learning

When we commit to learning a new language, the process is similar to when we first got married. In other words, we will have to make a commitment that lasts for our entire lives, since a language is not learned in a matter of days, but rather requires a lot of practice and experience over the years. When learning a new language, especially one as complex as Spanish, we must be willing to spend several hours a day practicing and be willing to do everything necessary so that each of the things we learn remains engraved in our memory forever. permanently. Many people learn languages at school, university, or even when they are just children, but over time they forget everything they learned.

This is because the languages must be practiced on a regular basis, and if possible, every day of the week. Practicing a language takes only a few minutes a day, especially if we use any of the methods that we saw in the previous section since they can help us achieve great things and learn much faster. People often believe that to learn a new language it is necessary that we have a lot of free time and that we spend all day practicing and studying when the truth is that just a few minutes a day are enough for us to learn a language permanently. and in a perfect way, as long as we maintain a high level of discipline and perseverance throughout the process since otherwise, everything will be in vain.

It's Not Easy, but It's Not Impossible

Many times people believe that Spanish is very difficult since it has some grammatical structures that are quite complex, and above all that sentences are usually much longer than those formed in English. However, it is important that we know that for many people English is the most difficult language because, despite the fact that it is a language that seems quite simple, it has certain things that can be very complex for the person who is learning. The most important thing is that we must know that learning to speak Spanish perfectly is not something impossible since all the people in this world have the ability to learn to speak a new language in a matter of a few months. The problem is that not all people are willing to invest in their education, as well as in taking the time to study and practice each of the things that we are going to learn in this book.

We must always keep a long-term vision and think about all the benefits that we will obtain once we have completely mastered this language since this will bring us many good things in life. Of course, this process is not easy, since it involves many aspects in which we will have to put our maximum effort and dedication, as well as our maximum potential to learn all these things. That is why I am sure that you will master each of the lessons that we are going to see next, just as you will strive to learn a little every day and thus become a true expert.

Things You Need to Know to Take Advantage of This Book

Throughout this book, we are going to see through the different chapters certain valuable lessons that are going to teach us the most important things that we must learn about Spanish. The good thing is that through these chapters we are not only going to learn the various meanings of some of the most important things in this language, but we are also going to see the exact pronunciations that should be given to each of the words. and phrases that we are learning. That is why, to get the most out of this book, we must make sure to review each of the lessons as many times as necessary, since usually once is not enough to learn perfectly.

In the same way, we must make sure to take note of everything that seems interesting to us, as well as all the things that seem difficult to us, since in this way we can put together a notebook where we put everything that we are learning and So have it on hand in case of any eventuality. Many times what happens to us during reading is that after we read we simply forget about the content, not because we did not want to learn it, but because as we have received so much information there are certain things that can confuse us or remain far behind in our memory. Instead, by taking notes we are going to make sure that each one of those things that we are learning we always have with us, and therefore everything we learn remains in our memory forever.

Another important factor that we must take into account when reading this book is that learning a language is not about translating what we want to say, but about understanding and interpreting everything we are saying, reading, hearing, or writing. so that we can develop this language naturally just as we do with English. All languages are made up of four extremely important factors, which are speaking, writing, listening, and reading. Each of them is extremely important and will help us learn that language perfectly. That is why this book is designed so that we can practice these four factors. Therefore, in addition to reading, we recommend that after each lesson, you write your own examples using the information learned in that lesson.

For example, when we are in the professions lesson, we can write several sentences detailing what we work at and what our parents work at. For the speaking part, it will be very important that after we see the examples, we not only read them but also pronounce them out loud so that we can practice the different forms of pronunciation that each of those phrases and words has. Finally, in the listening part, what we can do is watch a video on YouTube about the lesson we just read in the book, so that we can understand much more and see examples of everyday life in each of the lessons. those lessons.

Best of all is that at the end of the book we will have a short article available that will allow us to read it completely in Spanish. Don't worry, this article will be translated in its entirety so that we can compare each of the grammatical structures that we learned throughout the book and we can perfectly understand its meaning in English. This is one of the most basic but most complete ways we have to learn, so we must take advantage of this article to enhance our level of reading and interpretation in Spanish.

The good thing is that this article will be about something curious about some cities in South America, so that you not only practice Spanish, but you can also learn and have fun with some curiosities of that continent and learn more about its culture. That is why, without a doubt, this book is a complete adventure ideal for all those people who want to learn to speak Spanish once and for all and thus be able to achieve one of their most desired goals.

Also, Remember This is Not a Race

One of the most common mistakes people make when learning a new language, and one of the reasons why so many people end up giving up and abandoning this path, is that they think they will see immediate results. However, we must understand that this whole process is a marathon, and not a 100-meter race like the ones Usain Bolt used to do. This means that one of the keys to learning a new language is to have a lot of patience, otherwise, we will simply never be able to achieve our goals. When we are children, and our parents start talking to us and saying words that they want us to repeat, we do not learn to speak English immediately, but it is also a process of learning, growth, and development that occurs little by little.

That is why we cannot pretend to become experts speaking Spanish in a matter of just a few days since no one has ever achieved something like this. On the other hand, if we have the necessary patience, and above all, we make sure to practice every day, even for half an hour, then without a doubt we will be able to master this wonderful language much faster than we think.

Many times it can be a bit difficult to maintain that level of consistency when we are learning since in our daily routine we also have to study, work, take our children to school, cook, go to the market, and of course, socialize from time to time. when. However, everyone has the same 24 hours a day available, so it is not a valid excuse to say that we do not have time. It all depends on how we distribute our free hours and what we dedicate ourselves to right now. For example, if we only watch Netflix in our free time, then it is very likely that we will not be able to achieve our goals since we will not be dedicating the necessary time to learning.

Of course, each one of us loves to watch a good movie from time to time, but we have to know that there are moments that we have to dedicate to learning Spanish since otherwise we simply will not be able to achieve the objective to master this language perfectly. That is why we must put together a weekly schedule that includes at least half an hour every day, which we are going to dedicate to practicing Spanish. This is the only magic formula that will allow us to learn this language correctly.

The Technique of Shadowing

This is a great method to learn to speak Spanish (or any other language, of course). It is based on a very simple concept: listen and repeat what we have just heard by exactly reproducing the intonations, pauses, etc. That is to say, to act as if we were real parrots. For this, it is important that you know well what you are repeating. If you listen to a song in Spanish, print the lyrics. If you decide to watch a video, look for a subtitled file. He then listened to a phrase, paused, and repeated that process. It may seem like a very simple exercise at first glance, but don't be fooled; it is more complicated than it seems. It is a very effective activity that will allow you to learn by leaps and bounds. This is a method that is often quite underestimated, but that can give us many benefits if we do it consistently.

In the same way, it can be quite effective if you can learn together with a native person from a country where Spanish is spoken. However, if this is not possible, speak to yourself out loud in Spanish and record yourself. Try to think ahead about what words native speakers choose, as well as how they use the language. Also, try to imitate them in pronunciation, intonation, and melody. It may seem a little forced at first, but you think that over time it will help you have a more natural diction. This is a good practice that will only take you 10 minutes a day.

At the same time that you speak in Spanish, you will be recording your day. Plus, you can check your pronunciation later by listening to yourself. Many times, after hearing what we just said, we realize our mistakes so that we can correct them the next time. Also, repetition gives you the opportunity to assess whether you sound the same as a native speaker.

Chapter 2: Basics

We'll go over the fundamental points and words of the English language. Of course, the idea of this book is for us to learn to speak Spanish the right way, but in order to do that, we first need to understand certain fundamental concepts in English, and then we can go from there to learn Spanish or whatever other languages we want to learn. The problem of many people is that they want to learn a new language without having a perfect command of English, which is a problem because if we do not understand certain things in English, then we will not be able to interpret and learn many of the grammatical rules present in the Spanish language.

The good thing is that the vast majority of these things that we are going to see about the English language are things that we use on a daily basis. However, many times we do not realize certain things or certain technicalities since we do it automatically and we are not aware of that type of thing.

Fundamental Differences

As a native English speaker, you'll need to understand these concepts before you start learning Spanish. Little by little, we will realize that Spanish and English are very different in many things, and it is important that we know each of these differences so that we can have a much simpler and more efficient learning process. Knowing all these differences is one of the keys that we will need to learn to speak and understand Spanish perfectly.

Many people believe that they only have to learn to translate a few words and that way they will know how to speak another language, but the truth is that this learning process is much more complex than this, since we must also know each of the grammatical structures involved, as well as certain rules of the language. That is why the objective of this introductory chapter is for us to become much more familiar with this wonderful language.

Nouns Have Gender

English relies on pronouns to convey the gender of a person, but that's not exactly the case in Spanish. In Spanish, not only do people and animals have a gender, but also every other noun. So if you look at a word such as "máscara" (mask), it's feminine, while "cinturón" (belt) is a masculine noun. It's often the case that words that end with "o" or "e" are masculine, and those that end with "a" are feminine. However, there are far too many exceptions to this rule to take it as the only foundation for this rule.

Instead, practice is the only real way to learn the gender of all nouns. You'll learn the gender of any particular noun by paying attention to the articles, adjectives, and participle verbs used around it. These are the groups of words that change with the gender of the noun, and you'll learn about them further in the book.

Diacritic Acute

This is the name of the famous "tilde" (´) you'll see used often in Spanish. You don't need to concern yourself regarding when to use it and not to use it while you're writing; you'll learn this by reading Spanish texts. What you need to understand is that the job of the tilde is to mark the strong syllable of the word. It's true that all words have a strong syllable in their pronunciation, and not all Spanish words have a tilde.

However, this makes it easier to pronounce the words with a tilde, while the main use of the tilde is to differentiate two words that are written the same way but pronounced differently.

Let's see a couple of example words with their pronunciation to illustrate the use of the tilde:

Word	Pronunciation	Translation
Pájaro	PAH-hah-roh	Bird
Canción	Can-SEEOHN	Song
Árbol	AHR-bohl	Tree
Jardín	Har-DEEN	Garden

Punctuation Marks

Unlike English, Spanish uses two interrogation (question) marks (¿?) and/or two exclamation marks (¡!). Questions and exclamations are marked in Spanish from the beginning by an opening punctuation mark (in this case, "¡" for exclamations and "¿" for questions).

Here are two examples of how this would look like, with their respective pronunciations and translations:

¿Qué te gustaría comer?

Keh teh goos-tah-ree-ah coh-mehr

What would you like to eat?

¡Me alegra que estés aquí!

Meh ah-leh-grah keh ehs-tehs ah-kee

I'm glad you're here!

The Alphabet

Unlike letters in English, letters in Spanish are almost always pronounced the same way, especially the vowels. However, their pronunciation, if stable, is still slightly different from English pronunciation.

De igual manera, poco a poco nos vamos a ir dando cuenta que en el alfabeto del idioma español hay algunas letras que no existen en inglés. Por lo general, esas son las letras que generan una dificultad mayor a la hora de pronunciarlas, ya que es normal debido a que las personas nunca las han oído o visto anteriormente. Lo bueno es que de resto no existen diferencias tan abismales entre un alfabeto y otro, por lo que no se nos hará muy difícil poder aprenderlo.

A: Ah, as in "bar."

B: Beh, as in "ball."

C: Seh. It's pronounced like the C in "race" when it precedes I or E. However, it has a hard pronunciation that resembles more the K pronunciation when it precedes A, U, or O (as in "car").

CH: Cheh, as in "cheese." This letter is not always present in the Spanish alphabet.

D: Deh, as in "doll."

E: Eh, as in "get."

F: Eh-feh, as in "fall."

G: Heh, and it has a soft pronunciation and a hard pronunciation. It has a hard pronunciation when it appears before U, O, A, or any consonant, and the pronunciation

resembles that of the G in "good." It has a soft pronunciation that resembles the H in "horn" when it goes before E or I. There's an exception to this rule if the G appears before a U and then an E or an I, the U isn't pronounced and the G takes the hard pronunciation; and in that same case, if the U has an umlaut diaeresis (as "güe" or "güi"), the G still has the hard pronunciation, but the U is no longer silent.

H: Ah-cheh, and it's silent, as in "honor."

I: Ee, as in "think."

J: Hoh-tah, pronounced like the H in "hell."

K: Kah, as in "kebab."

L: Eh-leh, as in "loom." When two Ls are placed together, then it's pronounced like the hard Y in words like "yard."

M: Eh-meh, as in "Moon."

N: Eh-neh, as in "nose."

ñ: Ehn-nee-eh. This letter has no equivalent in the English language, and its pronunciation is difficult for native English speakers. Think about common Spanish words that have it such as "jalapeño" and you'll learn its pronunciation.

O: Oh, as in "boat."

P: Peh, as in "pear."

Q: Coo, and it's pronounced like the hard C, like the C in "car." The Q is always followed by a silent U before the main vowel.

R: Eh-reh, as in "race." When it's placed at the beginning of the word, or when two Rs are placed together, then it takes the pronunciation of the hard Spanish R that's made by rolling the Rs, very similar to the pronunciation of "rage," only stronger. When it's a single R in the middle of the word, then the pronunciation is a soft R, as in "art."

S: Eh-seh, as in "soft."

T: Teh, as in "tea."

U: Oo, as the oo in "good." The exception of this rule is when the U is silent (after a Q or a G without a diaeresis umlaut).

V: Veh, as in "vampire."

W: Doh-bleh beh (which means double v). Words with W in Spanish are adaptations of English words, so it also shares the pronunciation with these words, as it happens with "web."

X: Eh-kees, pronounced like the h in "has."

Y: Yeh, pronounced as a hard Y if it precedes a vowel, as in "yearn." However, if it stands alone, it's pronounced like the Spanish I as EE.

Z: Seh-tah, as in "zoo."

Numbers

Without a doubt, numbers are one of the most basic, yet most important things in any language. We can say that in each of the conversations that we carry out in our day to day, we use numbers, either to indicate some amount, some amount of money, or anything else. This means that when we learn a new language, it is mandatory that we learn the different ways in which numbers should be said. Many times people do not give much importance to this since they believe that it is only enough to write a number numerically.

The truth is that it is also very important that we know the correct way in which we should pronounce ourselves so that we can easily identify them when reading or talking to another person. Not knowing the numbers in Spanish is like wanting to learn to play baseball and not knowing what a bat or a ball is, that is, to learn this wonderful language correctly we have to learn everything we need about numbers. As in English, there are cardinal and ordinal numbers, so below we are going to see some of the main differences between them.

It is also important that we know how to differentiate some key factors between the way of pronouncing numbers between one language and the other. For example, when we are going to talk about the fortune that Elon Musk has, we say that he has 100 Billion dollars.

However, in Spanish we should not say that it has "100 billion dollars," but we say that it has "100 billion dollars." This is a rule that often confuses many people, and it is normal that it generates confusion since the translation is a little different from the way it is used in most Spanish-speaking countries. There are very few differences when we talk about numbers in Spanish and numbers in English.

Cardinal Numbers

In this section we are going to focus on cardinal numbers, which are all those that we use on a daily basis to express some quantity, an amount of money, or something similar. In other words, knowing these numbers is going to help us a lot to express ourselves in a better way, especially in certain situations where we must perfectly master this topic. Let's imagine that we are on vacation with our family, and we want to order a meal in a restaurant. In that case, we must know the numbers in order to be able to order the correct quantity, as well as to be able to ask what the various dishes on the menu cost.

In the same way, we are going to need to know the cardinal numbers for the vast majority of things that we are going to say or ask, especially if we are learning Spanish for work reasons. In the same way, as usual, we are going to have a small section dedicated to the pronunciation of each one of those numbers, so that you not only know how they are written but you can also have a practical guide that helps you in the pronunciation of each one. of those numbers.

Number	Spanish Cardinal Name	Pronunciation
0 CERO	Cero	Seh-roh
1 UNO	Uno	Oo-noh
2 Dos	Dos	Dohs
3 TRES	Tres	Trehs
4 Cuatro	Cuatro	Cooah-troh
5 Cinco	Cinco	Seen-coh
6 SEIS	Seis	Seh-ees
7 SIETE	Siete	See-eh-teh
8 Ocho	Ocho	O-choh
9 NUEVE	Nueve	Nooeh-beh
10 Diez	Diez	Dee-ehs
11 Once	Once	Ohn-seh
12 Doce	Doce	Doh-seh
13 TRECE	Trece	Treh-seh

14 *Cotorce*	Catorce	Cah-tohr-seh
15 *quince*	Quince	Keen-seh
16 *Diecisies*	Dieciséis	Dee-eh-see-seh-ees
17	Diecisiete	Dee-eh-see-eh-teh
18	Dieciocho	Dee-eh-seeoh-choh
19	Diecinueve	Dee-eh-see-nooeh-beh
20	Vcintc	Beh-een-teh
21	Veintiuno	Beh-een-teeoo-noh
22	Veintidós	Beh-een-tee-dohs
23	Veintitrés	Beh-een-tee-trehs
24	Veinticuatro	Beh-een-tee-cooah-troh
25	Veinticinco	Beh-een-tee-seen-coh
26	Veintiséis	Beh-een-tee-seh-ees
27	Veintisiete	Beh-een-tee-see-eh-teh
28	Veintiocho	Beh-een-teeoh-choh
29	Veintinueve	Beh-een-tee-nooeh-beh

30	Treinta	Treh-een-tah
31	Treinta y uno	Treh-een-tah ee oo-noh
32	Treinta y dos	Treh-een-tah ee dohs
33	Treinta y tres	Treh-een-tah ee trehs
40	Cuarenta	Cooah-rehn-tah
50	Sincuenta	Seen-cooehn-tah
60	Sesenta	Seh-sehn-tah
70	Setenta	Seh-tehn-tah
80	Ochenta	Oh-chehn-tah
90	Noventa	Noh-behn-tah
100	Cien	See-ehn
101	Ciento uno	See-ehn-toh oo-noh
200	Doscientos	Dohs-see-ehn-tohs
300	Trescientos	Trehs-see-ehn-tohs
400	Cuatrocientos	Cooah-troh-see-ehn-tohs

500	Quinientos	Kee-nee-ehn-tohs
600	Seiscentos	Seh-ees-see-ehn-tohs
700	Setecientos	Seh-teh-see-ehn-tohs
800	Ochocientos	Oh-choh-see-ehn-tohs
900	Novecientos	Noh-beh-see-ehn-tohs
1.000	Mil	Meel
1.500	Mil quinientos	Meel kee-nee-ehn-tohs
2.000	Dos mil	Dohs meel
100.000	Cien mil	See-ehn meel
150.000	Ciento cincuenta mil	See-ehn-toh seen-cooehn-tah meel
1.000.000	Un millón	Oon mee-yohn

Ordinal Numbers

Ordinal numbers are also important but are used to a lesser extent when compared to cardinal numbers. However, if we are learning this language for work purposes, it is very important that we know everything related to ordinal numbers since they are going to be very important when we talk about processes, positions, or anything else similar. We may not use them as much as the cardinal numbers, but it is still very important that we learn to identify and know the correct way to pronounce each of these numbers.

If we like sports, this is one of the most important things we must learn, since they will always be present in any event or competition of this magnitude.

Number	Spanish Ordinal Name	Pronunciation
1	Primero	Pree-meh-roh
2	Segundo	Seh-goon-doh
3	Tercero	Tehr-seh-roh
4	Cuarto	Cooahr-toh
5	Quinto	Keen-toh
6	Sexto	Sex-toh
7	Séptimo	Sehp-tee-moh
8	Octavo	Ohc-tah-boh
9	Noveno	Noh-beh-noh
10	Décimo	Deh-see-moh

We'll use a couple of example phrases with numbers to help you remember them. Remember, we'll always look at the pronunciation and translation of each Spanish phrase.

Esta es la segunda vez que veo esta película.

Ehs-tah ehs lah seh-goon-dah behs keh beh-oh ehs-tah peh-lee-coo-lah.

This is the second time I have seen this movie.

Ella tiene cinco perros en su casa.

Eh-yah tee-eh-neh seen-coh peh-rros ehn soo cah-sah

She has five dogs at her home.

Hay veinticuatro alumnos en mi clase.

Ah-ee beh-een-tee-cooah-troh ah-loom-nohs ehn mee clah-seh

There are twenty-five students in my class.

Personal Pronouns

Personal pronouns are another of the most important things when learning a language since all of them allow us to be able to refer to people in a correct way and thus they can understand us perfectly. If we don't know all these personal pronouns, then it will be very difficult for us to start a conversation with someone, since we don't know how to address them in conversation. The good thing is that, just like in English, personal pronouns are quite easy to understand and learn, since the vast majority of them are made up of just a few syllables.

Of course, nowadays the subject of personal pronouns has been expanding more and more, but to keep this book easy to understand, we are going to focus only on those traditional personal pronouns. Spanish has slightly more personal pronouns than English.

Pronoun Translation Mode

Yo	Yoh	I	First-person singular
Tú	Too	You	Second person singular
Él	Ehl	He	Third-person singular
Ella	Eh-yah	She	Third-person singular
Eso	Eh-soh	It	Third-person singular
Nosotros	Noh-soh-trohs	We	First-person plural
Ustedes	Oos-teh-dehs	You	Second-person plural
Ellos	Eh-yohs	They	Third-person singular

There's another second person singular pronoun, and it's reserved for formal conversations. The pronoun is "usted," pronounced "oos-ted," and it has its own conjugations.

We'll explore pronouns with a couple of examples:

Yo tomo café sin azúcar.

Yoh toh-moh cah-feh seen ah-soo-cahr.

I drink coffee without sugar.

Ellos viven en este edificio.

Eh-yohs bee-behn ehn ehs-teh eh-dee-fee-seeoh.

They live in this building.

Ella ama comer galletas.

Eh-yah ah-mah coh-mehr gah-yeh-tahs.

She loves eating cookies.

Days of the Week

The days of the week are one of the most important topics in any language since it is impossible for us not to use them every day. The good thing is that the days of the week in Spanish are quite easy to learn, although we must know that, unlike English, the days of the week in Spanish do not have the first letter in capital letters. Unless we are starting a paragraph or a sentence, we must write the entire word in lowercase.

Day	Pronunciation	Translation
Lunes	Loo-nehs	Monday
Martes	Mahr-tehs	Tuesday
Miércoles	Mee-ehr-coh-lehs	Wednesday
Jueves	Hoo-eh-behs	Thursday
Viernes	Bee-ehr-nehs	Friday
Sábado	Sah-bah-doh	Saturday
Domingo	Doh-meen-goh	Sunday

Let's see a couple of examples:

El viernes es mi día favorito de la semana.

Ehl bee-ehr-nehs ehs mee dee-ah fah-boh-ree-toh deh lah seh-mah-nah.

Friday is my favorite day of the week.

El jueves es dos días después del martes.

Ehl hooeh-behs ehs dohs dee-ahs dehs-pooehs dehl mahr-tehs.

Thursday is two days after Tuesday.

Voy a la iglesia todos los domingos.

Boh-ee ah lah ee-gleh-see-ah toh-dohs lohs doh-meen-gohs.

I go to church every Sunday.

Despues - After

Iglesia - Church

Related Definitions

These definitions that we are going to see next do not have so much to do with the days of the week but with expressions of time in which we refer to some moment of the day. In fact, we can say that these four words that we are going to learn next are even more used than the days of the week since we will always need them, no matter what type of conversation we are having.

Day Pronunciation Translation

Day	Pronunciation	Translation
Hoy	Oh-ee	Today
Mañana	Mahn-neeah-nah	Tomorrow
Ayer	Ah-yehr	Yesterday
Pasado mañana	Pah-sah-doh mahn-neeah-nah	Day After Tomorrow

Examples of uses for these terms:

Vamos a la playa mañana.

Bah-mohs ah lah plah-yah mahn-neeah-nah.

Let's go to the beach tomorrow.

Ayer comimos pescado.

Comimos - we ate

Ah-yehr coh-mee-mohs pehs-cah-doh.

Yesterday we ate fish.

The Months of the Year

The months of the year are one of the first things that are learned when one begins the path of learning in another language. Although these are not difficult to learn, we must know in advance that most of the months have a very different pronunciation than how they are said in English, but some months like June, July, February, March, December, October, and November have a different pronunciation. slightly similar pronunciation.

This will help us memorize each of those months in a much faster and more efficient way:

Month	Pronunciation	Translation
Enero	Eh-neh-roh	January
Febrero	Feh-breh-roh	February
Marzo	Mahr-soh	March
Abril	Ah-breel	April
Mayo	Mah-yoh	May
Junio	Hoo-neeoh	June
Julio	Hoo-leeoh	July
Agosto	Ah-gohs-toh	August
Septiembre	Sehp-tee-ehm-breh	September
Octubre	Ohc-too-breh	October
Noviembre	Noh-bee-ehm-breh	November
Diciembre	Dee-see-ehm-breh	December

A couple of phrases of common use within months:

Mi cumpleaños es en diciembre.

Mee coom-pleh-ahn-neeohs ehs ehn dee-see-ehm-breh.

My birthday is in December.

¿Cuánto falta para marzo?

Cooahn-toh fahl-tah pah-rah mahr-soh

How long is it until March?

Yo salgo de vacaciones en julio.

Yoh sahl-goh deh bah-cah-seeoh-nehs ehn hoo-leeoh.

I go on vacation in July.

Cuánto falta - How long (handwritten)

Verb Conjugation

As expected, verbs are one of the fundamental things to know when learning to speak a new language. Wanting to know a new language without learning the verbs is like starting to build a house starting from the roof, that is, it is simply impossible. That is why, below, we are going to see the correct forms in which each of the verbs must be conjugated, so that we know how to express ourselves when we speak using each of these verbs.

Regular verbs in Spanish are divided into three categories:

1. Those that end with "ar,"

2. Those that end with "er," and

3. Those that end with "ir."

These three groups of verbs have slightly different conjugation patterns, which is why it's important to divide them based on their last two letters. In this chapter we'll go over the three main conjugation patterns you'll use for verbs in the present tense.

It's important to point out that only regular verbs will follow this pattern. Irregular verbs, which won't be completely covered in this book, have different pronunciations. In any case, there's no better way to identify and learn the conjugation of irregular verbs than to read Spanish texts, so it's just a matter of time before you get the hang of it.

Verb That Ends With AR

We're going to use the example of the verb "amar" (to love).

Pronoun(s)	Conjugation	Pronunciation	Mode
Yo	Amo	Ah-moh	First-person singular
Tú	Amas	Ah-mahs	Second-person singular
Usted	Ama	Ah-mah	Second-person singular
Él/ Ella/ Eso	Ama	Ah-mah	Third-person singular
Nosotros	Amamos	Ah-mah-mohs	First-person plural
Ustedes	Aman	Ah-mahn	Second-person plural
Ellos / Ellas	Aman	Ah-mahn	Third-person plural

Verbs that End with "ER"

We will use the verb "correr" (to run).

Pronoun(s)	Conjugation	Pronunciation	Mode
Yo	Corro	Coh-rroh	First-person singular
Tú	Corres	Coh-rrehs	Second-person singular
Usted	Corre	Coh-rreh	Second-person singular
Él/ Ella/ Eso	Corre	Coh-rreh	Third-person singular

Nosotros	Corremos	Coh-rreh-mohs	First-person plural
Ustedes	Corren	Coh-rrehn	Second-person plural
Ellos/ Ellas	Corren	Coh-rrehn	Third-person plural

Verbs That End With "IR"

We will use the verb "vivir" (to live).

Pronoun(s)	Conjugation	Pronunciation	Mode
Yo	Vivo	Bee-boh	First-person singular
Tú	Vives	Bee-behs	Second-person singular
Usted	Vive	Bee-beh	Second-person singular
Él/ Ella/ Eso	Vive	Bee-beh	Third-person singular
Nosotros	Vivimos	Bee-bee-mohs	First-person plural
Ustedes	Viven	Bee-behn	Second-person plural
Ellos/ Ellas	Viven	Bee-behn	Third-person plural

Verb to Be

The Spanish language divides the English verb "to be" in two different verbs, "ser," and "estar." "Ser" means "to be" in a sense of identity and stable traits and situations, so it's used to express name, gender, nationality, among other permanent aspects.

Instead, "estar" also means "to be," but expressing a temporary situation, such as location, emotional state, mental state, among other temporary aspects. "Estar" is also the "to be" Spanish verb used to construct progressive time tenses.

"Ser" Simple Present Conjugation

Pronoun(s)	Conjugation	Pronunciation	Mode
Yo	Soy	Soh-ee	First-person singular
Tú	Eres	Eh-rehs	Second-person singular
Usted	Es	Ehs	Second-person singular
Él/ Ella/ Eso	Es	Ehs	Third-person singular
Nosotros	Somos	Soh-mohs	First-person plural
Ustedes	Son	Sohn	Second-person plural

Ellos/ Ellas Son Sohn Third-person plural.

"Estar" Simple Present Conjugation

Pronoun(s)	Conjugation	Pronunciation	Mode
Yo	Estoy	Ehs-toh-ee	First-person singular
Tú	Estás	Ehs-tahs	Second-person singular

Usted	Está	Ehs-tah	Second-person singular
Él/ Ella/ Eso	Está	Ehs-tah	Third-person singular
Nosotros	Estamos	Ehs-tah-mohs	First-person plural
Ustedes	Están	Ehs-tahn	Second-person plural
Ellos/ Ellas	Están	Ehs-tahn	Third-person plural

We'll illustrate the use of both verbs with a couple of examples:

Nosotros estamos cansados de comer arroz.

Noh-soh-trohs ehs-tah-mohs cahn-sah-dohs deh coh-mehr ah-rrohs.

We're tired of eating rice.

Ella es muy buena escritora.

escritora - writer

Eh-yah ehs mooee booeh-nah ehs-cree-toh-rah.

She's a very good writer.

Mi mamá está en el odontólogo.

Mee mah-mah ehs-tah ehn ehl oh-dohn-toh-loh-goh.

My mom is at the dentist.

Yo soy un abogado.

Yoh soh-ee oon ah-boh-gah-doh.

I'm a lawyer.

Verb to Have

As with the verb "to be," the Spanish language divides the verb "to have" into two different verbs "haber" and "tener." Both verbs work for expressing duty and obligation, but "haber" is the one used for verb tenses conjugation, while "tener" is the one used to express possession.

Verb to Do

The Spanish equivalent of the verb "to do" is "hacer," and it's used the same way. This verb mainly expresses actions, as it happens with "to do," however, it's not used to construct questions or conjugate verb tenses.

"Hacer" Simple Present Conjugation

Pronoun(s)	Conjugation	Pronunciation	Mode
Yo	Hago	Ah-goh	First-person singular
Tú	Haces	Ah-sehs	Second-person singular
Usted	Hace	Ah-seh	Second-person singular
Él/ Ella/ Eso	Hace	Ah-seh	Third-person singular
Nosotros	Hacemos	Ah-seh-mohs	First-person plural
Ustedes	Hacen	Ah-sehn	Second-person plural
Ellos/ Ellas	Hacen	Ah-sehn	Third-person plural

Here you'll have a couple of examples of how this verb is used:

Juan hace la tarea todas las tardes.

Hooahn ah-seh lah tah-reh-ah toh-dahs lahs tahr-dehs.

Juan does the homework every afternoon.

Nosotros hacemos quince ejercicios por tarde de entrenamiento.

Noh-soh-trohs ah-seh-mohs keen-seh eh-her-see-seeohs pohr tahr-deh deh ehn-treh-nah-mee-ehn-toh.

We do fifteen exercises per training afternoon.

Él hace la cena mientras yo limpio la sala.

Ehl ah-seh lah seh-nah mee-ehn-trahs yoh leem-peeoh lah sah-lah.

He does dinner while I clean the living room.

Articles

As with English articles, Spanish articles are divided between definite and indefinite articles. As it was explained at the beginning of this chapter, Spanish articles change with the gender of the noun they're affecting. They're also altered by whether the noun is singular or plural.

Definite Articles

The English determinate article is "the," and its equivalents in Spanish are "lo," "la," "los," and "las," depending on the gender and number of the nouns.

Article	Pronunciation	Use
El	Ehl	Masculine singular
La	Lah	Feminine singular
Los	Lohs	Masculine plural
Las	Lahs	Feminine plural

Here are some examples of this:

Los perros.

Lohs peh-rrohs.

The dogs.

Las peras.

Lahs peh-rahs.

The pears.

El piano.

The piano.

La ardilla.

Lah ahr-dee-yah.

The squirrel.

However, even if the noun is feminine, you shall use a masculine article if the noun starts with a strong syllable.

El águila.

Ehl ah-gee-lah

The eagle.

Indefinite Articles

These would be the equivalents of the English words "a" and "an." The Spanish indefinite articles are "un," "una," "unos," and "unas."

Article	Pronunciation	Use
Un	Oon	Masculine singular
Una	Oo-nah	Feminine singular
Unos	Oo-nohs	Masculine plural
Unas	Oo-nahs	Feminine plural

We'll take a look at a couple of examples. As with the definite articles, masculine indefinite articles are to be used with feminine nouns that start with a strong vowel.

Un gato.

Oon gah-toh.

A cat.

Una lagartija.

Oo-nah lah-gahr-tee-hah.

A lizard.

Unos monos.

Oo-nohs moh-nohs.

Some monkeys.

Unas sardinas.

Oo-nahs sahr-dee-nahs.

Some herrings.

Un ábaco.

Oon ah-bah-coh.

An abacus.

Chapter Exercises

Eng/Spa Matching

Match these words in English with their equivalent terms in Spanish.

#	English Term	Letter	Spanish Term
1 D	Monday Lunes	A	Octubre
2 K	Today Hoy	B	Sábado
3 M	March Marzo	C	Eres
4 J	Would Seria	D	Lunes
5 L	Am Soy	E	Mañana
6 N	Church Iglesia	F	Jardín
7 B	Saturday Sabado	G	Cumpleaños
8 C	Are Eres	H	Junio
9 G	Birthday Cumpleaños	I	El

10 **J**	The *EL*	J	Sería	
11 **A**	October *Octubre*	K	Hoy	
12 **O**	Glad *Alegra*	L	Soy	
13 **M**	June *Junio*	M	Marzo	
14 **E**	Tomorrow *Mañana*	N	Iglesia	
15 **F**	Garden *Jardín*	O	Alegra	

Fill in the Blank

Answer the questions by filling in the blanks.

1. Are months in Spanish capitalized? ~~Yes~~ *No*

2. What's the definite article to be used with the word "puerta" (door) in singular?

La

3. What's the conjugation of the verb "to have" for the following sentence: "Ustedes

Tienen que hacer la tarea" (you have to do the homework).

4. How do you say the number 1,005? *Mil cinco*

5. What's the formal equivalent of "you" in Spanish? *Usted*

Translation

Write the Spanish translation of these English phrases.

1. I'll go visit my grandmother next Friday.

2. I want you to hand me that pencil.

3. The eagle is a very large bird.

4. December is my favorite month of the year.

5. They're coming over this Monday.

Chapter 2– Answer Key

The answers for the Eng/Spa Matching exercises are the only ones that are strict. The other answers usually allow some freedom to adapt and rephrase the sentences as long as the core concept is intact.

Eng/Spa Matching

1:D, 2:K, 3:M, 4:J, 5:L, 6:N, 7: B, 8:C, 9:G, 10:I, 11:A, 12:O, 13:H, 14:E, 15:F

Fill in the Blank

1. No, they aren't.

2. La

3. Tienen

4. Mil cinco

5. Usted

Translation

1. Yo iré a visitar a mi abuela el próximo viernes.

2. Quiero que me pases ese lápiz.

3. El águila es un ave muy grande.

4. Diciembre es mi mes favorito del año.

5. Ellos van a venir este lunes.

Next, we are going to see a conversation that includes some of the topics that we have seen in this chapter. Of course, in this chapter, we saw some basic things that we should know whenever we are learning to speak a new language, and that is why we are going to see an informal conversation between two people so that we can see how to introduce each of these phrases and words to our regular conversations. I promise we will see this conversation in Spanish, and then we will see the English translation so that we can identify and learn to interpret each of the things that are being said.

In this way, not only will we learn new words and phrases, but we will also be able to practice reading in Spanish. It would be great if we read this conversation aloud so that it would also help us to practice our speaking and the correct way to pronounce each of those words. This is something that we are going to see in each of the chapters in order to strengthen the knowledge that we have acquired through each of the contents that we are learning. We must always remember that when we learn a new language, the key is always to practice as much as we can, otherwise, the effort we make will be in vain.

A Typical Conversation in Spanish

Juan: Voy a ir al juego de béisbol la semana que viene con mi papá

Kike: Me alegra mucho oír eso Juan, yo creo que también voy a ir a ese juego, aunque aún no estoy muy seguro. Estuve averiguando y los precios son un poco elevados, pero voy a intentar a ver si consigo alguna opción que sea barata.

Handwritten annotations: "Think" above "creo"; "Although" above "aunque"; "sure" under "seguro"; "I was" under "Estuve"; "options" under "opción".

Juan: Nosotros teníamos el mismo problema, todos los tickets que había estaban un poco caros. Lo que hicimos fue buscar algunas ofertas en internet y pudimos conseguir un precio especial.

Kike: Excelente, creo que también haré eso para así poder ir al juego con mi papá, es un gran fanatico del béisbol. Lo qué pasa es que el siempre tiene que trabajar los días de semana, pero lo intentaré convencer a ver si quiere ir al juego el sábado.

Juan: Nosotros pudimos comprar las entradas a 200 dólares, y la verdad es que considero que es un precio bastante alto. Sin embargo, mi papá se va de viaje el mes que viene y esta era nuestra última oportunidad de poder ir a un juego de béisbol.

Kike: ¿A qué parte se va tu papá de viaje? ¿Va por cuestiones de trabajo?

Juan: Si, va por cuestiones de trabajo dos semanas a México. Específicamente va a Guadalajara, ya que es allí en donde queda la empresa en la que trabaja.

Kike: He oído que México es un país bastante lindo, y que hay muchas cosas turísticas que son bastante interesantes y valen la pena conocer. Sin duda alguna tu papá se va a divertir muchísimo en México.

Juan: No me quedan dudas de que se va a divertir mucho. Lo único malo es que son aproximadamente 12 horas de viaje, y a mi papá no le gustan mucho los aviones porque le da miedo. Siempre prefiere viajar en carro o en bote.

Kike: Los aviones también me daban miedo cuando era niño, pero luego fui aprendiendo que hay muchas más posibilidades de tener un accidente en un carro o en un bote, así que no tengo dudas de que tu papá va a disfrutar mucho ese viaje.

Translation

Juan: I'm going to the baseball game next week with my dad.

Kike: I'm very happy to hear that Juan, I think I'm going to go to that game too, although I'm not sure yet. I've been researching and the prices are a bit high, but I'm going to try and see if I can find an option that is cheap.

Juan: We had the same problem, all the tickets that were available were a bit expensive. What we did was look for some deals on the internet and we were able to get a special price.

Kike: Great, I think I'll do that too so I can go to the game with my dad, who's a big baseball fan. What happens is that he always has to work on weekdays, but I will try to convince him to see if he wants to go to the game on Saturday.

Juan: We were able to buy the tickets for 200 dollars, and the truth is that I consider it to be quite a high price. However, my dad is going on a trip next month and this was our last chance to get to a baseball game.

Kike: Where is your dad going on a trip? Are you going for work reasons?

Juan: Yes, he goes to Mexico for two weeks for work reasons. Specifically, he goes to Guadalajara, since that is where the company where he works is located.

Kike: I've heard that Mexico is a pretty beautiful country and that there are many tourist things that are quite interesting and worth knowing. Without a doubt, your dad is going to have a lot of fun in Mexico.

Juan: I have no doubt that he is going to have a lot of fun. The only bad thing is that it's about a 12-hour drive, and my dad doesn't really like planes because they're scary. He always prefers to travel by car or by boat.

Kike: Planes also scared me when I was a child, but then I learned that there are many more chances of having an accident in a car or on a boat, so I have no doubt that your dad will enjoy that trip a lot.

Chapter 3: Small Talk and Normal Conversations

Throughout this chapter, we are going to review all those things that we are going to need to carry out a daily conversation. In other words, in this section, we are going to cover all those things that are necessary to be able to speak and understand other people in a clear and fluid way. Without a doubt, there is nothing more uncomfortable than not being able to communicate the way we want because we don't know what the other person is saying or because we simply can't find ways to communicate. That is why this is probably the most important chapter of the book as we are going to learn things of daily use. Of course, the other chapters are also of great importance and all the contents included in these chapters are also necessary.

However, everything that we are going to see in this chapter is things that we will always need, regardless of the circumstances in which our conversation with another person takes place. This is because we are not only going to use all this knowledge in conversations, but it will also be useful when we do a reading in Spanish, watch a movie, listen to a song, a podcast, or anything else that requires our knowledge of the Spanish language. Best of all, most of these things can be learned easily, as long as we have the necessary level of discipline to learn all these things and practice them as many times as necessary since we must remember that if we do not take care of practically everything we learn then we are going to end up forgetting all that very quickly.

Ideally, we could have another person who also speaks Spanish in order to practice in a much more fluid way. However, we know that this is not always easy, so we are also going to review some of the ways in which we can practice all these topics that we will see below in our day-to-day. One of those simple ways to practice Spanish on a daily basis is by reading. We all know how wonderful books are and all the wisdom that we can acquire from each of them, however, when we read in Spanish we will also be learning many new words, grammatical structures, verbs, and many other things that will help us a lot in our learning process.

In the same way, we can listen to songs in Spanish, which will also help us a lot to understand the way in which Spanish speakers normally express themselves. Also, while we are learning we are going to be having fun and learning about a new culture. Finally, we can try watching a movie in Spanish. In this way, we will be able to put the subtitles in English, and thus understand each of the things that he is saying in the film. Of course, it will not be easy at first, but little by little we will get used to it and do it in a much more natural way. All these methods will help us to practice all the topics and contents that we are going to see in this chapter so that we can learn them perfectly.

Past Tense

We'll cover the preterite imperfect of the indicative conjugations, and the preterite indefinite of the indicative conjugations. The first group is used to describe past events that have no clear beginning or end; on the other hand, the second group is used for exactly the opposite.

These are terms related to the weather and its expressions:

Term	Pronunciation	Translation
Soleado	Soh-leh-ah-doh	Sunny
Lluvia	Yoo-beeah	Rain
Llovizna	Yoh-bees-nah	Drizzle
Granizo	Grah-nee-soh	Hail
Cálido	Cah-lee-doh	Warmth
Frío	Freeoh	Cold
Calor	Cah-lohr	Heat
Nublado	Noo-blah-doh	Cloudy
Tormenta	Tohr-mehn-tah	Storm
Trueno	Trooeh-noh	Thunder
Nevada	Neh-bah-dah	Snowfall

Here are some example phrases about weather:

Me gusta más el frío que el calor.

Meh goos-tah mahs ehl free-oh keh ehl cah-lohr.

I like the cold more than the heat.

Nos encantan los días nublados.

Nohs ehn-cahn-tahn lohs dee-ahs noo-blah-dohs.

We love cloudy days.

Él odia las tormentas.

Hate

37

Ehl oh-deeah lahs tohr-mehn-tahs.

He hates storms.

Colors

This may be one of the easiest topics to learn in the entire book since we only have to memorize them and there are no rules or grammatical structures to learn. In fact, we may already know some of these colors because we have heard them in a song, heard them on the radio, seen them in a magazine, or something similar. Of course, in order not to make this section tedious and pointless, we are only going to focus on the main colors, since they are the ones that we probably need to use in a sentence or in a conversation.

Color Pronunciation Translation

Color	Pronunciation	Translation
Rojo	Roh-hoh	Red
Azul	Ah-sool	Blue
Blanco	Blahn-coh	White
Negro	Neh-groh	Black
Verde	Behr-deh	Green
Amarillo	Ah-mah-ree-yoh	Yellow
Marrón	Mah-rrohn	Brown
Púrpura	Poor-poo-rah	Purple
Violeta	Beeoh-leh-tah	Violet
Rosado	Roh-sah-doh	Pink
Anaranjado	Ah-nah-rahn-hah-doh	Orange

With some examples of how to use these terms in Spanish:

El amarillo te queda muy bien.

Ehl ah-mah-ree-yoh teh keh-dah mooee bee-ehn.

Yellow suits you.

Mi bolso es el negro.

Mee bohl-soh ehs ehl neh-groh.

My bag is the black one.

Deberíamos pintar la casa de azul.

Deh-beh-ree-ah-mohs peen-tahr lah cah-sah deh ah-sool.

We should paint the house blue.

Presentations

Presentations are always going to be important in whatever language we are communicating in. This is because there will be many occasions where we arrive at places where we do not know anyone and we have to introduce ourselves. However, introducing ourselves is not just saying our names, but many times we also add extra information such as our age, our occupation, if we have children or partners, and all that. Similarly, there will be many occasions when the opposite happens. That is, there will be times when we have to ask someone else to introduce themselves so that we can get to know them better and learn more about that person.

That is why if we do not know how to express ourselves in terms of presentations, it will be very difficult for us to meet new people or to reach a place where we do not know anyone and function correctly. That's why we'll go over phrases we use when we want to present ourselves, to present someone else, or ask someone to present themselves.

Presenting Oneself

Saludos, mi nombre es Carlos.

Sah-loo-dohs mee nohm-breh ehs cahr-lohs.

Greetings, my name is Carlos.

Yo soy de Brasil.

Yoh soh-ee deh brah-seel.

I come from Brazil.

Yo tengo treinta años de edad.

Yoh tehn-goh treh-een-tah ahn-neeohs deh eh-dahd.

I am thirty years old

Yo soy un contador.

Yoh soh-ee oon cohn-tah-dohr.

I'm an accountant.

Yo estoy casado y tengo dos hijos.

Yoh ehs-toh-ee cah-sah-doh ee tehn-goh dohs hee-hos.

I'm married and have two kids.

Presenting Another Person

Saludos, él se llama Andrés.

Sah-loo-dohs ehl seh yah-mah ahn-drehs.

Greetings, his name is Andrés.

Él tiene veinticuatro años de edad.

Ehl tee-eh-neh beh-een-tee-cooah-troh ahn-neeohs deh eh-dahd.

He's twenty-four years old.

Él es un periodista.

Ehl ehs oon peh-reeoh-dees-tah.

He's a journalist.

Él viene de México.

Ehl bee-eh-neh deh meh-hee-coh.

He comes from México.

Él es soltero.

Ehl ehs sohl-teh-roh.

He's single.

Asking Someone to Present Themselves

¿Cómo te llamas?

Coh-moh teh yah-mahs

What's your name?

¿De dónde eres?

Deh dohn-deh eh-rehs

Where are you from?

¿Cuántos años tienes?

Cooahn-tohs ahn-neeohs tee-eh-nehs

How old are you?

¿Cuál es tu profesión?

Cooahl ehs too proh-feh-seeohn

What's your profession?

¿Estás casado o soltero?

Ehs-tahs cah-sah-doh oh sohl-teh-roh

Are you married or single?

Adjectives

Adjectives in Spanish work the same way as in English. The only real difference is that Spanish adjectives are concerned with the gender of the noun. They'll end with "a" if the noun is feminine and "o" if the noun is masculine.

Here's a simple list of common adjectives you'll probably be using in small talk:

Adjective	Pronunciation	Meaning
Feliz	Feh-lees	Happy
Triste	Trees-teh	Sad
Enojado	Eh-noh-hah-doh	Angry
Hambriento	Ahm-bree-ehn-toh	Hungry
Cansado	Cahn-sah-doh	Tired
Dormido	Dohr-mee-doh	Asleep
Despierto	Dehs-pee-ehr-toh	Awake
Malo	Mah-loh	Bad
Bueno	Boo-eh-noh	Good
Sencillo	Sehn-see-yoh	Plain

Guapo	Goo-ah-poh	Handsome
Hermoso	Ehr-moh-soh	Beautiful
Feo	Feh-oh	Ugly
Limpio	Leem-peeoh	Clean
Sucio	Soo-seeoh	Dirty
Ordenado	Ohr-deh-nah-doh	Tidy
Desordenado	Dchs ohr-dch-nah-doh	Messy
Seco	Seh-coh	Dry
Mojado	Moh-hah-doh	Wet
Caliente	Cah-lee-ehn-teh	Hot
Fresco	Frehs-coh	Cool
Delicioso	Deh-lee-seeoh-soh	Delicious
Asqueroso	As-keh-roh-soh	Disgusting
Dulce	Dool-seh	Sweet
Salado	Sah-lah-doh	Salty
Amargo	Ah-mahr-goh	Bitter

Ácido	Ah-see-doh	Sour
Delgado	Dehl-gah-doh	Thin
Gordo	Gohr-doh	Fat
Alto	Ahl-toh	Tall
Bajo	Bah-hoh	Short
Pequeño	Peh-kehn-neeoh	Small
Grande	Grahn-deh	Big
Pesado	Peh-sah-doh	Heavy
Liviano	Lee-beeah-noh	Light
Lleno	Yeh-noh	Full
Vacío	Bah-seeoh	Empty
Rápido	Rah-pee-doh	Fast
Lento	Lehn-toh	Slow
Divertido	Dee-behr-tee-doh	Fun
Aburrido	Ah-boo-rree-doh	Boring

ssessive Adjectives

Spanish possessive adjectives work the same way as English possessive adjectives, so they replace words such as "my," "your," "his," "her," and so on. These would be the "atonic possessive adjectives," which are the most common ones and work exactly as adjectives. Besides the "atonic possessive adjectives," there are also "tonic possessive adjectives," which are written the same way as possessive pronouns, with the difference that tonic possessive adjectives are written next to the noun instead of replacing the noun altogether.

Atonic possessive adjectives are always written before the noun, while tonic possessive adjectives are written right after the noun. As with all adjectives, possessive adjectives end with an "a" or "o," depending on the gender of the object they're expressing possession of, they also add an "s" if the noun is plural.

Atonic Possessive Adjectives

Pronoun	Adjective	Pronunciation	Translation
Yo	Mi, Mis	Mee, Meehs	My
Tú	Tu, Tus	Too, Toos	Your
Usted	Su, Sus	Soo, Soos	Your
Él/ Ella/ Eso	Su, Sus	Soo, Soos	His/ Her/ Its
Nosotros	Nuestro, Nuestros	Nooehs-troh, Nooeh-strohs	Our
	Nuestra, Nuestras	Nooeh-strah, Nooeh-strahs	
Ustedes	Su, Sus	Soo, Soos	Your
Ellos/ Ellas	Su, Sus	Soo, Soos	Your

Tonic Possessive Adjectives

Pronoun	Adjective	Pronunciation
Yo	Mío, Míos	Meeoh, Meeohs
	Mía, Mías	Meeah, Meeahs
Tú	Tuyo, Tuyos	Too-yoh, Too-yohs
	Tuya, Tuyas	Too-yah, Too-yahs
Usted	Suyo, Suyos	Soo-yoh, Soo-yohs
	Suya, Suyas	Soo-yah, Soo-yahs
Él/ Ella/ Eso	Suyo, Suyos	Soo-yoh, Soo-yohs
	Suya, Suyas	Soo-yah, Soo-yahs
Nosotros	Nuestro, Nuestros	Nooehs-troh, Nooehs-trohs
	Nuestra, Nuestras	Nooehs-trah, Nooehs-trahs
Ustedes	Suyo, Suyos	Soo-yoh, Soo-yohs
	Suya, Suyas	Soo-yah, Soo-yahs
Ellos/ Ellas	Suyo, Suyos	Soo-yoh, Soo-yohs
	Suya, Suyas	Soo-yah, Soo-yahs

Here are some example phrases for the possessive adjectives:

Ellos siempre nos comparten su comida.

Eh-yohs see-ehm-preh nohs cohm-pahr-tehn soo coh-mee-dah.

They always share their food with us.

Yo cuido mucho a la novia mía.

Yoh cooee-doh moo-coh ah lah noh-beeah meeah.

I take care of my girlfriend.

Tú limpiabas tu casa todos los sábados.

Too leem-peeah-bahs too cah-sah toh-dohs lohs sah-bah-dohs.

You cleaned your house every Saturday.

Este perro tuyo es muy grande.

Ehs-teh peh-rroh too-yoh ehs mooee grahn-deh.

This dog of yours is too big.

Participle Verbs

Participle verbs are verbs used as adjectives. Instead of describing an action, they're adapted to speak about a quality of a noun, the same way an adjective does, and subjected to the same rules for adjectives: They change with the gender and number of the nouns. Participle verbs are conjugated in the past tense.

Here are a couple of examples that will make this concept easier to understand:

Los autos chocados se ven feos.

Lohs ah-oo-tohs choh-cah-dohs seh behn feh-ohs.

Crashed cars look ugly.

Me encantan las camisas teñidas.

Meh ehn-cahn-tahn lahs cah-mee-sahs tehn-nee-dahs.

I love dyed shirts.

Parts of the Body

As it happens in the case of colors, the parts of the body may not be the most common things to mention in an everyday conversation, but without a doubt some important ones that we learn the most important ones in order to be prepared for when the situation arises. chance.

Do not be scared, we are not going to review some parts of the body that can be very complicated or that are not entirely daily, since the important thing here is not to obtain a degree in medicine but to be able to learn some of the things that we are going to use on a daily basis in conversations, readings, when we watch a movie or any other situation that deserves it.

Word	Pronunciation	Tr
Cabeza	Cah-beh-sah	Head
Ojos	Oh-hos	Eyes
Nariz	Nah-rees	Nose
Orejas	Oh-reh-has	Ears
Cuero cabelludo	Cooeh-roh cah-beh-yoo-doh	Scalp
Cráneo	Crah-neh-oh	Skull
Boca	Boh-cah	Mouth
Dientes	Dee-ehn-tehs	Teeth
Lengua	Lehn-gooah	Tongue
Mandíbula	Mahn-dee-boo-lah	Jaw
Cuello	Cooeh-yoh	Neck
Hombros	Ohm-brohs	Shoulders
Pecho	Peh-choh	Chest
Corazón	Coh-rah-sohn	Heart
Pulmones	Pool-moh-nehs	Lungs

Brazo	Brah-soh	Arm
Codo	Coh-doh	Elbow
Mano	Mah-noh	Hand
Dedos	Deh-dohs	Fingers/ Toes
Espalda	Ehs-pahl-dah	Back
Abdomen	Ahb-doh-mehn	Abdomen
Panza	Pahn-sah	Belly
Estómago	Ehs-toh-mah-goh	Stomach
Hígado	Ee-gah-doh	Liver
Riñones	Reen-neeoh-nehs	Kidneys
Intestinos	Een-tehs-tee-nohs	Intestines/ Bowels
Trasero	Trah-sehr-oh	Ass
Piernas	Pee-ehr-nahs	Legs
Rodilla	Roh-dee-yah	Knee
Pies	Pee-ehs	Feet

Dolor	Doh-lohr	Pain
Duele	Dooeh-leh	Pains
Mareo	Mah-reh-oh	Dizzy
Fiebre	Fee-eh-breh	Fever
Tos	Tohs	Cough
Estornudo	Ehs-tohr-noo-doh	Sneeze

As usual, we'll go over a couple of examples:

Me duele el estómago.

Meh dooeh-leh ehl ehs-toh-mah-goh.

My stomach hurts.

Ayer tuve fiebre con tos y mareo.

Ah-yehr too-beh fee-eh-breh cohn tohs ee mah-reh-oh.

I had a fever yesterday with coughs and dizziness

Tengo dolor de cabeza.

Tehn-goh doh-lohr deh cah-beh-sah.

I have a headache.

Getting to Know Each Other

We'll explore some phrases that will be used when speaking about hobbies and things we like or dislike. Pay close attention to the words used to describe things like "gustar," love "amar ("encantar" is also used), dislike "desagradar" ("no me gusta" is also used), and so on.

Me gusta el fútbol.

Meh goos-tah ehl foot-bohl.

I like soccer.

¿Qué tipo de música escuchas?

Keh tee-poh deh moo-see-cah ehs-coo-chahs

What kind of music do you listen to?

¿Te gusta la música clásica?

Teh goos-tah lah moo-see-cah clah-see-cah

Do you like classical music?

A mi me gusta escuchar jazz.

Ah mee meh goos-tah ehs-coo-chahr yahs.

I like listening to jazz.

¿Cuál es tu equipo favorito?

Coo-ahl ehs too eh-kee-poh fah-boh-ree-toh

What's your favorite team?

Me encantan las películas románticas.

Meh ehn-cahn-tahn lahs peh-lee-coo-lahs roh-mahn-tee-cahs.

I love romantic movies.

¿Te gusta leer libros de terror?

Teh goos-tah leh-ehr lee-brohs deh teh-rrohr

Do you like to read horror books?

Me gusta ir a museos con mi pareja.

Meh goos-tah eer ah moo-seh-ohs cohn mee pah-reh-hah.

I like going to museums with my significant other.

Nos encanta salir a bailar juntos.

Nohs ehn-cahn-tah sah-leer ah bah-ee-lahr hoon-tohs.

We love going out to dance together.

A ellos les desagradan los clubes ruidosos.

Ah eh-yohs lehs deh-sah-grah-dahn lohs cloo-behs rooee-doh-sohs.

They dislike noisy clubs.

Ella es feliz siempre que puede ir a la playa.

Eh-yah ehs feh-lees see-ehm-preh keh pooeh-deh eer ah lah plah-yah.

She's happy as long as she can go to the beach.

Chapter Exercises

Eng/Spa Matching

Match these words in English with their equivalent terms in Spanish

#	English Term	Letter	Spanish Term
1	Black G	A	Mío
2	Kidneys C	B	Lengua
3	Nose F	C	Riñones
4	Red J	D	Azul
5	Teeth I	E	Cuero cabelludo
6	Blue D	F	Nariz
7	Tongue B	G	Negro
8	Rain M	H	Soleado
9	His N	I	Dientes

10	Fingers *O*	J	Rojo
11	Sunny *H*	K	Codo
12	Scalp *E*	L	Ojos
13	Mine *A*	M	Lluvia
14	Elbow *K*	N	Su
15	Eyes *L*	O	Dedos

Fill in the Blank

Answer the question by filling in the blank.

1. What's the preterite indefinite conjugation of the verb "cantar" (to sing) in the first person singular and plural? _Canté y Cantamos_

2. How do you ask someone to present themselves? _Como te llamas_

3. How would you say that the day is sunny? _El Dia Este Soleado_

4. What verb conjugation is the best fit for expressing situations with a clear starting point and ending point? _____

5. Which possessive adjectives are the same as possessive pronouns? _____

Translation

Write the Spanish translation of these English phrases.

1. I love dressing in black. _Me encanta vestirme de negro_

2. Nice to meet you, my name is Greg.

3. Sunny days like these are best for training.

4. I hope you enjoy my song.

5. Crops are thankful for rainy days.

Chapter 3– Answer Key

The answers for the Eng/Spa Matching exercises are the only ones that are strict. The other answers usually allow some freedom to adapt and rephrase the sentences as long as the core concept is intact.

Eng/Spa Matching

1:G, 2:C, 3:F, 4:J, 5:I, 6:D, 7:B, 8:M, 9:N, 10:O, 11:H, 12:E, 13:A, 14:K, 15:L

Fill in the Blank

1. Canté y cantamos.

2. Saludos ¿Cómo te llamas? ¿Te podrías presentar por favor?

3. El día está soleado.

4. Preterite indefinite.

5. Tonic possessive adjectives

Translation

1. Me encanta vestirme de negro.

2. Un placer conocerte, mi nombre es Greg.

3. Días soleados como estos son lo mejor para entrenar.

4. Espero que disfruten esta canción.

5. Los cultivos agradecen los días lluviosos.

En el capítulo anterior, vimos el ejemplo de una conversación cotidiana, que nos ayudó mucho a comprender todos los tópicos y contenidos que habíamos aprendido en ese capítulo. Para este nuevo capítulo, vamos a cambiar un poco la dinámica, ya que esta vez lo que vamos a hacer es un ejemplo ficticio en donde una persona se presenta y habla acerca de sí mismo. Esto se hace con el objetivo de que podamos ver un ejemplo de varios párrafos en un formato que incluya la mayoría de los contenidos y enseñanzas que hemos visto en este capítulo. Sin duda alguna, esto nos ayudará mucho a poder interpretar ciertas cosas y a que podamos tener mucha práctica a través de la lectura y de la pronunciación.

Como dijimos en el capítulo anterior, lo ideal es que leamos el siguiente párrafo en voz alta para que estemos practicando nuestro nivel de lectura en español, al igual que nuestro nivel de speaking, que son dos de los elementos más importantes cuando estamos aprendiendo un nuevo idioma. Esto nos va a permitir saber e identificar dónde podemos introducir cada una de las cosas que hemos ido aprendiendo a través de este capítulo para que así podamos tener un mejor nivel en nuestro español.

Presenting Pablo, a Student From Uruguay

¡Hola a todos! Mi nombre es Pablo. Nací en el año 1999 en Montevideo, capital de Uruguay. Sin embargo, durante los últimos tres años he estado viviendo en Inglaterra, ya que a mi papá lo transfirieron para trabajar en ese país hace algunos años. Mi infancia en Uruguay fue muy hermosa, ya que pude aprender todo acerca de esa maravillosa cultura y todas las ciudades bonitas que tiene.

Sin embargo, cuando tenía tres años, me tuve que mudar a Argentina, que es un país limítrofe con Uruguay, ya que mis papás creían que la economía sería mejor en ese país y que sería algo beneficioso para nosotros. Los primeros años viví en Buenos Aires, que es la capital de Argentina, pero luego me mudé a la ciudad de Rosario, que queda aproximadamente a una hora de Buenos Aires. En Rosario, todo era diferente, ya que las personas en Buenos Aires llevan un ritmo de vida mucho más rápido, se estresan mucho más fácilmente y suelen andar todo el tiempo preocupados. En cambio, en Rosario, todo era mucho más tranquilo, ya que las personas vivían con más calma y era mucho más fácil hacer amigos.

Cuando me mudé a Inglaterra, las cosas fueron un poco difíciles para mi, ya que no sabía hablar inglés y tuve que adaptarme a una cultura totalmente nueva y que era muy distinta a la cultura en la cual yo había crecido. Actualmente vivo en la ciudad de Londres, tengo un carro azul y voy a la Universidad de Oxford en donde estudio economía. Mi sueño desde que era muy pequeño siempre ha sido el de ser un economista bastante reconocido a nivel mundial, y sé que a través del tiempo y con la acumulación de experiencia lo voy a poder lograr sin ningún problema.

Por supuesto, va a requerir de mucho esfuerzo y dedicación, pero nada en la vida es imposible siempre y cuando tengamos mucha motivación en lo que hacemos y tengamos una pasión enorme. Sin duda alguna, yo amo a la economía,y estoy seguro de que, en el fondo, la economía me ama a mi. Actualmente mi nivel de inglés es bastante bueno, y soy uno de los mejores alumnos de mi clase. Eso ha hecho que mi camino universitario sea mucho más fácil. A todas aquellas personas que están aprendiendo a hablar español, les digo que es algo fascinante, y así como yo pude aprender su idioma con mucho esfuerzo y dedicación, ustedes van a poder aprender el mio sin ningún problema. Sólo requiere de mucha constancia, disciplina y motivación.

Translation

Hello everyone! My name is Pablo. I was born in 1999 in Montevideo, the capital of Uruguay. However, for the last three years I have been living in England, as my dad was transferred to work in that country a few years ago. My childhood in Uruguay was very beautiful, since I was able to learn everything about that wonderful culture and all the beautiful cities that country has. However, when I was three years old, I had to move to Argentina, which is a country bordering Uruguay, since my parents believed that the economy would be better in that country and that it would be beneficial for us.

The first years I lived in Buenos Aires, which is the capital of Argentina, but then I moved to the city of Rosario, which is about an hour from Buenos Aires. In Rosario, everything was different, since people in Buenos Aires lead a much faster pace of life, they get stressed much more easily and tend to be worried all the time. On the other hand, in Rosario, everything was much calmer since people lived more calmly and it was much easier to make friends.

When I moved to England, things were a bit difficult for me as I couldn't speak English and I had to adapt to a totally new culture that was very different from the one I had grown up in. I currently live in the city of London, I have a blue car and I go to the University of Oxford where I study economics. My dream since I was very little has always been to be a world-renowned economist, and I know that over time and with the accumulation of experience I will be able to achieve it without any problem. Of course, it will require a lot of effort and dedication, but nothing in life is impossible as long as we are highly motivated in what we do and have enormous passion.

Without a doubt, I love the economy, and I am sure that, deep down, economy loves me. Currently my level of English is quite good, and I am one of the best students in my class. That has made my college journey so much easier. To all those people who are learning to speak Spanish, I tell you that it is something fascinating, and just as I was able to learn your language with a lot of effort and dedication, you will be able to learn mine without any problem. It just requires a lot of perseverance, discipline and motivation.

Chapter 4: Addresses and Travels

It does not matter if we are learning to speak Spanish for work reasons or because we simply like this language. One of the things that we must always learn when we want to speak another language is things related to travel and directions. Suppose we are going on a trip to Spain or to a country in South America, then we are going to need to know each of these things so that we never get lost and always get to the place we want quickly and easily. All these things are usually a bit more complex, but without a doubt, with a little practice, we will be able to learn each of these things without any problem.

Future Simple Conjugation

This is included in this chapter because often we'll be speaking in the future tense while planning our vacations, buying tickets, stating our intentions for the day, etc.

Spanish has a traditional way to express the future where the conjugation of the verb changes, without needing anything else; this conjugation pattern is the same for verbs that end with "ar," "er," or "ir." There's another way to express future actions, and it's by using "voy a" (going to) in present tense + the main verb in infinitive. Both are equivalent and it depends on the speaker.

Future Simple Conjugation of Verbs that End with "AR," "ER," or "IR"

Pronoun(s)	Conjugation	Pronunciation	Mode
Yo	Amaré	Ah-mah-reh	First-person singular
Tú	Amarás	Ah-mah-rahs	Second-person singular
Usted	Amará	Ah-mah-rah	Second-person singular
Él/ Ella/ Eso	Amará	Ah-mah-rah	Third-person singular
Nosotros	Amaremos	Ah-mah-reh-mohs	First-person plural
Ustedes	Amarán	Ah-mah-rahn	Second-person plural

Present Tense Conjugation of the Verb "Ir" (to go)

Pronoun(s)	Conjugation	Pronunciation	Mode
Yo	Voy	Boh-ee	First-person singular
Tú	Vas	Bahs	Second-person singular
Usted	Va	Bah	Second-person singular
Él/ Ella/ Eso	Va	Bah	Third-person singular
Nosotros	Vamos	Bah-mohs	First-person plural

We'll have a couple of future tense sentences to illustrate this:

El año que viene nos vamos a Francia.

Ehl ahn-neeoh keh bee-eh-neh nohs bah-mohs ah eer ah frahn-seeah.

Next year we're going to France.

Pronto viajaremos a Chile.

Prohn-toh beeah-hah-reh-mohs ah chee-leh.

Soon, we'll travel to Chile.

El jueves vamos a comer en un restaurante.

Ehl hooeh-behs bah-mohs ah coh-mehr ehn oon rehs-tah-oo-rahn-teh.

This Thursday we're going to eat in a restaurant.

Compraremos los boletos de avión cuando estén de oferta.

Cohm-prah-reh-mohs lohs boh-leh-tohs deh ah-beeohn cooahn-doh ehs-tehn deh oh-fehr-tah.

We'll buy the plane tickets when they're on sale.

Means of Transportation

One of the most important things that we must know, especially when we are going to travel, are the means of transport. No one would like to be in the country on vacation and not know how to get around because they don't know how to communicate. That is why in this section we are going to see some of the means of transport most used by society on a day-to-day basis, as well as the correct pronunciation that we should give each of them.

It is important to note that many of them have the same meaning but the same pronunciation since in Spanish there are many words that have the same meaning. The good thing is that each of these means of transport is easy to learn and pronounce, so we shouldn't have any problem learning about them.

Vehicle	Pronunciation	Translation
Automóvil	Ah-oo-toh-moh-beel	Car
Carro	Cah-rroh	Car
Coche	Coh-cheh	Car
Motocicleta	Moh-toh-see-cleh-tah	Motorcycle
Barco	Bahr-coh	Ship
Bote	Boh-teh	Boat
Avión	Ah-beeohn	Airplane
Caminar	Cah-mee-nahr	Walk

Here are some examples of common phrases with vehicles:

Necesitamos ir a un alquiler de automóviles.

Neh-seh-see-tah-mohs eer ah oon ahl-kee-lehr deh ah-oo-toh-moh-bee-lehs.

We need to go to a car rental.

Sólo se puede llegar a la isla por avión.

Soh-loh seh pooeh-deh yeh-gahr ah la h ees-lah pohr ah-beeohn.

You can only reach the island by plane.

Las motocicletas no están permitidas por aquí.

Lahs moh-toh-see-cleh-tahs noh ehs-tahn pehr-mee-tee-dahs pohr ah-kee.

Motorcycles are not allowed around here.

Creo que mi coche está averiado.

Creh-oh keh mee coh-cheh ehs-tah ah-beh-reeah-doh.

I believe my car has broken down.

Giving Directions

It is possible that being in any part of the world, any day of the week, we need to ask for an address, or on the contrary, someone who is lost asks us to give him an address. This can happen any day and at any time, so we must be prepared to know how to respond in each of these situations. Of course, many times when we are giving directions we will have to use the names of the stores, the parks, or the places we want to go, but it is important to know the grammatical structures on which we are going to give or ask for those directions.

If we don't learn these things, then we will always depend on applications like Google Maps, which is undoubtedly something that will limit us a lot in our lives. On the contrary, learning everything related to addresses will mean that we never have to depend on these things.

Asking for Directions

This is mostly done with the interrogative adverb "dónde" (where). Here are some example phrases that illustrate this:

¿Dónde está el hospital?

Dohn-deh ehs-tah ehl ohs-pee-tahl

Where's the hospital?

Giving Directions

We'll go over verbs and nouns related to directions, then we'll have a couple of example phrases to illustrate it.

Term	Pronunciation	Translation
Continuar	Cohn-tee-nooahr	To continue
Girar	Hee-rahr	To turn
Ir	Eer	To go
Avanzar	Ah-bahn-sahr	To advance
Tomar	Toh-mahr	To take

Derecho	Deh-reh-coh	Straight
Izquierda	Ess-kee-ehr-dah	Left
Derecha	Deh-reh-chah	Right
Atrás	Ah-trahs	Back
Norte	Nohr-teh	North
Sur	Soor	South
Este	Ehs-teh	East
Oeste	Oh-ehs-teh	West

Sigue derecho y cruza tres calles.

See-geh deh-reh-coh ee croo-sah trehs cah-yehs.

Go straight and cross after three streets.

El parque queda atrás del hospital.

Ehl pahr-keh keh-dah ah-trahs dehls ohspee-tahl.

The park is behind the hospital.

El lago está al oeste de la ciudad.

Ehl lah-goh ehs-tah ahl oh-ehs-teh deh lah seeoo-dahd.

The lake is West of the city.

El hospital queda a tres calles a la derecha de aquí.

Ehl ohs-pee-tahl keh-dah ah trehs kah-yehs ah lah deh-reh-chah deh ah-kee.

The hospital is three blocks to the right of here.

The Four Seasons

Relevant to holiday planning, this is how the four seasons are named in Spanish. As it happens with months and days of the week, the seasons in Spanish aren't capitalized.

Season	Pronunciation	Translation
Primavera	Pree-mah-beh-rah	Spring
Verano	Beh-rah-noh	Summer
Otoño	Oh-tohn-neeoh	Autumn/Fall
Invierno	Een-bee-ehr-noh	Winter

Here are a couple of example sentences that include seasons:

Los inviernos son demasiado fríos por aquí.

Lohs een-bee-ehr-nohs sohn deh-mah-seeah-doh free-ohs pohr ah-kee.

The winters are too cold around here.

Me gusta lo soleado que es el verano.

Meh goos-tah loh soh-leh-ah-doh keh ehs ehl beh-rah-noh.

I like how sunny the summer is.

Japón es hermoso en primavera.

Hah-pohn ehs ehr-moh-soh ehn pree-mah-beh-rah.

Japan is beautiful in spring.

Other Relevant Sentences

We'll go over important phrases that you should learn before going to a foreign country:

¿Dónde queda inmigración?

Dohn-deh keh-dah een-mee-grah-seeohn.

Where's immigration?

¿Qué hoteles hay en la zona?

Keh oh-teh-lehs ah-ee ehn lah soh-nah

What hotels are in the area?

Tiene hospedaje por 72 horas.

Tee-eh-neh ohs-peh-dah-heh pohr seh-tehn-tah ee dohs oh-rahrs.

Has lodging for 72 hours.

Vas a perder tu vuelo.

Bahs ah pehr-dehr too booeh-loh.

You're going to miss your flight.

¿Dónde está la piscina?

Dohn-deh ehs-tah lah pees-see-nah

Where's the pool?

Chapter Exercises

Eng/Spa Matching

Match these words in English with their equivalent terms in Spanish.

#	English Term	Letter	Spanish Term
1 *D*	Car	A	Vuelo
2 *G*	Winter	B	Primavera
3 *J*	Left	C	Verano
4 *F*	Where	D	Motocicleta
5 *A*	Flight	E	Derecho
6 *C*	Summer	F	Dónde

7 M	Ship	G	Invierno
8 N	Zone	H	Coche
9 K	Allowed	I	Piscina
10 E	Straight	J	Izquierda
11 D	Motorcycle	K	Permitido
12 O	College	L	Derecha
13 I	Pool	M	Barco
14 L	Right	N	Zona
15 B	Spring	O	Universidad

Fill in the Blank

Answer the questions by filling in the blanks.

1. How do you do the alternative future tense conjugation? _____

2. Name three ways to say "car" in Spanish. _____

3. What's the traditional future tense conjugation of the verb "vivir" (to live). _____

4. How do you say "turn left" in Spanish? _____

5. Are seasons capitalized in Spanish? _____

Translation

Write the Spanish translation of these English phrases.

1. It's better to call a cab so it can take us.

2. To reach the hospital you'll need to turn right on the next street and then go straight from there.

3. I enjoy sailing on large ships.

4. Riding a motorcycle makes me feel free.

5. My girlfriend loves taking pictures in the fall.

En este capítulo estuvimos enfocados en hablar de cosas muy elementales como los viajes y las cuestiones básicas que debemos saber al irnos de vacaciones y dar o recibir direcciones. Sin duda alguna, estos son tópicos súper importantes a la de hora de irnos de vacaciones, ya que es imposible estar en un país o en una ciudad que no conocemos si no sabemos la forma correcta de pedir y dar direcciones. Es por eso, que siguiendo lo que hemos hecho en capítulos anteriores, en donde hacíamos ejemplos de conversaciones o de algún monólogo, en este capítulo vamos a ver un pequeño artículo que nos va a hablar sobre algún destino turístico bastante conocido en Sudamérica. No sólo podremos reforzar nuestro nivel de lectura en español, sino que también podremos aprender un poco más acerca de otras culturas.

De esta manera, estaremos aprendiendo dos cosas a la misma vez. Recuerda que es muy importante que hagas la lectura en voz alta. Al principio, es normal que te cueste un poco, ya que es un idioma completamente nuevo, pero no te tienes que sentir apenado o algo por el estilo, ya que todos nos equivocamos durante este proceso de aprendizaje.

How Machu Picchu Was Built

Sin duda alguna, uno de los atractivos turísticos más grandes de Perú (y de toda Latinoamérica) es Machu Picchu, que es una zona que fue construida por los incas hace cientos de años, y que aún permanece intacta. Machu Picchu fue construida en la parte oriental de la Cordillera de los Andes, en la selva del Cusco. El increíble entorno natural que se encuentra a los alrededores de esta maravillosa ciudad inca no es la única razón por la que fue construida esa gran maravilla del mundo. Existen muchas teorías que tratan de explicar el porqué de la existencia de este monumento histórico de la humanidad. La mayoría de los expertos en geología e historia coinciden en que sirvió de puesto de control, centro agrícola, centro religioso y urbano.

A lo largo de los años, han habido muchas investigaciones en Machu Picchu que señalan que esta ciudad fue construida sobre una gran falla geológica, que tuvo como consecuencia principal la proliferación de bancos de piedra granítica, ideal para la edificación de esos maravillosos monumentos que podemos ver en internet (o si tenemos suerte, en vivo y en directo). Debido a eso, los incas construyeron los muros con una posición antisísmica, que ha logrado mantener el sitio sin mayores daños a lo largo de todos estos siglos.

Se dice que los incas construyeron sus principales ciudadelas en las partes elevadas e inaccesibles de las montañas, ya que así podrían tener una vista estratégica y privilegiada del entorno, al igual que se podían acercar a sus dioses celestiales, que debemos recordar eran muy importantes para ese tipo de tribus indígenas. Así como Machu Picchu, los incas edificaron otras ciudades en las altas montañas como por ejemplo: Sacsayhuaman, Pisac, Ollantaytambo, Choquequirao, etc. Machu Picchu también es conocido como 'Ciudad en las nubes' puesto que está situado en una montaña alta y rodeada de un bosque nuboso. Su ubicación privilegiada les permitió a sus habitantes observar los fenómenos astronómicos con gran claridad.

Estas estructuras fueron ideales para la observación astronómica y así predecir los ciclos del sol durante la siembra y cosecha de productos agrícolas. El Intihuatana, por ejemplo, indica la fecha exacta de los solsticios, equinoccios y otros eventos astronómicos importantes. Sin duda alguna, esto nos habla de lo avanzada que eran esas tribus, y de la importancia que le daban al diseño arquitectónico de cada una de sus ciudades. Muchas veces las construcciones de hoy en día sólo tienen los costos y las cuestiones relacionadas a los tiempos de construcción, pero en aquel entonces, era muy importante darle una estructura arquitectónica hermosa a cada una de las obras que realizaban estas tribus.

Translation

Without a doubt, one of the biggest tourist attractions in Peru (and in all of Latin America) is Machu Picchu, which is an area that was built by the Incas hundreds of years ago, and that still remains intact. Machu Picchu was built in the eastern part of the Andes Mountains, in the jungle of Cusco. The incredible natural environment that surrounds this wonderful Inca city is not the only reason why this great wonder of the world was built. There are many theories that try to explain the reason for the existence of this historical monument of humanity. Most experts in geology and history agree that it served as a checkpoint, agricultural center, religious and urban center.

Over the years there have been many investigations in Machu Picchu that indicate that this city was built on a great geological fault, which had as its main consequence the proliferation of granite stone benches, ideal for the construction of those wonderful monuments that we can see on the internet (or if we're lucky, live and direct). Due to this, the Incas built the walls with an anti-seismic position, which has managed to maintain the site without major damage throughout all these centuries.

It is said that the Incas built their main citadels in the high and inaccessible parts of the mountains since that way they could have a strategic and privileged view of the environment, just as they could get closer to their celestial gods, which we must remember were very important. for that type of indigenous tribe. As well as Machu Picchu, the Incas built other cities in the high mountains such as: Sacsayhuaman, Pisac, Ollantaytambo, Choquequirao, etc. Machu Picchu is also known as 'City in the clouds' since it is located on a high mountain and surrounded by a cloud forest. Its privileged location allowed its inhabitants to observe astronomical phenomena with great clarity.

These structures were ideal for astronomical observation and thus predict the cycles of the sun during the planting and harvesting of agricultural products. The Intihuatana, for example, indicates the exact date of the solstices, equinoxes, and other important astronomical events. Without a doubt, this tells us how advanced these tribes were, and the importance they gave to the architectural design of each of their cities. Many times today's constructions only have costs and issues related to construction times, but back then, it was very important to give a beautiful architectural structure to each of the works carried out by these tribes.

Chapter 5: Household, Food, and Shopping

In all daily conversations we will find ourselves talking about things related to the home, food, and of course, the various purchases that we can make during the week. That is why it is extremely necessary that we know how to use the correct expressions to refer to all these kinds of things since we will always use them. It does not matter if we are talking to a friend, a family member, or even a stranger, since in the same way, these types of topics are always present in any type of formal or informal conversation that we carry out. Of course, most of what we are going to look at in this chapter have to do with specific words, and not with grammatical structures or some sentence rules.

In other words, to be able to use all the phrases and words that we are going to learn next, you must master all the content that we have been learning throughout the three previous chapters. Therefore, if we are still not sure that we have perfectly mastered any of the previous chapters or sections, we must review them again so that we can understand this chapter correctly. We must always remember that many times the contents that we are learning can be easily forgotten, so it is always important to practice them and review them as many times as necessary so that we can ensure that all these contents will remain engraved in our heads in the long term, which is the goal that all of us have.

Pricing

If we are learning to speak Spanish for work reasons, without a doubt this is a very important section for us. This is because in this section we are going to learn some of the most important terms in relation to financial, economic, and cost factors. This is something vital that we must know to carry out most of the works, for which it is important that we pay close attention to all the terms that we are going to learn next, as well as the various examples that we are going to review.

Of course, let's not be scared, because if we are not learning to speak Spanish for work reasons but more for tourism or a matter of personal growth, this section will also be very useful to us. We all need to ask the price of something before buying it, as well as knowing terms related to tariffs and taxes since they are very important when we are going to a city or country as tourists. That is why this section may seem a bit simple, but it is undoubtedly much more important than it seems since it is possible that we are going to use each of these terms a lot. We'll go over some terms that are important to study value and ask about the cost of items in stores; and then, as always, we'll cover a couple of phrases to illustrate this.

Term	Pronunciation	Translation
Precio	Preh-seeoh	Price
Costo	Cohs-toh	Cost
Cuesta	Cooehs-tah	Cost

Valor	Bah-lohr	Value
Vale	Bah-leh	Values

Este pantalón vale doscientos.

Ehs-teh pahn-tah-lohn bah-leh dohs-see-ehn-tohs.

These pants are worth two hundred.

El precio por mis servicios es de veinte la hora.

Ehl preh-seeoh pohr mees sehr-bee-seeohs ehs deh beh-een-teh lah oh-rah.

The price for my services is twenty per hour.

Appreciating Food

When we talk about food, it is impossible not to use adjectives, since we will always need them to describe how good or how bad the food was. That is, adjectives help us describe how our experience has been after having eaten something, whether we have prepared it ourselves or it is food from a restaurant. As we all know, it is normal that when we are in a city or a country as tourists, we eat in many restaurants and try a lot of new food, since that is one of the most wonderful experiences of traveling and learning about other cultures. Knowing each of these adjectives and expressions will help us communicate much better when we are eating in a restaurant, or simply when we are going to eat with a friend or family member.

Of course, we can describe how the food was with many other adjectives, which will vary especially depending on the country we are in. However, below we are going to see some of the most common adjectives and terms that we are going to use on a daily basis when we are going to refer to food. We'll go over some words and phrases used when we want to rate the food and express gratitude for it.

Term	Pronunciation	Translation
Delicioso	Deh-lee-seeoh-soh	Delicious
Rico	Ree-coh	Rich, tasty
Sabroso	Sah-broh-soh	Tasty
Salado	Sah-lah-doh	Salty

Dulce	Dool-seh	Sweet
Sour	Soh-oor	Agrio
Amargo	Ah-mahr-goh	Bitter
Sabor	Sah-bohr	Taste
Textura	Tex-too-rah	Texture

Mi sopa está rica, pero demasiado caliente.

Mee soh-pah ehs-tah ree-cah peh-roh deh-mah-seeah-doh cah-lee-ehn-teh.

My soup is good but way too hot.

Me encanta la textura de la nieve.

Meh ehn-cahn-tah lah tex-too-rah deh lah nee-eh-beh.

I love the texture of the snow.

Me encantan las cerezas dulces y amargas.

Meh ehn-cahn-tahn lahs seh-reh-sahs dool-sehs ee ah-mahr-gahs.

I love bitter and sweet cherries.

Food Items

The goal of this section is for us to learn the correct way in which we should pronounce some of the main foods that we are likely to interact with every day. In other words, in this chapter, we are going to learn about the main fruits, the most common drinks, some proteins, and everything related to the basic and most consumed foods in general. Of course, everyone has different tastes and it is possible that some of the foods that we are going to mention below may not be part of our daily diet, but in the same way, we are going to review them so that we can identify them quickly and simply in any store, market, restaurant or simply in any conversation in which any of these topics arise.

Here's a simple list of food items for every home:

Item	Pronunciation	Translation
Manzanas	Mahn-sah-nahs	Apples
Naranjas	Nah-rahn-has	Oranges
Cerezas	Seh-reh-sahs	Cherries
Fresas	Freh-sahs	Strawberries
Carne	Cahr-neh	Meat
Cerdo	Sehr-doh	Pork
Agua	Ah-gooah	Water
Pollo	Poh-yoh	Chicken
Harina	Ah-ree-nah	Flour
Maíz	Mah-ees	Corn
Champiñones	Cham-peen-neeoh-nehs	Mushrooms
Limón	Lee-mohn	Lemon
Melón	Meh-lohn	Melon
Jalea	Hah-leh-ah	Jam
Mantequilla de maní	Mahn-teh-kee-yah deh mah-nee	Peanut butter

Azúcar	Ah-soo-cahr	Sugar
Huevos	Oo-eh-bohs	Eggs
Arroz	Ah-rrohs	Rice
Pasta	Pahs-tah	Pasta
Pan	Pahn	Bread
Tomate	Toh-mah-teh	Tomato
Cebolla	Sch-boh-yah	Onion
Lechuga	Leh-choo-gah	Lettuce
Perejil	Peh-reh-heel	Parsley
Leche	Leh-cheh	Milk
Queso	Keh-soh	Cheese
Jamón	Hah-mohn	Ham
Salsa	Sahl-sah	Sauce
Papa	Pah-pah	Potatoe
Zanahoria	Sah-nah-oh-reeah	Carrot

Repollo	Reh-poh-yoh	Cabbage
Salsa de tomate	Sahl-sah deh toh-mah-teh	Ketchup
Mayonesa	Mah-yoh-neh-sah	Mayonnaise
Mostaza	Mohs-tah-sah	Mustard
Pimienta	Pee-mee-ehn-tah	Pepper
Sal	Sahl	Salt

We'll go over a couple of sentences with food items:

Me gustan los huevos con sal y pimienta.

Meh goos-tahn lohs ooeh-bohs cohn sahl ee pee-mee-ehn-tah.

I like eggs with salt and pepper.

Mi mamá cocina muy bien el cerdo.

Mee mah-mah coh-see-nah mooee bee-ehn ehl sehr-doh.

My mother cooks the pork very well.

Ella prefiere comer pasta antes que arroz.

Eh-yah preh-fee-eh-reh coh-mehr pahs-tah ahn-tehs keh ah-rrohs.

She prefers to eat pasta rather than rice.

Shopping

Without a doubt, one of the things that identify us all equally, regardless of our tastes or preferences, is that all of us must make purchases in our day to day, since we must go to the pharmacy, to the supermarket, to the hardware store or any other store to buy the things we need for our daily routine at home. Therefore, when we go on a trip or we are doing tourism, we must also know how to express ourselves regarding these situations, since we will always need to go shopping, whatever the specific circumstances that arise that day.

In the same way, each of these phrases and words is usually very common in people's daily conversations. So, this section will also help us identify each of those things so that we can carry out communication and conversation. much more fluid.

Here's a list of various types of stores and phrases that are relevant to shopping:

Types of Stores

Store	Pronunciation	Translation
Farmacia	Fahr-mah-seeah	Drugstore
Ferretería	Feh-rreh-teh-ree-ah	Hardware store
Mercado	Mehr-cah-doh	Market
Supermercado	Soo-pehr-mehr-cah-doh	Supermarket
Panadería	Pah-nah-deh-ree-ah	Bakery
Floristería	Floh-rees-teh-ree-ah	Flower store
Tienda	Tee-ehn-dah	Store
Restaurante	Rehs-tah-oo-rahn-teh	Restaurant

Relevant Phrases

Necesito llegar al mercado más cercano.

Neh-seh-see-toh yeh-gahr ahl mehr-cah-doh mahs sehr-cah-noh.

I need to get to the closest market.

¿Tiene vuelto de cien?

Tee-eh-neh booehl-toh deh see-ehn

Do you have change for a 100 bill?

¿Cuánto le debo?

Cooahn-toh leh deh-boh

How much do I owe you?

No lo quiero, no me gusta.

Noh loh kee-eh-roh noh meh goos-tah.

I don't want it; I don't like it.

¿Aceptan crédito?

Ah-sehp-tahn creh-dee-toh

Do you accept credit?

¿Esto viene con garantía?

Ehs-toh bee-eh-neh cohn gah-rahn-tee-ah

Does this come with a warranty?

Necesito comprar regalos para mi familia. ¿Dónde consigo una tienda de regalos?

Neh-seh-see-toh cohm-prahr reh-gah-lohs pah-rah mee fah-mee-leeah dohn-deh cohn-see-goh oo-nah tee-ehn-dah deh reh-gah-lohs

I need to buy gifts for my family. Where shall I find a gift shop?

Vamos a la panadería que tienen muestras gratis.

Bah-mohs ah lah pah-nah-deh-ree-ah keh tee-eh-nehn mooehs-trahs grah-tees.

Let's go to the bakery, they have free samples.

¿En qué talla necesita?

Ehn keh tah-yah neh-seh-see-tah

What size do you need?

Me gusta este modelo, ¿lo tienen en verde?

Meh goos-tah ehs-teh moh-deh-loh loh tee-eh-nehn ehn behr-deh

I like this model, do you have it in green?

Hoy tenemos rebajas en la tienda.

Oh-ee teh-neh-mohs reh-bah-has ehn lah tee-ehn-dah.

Today we have sales in the store.

Home

Another of the topics that we undoubtedly have to learn about is everything related to real estate. This is something basic that we have to learn when we are starting to speak a language, since it does not matter if it is for work, curiosity, tourism or anything else, we will always need this set of words when we carry out a conversation, for more indifferent than it seems at first. That is why in this section we are going to see some of the most important concepts related to real estate and everything that has to do with the objects that we find in our homes.

Types of Homes
Home Pronunciation

Casa Cah-sah

Apartamento Ah-pahr-tah-mehn-toh

Mansión Mahn-seeohn

Cabaña Cah-bahn-neeah

Objects in the Living Room

Object	Pronunciation	Translation
Sofá	Soh-fah	Couch
Mesa	Meh-sah	Table
Butaca	Boo-tah-cah	Armchair
Alfombra	Ahl-fohm-brah	Carpet
Escritorio	Ehs-cree-toh-reeoh	Desk
Biblioteca	Bee-bleeoh-teh-cah	Library
Chimenea	Chee-meh-neh-ah	Chimney
Escultura	Ehs-cool-too-rah	Sculpture
Pintura	Peen-too-rah	Painting
Candelabro	Cahn-deh-lah-broh	Candelabra
Lámpara de techo	Lahm-pah-rah deh teh-choh	Ceiling lamp
Silla	See-yah	Chair
Televisión	Teh-leh-bee-seeohn	Television

Objects in the Bedroom

Object	Pronunciation	Translation
Cama	Cah-mah	Bed
Litera	Lee-teh-rah	Bunk bed
Ropero	Roh-peh-roh	Wardrobe
Armario	Ahr-mah-reeoh	Closet
Mesa	Meh-sah	Table
Espejo	Ehs-peh-hoh	Mirror
Tocador	Toh-cah-dohr	Dresser
Cortinas	Cohr-tee-nahs	Curtains
Sábana	Sah-bah-nah	Sheet
Almohadas	Ahl-moh-ah-dahs	Pillows
Lámpara	Lahm-pah-rah	Lamp
Computadora	Cohm-poo-tah-doh-rah	Computer
Escritorio	Ehs-cree-toh-reeoh	Desk

Objects in the Dining Room

Object	Pronunciation	Translation
Mesa	Meh-sah	Table
Sillas	See-yahs	Chairs
Alfombra	Ahl-fohm-brah	Carpet
Platos	Plah-tohs	Dishes
Vasos	Bah-sohs	Glasses
Jarra	Hah-rrah	Jar
Cubiertos	Coo-bee-ehr-tohs	Cutlery

Objects in the Bathroom

Object	Pronunciation	Translation
Ducha	Doo-chah	Shower
Bañera	Bahn-nee-eh-rah	Bathtub
Lavamanos	Lah-bah-mah-nohs	Sink
Espejo	Ehs-peh-hoh	Mirror

Objects in the Kitchen

Object	Pronunciation	Translation
Refrigerador	Reh-free-heh-rah-dohr	Fridge
Lavaplatos	Lah-blah-plah-tohs	Sink
Lavadora	Lah-bah-doh-rah	Washing machine
Lavavajillas	Lah-bah-bah-hee-yahs	Dishwasher
Grifo	Gree-foh	Tap
Horno microondas	Ohr-noh mee-croh-ohn-dahs	Microwave
Horno	Ohr-noh	Oven
Licuadora	Lee-cooah-doh-rah	Blender
Gabinetes	Gah-bee-nehts	Cabinets
Tostadora	Tohs-tah-doh-rah	Toaster
Estufa	Ehs-too-fah	Stove

Objects in the Garage

Object	Pronunciation	Translation
Lámpara	Lahm-pah-rah	Lamp

Automóvil	Ah-oo-toh-moh-beel	Car
Cobertizo	Coh-behr-tee-soh	Shed
Tanque de agua	Tahn-keh deh ah-gooah	Water tank

Objects in the Garden

Object	Pronunciation	Translation
Piscina	Pees-see-nah	Pool
Estanque	Ehs-tahn-keh	Pond
Árbol	Ahr-bohl	Tree
Fuente	Fooehn-teh	Fountain
Casa del perro	Cah-sah dehl peh-rroh	Doghouse
Pala	Pah-lah	Shovel
Manguera	Mahn-gueh-rah	Hose

Phrases for Eating

In this section, we are going to see some of the most important and common words and phrases that we are going to need when we want to express something related to eating or food in general. That is, these are the words that we are going to use when we want to say that we want to eat, that we want to see the restaurant menu, that we want to go eat at a specific place, and all those things. Each of these phrases is going to have great importance since we are going to need them whenever we go out to eat with friends, family, at home, or in a restaurant.

Similarly, it is likely that many times, in everyday conversations, we use some of these phrases to refer to something we ate or some gastronomic experience we have had. Without a doubt, learning all these things will help us a lot to expand our vocabulary in Spanish and to know how we should develop a conversation at certain times.

Tengo hambre, quiero comer.

Tehn-goh ahm-breh kee-eh-roh coh-mehr.

I'm hungry, I want to eat.

Me gustaría ver el menú, por favor.

Meh goos-tah-ree-ah behr ehl meh-noo pohr fah-bohr.

I'd like to see the menu, please.

Me gustaría comer pizza.

Meh goos-tah-ree-ah coh-mehr pee-sah.

I'd like to eat pizza.

La cuenta, por favor.

Lah cooehn-tah pohr fah-bohr.

The check, please.

Quiero comer ensalada con mi pollo frito.

Kee-eh-roh coh-mehr ehn-sah-lah-dah cohn mee poh-yoh free-toh.

I'd like to have a salad with my fried chicken.

Esta comida está un poco cruda.

Ehst-ah coh-mee-dah ehs-tah oon poh-coh croo-dah.

This meal is a little bit raw.

Sólo puedo comer productos sin azúcar.

Soh-loh pooeh-doh coh-mehr proh-dooc-tohs seen ah-soo-cahr.

I can only eat sugar-free products.

Prueba un poco de esto.

Prooeh-bah oon poh-coh deh ehs-toh.

Have a taste of this.

Chapter Exercises

Eng/Spa Matching

Match these words in English with their equivalent terms in Spanish.

#		English Term	Letter	Spanish Term
1	C	Costs	A	Valor
2	D	Apples	B	Panadería
3	I	Market	C	Cuesta
4	L	Bathroom	D	Manzanas
5	O	Library	E	Tienda
6	A	Value	F	Farmacia
7	B	Bakery	G	Cebolla
8	J	Pork	H	Agua
9	N	Basement	I	Mercado

10 M	Mushrooms	J	Cerdo
11 G	Onion	K	Cocina
12 F	Drugstore	L	Baño
13 K	Kitchen	M	Champiñones
14 E	Store	N	Sótano
15 H	Water	O	Biblioteca

Fill in the Blank

Answer the questions by filling in the blanks.

1. How would you say that you're hungry in Spanish? _Tengo Hambre_

2. Name five objects in Spanish that you would find in most bedrooms._____

3. What does it mean if a Spanish store clerk tells you "estamos de oferta!"? _____

4. How would you ask for the price of a pair of shoes in Spanish? _Cuanto Cuesta_

5. How would you ask for the bill at a restaurant in Spanish? _me gustan La cuenta_

Translation

Write the Spanish translation of these English phrases.

1. My kitchen has a sharp set of knives that I love to use every day.

2. My brother's bedroom is very tidy, he's an organized person.

83

3. All families should spend time together in the living room, even if it's just watching TV.

4. I loved the sweet and sour flavors of this cream pie!

5. My family loves it when I cook pasta with mushrooms.

Chapter 5– Answer Key

The answers for the Eng/Spa Matching exercises are the only ones that are strict. The other answers usually allow some freedom to adapt and rephrase the sentences as long as the core concept is intact.

Eng/Spa Matching

1:C, 2:D, 3:I, 4:L, 5:O, 6:A, 7:B, 8:J, 9:N, 10:M, 11:G, 12:F, 13:K, 14:E, 15:H

Fill in the Blank

1. Tengo mucha hambre.

2. In this case, the list is long, but you should name at least five of the following: cama, armario, mesa, lámpara, espejo, ropero, tocador, cortinas, sábana, almohadas, litera, etc.

3. It means that they're on sale.

4. ¿Cuánto cuesta ese par de zapatos?

5. Mesero, la cuenta, por favor.

Translation

1. Mi cocina tiene un lote de cuchillos afilados que me encanta usar todos los días.

2. La habitación de mi hermano está muy ordenada, él es una persona organizada.

3. Todas las familias deberían pasar tiempo juntos en la sala de estar, al menos si están viendo televisión como mínimo.

4. Yo amé los sabores dulces y agrios de este pie de crema.

5. A mi familia le encanta cuando cocino pasta con champiñones.

Al igual que hemos hecho en los capítulos anteriores, a continuación vamos a ver un artículo que nos explica un poco sobre cómo debemos ordenar nuestra casa para que esta sea mucho más espaciosa. De esta forma, no solo vamos a tener todo ordenado, sino que también vamos a poder contar con mucho más espacio y conseguir todas nuestras cosas de una forma más rápida. Por supuesto, la idea no es enseñar una lección de vida, sino que podamos obtener un poco de práctica al leer y hablar en voz alta un artículo entero en español.

How to Keep our house in Order

Una de las cosas que nos hace estar cómodos en nuestro hogar, sintiéndonos relajados, libres de estrés y también más felices, es tener nuestra casa limpia y recogida. Sin embargo, lograrlo no es fácil para todo el mundo, ya que a veces las personas no saben cómo llevar un orden en la casa, no pueden organizar sus cosas, o simplemente les parece algo demasiado fastidioso. Una de las primeras cosas que deberíamos hacer es deshacernos de todas aquellas cosas que no usamos ya que las consideramos como inservibles. A veces tenemos en nuestra casa un montón de cosas que no usamos o que ya no necesitamos, incluso es habitual encontrarnos con cosas que ni siquiera nos son útiles porque ya no funcionan.

Tendemos a guardar mucha "basura" que nos quita espacio para guardar las cosas realmente importantes. De igual manera, siempre se recomienda que cuando decidamos ordenar nuestra casa debemos hacerlo en el menor tiempo posible ya que así las posibilidades de éxito serán mayores debido a que estaremos más motivados durante todo el proceso. Si por el contrario ordenamos hoy una parte y dejamos el resto para dentro de varios días, esto puede hacer que vayamos retrasando la tarea hasta llegar incluso a no completarla.

Otra de las cosas que nos puede ayudar mucho (aunque ya eso pertenece a la etapa previa a mudarnos a nuestra casa), es tener muebles a medida. Tener una casa con muebles a medida nos va a ayudar mucho a aprovechar mejor todos los rincones de la casa. Aprovechar un rincón para poner una estantería o una repisa nos proporcionará más espacio de almacenaje. No obstante, debemos de tener cuidado de no cargar demasiado los espacios ya que no nos ayudan a liberarnos del estrés y tampoco ayudará a que posteriormente mantengamos el orden y la limpieza. Una vez que hemos ordenado nuestra casa, el trabajo que tenemos por delante es de mantenimiento.

De nada sirve todo el esfuerzo realizado en organizar la casa si a los tres días todo va a estar de nuevo patas arriba. Lo que ocurre con muchas personas es que limpian la casa el sábado o el domingo, pero después se pasan la semana entera desordenando o ensuciando. Sin duda alguna, el orden depende solamente de nosotros, así que debemos tener mucho más cuidado con nuestros hábitos y nuestra higiene alrededor de la casa.

Translation

One of the things that makes us feel comfortable in our home, feeling relaxed, stress-free, and also happier, is having our house clean and tidy. However, achieving this is not easy for everyone, since sometimes people do not know how to keep order in the house, they cannot organize their things, or it simply seems too annoying. One of the first things we should do is get rid of all those things that we do not use since we consider them useless. Sometimes we have a lot of things in our house that we do not use or that we no longer need, it is even common to find things that are not even useful to us because they no longer work.

We tend to keep a lot of "junk" that takes away space to store the really important things. In the same way, it is always recommended that when we decide to tidy up our house we should do it in the shortest time possible since this way the chances of success will be greater because we will be more motivated throughout the process. If, on the other hand, we order a part today and leave the rest for several days, this can cause us to delay the task until we even fail to complete it.

Another thing that can help us a lot (although that already belongs to the stage prior to moving into our house), is having custom-made furniture. Having a house with custom furniture will help us a lot to make better use of every corner of the house. Taking advantage of a corner to put a shelf or a shelf will provide us with more storage space. However, we must be careful not to load the spaces too much since they do not help us to free ourselves from stress and neither will it help us to maintain order and cleanliness later. Once we have tidied up our house, the job ahead of us is maintenance.

All the effort made in organizing the house is useless if after three days everything is going to be upside down again. What happens with many people is that they clean the house on Saturday or Sunday, but then they spend the whole week messing or dirty. Without a doubt, the order depends only on us, so we must be much more careful with our habits and our hygiene around the house.

Chapter 6: Business, Work, and Relationships

As we said at the beginning of this book, there are many people who want to learn to speak Spanish for work reasons, or simply to add one more skill to their resumes. Without a doubt, learning to speak a language as popular as Spanish is one of the best things that we are going to be able to do for our professional careers. Since in this globalized world in which we live today we have to have all those skills that allow us to work from anywhere in the world and thus, have many more opportunities.

Of course, we are not only going to need to learn these topics if we are learning for business because if we are doing it for personal reasons we must also know all these terms and phrases so that we can communicate in a much more effective way. Business topics today are very common in everyday conversations, so it is very important that we know how to recognize each one of them so that we are not caught off guard when someone is talking to us about business in Spanish. In the same way, we are going to see some things that are related to regular labor issues, as well as various topics related to family ties, relationships, and of course, social networks, which are so popular today.

Possessive Pronouns

Possessive pronouns in Spanish work the same way as they do in English, they replace the noun of the sentence. These are the same as the tonic possessive adjectives, and they have the same meaning. However, they're used in sentences where there's no noun. We'll go over these pronouns and then we'll illustrate this with a couple of examples.

Personal	Possessive	Pronunciation	Translation
Yo	Mío	Mee-oh	Mine
Tú	Tuyo	Too-yoh	Yours
Usted	Suyo	Soo-yoh	Yours
Él/ Ella/ Eso	Suyo	Soo-yoh	His/ Hers/ Its
Nosotros	Nuestro	Nooehs-troh	Ours
Ustedes	Suyo	Soo-yoh	Yours

| Ellos/ Ellas | Suyo | Soo-yoh | Theirs |

El mío está guardado en mi bolso.

Ehl meeoh ehstah gooahr-dah-doh ehn mee bohl-soh.

Mine is kept in my bag.

El tuyo quedó mejor después de tu corte de cabello.

Ehl too-yoh keh-doh meh-hohr dehs-pooehs deh too cohr-teh deh cah-beh-yoh.

Yours was better after your haircut.

Nosotros veremos a los nuestros esta navidad.

Noh-soh-trohs beh-reh-mohs ah lohs nooehs-trohs ehs-tah nah-bee-dahd.

We'll see our family this Christmas.

Como pudimos ver al principio de esta sección, cuando aprendimos acerca de las formas correctas de pronunciar y escribir cada uno de esos pronombres posesivos, vemos que hay muchos que se repiten, pero que sin embargo, según el sujeto de la oración, van a tener diferentes significados. Muchas personas tienen algunos pequeños problemas con esto, por lo cual debemos estar bien atentos para evitar caer en esos pequeños errores que nos puedan llevar a traducir alguna información de forma incorrecta, o simplemente a tener algunos problemas a la hora de expresar algún mensaje.

Telling Time

Knowing how to tell the time is something much more important than is often believed. I mean, people may think that this is basic and not that important, however, in the business world, it's important to know how to make appointments and all that. In the same way, if we are going to see a friend or family member, we must tell them what time we expect them, and that way we will be much more organized. Not many things are more important in the world of business than telling the time and setting up appointments. We must learn how to tell the time in Spanish.

What Time Is It?

These are a couple of examples of how to ask for the time:

¿Qué hora es?

Keh oh-rah ehs

What time is it?

Disculpe, ¿podría por favor decirme la hora?

Dees-cool-peh poh-dree-ah pohr fah-bohr deh-seer-meh lah oh-rah

Excuse me, could you please tell me the time?

¿Qué hora marca el reloj?

Keh oh-rah mahr-cah ehl reh-loh

What time does the clock show?

Parts of a Day

It's important to learn how to tell morning, afternoon, evening, and night:

Mañana	Mah-gnaa-nna	Morning
Mediodía	Meh-deeoh-dee-ah	Noon
Tarde	Tahr-deh	Afternoon
Atardecer	Ah-tahr-deh-sehr	Sunset
Noche	Noh-cheh	Night
Medianoche	Meh-deeah-noh-cheh	Midnight
Madrugada	Mah-droo-gah-dah	Early morning
Amanecer	Ah-mah-neh-sehr	Sunrise

Telling the Time

The usual way to tell time is by dividing the twenty-four hours into two halves, AM for the morning and PM for the afternoon/night. Time in Spanish is told by the following pattern: hours in numbers + "y" (and) + minutes in the hour.

In this respect, you can always say the number of minutes. There are also names for a specific number of minutes. In particular, when it's the hour "o'clock" this is replaced by the expression "en punto" (at that point).

Here are some examples of times and how they're told in Spanish:

07:00 AM	Siete AM en punto	See-eh-teh ah-eh-meh ehn poon-toh
08:40 PM	Ocho y cuarenta PM	Oh-choh ee cooah-rehn-tah peh-eh-meh

03:15 PM	Tres y cuarto PM	Trehs ee cooahr-toh peh-eh-meh
12:45 AM	Un cuarto para la una AM	Oon cooahr-toh pah-rah lah oo-nah ah-eh-meh
05:30 AM	Cinco y media AM	Seen-coh ee meh-deeah ah-eh-meh

We'll go over a couple of examples regarding time:

Quiero que llames al cliente a las siete de la mañana.

Kee-eh-roh keh yah-mehs ahl clee-ehn-teh ah lahs see-eh-teh deh lah mahn-neeah-nah.

I want you to call the client at seven AM.

La reunión será a las cuatro y media.

Lah reh oo-neeohn seh-rah ah lahs cooah-troh ee meh-deeah.

The meeting will be at four-thirty.

Quiero el informe a las tres y cuarto.

Kee-eh-roh ehl een-fohr-meh ah lahs trehs ee cooahr-toh.

I want the paper at quarter past three.

Professions

Next, we are going to see a list that contains the majority of the professions, or at least the most popular, so that we can have a much broader idea of the professions most used in everyday conversations. Each of these professions is usually the most used since they are the most popular in most countries, although, of course, we must know that there are many other professions besides these, but that we have decided to only mention some of the most popular for don't make this section so long and tedious.

We may have already heard some of these professions mentioned in a television series, or even in a song, so we will realize that while some of these may be a bit difficult to pronounce, most are quite basic and contain few syllables. Best of all, in the examples section, we are going to see the context in which we could use each of these words. In the same way, we are going to see that there are certain professions that are pronounced the same as in English, as well as others that, although they are written exactly the same, have a slightly different pronunciation.

Profession	Pronunciation	Translation
Conductor	Cohn-dooc-tohr	Driver
Abogado	Ah-boh-gah-doh	Lawyer
Artista	Ahr-tees-tah	Artist
Contador	Cohn-tah-dohr	Accountant
Periodista	Peh-reeoh-dees-tah	Journalist
Dentista	Dehn-tees-tah	Dentist
Director	Dee-rech-tor	Director
Doctor	Dohc-tohr	Doctor
Enfermero	Ehn-fehr-meh-roh	Nurse
Cartero	Cahr-teh-roh	Mailman
Empresario	Ehm-preh-sah-reeoh	Businessman
Secretario	Seh-creh-tah-reeah	Secretary
Policía	Poh-lee-see-ah	Police officer
Mesero	Meh-seh-roh	Waiter
Mecánico	Meh-cah-nee-coh	Mechanic

Programador	Proh-grah-mah-dohr	Programmer
Ingeniero	Een-heh-nee-eh-roh	Engineer
Vendedor	Behn-deh-dohr	Salesman

Here are a couple of phrases using professions:

Tenemos una cita con el abogado a las dos de la tarde.

Teh-neh-mohs oo-nah see-tah cohn ehl ah-boh-gah-doh ah lahs dohs deh lah tahr-deh.

We have an appointment with the lawyer at two o'clock in the afternoon.

Te desempeñarás como vendedor en esta compañía.

Teh deh-sehm-pehn-neeah-rahs coh-moh behn-deh-dohr ehn ehs-tah cohm-pahn-neeah.

You'll perform as a salesman in this company.

Agenda una cita con mi secretaria.

Ah-hen-dah oo-nah see-tah cohn mee seh-creh-tah-reeah.

Set an appointment with my secretary.

Te presento a mi contadora, trabajarás con ella de ahora en adelante.

Teh preh-sehn-toh ah mee cohn-tah-doh-rah trah-bah-hah-rahs cohn eh-yah deh ah-oh-rah ehn ah-deh-lahn-teh.

I present to you my accountant, you'll work with her from now on.

Relevant Business Phrases

In this section, what we are going to see are some of the most popular phrases that we are going to use in terms of everything related to business. Of course, these phrases are going to be very necessary if we are learning to speak Spanish for work issues. However, if this is not the case, it will also be necessary for us to learn all these topics since we will be able to use them in any instance that comes our way in our work or in any other circumstance of our daily lives. The good thing is that each of these phrases is easy to learn and that we will be able to use all the words that we learned earlier when we were talking about the professions.

In other words, below we are going to see the grammatical structures and sentences that we can use in each of the cases that we want to talk about the professions mentioned above. We are going to realize that, unlike previous sections, in this section, we have included many examples so that in this way we have a practical guide on each of the situations in which we can talk about professions, as well as the easier ways on how we can pronounce each of those phrases.

Soy graduado en leyes.

S-oh-ee grah-dooah-doh ehn leh-yehs.

I have a degree in law.

Le dejé el informe en el escritorio de su oficina.

Leh deh-heh ehl een-fohr-meh ehn ehl ehs-cree-toh-reeoh deh soo oh-fee-see-nah.

I left the report for him on his office desk.

Tiene mucho trabajo que hacer y está llegando tarde.

Tee-eh-neh moo-choh trah-bah-hoh keh ah-sehr ee ehs-tah yeh-gahn-doh tahr-deh.

You have a lot of work to do and you're running late.

La reunión será a las tres de la tarde.

Lah reh-oo-neeohn seh-rah ah lahs trehs deh lah tahr-deh.

The meeting will be at three PM.

Estoy desempleado, busco trabajo aquí.

Aest-oh-e daes-am-plae-do boos-coh trah-bah-hoh ah-keeh.

I'm unemployed, I'm looking for a job here.

La despidieron ayer y su amiga renunció hoy.

Lah dehs-pee-dee-eh-rohn ah-yehr ee soo ah-mee-gah reh-noon-seeoh oh-ee.

She got fired yesterday, and her friend resigned today.

Necesitamos que firme el contrato, por favor.

Neh-seh-see-tah-mohs keh feer-meh ehl cohn-trah-toh pohr fah-bohr.

We need you to sign the contract, please.

Yo dejé un currículum aquí la semana pasada.

Yoh deh-heh oon coo-rree-coo-loom ah-kee lah seh-mah-nah pah-sah-dah.

I left a resume here last week.

Que pase el siguiente candidato a la entrevista de trabajo.

Keh pah-seh ehl see-gee-ehn-teh cahn-dee-dah-toh ah lah ehn-treh-bees-tah deh trah-bah-hoh.

Let the next candidate for the job interview come in.

Buenas tardes. ¿Por qué busca trabajar en esta compañía?

Booeh-nahs tahr-dehs pohr keh boos-cah trah-bah-hahr ehn ehs-tah cohm-pahn-neeah

Good afternoon. Why are you looking to work in this company?

Está contratado, nos vemos la próxima semana.

Ehs-tah cohn-trah-tah-doh nohs beh-mohs lah proh-xee-mah seh-mah-nah.

You're hired, see you next week.

Family Tree

Without a doubt, family is one of the most important things we have in life. In any country in the world, and in whatever language we are speaking, we are going to need to know how to pronounce the different terms used for relatives, as well as knowing the proper pronunciation for each of these. One of the main differences that the familiar April has in Spanish compared to English is that cousins have different terms depending on whether they are feminine or masculine. In English, the word cousin encompasses both the feminine and the masculine, but in Spanish these are different depending on each case.

Beyond that, the truth is that there are not many differences in the grammatical structures that are found in each case, but we must be alert to learn each of these words perfectly so that we can address our relatives or the relatives of another person correctly. Without a doubt, these are words that we are going to use on a daily basis since in everyday conversations it is very common to refer to a family member or a close person. Similarly, in the examples, we are going to see some of the most repeated phrases when we talk about a family member so that we know where to insert each of these words in a conversation or in a sentence. We'll start by teaching you how to talk about your relatives.

Profession	Pronunciation	Translation
Madre	Mah-dreh	Mother
Padre	Pah-dreh	Father
Abuela	Ah-booeh-lah	Grandmother
Abuelo	Ah-booeh-loh	Grandfather
Hermana	Ehr-mah-nah	Sister
Hermano	Ehr-mah-noh	Brother
Hija	Ee-hah	Daughter
Hijo	Ee-hoh	Son
Tía	Tee-ah	Aunt
Tío	Tee-oh	Uncle
Prima	Pree-mah	Cousin (female)
Primo	Pree-moh	Cousin (male)

Sobrina	Soh-bree-nah	Niece
Sobrino	Soh-bree-noh	Nephew

Other Relatives

Relative	Pronunciation	Translation
Padrastro	Pah-drahs-troh	Father-in-law
Madrastra	Mah-drahs-trah	Mother-in-law
Esposa	Ehs-poh-sah	Wife
Esposo	Ehs-poh-soh	Husband
Hermanastra	Ehr-mah-nahs-trah	Sister-in-law
Hermanastro	Ehr-mah-nahs-troh	Brother-in-law
Yerna	Yehr-nah	Daughter-in-law
Yerno	Yehr-noh	Son-in-law
Madrina	Mah-dree-nah	Godmother
Padrino	Pah-dree-noh	Godfather

We'll go over a couple of family-related phrases:

Tus hijos están más grandes cada vez que los veo.

Toos ee-hos ehs-tahn mahs grahn-dehs cah-dah behs keh lohs beh-oh.

Your children are bigger every time I see them.

Mi abuela hornea las mejores galletas del mundo.

Mee ah-booeh-lah ohr-neh-ah lahs meh-hoh-rehs gah-yeh-tahs dehl moon-doh.

My grandmother bakes the best cookies in the world.

Sal a la sala, tu padrino te trajo un regalo.

Sahl ah lah sah-lah too pah-dree-noh teh trah-hoh oon reh-gah-loh.

Come out to the living room, your godfather brought you a present.

Mi mamá nos está invitando a todos los primos a la playa.

Mee mah-mah nohs ehs-tah een-bee-tahn-doh ah toh-dohs lohs pree-mohs ah lah plah-yah.

My mother is inviting all of us cousins to the beach.

Social Media

Without a doubt, one of the things that people use the most on a daily basis is social networks. It doesn't matter if we are in school, if we are in university, if we are parents or if we are older adults since each of us uses at least one social network daily. Of course, not all of us use the same social networks, but it is important that we know some of the terms and phrases that are related to all these topics since conversations about these topics can arise in any member and we have to be prepared. Many times people believe that social networks are just for seeing photos or news, but the truth is that they often help us connect with people from other countries and make business relationships or any other type of thing. That is why learning to pronounce all the phrases and words related to social networks is something fundamental today, especially since we live in a world that is always connected through the internet.

For example, if we go to eat at a restaurant, we are likely to ask what their Instagram account is or if they have a Facebook page. The same goes for every other tourist attraction we go to, as well as every conversation we have with our friends and family. That's why we'll study some terms relevant to social media and then we'll go over a couple of phrases that are extremely useful to use social media in Spanish.

Phrases Relevant to Social Media

No compartas tu clave con nadie.

Noh cohm-pahr-tahs too clah-beh cohn nah-dee-eh.

Don't share your password with anyone.

Yo te sigo en Instagram.

Yoh teh see-goh ehn eens-tah-grahm.

I follow you on Instagram.

Me gusta lo que publicas en Twitter.

Meh goos-tah loh keh poo-blee-cahs ehn tooee-tehr.

I like what you post on Twitter.

Comparte mi publicación de venta, por favor.

Cohm-pahr-teh mee poo-blee-cah-seeohn deh behn-tah pohr fah-bohr.

Please share my sales post.

Vamos a conectarnos en LinkedIn.

Bah-mohs ah coh-nehc-tahr-nohs ehn leen-kehd-een.

Let's connect on LinkedIn.

No publiques esa fotografía por favor.

Noh poo-blee-kehs eh-sah foh-toh-grah-fee-ah pohr fah-bohr.

Don't post that photograph, please.

Chapter Exercises

Eng/Spa Matching

Match these words in English with their equivalent terms in Spanish

#	English Term	Letter	Spanish Term
1	Accountant	A	Mediodía
2	Aunt	B	Abuela
3	Morning	C	Abogado
4	Son	D	Ingeniero
5	Lawyer	E	Publicar
6	Nurse	F	Noche

7	Noon	G	Hijo

8	Account	H	Periodista
9	Secretary	I	Perfil
10	Engineer	J	Tía
11	Journalist	K	Mañana
12	Post	L	Cuenta
13	Night	M	Contador
14	Grandmother	N	Enfermero
15	Profile	O	Secretario

Fill in the Blanks

Answer the questions by filling in the blanks.

1. The word "mío" is a _____ in the following sentence: "Tu perro y el mío juegan cada vez que se ven".

2. The word "tuya" is a _____ in the following sentence: "La casa tuya vive durmiendo en la sala de estar".

3. Tell these following times in Spanish: 08:36 AM, 04:15 PM, 09:12 AM.

4. How would you ask someone to add him on Facebook and follow him on Twitter in Spanish?

5. How would you set a meeting in your office at 05:00 PM in Spanish?

Translation

Write the Spanish translation of these English phrases.

1. My grandfather and my dad look very much alike.

2. The mechanic told us that our car would be ready next Friday.

3. I want you to introduce me to your boss on LinkedIn.

4. We'll be leaving on our fishing trip by dawn.

5. Tomorrow morning we'll have a "bring your son to the office" day.

Chapter 6 – Answer Key

The answers for the Eng/Spa Matching exercises are the only ones that are strict. The other answers usually allow some freedom to adapt and rephrase the sentences as long as the core concept is intact.

Eng/Spa Matching

1:M, 2:J, 3:K, 4:G, 5:C, 6:N, 7:A, 8:L, 9:O, 10:D, 11:H, 12:E, 13:F, 14:B, 15:I

Fill in the Blank

1. Possessive pronoun.

2. Possessive adjective.

3. Ocho y treinta y seis de la mañana, cuatro y cuarto de la tarde, y nueve y doce de la mañana.

4. ¿Podría agregarte en Facebook y seguirte en Twitter?

5. La reunión de hoy será a las cinco de la tarde en la oficina.

Translation

1. Mi abuelo y mi padre se parecen mucho.

2. El mecánico nos dijo que nuestro coche estaría listo para el próximo viernes.

3. Quiero que me presentes a tu jefe en LinkedIn.

4. Estaremos saliendo en nuestro viaje de pesca para el amanecer.

5. Mañana en la mañana tendremos un día de "trae a tu hijo a la oficina".

De igual forma, a continuación vamos a ver el ejemplo de una conversación entre dos personas que están hablando de algunos de los tópicos que aprendimos en este capítulo, como por ejemplo cuestiones relacionadas al trabajo y a las redes sociales. De esta forma vamos a poder ver cómo todas las frases y palabras aprendidas en este capítulo nos van a servir para desarrollar e interactuar en conversaciones habituales y así poder interpretar todo lo que nos dicen.

Muchas veces las personas creen que porque no están aprendiendo a hablar español por cuestiones laborales entonces no necesitan saber este tipo de cosas, pero la verdad es que siempre serán importantes ya que pueden surgir en cualquier conversación que tengamos, bien sea con un amigo, colega o algún familiar. En la conversación que vamos a ver a continuación, como de costumbre, primero la vamos a ver en español y luego en inglés, para que así sepamos de forma perfecta la traducción de cada una de las cosas que dicen, y podamos tomar nota de aquellas frases o estructuras gramaticales que nos parezcan interesantes.

Example of a Conversation Related to Businesses

Freddie: John, ¿dónde pusiste los documentos que había dejado encima del escritorio? ¡Los necesito urgentemente!

John: Hace una hora vino el jefe y me pidió que le entregara esos documentos. Me dijo que los necesitaba para poder realizar el informe acerca del nuevo cliente.

Freddie: No debió haberlos llevado, ya que aún no he terminado de redactar todo lo que hacía falta para el informe del nuevo cliente. Supongo que ahora tendré que pasarle esa información a través de un email.

John: Lamento mucho oír eso. La verdad no sabía que esos documentos estaban incompletos.

Freddie: ¿Sabes cuál es la ocupación del nuevo cliente? Necesito saber esa información para así poder saber qué incluir en el informe.

John: He oído que el nuevo cliente es un ingeniero químico que trabaja en una empresa farmacéutica. Pero la verdad es que nunca lo he conocido, así que mejor deberías preguntarle directamente al jefe para asegurarnos que de verdad es un ingeniero.

Freddie: Perfecto, voy a preguntarle al jefe para así incluir ese dato en el informe.

John: Genial. También puedes ver la información que aparece en el perfil de LinkedIn del cliente, ahí probablemente salga cuál es su trabajo.

Freddie: ¿Qué es LinkedIn?

John: Es una red social con motivos laborales en donde las personas pueden hacer networking y conocer a otras personas de la industria. Deberías abrir una cuenta.

Freddie: La verdad nunca había oído hablar de esa red social, pero suena muy interesante, voy a abrir mi cuenta ahora mismo.

John: Genial, Freddie, avísame si necesitas ayuda.

Translation

Freddie: John, where did you put the documents that I had left on the desk? I need them urgently!

John: An hour ago the boss came and asked me to give him those documents. He told me that he needed them to be able to make a report about the new client.

Freddie: He shouldn't have brought them, since I haven't finished writing everything that was needed for the new client's report yet. I guess now I'll have to pass that information on to him via email.

John: I'm so sorry to hear that. The truth is I didn't know that those documents were incomplete.

Freddie: Do you know what the new client's occupation is? I need to know that information so I can know what to include in the report.

John: I heard that the new client is a chemical engineer who works for a pharmaceutical company. But the truth is that I have never met him, so you should ask the boss directly to make sure that he really is an engineer.

Freddie: Perfect, I'm going to ask the boss to include that information in the report.

John: Great. You can also see the information that appears in the client's LinkedIn profile, it will probably show what their job is.

Freddy: What is LinkedIn?

John: It is a social network for work purposes where people can network and meet other people in the industry. You should open an account.

Freddie: The truth is that I had never heard of that social network, but it sounds very interesting, I'm going to open my account right now.

John: Great Freddie, let me know if you need any help.

Chapter 7: Sports and Hobbies

Without a doubt, sports, and physical activities are some of the most important things in life. All these activities not only allow us to maintain a healthy lifestyle but also allow us to relax and enjoy our free time much more. In general, people who are fans of some sport usually practice it. That is, if someone is a big fan of basketball, it is very likely that person meets with his friends or family to play basketball from time to time. However, there are many people who like to do physical activities but are not sports fans. That is to say, there are people who usually go to the gym every day, go for a run or simply do any other physical activity, and although they like it a lot, it is very unlikely that they will ever watch a baseball game or play a game of football with their friends.

The important thing is that whatever our passion is in the world of sports or physical activities, it is very important that we learn the correct way in which we should use each term related to sports, since many times they are usually pronounced in a different way to how we would do it in English. However, this is a subject that can be learned quickly, since the words are usually not that difficult and the phrases used in this context are also usually simple.

Of course, you may not like sports or you are not a person who likes physical activities. That is totally understandable, but we must know that knowing each of these terms is extremely important since they can be present in any type of daily conversation. It may be that a friend is telling us about his passions, that we are talking to a family member, that we are watching television or something else, and it is very possible that some topic related to sports will come up. In fact, in many countries, there are sports that are part of the culture, and we must know to say that we truly visited those countries.

For example, if we go to Argentina or Brazil, soccer is part of the culture of both countries, since people do not see it as a simple game or a simple sport, but for them, it is something sacred. In fact, in Argentina they often say that soccer is a religion for them, so we can see people of all ages enjoying a game in the stadiums at any time of the day. The same happens in Brazil since soccer is one of the things that has lifted more children out of poverty and has allowed them to dream of a bright future. The point is, if we ever visit those two countries, we should know some super important terms around the world of sports.

Football: Fútbol americano

Basketball: Baloncesto

Soccer: Fútbol

Tennis: Tenis

Golf: Golf

Baseball: Béisbol

Score: Anotación

Goal: Gol

Net: Malla

Baseball bat: Bate

Ball: Pelota

Glove: Guante

Basket: Aro

Points: Puntos

Runs: Carreras

Home run: Jonrón

Field: Terreno

Stadium: Estadio

Sports: Deportes

Gym: Gimnasio

Workout: Ejercicio

Training: Entrenamiento

Athlete: Atleta

Marathon: Maratón

Running: Correr

Game: Juego

Play: Jugar

Field goal: Gol de campo

Game over: Juego terminado

Sports are a fundamental section when learning a sport, since they will always be necessary topics in any type of conversation. Similarly, not only will they be very important in regular conversations, but it is very likely that we will also hear about all these topics in movies or television series. We will have realized in this section that most sports have general terms that are said in the same way in each of the languages, and that is why they do not have a specific translation into Spanish, such as touchdown, which is a term that is always used in English.

However, the vast majority of other sports have specific terms for each of the things that we must learn to say in Spanish. Best of all is that each of these words is very easy to learn since it is very likely that we have heard or seen them before. Of course, if we are fans of sports or physical activities, it will be even easier since we may be familiar with some of these terms.

Phrases Related to Sports

As well as knowing how to pronounce and write the main sports, it is also very important that we know what are some phrases and words related to sports and physical activities. It is very likely that when we have conversations related to sports or different physical activities, some of these phrases or words will come up, which is why it is very important that we not only know how to pronounce them but also know their meaning. We may have heard these phrases a few times on television, on social networks, or even in a television series. Of course, it is very rare that we watch television or use social networks in another language, but this can help us a lot to continue developing our Spanish-speaking skills.

In the same way, many times when we watch international sports or we are watching foreign television channels, we have no choice but to interpret what they are saying based on the context of the conversion. On the other hand, if we learn all these phrases perfectly, we will be making sure that we do not have any problem related to the fluency of our understanding in each of these conversations or situations. Of course, as we have done in previous chapters, at the end of this section we are going to see some sentences and examples that will allow us to better understand all this.

Winner: ganador

Loser: perdedor

Player: jugador

Sore loser: mal perdedor

¡Gané!: I won!

Let's go!: ¡Vamos!

Rendirse: giving up

Win: ganar

Lose: perder

Effort: esfuerzo

Fun: diversión

Sweat: sudor

Algunos ejemplos que podemos dar en relación a estos tópicos son los siguientes:

Mario scored a goal last night in his soccer game.

Mario anotó un gol en su juego de fútbol anoche.

She was having a lot of fun while she was swimming in the pool.

Ella estaba divirtiéndose mucho mientras estaba nadando en la piscina.

He is a sore loser, he needs to change thy and behave better.

El es un mal perdedor, necesita cambiar y comportarse mejor.

You can see the effort she is putting in every day at the gym.

Puedes ver el esfuerzo que ella está haciendo todos los días en el gimnasio.

He sweats too much when he goes to the gym.

Él suda mucho cuando va al gimnasio.

How to Ask Someone His/Her About Favorite Sport

Believe it or not, most people love to talk about their favorite sports and physical activities they do every day. This is undoubtedly one of the most common topics in everyday conversations, as people like to talk about their favorite team, the previous day's baseball game, or the routine they did in the gym. That's why it's important to know how to ask the right questions when we want to learn more about a person's lifestyle or passions.

In fact, this is a very useful topic when we are getting to know someone since we will want to know what their main hobbies are, as well as the things that person is interested in. People love to talk about their passions, as they are things that are very important to them and that have a deep meaning in many cases. That is why if we know how to ask people questions about their favorite sports or physical activities, it not only guarantees us that we will be able to make many new friends, but we will also be able to understand and interpret much better what our friends tell us.

What's your favorite sport?: ¿Cuál es tu deporte favorito?

What's your favorite physical activity?: ¿Cuál es tu actividad física favorita?

Which days do you go training?: ¿Qué días vas a entrenar?

What's your favorite team?: ¿Cuál equipo es tu favorito?

How often do you work out?: ¿Qué tan seguido entrenas?

Sin duda alguna, cada una de esas frases y palabras se pueden utilizar en cualquiera de las conversaciones habituales que tengamos con alguien, sin importar si nos gustan los deportes o no, al igual que no importa de lo que estemos hablando ya que son temas que pueden surgir de forma espontánea. Si nos enfocamos en aprender todas estas cosas, entonces estaremos preparados para poder desarrollar e interpretar de la mejor manera cualquier conversación en donde puedan surgir algunos de estos temas, ya que como hemos dicho de forma repetida, no importa si no somos fanáticos de los deportes o no hacemos alguna actividad física, estos temas suelen ser bastante comunes en cada una de las conversaciones.

De igual forma, a continuación vamos a ver un ejemplo de una conversación en donde dos personas se encuentran hablando acerca de estos temas, para que así podamos ver un contexto de una conversación que puede surgir en cualquier momento, y podamos ver en donde introducir cada una de esas frases, palabras y oraciones. Primero, la vamos a ver en español, y luego tendremos la traducción en inglés para que podamos ver de forma práctica cómo utilizar cada una de estas frases y oraciones.

Example of a Conversation Related to Sports and Physical Activities

José: ¡Hola! ¿Cómo estás Peter? Tanto tiempo sin verte.

Peter: ¡Hola José! Estoy muy bien, gracias por preguntar. ¿Tú cómo estás?

José: Muy bien, Peter. Hace un rato estaba en el gimnasio y en unas horas voy al partido de béisbol con mi hermano.

Peter: ¡Qué bueno, José! ¿Te gustan otras actividades físicas o sólo el gimnasio?

José: A veces voy a correr por el parque, a hacer CrossFit o alguna de esas actividades que exigen un poco más de esfuerzo, pero por lo general sólo voy al gimnasio.

Peter: ¡Me parece excelente! Yo solía ir al gimnasio hace algunos años, pero desde que nació mi hijo menor no he ido más. Tengo que intentar volver algún día de estos, la verdad me gustaba mucho ir al gimnasio.

José: De verdad es algo muy bueno. En el gimnasio no sólo te diviertes y entrenas, sino que también liberas mucho estrés de tu cuerpo.

Peter: Eso es correcto José. ¿Vas al partido de béisbol de los Tigres?

José: ¡Sí! ¿Tú también vas?

Peter: No, lo voy a ver por televisión ya que no logré conseguir entradas.

José: Bueno está bien. ¡Espero que ganen los Tigres!

Peter: ¡Yo también!

Translation

Jose: Hi! How are you Peter? Long time no see.

Peter: Hi Jose! I'm very good, thanks for asking. How are you?

Jose: Very good Peter. A while ago I was in the gym, and in a few hours I'm going to the baseball game with my brother.

Peter: Good job Jose! Do you like other physical activities or just the gym?

José: Sometimes I go for a run in the park, do CrossFit or one of those activities that require a little more effort, but usually I just go to the gym.

Peter: Sounds great to me! I used to go to the gym a few years ago, but since my youngest son was born I haven't been there anymore. I have to try to go back one of these days, I really liked going to the gym.

José: It really is a very good thing. In the gym you not only have fun and train, but also release a lot of stress from your body.

Peter: That's right Jose. Are you going to the Tigers baseball game?

Jose: Yes! Are you going too?

Peter: No, I'm going to watch it on TV since I couldn't get tickets.

Jose: Well that's fine. I hope the Tigers win!

Peter: Me too!

Conclusion

Without a doubt, learning a new language is one of the most wonderful things we can do, especially when it comes to a language as popular as Spanish. Of course, English is the most widely spoken language in the world, but Spanish is one of the main ones and one of the languages that has become more relevant in recent times. As we all know, the world has gone through a process of globalization in recent years, which is why today it is much easier to be in contact with other cultures, languages, people, and much more around the world.

That is why learning a new language will not only help us expand our knowledge and entertain ourselves, but it will also help us open up new job opportunities since the language will not be a limiting barrier for us. Of course, it's also fine that we want to learn this language just out of curiosity or because we just like to know about other cultures. The most important thing of all is that learning a new language is useful for many things, and there is no age limit in which we must learn it since we can do this whenever we want.

After having read this book, we are undoubtedly in a position to say that we can speak Spanish perfectly, as long as we never forget that we must constantly practice so that we do not forget everything we have learned. The problem of many of the people who start learning new languages is that they believe that it is only enough to read a book like this, attend a course or something similar to speak another language perfectly when the truth is that practice is what will lead us to perfection.

Knowing how to speak a language, but not practicing it, is like having muscles and not exercising them, because sooner or later if we don't go to the gym or do some physical activity then we will lose those muscles. The good news is that, as we have said several times throughout the book, each of us can practice consistently and easily through many different methods.

In the same way, it is very important to emphasize that learning a new language is not only good from a professional point of view and that it will be very useful in other facets of our lives, but it is also something that will help us strengthen our mind in many ways. For example, it is proven that when we learn a new language, our memory is strengthened, since we have to learn many completely new words, grammatical structures, sentences, and phrases. Similarly, when we learn a language we also increase our ability to do different tasks at the same time and increase our level of proactivity. As we all know, learning a new language requires a lot of attention and effort, just like learning to think in another language. That is why when we are learning Spanish we are also going to strengthen our ability to do several things at the same time.

Finally, it is also important that we know that many times learning a new language will help us a lot to improve our performance in other types of academic activities since it increases our level of concentration and the mental effort we make to learn. The point of all this is that we must know that learning a language not only helps us in terms of professional and personal growth but also helps us a lot in terms of our mental health.

Without a doubt, this path may not be easy at first, since learning a new language also requires a lot of patience and discipline, because otherwise, we will not be able to achieve our goals. But if we have enough discipline to practice every day, as well as the necessary level of patience to not give up in the middle of the process, without a doubt we will be able to achieve all those results that we want to achieve, and we can become bilingual. What do you say? Are you ready to start on this wonderful adventure? If your answer was yes (and I'm sure it was) then I'm sure you will achieve every one of your goals.

Bonus Chapter (Articles)

In this chapter, the objective is that we see some articles that we can use to practice our reading in Spanish, as well as different aspects of our pronunciation. In the same way, this is an excellent technique that will help us a lot to not only exercise our reading level and our pronunciation, but we will also be able to learn many new words and phrases that are commonly used in Spanish. Without a doubt, this is one of the most effective techniques that we can use when we are learning a new language, and that is why we have decided to include it in this book.

The important thing, so that we can get the most out of this section, is that we can try to understand and interpret each of the sentences that appear in the text that is in Spanish, and so that later we can verify if we understood everything perfectly when we are reading the English translation. Many people underestimate the power of reading, but it can help us achieve great things, especially when it comes to reading in another language since in this way we will understand everything we have been learning throughout this book. in a better way. On the other hand, if we do not focus on understanding each of these things, it is very likely that we will forget many of the phrases and words that we have learned so far.

La Evolución de la Música Latina (The Evolution of the Latin Music)

Sin duda, la historia de la música latina es muy extensa y muy interesante. A diferencia de muchísimos otros géneros musicales, la música latina es una de las más movidas y emocionantes del mundo artístico. De hecho, muchas personas alrededor del mundo se fascinan cuando escuchan este tipo de música, ya que sienten una vibra positiva en el cuerpo que se genera gracias a los variados ritmos latinos que se producen en estos géneros musicales. Entre los más famosos de la música latina tenemos a la salsa, la bachata, el reggaetón, el tango, la cumbia y muchos otros que han sido los géneros encargados de representar no sólo a la música sino a la cultura latina alrededor del mundo.

Sin embargo, muchos de esos géneros son más famosos en algunos países y menos escuchados en otros. Por ejemplo, el tango es uno de los géneros musicales más famosos de Argentina, pero la verdad es que es muy poco escuchado en otros países. En cambio, la bachata es uno de los géneros musicales más escuchados en República Dominicana y en otros países del Caribe. Es por eso que cada país tiene una música en específico que se encarga de representar a la cultura y de expresar lo que la gente piensa y siente.

Sin duda alguna, la música tiene el poder de transportarnos a otros lugares y de hacernos sentir muchísimas emociones que no se pueden sentir con ningún otro tipo de arte. Lo qué pasa con la música latina es que está llena de alegría y de muchos colores, que nos generan una enorme satisfacción al escucharla. Es por eso que la música latina se ha ido expandiendo hacia muchos otros países en el mundo, y ha sido bien recibida por el público internacional. Hoy en día hay artistas que son escuchados en todo el mundo, como por ejemplo, Bad Bunny, Ozuna, J Balvin, Maluma, Daddy Yankee y otros más que representan al género musical del reggaetón.

Por supuesto, existen muchos otros géneros que se han ido popularizando alrededor del mundo, pero el reggaetón tiene la principal característica de que es un estilo de música que es muy popular entre los jóvenes, cuyos artistas se han vuelto muy famosos en las principales plataformas digitales como por ejemplo Spotify, Apple Music, Deezer y muchos otros. Sin duda alguna, es probable que hayamos escuchado alguna de esas canciones en la radio, en la televisión o en esas principales plataformas digitales. Popularmente se dice que nunca es un mal día para escuchar música latina, así que debemos seguir ese consejo para alegrar cada uno de nuestros días.

Translation

Without a doubt, the history of Latin music is very extensive and very interesting. Unlike so many other musical genres, Latin music is one of the busiest and most exciting in the art world. In fact, many people around the world are fascinated when they listen to this type of music, since they feel a positive vibe in the whole body that is generated thanks to the varied Latin rhythms that are produced in these musical genres. Among the most famous musical genres of Latin music, we have salsa, bachata, reggaeton, tango, cumbia and many others that have been the genres in charge of representing not only music but also Latin culture around the world. world.

However, many of those genres are more famous in some countries and less listened to in others. For example, tango is one of the most famous musical genres in Argentina, but the truth is that it is rarely heard in other countries. Instead, bachata is one of the most listened to musical genres in the Dominican Republic and in some Caribbean countries. That is why each country has a specific music that is responsible for representing the culture and expressing what people think and feel.

Without a doubt, music has the power to transport us to other places and make us feel many emotions that cannot be felt with any other type of art. What happens with Latin music is that it is full of joy and many colors, which give us enormous satisfaction when listening to it. That is why Latin music has been expanding to many other countries in the world, and has been well received by the international public. Today there are artists who are heard all over the world such as Bad Bunny, Ozuna, J Balvin, Maluma, Daddy Yankee and others who represent the musical genre of reggaeton.

Of course, there are many other genres that have become popular around the world, but reggaeton has the main characteristic that it is a style of music that is very popular among young people, whose artists have become very famous on the main digital platforms. such as Spotify, Apple Music, Deezer and many others. Without a doubt, it is likely that we have heard some of those songs on the radio, on television or on those main digital platforms. It is popularly said that it is never a bad day to listen to Latin music, so we must follow that advice to brighten each of our days.

La Historia de las Capitales Sudamericanas (The History of the South American Capitals)

Sin duda alguna, Sudamérica es uno de los continentes más interesantes del mundo, ya que cuenta con países increíbles, culturas interesantes, y sobre todo, gente que es muy cálida y que tienen un carisma increíble. Sin embargo, lo verdaderamente impresionante de este continente son todas las capitales hermosas que tiene a lo largo de todos sus territorios y países. Debemos recordar que Sudamérica está compuesto por 10 países principales y, adicionalmente, otros países no tan conocidos como Surinam y Guyana. Una de las capitales más importantes (y más famosas) del continente es Brasilia. La mayoría de las personas usualmente cree que la capital de Brasil es Rio de Janeiro, pero la verdad es que la ciudad de Brasilia es una de las más hermosas del continente, pese a no compararse con el paraíso tropical de Río de Janeiro.

Luego, una de las capitales más bonitas no sólo de este continente sino del mundo entero es Buenos Aires. Esta es una ciudad cargada de bastante historia y cultura en la que podemos ver muchísimos recitales de tango, comer una de las mejores carnes del mundo, y por supuesto, ver un partido de fútbol en vivo y sentir la enorme pasión de los fanáticos argentinos. Todo esto hace que Buenos Aires sea uno de los destinos preferidos por muchos viajeros del continente, por lo que es muy recomendable que cuando podamos, no dudemos en visitar esta hermosa ciudad.

Luego tenemos a Bogotá, que es la capital de Colombia. Esta es una ciudad que se caracteriza por tener uno de los mejores cafés del mundo, así que si algún día vamos, no podemos dejar de probar el exquisito café de la marca Juan Valdez, que es uno de los cafés más aclamados en el mundo entero. De igual forma, el clima de Bogotá hará que simplemente queramos vivir ahí por siempre. Unos kilómetros más al sur, nos vamos a encontrar con Montevideo, que es la capital de Uruguay. En los últimos años, esta es una ciudad que ha tenido un crecimiento económico impresionante, lo que ha llevado a muchísimas personas del continente a emigrar a ese país en búsqueda de mejores oportunidades laborales y de aumentar el nivel de sus estilos de vida. De igual forma, esta es una ciudad que tiene muchísimos destinos turísticos por recorrer, por lo cual es un destino sumamente recomendado para todo tipo de personas.

Por último, tenemos a Quito, que es la capital de Ecuador. Esta es una ciudad bastante famosa alrededor del mundo, ya que hay un punto en el que existe lo que se le conoce como la mitad del mundo. Es decir, cuando visitemos ese parque, nos vamos a dar cuenta que hay una enorme línea amarilla, que indica que en ese mismo punto estamos parados en la mitad del mundo. De igual forma, Ecuador tiene muchísimos sitios turísticos que vale la pena recorrer, tales como Machu Pichu y muchas otras obras arquitectónicas ancestrales que hacen que este país sea único y maravilloso. Estas fueron tan solo cinco de las capitales más importantes e históricas de Sudamérica, que no debemos dudar en visitar si alguna vez se nos presenta la oportunidad.

Translation

Without a doubt, South America is one of the most interesting continents in the world, as it has incredible countries, interesting cultures, and above all, people who are very warm and have incredible charisma. However, what is truly impressive about this continent are all the beautiful capitals that it has throughout all its territories and countries. We must remember that South America is made up of 10 main countries, and additionally other less well-known countries such as Suriname and Guyana. One of the most important (and most famous) capitals of the continent is Brasilia. Most people usually believe that the capital of Brazil is Rio de Janeiro, but the truth is that the city of Brasilia is one of the most beautiful on the continent, despite not being compared to the tropical paradise of Rio de Janeiro.

Then, one of the most beautiful capitals not only in this continent but in the whole world is Buenos Aires. This is a city full of history and culture, where we can see many tango recitals, eat one of the best meats in the world, and of course, watch a live soccer game and feel the enormous passion of Argentine fans. All this makes Buenos Aires one of the favorite destinations for many travelers from the continent, so it is highly recommended that when we can, we do not hesitate to visit this beautiful city.

Then we have Bogotá, which is the capital of Colombia. This is a city that is characterized by having one of the best coffees in the world, so if one day we go, we cannot miss out on trying the exquisite coffee from the Juan Valdez brand, which is one of the most acclaimed coffees in the entire world. Similarly, the climate of Bogotá will make us simply want to live there forever. A few kilometers further south, we will find Montevideo, which is the capital of Uruguay. In recent years, this is a city that has had impressive economic growth, which has led many people from the continent to emigrate to that country in search of better job opportunities and to increase the level of their lifestyles. Similarly, this is a city that has many tourist destinations to visit, which is why it is a highly recommended destination for all types of people.

Finally, we have Quito, which is the capital of Ecuador. This is quite a famous city around the world, as there is a point where there is what is known as the middle of the world. That is to say, when we visit that park, we are going to realize that there is a huge yellow line, which indicates that at that same point we are standing in the middle of the world. Similarly, Ecuador has many tourist sites that are worth visiting, such as Machu Picchu and many other ancient architectural works that make this country unique and wonderful. These were just five of the most important and historical capitals of South America, which we should not hesitate to visit if the opportunity ever arises.

La Mejor Comida Hispana (The Best Hispanic Food)

Una de las mejores cosas que tienen los países hispanohablantes es, sin duda alguna, la comida. La gran mayoría de los países latinoamericanos, al igual que países de Centroamérica, México y España se caracterizan por tener una gastronomía privilegiada, cuyos amantes van mucho más allá de sus fronteras. Cuando hablamos de la buena comida hispana, no nos referimos a esas falsas imitaciones que podemos encontrar en Taco Bell, Chipotle, La Cantina o alguno de estos restaurantes o franquicias. En cambio, nos estamos refiriendo a la verdadera comida hispana, hecha por las personas que de verdad saben darle una buena sazón a esa comida, y usan los típicos ingredientes de cada uno de esos países.

Por supuesto, puede que aún no hayamos probado algunos de esos platos, pero en este artículo vamos a hacer un repaso por algunos de los mejores platos hispanos. Uno de esos es la empanada argentina. Este es un plato bastante típico que consiste en un pastel de masa que está relleno de diversos ingredientes previamente cocinados y que sirve caliente. Esto se puede comer como entrada, aperitivo o simplemente una comida fuerte si nos comemos varias empanadas. Estas no sólo son famosas en Argentina, sino que también las podemos encontrar en otros países como Colombia y Venezuela.

Otra de las mejores comidas hispanas es el Ceviche peruano. Esto consiste en un tipo de pescado picado en trocitos, acompañado de otros ingredientes como limón, papas, arroz y muchas otras cosas. Sin duda alguna, muy pocas recetas de pescado son tan deliciosas como el ceviche peruano, ya que simplemente es algo único. Otro plato típico es el de la Bandeja Paisa en Colombia, que es un plato que incluye huevo, salchicha, arroz, aguacate y muchas otras cosas deliciosas que nos van a dejar muy satisfechos.

Por último, tenemos a los tamales, que son una de las comidas mexicanas más deliciosas. Estos están hechos a base de harina de maíz y suelen estar rellenos con carne o pollo, al igual que diversas salsas a base de aguacate e ingredientes variados. Sin duda alguna, no podemos dejar de comer alguno de esos deliciosos platos si tenemos alguna vez la oportunidad, ya que sencillamente no nos vamos a arrepentir. De igual forma, podemos buscar todas esas recetas en YouTube e intentar hacerlas en casa, ya que sin duda alguna también será un experimento que valga la pena.

Translation

One of the best things that Spanish-speaking countries have is, without a doubt, the food. The vast majority of Latin American countries, as well as countries in Central America, Mexico and Spain are characterized by having a privileged gastronomy, whose lovers go far beyond their borders. When we talk about good Hispanic food, we are not referring to those false imitations that we can find in Taco Bell, Chipotle, La Cantina or any of these restaurants or franchises. Instead, we are referring to real Hispanic food, made by people who really know how to give that food a good seasoning, and use the typical ingredients of each of those countries.

Of course, we may not have tried some of those dishes yet, but in this article we are going to take a look at some of the best Hispanic dishes. One of those is the Argentine empanada. This is a fairly typical dish that consists of a dough cake that is filled with various previously cooked ingredients, and served hot. This can be eaten as a starter, an appetizer or simply a strong meal if we eat several empanadas. These are not only famous in Argentina, but we can also find them in other countries such as Colombia and Venezuela.

Another of the best Hispanic foods is the Peruvian Ceviche. This consists of a type of fish chopped into small pieces, accompanied by other ingredients such as lemon, potatoes, rice and many other things. Without a doubt, very few fish recipes are as delicious as Peruvian ceviche, as it is simply something unique. Another typical dish is the Paisa Tray in Colombia, which is a dish that includes eggs, sausage, rice, avocado, and many other delicious things that will leave us very satisfied.

Finally, we have tamales, which are one of the most delicious Mexican foods. These are made from corn flour, and are usually filled with meat or chicken, as well as various avocado-based sauces, and assorted ingredients. Without a doubt, we cannot stop eating any of these delicious dishes if we ever have the opportunity, since we simply will not regret it. In the same way, we can look for all those recipes on YouTube and try to make them at home, since without a doubt it will also be a worthwhile experiment.

El Fútbol, Deporte Rey en Argentina (Soccer, the King of Sports in Argentina)

Sin duda alguna, el fútbol es el deporte más popular en Argentina y es el encargado de hacer vibrar a la sociedad en cada uno de los partidos que disputan los equipos más populares del país. Pese a que Argentina solo ha ganado dos copas mundiales en la historia, es uno de los países que tiene futbolistas más talentosos alrededor del mundo, teniendo entre los más famosos a dos de los mejores jugadores de la historia como Diego Maradona y Lionel Messi. Estos dos jugadores, uno que lastimosamente falleció en 2020 y el otro que aún sigue activo, han llevado no solo la pasión del deporte argentino alrededor del mundo, sino que también se han encargado de esparcir un poco de cultura de ese país hacia otros rincones del mundo, incluyendo a países de Europa, Asia y África.

De hecho, el estadio de Nápoles, que es uno de los estadios de fútbol más importantes en Argentina, se llama Estadio Diego Armando Maradona en honor a este enorme jugador que es considerado el mejor jugador en la historia de ese equipo. Por otro lado, Lionel Messi es considerado el mejor futbolista en la actualidad y de la historia por muchos expertos en ese deporte.

En Argentina, se dice usualmente que el fútbol no es solo un deporte, sino que es como una religión para todos los argentinos. No importa qué edad tengas, cuál es tu religión, tu nivel de educación o tu nivel económico, si eres argentino es muy probable que te guste el fútbol. De hecho, tan solo en la Ciudad de Buenos Aires (que es la capital de Argentina) hay más de 50 equipos de fútbol profesionales. Esto nos habla de la enorme pasión que genera este deporte, al igual que la enorme cantidad de dinero que se mueve en torno a este maravilloso deporte. De hecho, los canales de televisión en Argentina básicamente sólo hablan de fútbol, ya que saben que es el deporte que más le interesa a las personas.

Los dos equipos argentinos más famosos son Boca Juniors y River Plate (ambos de la Ciudad de Buenos Aires). Ambos son considerados como los equipos más importantes de la historia en el fútbol sudamericano, ya que las personas saben que estos no solo han sido los equipos con más trofeos en la historia del continente, sino que también son los equipos con más aficionados no solo en Argentina sino en Sudamérica. Los argentinos dicen que no podemos ir al país y no ir a un partido de fútbol, ya que sería similar a ir a París y no ver la Torre Eiffel. El punto es que si vamos a Argentina, no podemos dejar de ir a un emocionante partido de fútbol, ya que sin duda alguna estaremos conociendo uno de los aspectos más importantes de la cultura argentina.

Translation

Without a doubt, soccer is the most popular sport in Argentina, and it is responsible for making society vibrate in each of the matches played by the most popular teams in the country. Despite the fact that Argentina has only won two world cups in history, it is one of the countries that have the most talented soccer players around the world, having among the most famous two of the best players in history such as Diego Maradona and Lionel Messi. These two players, one who unfortunately passed away in 2020 and the other who is still active, have not only brought the passion of Argentine sports around the world, but have also been responsible for spreading a bit of culture from that country to other corners of the world. world, including countries in Europe, Asia and Africa.

In fact, the stadium in Naples, which is one of the most important soccer stadiums in Argentina, is called Estadio Diego Armando Maradona, in honor of this huge player who is considered the best player in the history of that team. On the other hand, Lionel Messi is considered the best footballer today, and also the best in history by many experts in the sport.

In Argentina, it is usually said that soccer is not just a sport, but rather it is like a religion for all Argentines. No matter how old you are, what your religion is, your level of education or your economic level, if you are Argentine it is very likely that you like soccer. In fact, in the City of Buenos Aires alone (which is the capital of Argentina), there are more than 50 professional soccer teams. This tells us about the enormous passion that this sport generates, as well as the enormous amount of money that moves around this wonderful sport. In fact, the television channels in Argentina basically only talk about soccer, since they know that it is the sport that most interests people.

The two most famous Argentine teams are Boca Juniors and River Plate (both from the City of Buenos Aires). Both are considered as the most important teams in the history of South American football, as people know that these have not only been the teams with the most trophies in the history of the continent, but they are also the teams with the most fans not only in Argentina but in South America. Argentines say that we cannot go to the country and not go to a football match, since it would be similar to going to Paris and not seeing the Eiffel Tower. The point is that if we go to Argentina, we can't stop going to an exciting soccer game, since without a doubt we will be getting to know one of the most important aspects of Argentine culture.

BOOK 2

Learn Spanish for Adult Beginners Handbook

Your Proven Guide to Speaking Spanish in 30 Days!

Explore to Win

Book 2 Description

$\sim$

If you've always wanted to learn Spanish, but still can't, keep reading...

Are you sick of not being able to learn Spanish? Have you tried countless language courses, but none seem to work? Do you finally want to say goodbye to boring Spanish textbooks and discover something that really works for you?

Then, we have the perfect book for you.

You see, learning Spanish doesn't have to be complicated. The truth is that it's much simpler than you think.

In this book, you can become a Spanish beginner in just 30 days. But why 30 days? Isn't a month a short time? Well, no. Setting a time frame is a great way to reach a goal, and 30 days is enough time to learn a lot of things.

In *Learn Spanish for Adult Beginners Handbook: Your Proven Guide to Speaking Spanish in 30 Days*, you'll discover:

- The most common grammar mistakes in Spanish and how to overcome them

- Lots of useful Spanish phrases for everyday life

- Secrets to pronouncing Spanish like a true native

- The most important verbs in Spanish and how to conjugate them

- The days of the week, the months, and the seasons

- All the vocabulary you'll need in your next trip

...and much more!

That's right: this is the perfect book to dive head-first into Spanish. No matter how old you are, and no matter if you already know some basic Spanish or if you don't know a word. This is a book for everyone and it will cover all the necessary topics so that, in just 30 days, you will already have all the skills you need to be able to communicate and have conversations in Spanish.

So, even if you've never had any contact with the Spanish language, you can learn to speak it in only a month with *Learn Spanish for Adult Beginners Handbook: Your Proven Guide to Speaking Spanish in 30 Days!*

If you are ready to learn Spanish in one month, scroll up and click "Add to cart" now. *¡Buena suerte!*

Introduction

❧

Are you ready to begin your Spanish-learning journey but feel like you're wasting your time with language courses? Or, perhaps you already know some Spanish but don't want to go at someone else's pace? Or maybe you need a book that makes grammar easy to understand to complement your Spanish lessons? Well, then you've got your hands on the right book!

Learn Spanish for Adult Beginners Handbook: Speak Spanish in 30 Days! is the perfect book to dive head-first into Spanish.

With this book, you will learn everything you need not only for your next trip but also for all the ones that follow! And though we suggest you take 30 days to take all of it in, we also encourage you to do it at your own pace!

In this book, you will find useful phrases and real-life situations and you will also learn all the grammar, vocabulary, and pronunciation you need to set the foundations to keep on learning Spanish.

This book contains all the vocabulary you need to understand people on your next trip to a Spanish-speaking country. You will find lists of nouns, adjectives, and the most used verbs, but we don't expect you to simply read them and remember them. We will give you many examples of the words in use so that you can learn how to use them yourself. It is also accompanied with some easy pronunciation guides.

You won't just learn to introduce yourself to strangers and answer basic questions. In this book, you will learn how to buy things at a shop, ask for prices, and choose the best item for you. You will also learn how to interact with staff at a restaurant, including asking for recommendations and talking about your eating habits.

And, of course, you will become the master of the present tense without even realizing it: all of the grammar explanations are simple and easy-to-access for English speakers. And we will give you simple examples so that you learn more from practice than from reading.

And all of this content will then be summarized at the end of the chapter so that you can review everything and also double-check that you've learned everything you've seen so far. Additionally, you will also find some really useful exercises to start practicing for real-life interactions at the end of each chapter. You will also find the answers key so that you can go on this Spanish-learning journey on your own and check your own progress!

You can actually use this book in different ways. It is useful to study on your own, following its explanations, practicing with the exercises and answer keys. Of course, it can also be a great complement to your Spanish courses because it is filled with easy explanations and extra practice for you! You can also take this book on your trips, for example, and find the chapter you need for every particular situation in case you can't remember exactly what you needed to say. So, don't forget it next time you're at a restaurant.

The authors of this book are actually native Spanish-speaking linguists themselves, which means they know exactly what they're talking about and can give you excellent tips on how to use and pronounce the language and phrases that are in this book.

When you're done with this book, you won't believe how much you've learned in such a short time. So, it's time to get started! What are you waiting for? Our 30 days start **today**!

Chapter 1: Basics

❦

El lenguaje nos ayuda a capturar el mundo.

- Fernando Lázaro Carreter

In this chapter, for the first three days of this course, we will be dealing with a basic kit to start your Spanish-learning journey. In this kit, you will find a guide to the Spanish alphabet, sounds, and numbers, and some vocabulary with basic greetings, farewells and useful phrases. Are you ready?

The Alphabet

First, we will see the Spanish alphabet, which is almost the same as the English alphabet. We will learn the names of each letter before we get into the Spanish sounds in the following section. In Spanish, the alphabet is called *abecedario* or *alfabeto*.

- A is called *a*.
- B is called *be* o *be larga*.
- C is called *ce*.
- D is called *de*.
- E is called *e*.
- F is called *efe*.
- G is called *ge*.
- H is called *hache*.
- I is called *i* or *i latina*.
- J is called *jota*.
- K is called *ca*.
- L is called *ele*.
- M is called *eme*.
- N is called *ene*.
- Ñ is called *eñe*.
- O is called *o*.
- P is called *pe*.
- Q is called *cu*.
- R is called *erre*.
- S is called *ese*.
- T is called *te*.

- U is called *u.*
- V is called *uve, ve* or *ve corta.*
- W is called *uve doble, doble u,* or *doble ve.*
- X is called *equis.*
- Y is called *i griega.*
- Z is called *zeta.*

The Spanish Sounds

Let's start with a quick and easy guide to Spanish sounds so that you can start practicing your pronunciation from the get-go. The first thing that you need to know is that Spanish pronunciation is much simpler than English pronunciation. For example, in English, you can have many different sounds for one single vowel, but in Spanish each vowel has only one sound. What a relief, right? Let's get started.

The Spanish Vowel Sounds

In Spanish, we have the same five vowels as in English, but they always have the same pronunciation. Let's see these sounds and some examples of them in use!

Vowel	English Sound	Example	Pronunciation	Translation
A	ah	m<u>a</u>nz<u>a</u>n<u>a</u>	mahn-ZAH-nah	apple
E	eh	t<u>e</u>n<u>e</u>r	teh-NEHR	to have
I	ee	f<u>i</u>n	feen	end
O	oh	<u>o</u>lm<u>o</u>	OHL-moh	elm tree
U	oo	s<u>u</u>r	soor	south

Note: To better understand this table (and all pronunciation tables to come), you need to know that the pronunciation of the words are separated in syllables with dashes (-) to make pronunciation simple, and that the syllables capitalized are the ones where the stress is.

To make a long explanation simple enough for this level, we recommend you use these pronunciation guides to see where the stress falls on each word. Remember that whenever you see a tilde on top of a vowel (that is, this symbol ´ in the following way: *á, é, í, ó, ú*), you should put the stress on that vowel.

Whenever any of these vowels appear together, we pronounce them separately, unlike in English. This means that a word like *Alegría,* which means "happiness", is pronounced ah-leh-GREE-ah.

However, there are two exceptions to this rule:

121

- **UE after Q or G.** When the vowels U and E appear together after a Q or a G, the U is not pronounced, which means that it is as if there was only an E. An example of this could be the word *guerra*, which means "war" and is pronounced GEH-rrah.

- **UI after Q or G.** The same happens when there is a U and an I together after a Q and a G. One example of this is the word *águila*, which means "eagle" and is pronounced AH-gee-lah.

Let's see some examples of combinations of vowels and their pronunciations.

Vowel Combination	Example	Pronunciation	Translation
AE	m<u>ae</u>stra	mah-EHS-trah	teacher
AI	c<u>aí</u>da	kah-EE-dah	fall
AO	<u>ao</u>rta	ah-OHR-tah	aorta
AU	<u>au</u>xilio	ah-oo-xee-LEE-oh	help
EA	pel<u>ea</u>	pch-LEH-ah	fight
EI	r<u>eí</u>r	rreh-EEHR	to laugh
EO	empl<u>eo</u>	em-PLEH-oh	job
EU	<u>eu</u>ropa	eh-oo-ROH-pah	europe
IA	al<u>ia</u>nza	ah-lee-AHN-sah	alliance
IE	m<u>ie</u>l	mee-EHL	honey
IO	glor<u>io</u>so	glo-ree-OH-soh	glorious
IU	tr<u>iu</u>nfo	tree-OON-foh	triumph
OA	<u>oa</u>sis	oh-ah-sees	oasis
OE	p<u>oe</u>ta	poh-eh-tah	poet
OI	<u>oí</u>r	oh-EER	to hear
OU	estad<u>ou</u>nidense	ehs-tah-doh-oo-nee-DEHN-seh	American
UA	g<u>ua</u>nte	goo-AHN-teh	glove
UE	m<u>ue</u>stra	moo-EHS-trah	sample

Q/G + UE	queso	KEH-soh	cheese
UI	fluido	floo-EE-doh	fluid
Q/G + UI	guiar	gee-AHR	to guide
UO	continuo	con-TEE-noo-oh	continuous

The Spanish Consonant Sounds

Since Spanish is the official language of 21 countries located in very different parts of the globe and with different cultures and customs, it is no wonder we can hear very different Spanish accents around the world. This has a great impact on the way some Spanish consonants are pronounced in different Spanish-speaking regions. Sometimes, we can even find different pronunciations and accents within a country. Spanish is really diverse!

This makes consonants a bit more complicated than vowels, but, as we promised, we will make it simple!

- B sounds similar to an English B, but we let out less air to pronounce it.
- The consonant C has four possible pronunciations:
  - When it comes before vowels A, O, and U, it has a sound similar to an English K.
  - When it comes before vowels E and I, it has a sound similar to an English S.
  - When it comes before an H, it is pronounced like the CH sound in "choose".
  - When there are two Cs together, the first C is pronounced like an English K and the second C is pronounced like an English S.
- Spanish D has a similar sound to English D.
- F is pronounced the same as an English F.
- The consonant G has two possible pronunciations:
  - It is soft when it comes before A, O, and U or a consonant. Then, it has a sound similar to the English G in "goat"
  - It is strong when it comes before E and I. Then, it has a sound similar to the H sound in "hello".
  - What happens when it comes before the combinations UE and UI? Is it soft or strong? We learned earlier that the U is silent in these cases, but since it is there, we read these combinations with a soft G!
- The consonant H in Spanish has no sound. It is always silent!
- J is pronounced like a strong G (the one from "hello").
- K is pronounced like the C that comes before A, O, and U, which means that it is pronounced like an English K.
- The consonant L is pronounced very similarly to an English L!

- In Spanish, the L can appear duplicated. We call this *doble ele* and its pronunciation varies depending on the region.
  - It can be pronounced similar to the English Y in "yet".
  - It can be pronounced as the English J in "jeans". This is the sound that we will use for *doble ele* in this course.
  - In some countries, it is pronounced almost as an L with an I together.
  - Finally, in a few other countries it is pronounced as the SH sound in "shutter".
- M is pronounced just like an English M.
- N is also pronounced just like an English N.
- Ñ is the one letter that exists in Spanish but doesn't in English. This is pronounced similarly to the letters N and Y together. For example, in the name of the rapper Kanye.
- P is pronounced just like an English P, only letting out less air.
- The consonant Q is pronounced like the Spanish K (and C before A, U, and O).
- Consonant R also has two possible pronunciations:
  - The soft R is used when there is a single R in the middle or end of a word. This R sounds like the T sound some American speakers use in words like "better".
  - The famous "rolled R" sound is pronounced putting your tongue in the same position as you would to pronounce a normal English R, but making a trill between your tongue and the ridge of bone behind your teeth. This sound is used whenever there is a single R at the beginning of a word or when there is a double R in the middle of a word.
- S is pronounced just like an English S.
- T is pronounced similar to the English Y sound in "stay."
- Consonants B and V have the same pronunciation in most Spanish-speaking countries.
- Consonant W is barely used in Spanish, but when it is, it's pronounced like an English W sound.
- Consonant X has three possible pronunciations:
  - If it appears at the beginning of a word, it is pronounced like an S.
  - If it is in the middle or at the end of a word, it is pronounced like the English X in "fox".
  - As an exception, it can sometimes be pronounced similar to a Spanish J and strong G in words like Mexico.
- The pronunciation of Y can vary depending on the region. In most countries, it is pronounced exactly the same as a LL.
  - It can be pronounced as the English Y sound in "yet"
  - It can also be pronounced as the English J sound in "jeans". This is the sound we will use throughout this course.
  - It can also be pronounced as an SH sound.
  - However, when the Y is on its own or at the end of a word, it is pronounced exactly like a Spanish I: *ee*.

- In some regions, the S and the Z have the same pronunciation, but in some others, the Z has a different sound which is similar to the English TH sound in "thing".

Spanish Consonant	English Sound	Example	Pronunciation	Translation
B / V	b	bravo	BRAH-boh	bravo
C / K / Q	k	cacique kilo	kah-SEE-keh KEE-loh	chieftain kilo
C / S / X	s	cesárea xilofón	seh-SAH-reh-ah see-loh-FOHN	cesarean xylophone
CH	ch	chancho	CHAHN-choh	pig
D	d	dar	dahr	to give
F	f	fácil	FAH-seel	easy
G	g	gorro	GOH-rroh	hat
G / J /X	h	jorge Texas	HOHR-heh TEH-hahs	george texas
H	[silent]	hondo	OHN-doh	deep
L	l	lila	LEE-lah	lilac
LL / Y	j	pollo yacer	POH-joh jah-SEHR	chicken to lie
M	m	mimar	mee-MAHR	to pamper
N	n	ninfa	NEEN-fah	nymph
Ñ	ny	ñandú	nyahn-DOO	rhea
P	p	papel	pah-PEHL	paper
R	r	comer	koh-MEHR	to eat
RR	rr	burro rápido	BOO-rroh RRAH-pee-doh	donkey fast

T	t	<u>t</u>oma<u>t</u>e	toh-MAH-teh	tomato
W	w	<u>w</u>eb	wehb	web
X	cs	sa<u>x</u>o	SAH-csoh	sax
Y	ee	ho<u>y</u>	oh-EE	today
Z	z	<u>z</u>afiro	zah-FEE-roh	sapphire

I know the charts we've seen might seem like a lot, but you can always come back to this page to check if you're pronouncing things correctly. We also encourage you to practice by pronouncing the words in this chart out loud–don't be embarrassed!

Saying 'Hello' and 'Goodbye'

Now that we know a bit about pronunciation, we can finally get into some of the vocabulary of this chapter. In this section we will deal with different ways of saying "hello" and "goodbye" in Spanish because, even if you can't speak Spanish (yet!), you will surely need to greet people when you enter hotels, bars, restaurants, etc. in a foreign country... So let's get to it!

Greetings

Greeting	Pronunciation	Explanation
hola	OH-lah	It means "hello".
buenos días	boo-EH-nohs DEE-ahs	It is used to greet someone during the morning (until noon).
buenas tardes	boo-EH-nahs TAHR-dehs	It is used to greet people during the afternoon. From around noon until sundown.
buenas noches	boo-EH-nahs NOH-chehs	It is used to greet people at night, but we can also use it to say goodbye before going to bed.
buenas	boo-EH-nahs	This is a short version of *buenas tardes* or *buenas noches*, but we can also use it during the morning.
buen día	boo-EHN DEE-ah	We can use it at any point during the day.

¿cómo estás?	KOH-moh ehs-TAHS	It means "how are you?" and it is commonly used after some of the other ways of greeting. It is more an expression than a question, but we can always answer!
¿qué tal?	keh tahl	It is another way of asking someone how's it going and works like ¿cómo estás?

Farewells

Farewell	Pronunciation	Explanation
adiós	ah-dee-OHS	It means "goodbye".
chao / chau	CHAH-oh / CHAH-oo	It also means "goodbye" and, in some countries, it is even more common than *adiós*.
nos vemos	nohs VEH-mohs	It means "see you" and it's used to say goodbye. We can also use it after *adiós* or *chao*.
hasta luego	AHS-tah loo-EH-goh	It means "see you later" and is a bit more formal than *nos vemos*. We can also change *luego* with the time we are going to see someone next, for example *hasta mañana* means "see you tomorrow".

The Numbers

Of course, learning the numbers is part of the basics. It's one of the first things we learn in every language and this Spanish course won't be the exception. You need to be able to say how many bottles of water you want at a restaurant or how many tickets you want to buy!

Let's see the numbers from 1 to 100 with their written form and their pronunciation!

Number	Written Form	Pronunciation
0	cero	SEH-roh
1	uno	OHH-noh
2	dos	dohs
3	tres	trehs

4	cuatro	koo-AH-troh
5	cinco	seen-koh
6	seis	SEH-ees
7	siete	see-EH-teh
8	ocho	OH-choh
9	nueve	noo-EH-beh
10	diez	DEE-ehz
11	once	OHN-seh
12	doce	DOH-seh
13	trece	TREH-seh
14	catorce	kah-TOHR-seh
15	quince	KEEN-seh
16	dieciséis	dee-eh-see-SEH-ees
17	diecisiete	dee-eh-see-seeh-EH-teh
18	dieciocho	dee-eh-see-OH-choh
19	diecinueve	dee-eh-see-noo-EH-beh
20	veinte	beh-EEN-teh
21	veintiuno	beh-een-tee-OO-noh
22	veintidós	beh-een-tee-DOHS
23	veintitrés	beh-een-tee-TREHS
24	veinticuatro	beh-een-tee-koo-AH-troh
25	veinticinco	beh-een-tee-SEEN-koh

26	veintiséis	beh-een-tee-SEH-ees
27	veintisiete	beh-een-tee-see-EH-teh
28	veintiocho	beh-een-tee-OH-choh
29	veintinueve	beh-een-tee-noo-EH-beh
30	treinta	treh-EEN-tah
31	treinta y uno	treh-EEN-tah ee OO-noh
32	treinta y dos	treh-EEN-tah ee dohs
33	treinta y tres	treh-EEN-tah ee trehs
34	treinta y cuatro	treh-EEN-tah ee koo-ah-troh
35	treinta y cinco	treh-EEN-tah ee seen-koh
36	treinta y seis	treh-EEN-tah ee seh-EES
37	treinta y siete	treh-EEN-tah ee see-EH-teh
38	treinta y ocho	treh-EEN-tah ee OH-choh
39	treinta y nueve	treh-EEN-tah ee noo-EH-beh
40	cuarenta	koo-ah-REHN-tah
50	cincuenta	seen-koo-EHN-tah
60	sesenta	seh-SEHN-tah
70	setenta	seh-TEHN-tah
80	ochenta	oh-CHEHN-tah
90	noventa	noh-BEHN-tah
100	cien	see-EHN

We didn't include the numbers between the tens after 40 in this chart because they are formed in the same way as the thirties. We use the ten we are talking about (*cuarenta, cincuenta, sesenta, setenta, ochenta,* or *noventa*), and then we add "y" and the number of the units digit we need (*uno, dos, tres, cuatro, cinco, seis, siete, ocho,* or *nueve*). So, for example, 58 is *cincuenta y ocho*, 75 is *setenta y cinco*, and 87 is *ochenta y siete*.

Some Useful Phrases

To finish off this chapter, we will see some useful phrases that will probably come in handy wherever you go! They are just some basic phrases, but they are used in everyday life.

Let's have a look at them, their pronunciation, and their translation in the following table!

Word or phrase	Pronunciation	Translation
sí	see	yes
no	noh	no
no lo sé	noh loh seh	I don't know
quizás	kee-ZAHS	maybe
gracias	grah-SEE-ahs	thank you
de nada	deh NAH-dah	you're welcome
perdón	pehr-DOHN	sorry
lo siento	loh see-EHN-toh	I'm sorry
disculpa	dees-KOOL-pah	excuse me
Bien, ¿y tú?	bee-EHN ee too	Fine, and you?
¡Mucho gusto!	MOO-choh GOOS-toh	Nice to meet you!
¡Es un placer conocerte!	ehs oon plah-sehr ko-noh-SEHR-teh	It's a pleasure to meet you!

Key Takeaways

In this first chapter, we saw some basic things that will allow us to start our Spanish-learning journey. Everything we've learned in this chapter will be useful to us throughout the entire course, so we should make sure that we've understood all of the topics. Let's recap:

- The alphabet
- The Spanish vowel sounds

- The Spanish vowels
- The Spanish vowel combinations
- The Spanish consonant sounds depending on the context of the consonant and the different regions
- Greetings
  - *Hola*
  - *Buenos días*
  - *Buenas tardes*
  - *Buenas noches*
  - *Buenas*
  - *Buen día*
  - *¿Cómo estás?*
  - *¿Qué tal?*
- Farewells
  - *Adiós*
  - *Chau / Chao*
  - *Nos vemos*
  - *Hasta luego*
- The numbers from *uno* to *cien*
- Some useful phrases
  - *Sí*
  - *No*
  - *No lo sé*
  - *Quizás*
  - *Gracias*
  - *De nada*
  - *Perdón*
  - *Lo siento*
  - *Disculpa*
  - *Bien, ¿y tú?*
  - *¡Mucho gusto!*
  - *¡Es un placer conocerte!*

Now that we've got the basics, the sky's the limit! After some exercises, we will move on to the next chapter, where you will learn to introduce yourself and ask questions about someone else. Let's meet new people!

Exercises

It's time to check if you've understood everything we saw in this chapter. You will find the answers to these exercises in the following section.

Don't be discouraged if you don't get all of the questions right the first time. You can always go back and revise the chapter and do the exercises again.

1. There's a quote at the beginning of the chapter. To practice the alphabet, can you spell out in Spanish the full name of its author out loud?

2. Can you spell out your own name?

3. True or false. In Spanish, the vowels can have many different pronunciations.

4. What happens when there are two vowels together?

    a. They create one new sound.

    b. Each vowel is pronounced separately.

    c. One of them isn't pronounced.

5. How do you pronounce *que*?

    a. koo

    b. kooeh

    c. keh

6. In Spanish, some consonants have different sounds depending on their position in the word or the letters that surround them. When do we pronounce a soft G?

    a. Before A, O, and U.

    b. Before E and I.

7. True or false. The consonants C, K and Q can be pronounced in the same way.

8. If you go into a restaurant to have dinner at night, which of the following words cannot be used to greet?

    a. Buenas

    b. ¿Qué tal?

    c. Buenos días

    d. Hola

    e. Buenas noches

9. How do you say 63 in Spanish?

    a. Setenta y tres

    b. Sesenta y tres

    c. Tres y sesenta

    d. Sesentitrés

10. If someone tells you *Gracias*, what would you answer?

    a. Sí.

b. Lo siento.

c. Bien, ¿y tú?

d. De nada.

Answer Key

1. eme-a-erre-i-o be-u-ene-ge-e
2. False. Vowels have only one pronunciation.
3. b. Each vowel is pronounced separately.
4. c. keh
5. a. Before A, O, and U.
6. True.
7. c. Buenos días
8. b. Sesenta y tres
9. d. De nada.

Chapter 2: Who Are You?

⌘

¿Quién soy? Estoy tratando de averiguarlo.

- Jorge Luis Borges

It's time for us to get to know you and to give you the tools for you to get to know others. In this chapter, you will learn to introduce yourself and to ask questions to others so that you can get to know them. Socializing is an important part of life, even if you're only planning on using your Spanish knowledge for a trip. You'll see that it will come in really handy!

Subject Pronouns

Before we start to introduce ourselves, we will talk about Spanish subject pronouns. Subject or personal pronouns are used to replace nouns in the subject position when we don't need to specify who that person is because of context or because we've already been talking about them.

While there are only 7 pronouns in English, Spanish has 12. That sounds like a lot, I know, but it's not as hard as it seems.

First, let's have a look at them in the following table, and I'll break it down for you afterwards.

	Pronoun	Pronunciation	Translation
1st person singular	yo	joh	I
2nd person singular	tú	too	you
	usted	oos-TEHD	
3rd person singular	él	ehl	he
	ella	EH-jah	she
1st person plural	nosotros	noh-SOH-trohs	we
	nosotras	noh-SOH-trahs	
2nd person plural	vosotros	voh-SOH-trohs	you
	vosotras	voh-SOH-trahs	
	ustedes	oos-TEH-dehs	

3rd person plural	ellos	EH-johs	them
	ellas	EH-jahs	

Now, let's see these pronouns one by one with a simple explanation and some examples.

Yo is the first person singular pronoun and can be translated as "I". Here's an example: *Yo soy inteligente* ("I'm intelligent").

Tú and *usted* are both second person singular pronouns, but we can't use them in the same contexts. We use *tú* for informal contexts and *usted* in formal contexts. For example, if I was with a friend, I could tell her <u>*Tú* eres inteligente</u> ("You're intelligent"), but if I was with a professor or my boss, I would say <u>*Usted* es inteligente</u> ("You're intelligent").

For the third person singular, we also have two options: *él* and *ella*. However, in this case, we are not talking about a formal and an informal pronoun, but a masculine (*él*) and a feminine (*ella*) pronoun, just like in English. This means that whenever we are talking about a man or a boy, we will use *él*, for example in: <u>*Él* es inteligente</u> ("He is intelligent"). However, when we are talking about a woman or a girl, we will use *ella*, for example in: <u>*Ella* es inteligente</u> ("She is intelligent").

Now we're moving on to the plural pronouns. The Spanish counterparts for the first person plural in English are *nosotros* and *nosotras*. In this case, just like with *él* and *ella*, we are talking about a masculine and a feminine pronoun. We use *nosotras* to talk about a group of women or girls when we're a part of it, for example: <u>*Nosotras* somos inteligentes</u> ("We're intelligent"). And we use *nosotros* when we talk about a group of men or boys we're a part of, for example: <u>*Nosotros* somos inteligentes</u> ("We're intelligent"). But what if we're part of a group of both men and women? Well, then we use the masculine to generalize: <u>*Nosotros* somos inteligentes</u>.

For the second person plural we have the pronouns *vosotros* and *vosotras*. As you may have already guessed, *vosotros* is the masculine form and *vosotras* is the feminine one. We can say <u>*Vosotros* sois inteligentes</u> ("You're intelligent") when we are talking to and about a group of men or boys, and we say <u>*Vosotras* sois inteligentes</u> ("You're intelligent") when we are talking to and about a group of women or girls. And in this case, we also use the masculine form to talk about a mixed group of men and women. But in the table we also have the pronoun *ustedes*, what do we use it for? Well, despite your guesses, it's not a formal version of the second person plural. Actually, many Latin American countries don't use *vosotros* and *vosotras*, but use *ustedes* instead. We can say <u>*Ustedes* son inteligentes</u> ("You're intelligent") to refer to a group of men, women or both!

Finally, we have the third-person plural pronouns *ellos* and *ellas*. *Ellos* is used to talk about a group of men, boys or a mixed group of men and women. For example: <u>*Ellos* son inteligentes</u> ("They're intelligent"). And we use *ellas* tu refer to a group of women or girls, for example: <u>*Ellas* son inteligentes</u> ("They're intelligent")

And you may be wondering, 'What about the English pronoun "it"?' Well, we have no equivalent for the neuter third person singular pronoun "it" in Spanish because every noun in Spanish is gendered. We must always use *él* or *ella*, even when we are talking about objects. We'll talk about that in the following section.

Gender and Number of Words

As we've just mentioned, every word in Spanish has a gender, but it also always has a number. Let's explain what this means: the gender of a word, in Spanish, is whether it is feminine or masculine. Nouns, adjectives, pronouns, and articles in Spanish have a gender. As a rule of thumb, we could say that nouns that end in -*a* are usually feminine, while nouns that end in -*o* are usually masculine. The number of a word is whether it is plural or singular. Nouns, adjectives, pronouns, articles, and verbs in Spanish have a number.

The heart and soul of the sentence is always the noun. So, in Spanish, the adjectives, pronouns, articles and verbs need to agree in gender and number (or only in number in the case of verbs) with the noun.

Let's see an example. In Spanish, a door isn't neutral, it's feminine and it's singular, so we refer to it as *la puerta*. In this phrase, we use the singular feminine article *la* because *puerta* is feminine and singular. If we wanted to add an adjective, we would also need to use a singular feminine adjective, for example: *La puerta es vieja* ("The door is old"). In this sentence, *es* is the third-person singular form of the verb *ser* ("to be"). And, if we wanted to refer to the door without naming it, we could say *Ella es vieja* ("It is old").

As you can see, in Spanish, the gender and number of the elements that surround the noun help us understand what object or person we're talking about. That's why we don't generally say *Ella es vieja* to refer to a door, we simply say *Es vieja* ("It's old"). And you might be thinking, 'Wait, but that sentence doesn't have a subject!' and you would be partially right. *Es vieja* doesn't have an overt subject. Its subject is *la puerta* or *ella*, but it isn't there, it is implicit. While we always need to have a subject in English, we can have implicit subjects in Spanish because the other elements of the sentence and the context are telling us exactly what noun we're referring to.

For example, if we say *La puerta es vieja* and then add another sentence about the door, we don't need to say *la puerta* again or even use the pronoun *ella*, we can just add a sentence without a subject. For example, we could have something like: *La puerta es vieja. Es linda.* ("The door is old. It's pretty.")

Now let's see an example with a plural masculine noun like *asientos* ("seats"). We could say *Los asientos son viejos. Son lindos* ("The seats are new. They're pretty"). In this sentence, *los* is the masculine plural article, *son* is the third-person plural conjugation of *ser*, *viejos* is the masculine plural form of the adjective *viejo* we've seen with the previous example, and *lindos* is the plural masculine form of the adjective *lindo*, which we've also seen in the previous example.

Getting to Know Someone

Now, it's time to get to know you and ask you some questions. We'll start by learning some questions we can ask anyone we're meeting for the first time, and we'll see how to answer those questions in the following section.

Here's a list of simple questions, their pronunciation, and their translation into English:

Question	Pronunciation	Translation
¿Cómo te llamas?	KOH-moh teh JAH-mahs	What's your name?
¿Cuál es tu nombre?	koo-AHL ehs too NOHM-breh	What's your name?

¿Cuál es tu apellido?	koo-AHL ehs too ah-PEH-jee-doh	What's your last name?
¿De dónde eres?	deh DOHN-deh eh-rehs	Where are you from?
¿Cuántos años tienes?	koo-AHN-tohs ah-NYOHS tee-EH-nehs	How old are you?
¿En qué trabajas?	ehn keh trah-bah-hahs	What do you do for work?
¿A qué te dedicas?	a keh teh deh-DEE-kahs	What do you do?

As you can see, all Spanish questions need an opening question mark and a closing question mark. In informal writing (for example, in chats), you might see that sometimes people only use a closing question mark, like in English, but this isn't correct.

Answering Questions

Now, let's learn how to answer the questions we've seen with their pronunciations and translations. To do this, we will use a fictional person called Carlos García from Spain who is 53 years old and works as an engineer so that we can give full answers. However, you need to change Carlos's information for your own when you answer questions about yourself.

¿Cómo te llamas? and _¿Cuál es tu nombre?_

Phrase	Pronunciation	Translation
Me llamo Carlos	meh JAH-moh KAHR-lohs	My name is Carlos
Mi nombre es Carlos	mee NOHM-breh ehs KAHR-lohs	My name is Carlos
Soy Carlos	SOH-ee KAHR-lohs	I'm Carlos

¿Cuál es tu apellido?

We can answer this question with the phrases:

Phrase	Pronunciation	Translation
Mi apellido es García	mee ah-peh-JEE-doh ehs gahr-SEE-ah	My last name is García
Es García	ehs gahr-SEE-ah	It's García

¿De dónde eres?

Phrase	Pronunciation	Translation

Soy de España	SOH-ee deh ehs-PAH-nya	I'm from Spain
Soy español	SOH-ee ehs-PAH-nyohl	I'm a Spaniard
Vengo de España	BEHN-goh deh ehs-PAH-nya	I come from Spain
Vivo en España	BEE-boh ehn ehs-PAH-nya	I live in Spain

¿Cuántos años tienes?

Phrase	Pronunciation	Translation
Tengo 53 años	TEHN-goh seen-koo-EHN-tah ee trehs AH-nyos	I'm 53 years old
53	seen-koo-EHN-tah ee trehs AH-nyos	I'm 53

We should note that even though we can use the verb to be to talk about our age in English, we can never say *Soy 53 años* or *Estoy 53 años*, we should always use the verb *tener* in Spanish.

¿En qué trabajas? and *¿A qué te dedicas?*

Phrase	Pronunciation	Translation
Soy ingeniero	SOH-ee een-heh-nee-EH-roh	I'm an engineer
Trabajo de ingeniero	trah-BAH-hoh deh een-heh-nee-EH-roh	I work as an engineer
Trabajo como ingeniero	trah-BAH-hoh koh-moh een-heh-nee-EH-roh	I work as an engineer

Verbs: Ser, Tener, Llamarse

As you may have noticed, to ask and answer the questions, we've used three verbs: *ser, tener,* and *llamarse.*

As we've seen, in Spanish, verbs need to agree in number and person with the noun, which means that in Spanish each verb has 6 different conjugations per tense.

Now, we'll see the present conjugations of the verbs *ser* (to be), *tener* (to have), and *llamarse* ("to be called") and we'll follow this with a simple explanation of the table.

	Pronoun	Ser	Tener	Llamarse
1st person singular	(yo)	soy	tengo	me llamo
2nd person singular	(tú)	eres	tienes	te llamas
3rd person singular	(él / ella / usted)	es	tiene	se llama
1st person plural	(nosotros / nosotras)	somos	tenemos	nos llamamos
2nd person plural	(vosotros / vosotras)	sois	tenéis	os llamáis
3rd person plural	(ellos / ellas / ustedes)	son	tienen	se llaman

Firstly, the pronouns in this table appear between parentheses because, as you might remember, they don't necessarily need to appear in the sentence. You might have realized that the pronouns *usted* and *ustedes* are misplaced, though. *Usted* is a second person singular pronoun, but it's grouped up with *él* and *ella*, which are third person singular pronouns. This is because *usted* is conjugated in the same way as *él* and *ella*, and not like *tú*. The same happens with *ustedes*, which is a second person plural pronoun but is conjugated like the third person plural pronouns *ellos* and *ellas*.

Now that we know these conjugations, we can, for example, answer questions about Carlos in the third person. We could ask and answer the questions in the following way:

- *¿Cómo se llama?* ("What's his name?")
  - *Se llama Carlos.* ("His name is Carlos")
- *¿Cuál es su apellido?* ("What's his last name?")
  - *Es García.* ("His last name is García")
- *¿De dónde es?* ("Where is he from?")
  - *Viene de España.* ("He's from Spain")
- *¿Cuántos años tiene?* ("How old is he?")
  - *Tiene 53 años.* ("He's 53 years old")
- *¿En qué trabaja?* ("What does he do for work?")
  - *Es ingeniero.* ("He's an engineer")

Finally, let's do a similar exercise but let's talk about Paula and Pedro now–Carlos's twin children.

- *¿Cómo se llaman?* ("What are their names?")
  - *Son Paula y Pedro.* ("They're Paula and Pedro")

- *¿Cuál es su apellido?* ("What's their last name?")
  - *Su apellido es García.* ("Their last name is García")
- *¿De dónde son?* ("Where are they from?")
  - *Son españoles.* ("They're from Spain")
- *¿Cuántos años tienen?* ("How old are they?")
  - *Tienen 16 años.* ("They're 16 years old")
- *¿A qué se dedican?* ("What do they do?")
  - *Son estudiantes.* ("They're students")

Countries and Nationalities

Now, it's time to see some vocabulary so that you can answer questions and understand the answers people give you. We'll start with some nationalities.

In the following table, you will find the English name of the country, the Spanish name of the country, its Spanish pronunciation, the masculine and feminine forms of the nationality of that country, and the Spanish pronunciation of the nationality.

Country in English	Country in Spanish	Pronunciation	Nationality	Pronunciation
Spain	España	ehs-PAH-nya	español española	ehs-PAH-nyol ehs-PAH-nyo-lah
Portugal	Portugal	pohr-TOO-gahl	portugués portuguesa	pohr-TOO-gehs pohr-TOO-geh-sah
Italy	Italia	ee-TAH-lee-ah	italiano italiana	ee-tah-lee-AH-noh ee-tah-lee-AH-nah
France	Francia	frahn-SEE-ah	francés francesa	frahn-SEHS frahn-SEH-sah
England	Inglaterra	een-glah-TEH-rrah	inglés inglesa	een-GLEHS een-GLEH-sah
Germany	Alemania	ah-leh-MAH-nee-ah	alemán alemana	ah-leh-MAHN ah-leh-MAH-nah
Russia	Rusia	ROO-see-a	ruso rusa	RROO-soh RROO-sah

United States	Estados Unidos	Ehs-TAH-dohs oo-NEE-dohs	estadounidense	ehs-tah-doh-oo-nee-DEHN-seh
Canada	Canadá	kah-nah-DAH	canadiense	kah-nah-dee-EHN-seh
China	China	CHEE-nah	chino china	CHEE-noh CHEE-nah
Japan	Japón	hah-POHN	japonés japonesa	hah-poh-NEHS hah-poh-NEH-sah
Korea	Corea	koh-REH-ah	coreano coreana	koh-reh-AH-no koh-reh-AH-nah
Mexico	México	MEH-hee-koh	mexicano mexicana	meh-hee-KAH-noh meh-hee-KAH-nah
Colombia	Colombia	koh-LOHM-bee-ah	colombiano colombiana	koh-lohm-bee-AH-noh koh-lohm-bee-AH-nah
Cuba	Cuba	KOO-bah	cubano cubana	koo-BAH-noh koo-BAH-nah
Costa Rica	Costa Rica	KOHS-tah REE-kah	costarricense	kohs-tah-rree-SEHN-seh
Puerto Rico	Puerto Rico	poo-EHR-toh ree-koh	puertorriqueño, puertorriqueña	poo-ehr-toh-rree-KEHN-yoh poo-ehr-toh-rree-KEHN-yah
Argentina	Argentina	ahr-hen-TEE-nah	argentino argentina	ahr-hehn-TEE-noh ahr-hehn-TEE-nah
Chile	Chile	CHEE-leh	chileno chilena	chee-LEH-noh chee-LEH-nah
Peru	Perú	peh-ROO	peruano peruana	peh-roo-AH-noh peh-roo-AH-nah

Brazil	Brasil	BRAH-seel	brasilero	brah-see-LEH-roh
			brasilera	brah-see-LEH-rah
Uruguay	Uruguay	oo-roo-goo-AH-ee	uruguayo	oo-roo-goo-AH-yo
			uruguaya	oo-roo-goo-AH-ya
Ecuador	Ecuador	eh-koo-AH-dohr	ecuatoriano	eh-koo-ah-toh-ree-ah-noh
			ecuatoriana	eh-koo-ah-toh-ree-ah-nah

In some cases, there is only one option in the nationality column because there is only one way to call a person from that country, regardless of their gender.

Finally, it's worth noting that, unlike in English, the nationalities in Spanish are never capitalized, but the names of the countries always are.

Jobs and Professions

Now, let's see some jobs and occupations! In the following table, you will find the masculine and feminine form of some jobs, their pronunciation, and their translation.

Like in the previous table, you will find that some jobs have only one option, which is used for both men and women.

Job	Pronunciation	Translation
estudiante	ehs-too-dee-AHN-teh	student
arquitecto	ahr-kee-TEHK-toh	architect
arquitecta	ahr-kee-TEHK-tah	
ingeniero	een-heh-nee-EH-roh	engineer
ingeniera	een-heh-nee-EH-rah	
abogado	ah-boh-GAH-doh	lawyer
abogada	ah-boh-GAH-dah	
secretario	seh-kreh-tah-REE-oh	secretary
secretaria	sek-kreh-tah-REE-ah	
artista	ahr-tees-tah	artist

actor actriz	ahk-TOHR ahk-TREEZ	actor actress
doctor doctora	dohk-TOHR dohk-TOH-rah	doctor
empresario empresaria	ehm-preh-SAH-ree-oh ehm-preh-SAH-ree-ah	businessperson
cocinero cocinera	koh-see-NEH-roh koh-see-NEH-rah	cook
cantante	kahn-TAHN-teh	singer
bombero bombera	bohm-BEH-roh bohm-BEH-rah	firefighter
policía	poh-lee-SEE-ah	police officer
mecánico mecánica	meh-kah-NEE-koh meh-kah-NEE-kah	mechanic
enfermero enfermera	ehn-fehr-MEH-roh ehn-ferh-MEH-rah	nurse
veterinario veterinaria	beh-teh-ree-NAH-ree-oh beh-teh-ree-NAH-ree-ah	vet
profesor profesora	proh-feh-SOHR proh-feh-SOH-rah	professor
traductor traductora	trah-dook-TOHR trah-dook-TOH-rah	translator
mesero mesera	meh-SEH-roh meh-SEH-rah	waiter

Key Takeaways

In this chapter, we've learned to introduce ourselves and to ask questions to get to know others. In order to do this, we've learned:

- The subject pronouns:
    - 1st person singular: *yo*
    - 2nd person singular: *tú* and *usted*
    - 3rd person singular: *él* and *ella*
    - 1st person plural: *nosotros* and *nosotras*
    - 2nd person plural: *vosotros, vosotras,* and *ustedes*
    - 3rd person plural: *ellos* and *ellas*
- The gender and number of words:
    - Adjectives, pronouns and articles need to agree in <u>gender</u> with the main noun
    - Adjectives, pronouns, articles, and verbs need to agree in <u>number</u> with the main noun
- That the subject in Spanish can be omitted when the people in the conversation know what we're talking about.
- Some basic questions to ask someone we've just met and how to answer those questions:
    - *¿Cómo te llamas?* or *¿Cuál es tu nombre?*
        - *Me llamo...* + your name
        - *Mi nombre es...* + your name
        - *Soy...* + your name
    - *¿Cuál es tu apellido?*
        - *Mi apellido es...* + your last name
        - *Es...* + your last name
    - *¿De dónde eres?*
        - *Soy de...* + your country
        - *Soy...* + your nationality
        - *Vengo de* + your country
        - *Vivo en* + your country
    - *¿Cuántos años tienes?*
        - *Tengo...* + your age
        - Your age
    - *¿En qué trabajas?* or *¿A qué te dedicas?*
        - *Soy* + your profession
        - *Trabajo de* + your profession
        - *Trabajo como* + your profession

- The present conjugations of the verbs *ser, tener,* and *llamarse.*
- A list of countries and nationalities.
  - And that nationalities should never be capitalized!
- A list of jobs and professions.

In conclusion, we've covered a lot in this second chapter, but there's still a long way to go! In the next chapter, we'll go deeper into the Spanish present tense and we'll also talk about articles, adjectives, and how to describe places. But before that, it's time for some exercises!

Exercises

1. What's the difference between *tú* and *usted*? (More than one option can be right)
   a. *Tú* is a second-person pronoun and *usted* is a third-person pronoun.
   b. *Tú* is informal and the *usted* is formal.
   c. *Tú* is a masculine pronoun and *usted* is a feminine pronoun.
   d. *Tú* is conjugated in the second-person and *usted* is conjugated in the third-person.

2. What's the difference between *vosotras* and *ustedes*? (More than one option can be right).
   a. *Vosotras* is a feminine pronoun and *ustedes* is a masculine pronoun.
   b. *Vosotras* is a third person pronoun and *ustedes* is a second person pronoun.
   c. *Vosotras* is a feminine pronoun and *ustedes* can be used for men and women.
   d. *Vosotras* is an informal pronoun and *ustedes* is a formal pronoun.
   e. *Vosotras* is conjugated in the second person and *ustedes* is conjugated in the third person.
   f. *Vosotras* is used in Spain and *ustedes* is used in Latin America.

3. Which part of the sentence determines the gender and number of other elements in the sentence?
   a. The noun
   b. The verb
   c. The article
   d. The adjective

4. If the word *ventana* (window) is a feminine word, which of the following sentences is correct?
   a. El ventana es lindo.
   b. La ventana es linda.
   c. La ventana es lindo.
   d. El ventana es linda.

5. Which of the following answers is an appropriate answer to the question *¿De dónde eres?*
   a. Es García.
   b. Soy Carlos.

    c. Soy ingeniero.

    d. Soy de España.

6. Which of the following answers is an appropriate answer to the question *¿Cuántos años tienes?*

    a. Tengo 53 años.

    b. Soy 53 años.

    c. Vivo en 53 años.

    d. Me llamo 53 años.

7. What question has someone asked me if my answer is *Me llamo Susana*?

    a. ¿Cuál es tu apellido?

    b. ¿Cómo te llamas?

    c. ¿A qué te dedicas?

    d. ¿De dónde eres?

8. If I meet a woman who comes from Germany, she is...?

    a. Italiana

    b. Mexicana

    c. Francesa

    d. Alemana

9. If I'm a woman who works at a restaurant cooking for customers, what's my job?

    a. Bombero

    b. Mesera

    c. Cocinera

    d. Actor

10. Write short sentences about yourself to answer the following questions. This will allow you to practice your introduction for the next time you meet someone!

    a. ¿Cuál es tu nombre?

    b. ¿Cuál es tu apellido?

    c. ¿De dónde eres?

    d. ¿Cuántos años tienes?

    e. ¿A qué te dedicas?

Answer Key

1. b. *Tú* is informal and *usted* is formal.
   d. *Tú* is conjugated in the second-person and *usted* is conjugated in the third-person.

2. c. *Vosotras* is a feminine pronoun and *ustedes* can be used for men and women.
   e. *Vosotras* is conjugated in the second person and *ustedes* is conjugated in the third person.
   f. *Vosotras* is used in Spain and *ustedes* is used in Latin America.

3. a. The noun

4. b. La ventana es linda.

5. d. Vivo en España.

6. a. Tengo 53 años.

7. b. ¿Cómo te llamas?

8. d. Alemana

9. c. Cocinera

Chapter 3: Such a Beautiful Place!

Si no escalas la montaña, jamás podrás disfrutar el paisaje.

- Pablo Neruda

Hey! We're already two chapters and, also, six days in. I hope you're starting to feel comfortable because we're hardly there yet! In this chapter, we're going to delve a little deeper into some of the topics we saw in the previous chapter. We will see some definite and indefinite articles so that you know how to make them agree with the noun, we will go into how to form plural nouns, we will learn how to describe places (with a vocabulary list containing many adjectives), and we will also talk about the regular form of verbs in the present and learn to conjugate one irregular verb.

Since we've got a lot to cover in these next three days, we better get started!

Definite and Indefinite Articles

We've already talked about articles in the previous chapter. Like we said, they need to agree in gender and number with the noun, and we saw that *la* and *el* were two examples.

But what is an article? To make it simple, let's say that an article is a word that comes before a noun and tells us something about that noun. It tells us whether it is a known noun (called "definite articles") or an unknown noun (called "indefinite articles"). We have these in English too, of course. In English, we have the article "the" which is used to talk about known nouns, and the articles "a" and "an" to talk about unknown nouns. In Spanish, however, we have a few more... We have nine articles in Spanish!

Why do we have so many? Well, because we need to make them agree in gender and number with the noun, so we have four different variants of definite articles and four different variants for indefinite articles.

Wait! That doesn't add up, those are eight and I said nine! Well, in Spanish we have one last article which is neuter and isn't exactly used with nouns–it is used to turn adjectives or adverbs into nouns. This means that whenever we see an adjective or an adverb with this article (*lo*) before, that adjective or adverb is now a noun. And the article *lo* doesn't have a feminine, maculine, singular or plural form, it is always *lo*.

Now, let's have a look at the following table in which you'll find all nine Spanish articles and then it's time to see some examples!

	Singular		Plural	
	Masculine	Feminine	Masculine	Feminine
Definite	El	La	Los	Las
Indefinite	Un	Una	Unos	Unas

Neuter	Lo

Now that we've got the table to help us, let's see some examples. For these examples, we'll use the masculine noun *árbol* ("tree") and the feminine noun *flor* ("flower").

- Masculine singular: *En el patio hay <u>un</u> árbol. <u>El</u> árbol es hermoso.* ("In the garden there's <u>a</u> tree. <u>The</u> tree is beautiful").

- Feminine singular: *El árbol tiene <u>una</u> flor. <u>La</u> flor es roja.* ("The tree has <u>a</u> flower. <u>The</u> flower is red").

- Masculine plural: *En el patio hay <u>unos</u> árboles. <u>Los</u> árboles son hermosos.* ("In the garden there are trees. <u>The</u> trees are beautiful").

- Feminine plural: *El árbol tiene <u>unas</u> flores. <u>Las</u> flores son hermosas.* ("The tree has flowers. <u>The</u> flowers are beautiful").

- Neuter: *<u>Lo</u> hermoso del árbol son las flores.* ("The beautiful things in the tree are the flowers").

As you can see in these examples, we use the indefinite article first because we're introducing a new noun, and then, once we already know what noun we're talking about, we can use the definite article, just like in English!

Learning the articles will be helpful to us from now on because every time we see a feminine noun, we will add a *la* before it so that you can tell that it is a feminine noun and we will add an *el* before masculine nouns.

Nouns to Describe

Now that we've talked about nouns and how we will identify whether they are feminine or masculine, we can look at a list with some nouns of things we might want to describe in a new place. For example, if we're on a trip!

Noun	Pronunciation	Translation
la cama	KAH-mah	bed
la silla	SEE-jah	chair
la televisión	teh-leh-vee-see-OHN	TV
la mesa	MEH-sah	table
la puerta	poo-EHR-tah	door
la ventana	behn-TAH-nah	window
el armario	ahr-MAH-ree-oh	wardrobe

el despertador	dehs-pehr-TAH-dohr	alarm clock
la toalla	toh-AH-jah	towel
el espejo	ehs-PEH-hoh	mirror
la playa	PLAH-jah	beach
la montaña	mohn-TAH-nya	mountain
el lago	LAH-goh	lake
el río	REE-oh	river
la laguna	lah-GOO-nah	lagoon
el edificio	eh-dee-FEE-see-oh	building
la casa	KAH-sah	house
el paisaje	pah-ee-SAH-heh	view
la vista	VEES-tah	view
el hotel	oh-TEHL	hotel
la habitación	ah-bee-tah-see-OHN	room
la luz	loos	light
la ciudad	see-oo-DAHD	city
el país	pah-EES	country

Plural Forms

We've already learned that articles, adjectives, pronouns and verbs need to agree in number with the noun. And we also know that nouns can be singular or plural, but how do we pluralize nouns? Well, in some cases, it's a bit similar to English: we add an -s. But in some other cases, we must add -es or -ces. Let's have a look at the rule in the following table:

	Rule	Examples
Vowel + -s	If the singular ends in a vowel, we simply need to add an -s.	la cas<u>a</u> ("house") → las casa<u>s</u> el salud<u>o</u> ("greeting") → los saludos el viaj<u>e</u> ("trip") → los viaje<u>s</u>
Consonant or stressed vowel + -es	If the singular ends in a consonant or stressed vowel, we add -es.	el ba<u>r</u> ("bar") → los bar<u>es</u> el igl<u>ú</u> ("igloo") → los iglú<u>es</u> la pare<u>d</u> ("wall") → las pared<u>es</u>
-z → -ces	If the singular ends in -z, we replace the z for -ces.	el pe<u>z</u> ("fish") → los pe<u>ces</u> la lu<u>z</u> ("light") → las lu<u>ces</u>
-s or -x → remains the same	If the singular ends in -s or -x, the plural stays the same.	el lune<u>s</u> ("Monday") → los lunes el tóra<u>x</u> ("thorax") → los tórax

Now, before we move on to adjectives, let's talk about how we pluralize them. And, the good news is... We pluralize them in the same way! Now, you will only need to keep in mind one set of rules when pluralizing nouns, and then the same rule when you're trying to make the adjective(s) agree with that plural noun.

Present Indicative

We haven't formally introduced this tense, but we've already seen the present indicative form of three verbs in this tense: *ser, tener,* and *llamarse.*

First, let's understand what it is. The present is, of course, used to talk about the present, but it is also used to talk about facts, routines, recurring actions, stable situations or even a close future. It's a rather multifaceted verb! But, why is it called the present *indicative* and not just the present? Well, the indicative is one of the three Spanish verbal moods: the indicative, the subjunctive, and the imperative. The indicative is used to talk about real things.

This is the tense that we will be dealing with throughout this whole book, so we will see its different functions and uses as we go. For now, we will focus on using it to describe things.

Conjugations: -ar, -er and -ir

We've already covered a few conjugations of verbs and we know that verbs need to agree in person and number with the main noun, so we have six possible conjugations for every verb.

In Spanish, we have three possible infinitive verb endings: *-ar, -er,* and *-ir.* But why are infinitive verb endings relevant to learning the present indicative conjugations? Well, in Spanish, we don't have one regular form for each tense but three, and they depend on the infinitive ending of the verb. This means that you should keep in mind the infinitive ending of the verb in order to conjugate it in any tense.

To see the conjugations of the present indicative with these three different endings, we will use three prototypical regular verbs so that you can use them as an example. They are: *cantar* ("to sing"), *comer* ("to eat"), and *vivir* ("to live").

First, we will see a table with the present indicative conjugations of these three verbs, after that, we will break the table down and see some useful examples with these and other regular verbs.

	Cantar	Comer	Vivir
(yo)	cant<u>o</u>	com<u>o</u>	viv<u>o</u>
(tú)	cant<u>as</u>	com<u>es</u>	viv<u>es</u>
(él / ella / usted)	cant<u>a</u>	com<u>e</u>	viv<u>e</u>
(nosotros / nosotras)	cant<u>amos</u>	com<u>emos</u>	viv<u>imos</u>
(vosotros / vosotras)	cant<u>áis</u>	com<u>éis</u>	viv<u>ís</u>
(ellos / ellas / ustedes)	cant<u>an</u>	com<u>en</u>	viv<u>en</u>

Firstly, remember that the pronoun *usted* is a second person singular pronoun but it is conjugated like the verbs in the third person singular. And that the pronoun *ustedes* is a second person plural pronoun but is conjugated like the verbs in the third person plural.

As you can see, every verb has a root which is the part of the verb that remains unchanged: in the case of *cantar* it is *cant*, in the case of *comer* it is *com*, and in the case of *vivir* it is *viv*; that is to say that the root is basically the verb without the *-ar*, *-er*, or *-ir* ending. In regular verbs, the roots do not change, what changes is the ending in order to make the conjugations in the different persons and numbers.

For the present indicative, the first person singular form of regular verbs ends in *-o* in the three verbs: *cant<u>o</u>, com<u>o</u>,* and *viv<u>o</u>.* The second person singular form in all cases ends with an *-s*, however, in the verbs ending in *-ar* the *-s* is preceded by an *-a* while in the other two cases it is preceded by an *-e*: *cant<u>as</u>, com<u>es</u>,* and *viv<u>es</u>.* The third person singular form is like the second person without the *-s*. This means that the verbs ending in *-ar* simply end in *-a*, and the verbs ending in *-er* and *-ir* end in *-e*: *cant<u>a</u>, com<u>e</u>, and viv<u>e</u>.*

Now let's move on to the plurals. For the first person plural, the three verbs end in *-mos*, but this is preceded by an *-a*, an *-e*, or an *-i* depending on the infinitive form of the verb: *cant<u>amos</u>, com<u>emos</u>, viv<u>imos</u>.* The second person plural forms all have an accent mark and all end in *-is*. In the case of verbs ending in *-ar*, there is an *-á* with an accent mark before *-is: cant<u>áis</u>.* In the case of verbs ending in *-er*, there is an *-é* with an accent mark before *is: com<u>éis</u>.* And in the case of verbs ending in *-ir*, the same *-í* is the one with the accent: *viv<u>ís</u>.* Finally, the third person plural is just like the third person singular but with an added *-n* at the end: *cant<u>an</u>, com<u>en</u>,* and *viv<u>en</u>.*

I hope that made it a bit easier to grasp! Now, it's time to see some examples using these verbs and other regular verbs so that you can see that the endings are the same!

- *cantar* ("to sing"): *Lucas y yo cant<u>amos</u> el himno nacional* ("Lucas and I sing the national anthem")

- *hablar* ("to talk"): *Carlos habla con María todos los días* ("Carlos talks to María every day")
- *amar* ("to love"): *Yo amo a Lucía* ("I love Lucía")
- *comer* ("to eat"): *Sandra y Juana comen mucho* ("Sandra and Juana eat a lot")
- *leer* ("to read"): *Lees todo el día* ("You read all day long")
- *correr* ("to run"): *Vosotros corréis una vez por semana, ¿verdad?* ("You run once a week, right?")
- *vivir* ("to live"): *Manuel y Sofía viven cerca de mi casa* ("Manuel and Sofía live near my house")
- *recibir* ("to receive"): *Federico recibe regalos solo para su cumpleaños* ("Federico receives gifts only for his birthday")
- *escribir* ("to write"): *Escribo en mi diario todos los días* ("I write on my diary every day")

Expressing Existence: *Hay*

The verb *hay*, as the title suggests, is used to express existence. In Spanish, we use this form (which is a third-person impersonal present form of the verb *haber*, which is mainly an auxiliary verb similar to "have") to express existence, without conjugating it.

You may not have noticed, but we've already seen some examples of this verb in this very same chapter. When we saw the articles in the first section, one of the examples was: *En el patio hay un árbol* which, if you remember, means "In the garden there's a tree".

Let's look at some other examples of this verb in use, so that you can see how it works with different types of nouns and check for yourself that we don't have to conjugate it:

- *En España hay naranjas* ("In Spain there are oranges")
- *En Perú hay ruinas* ("In Peru there are ruins")
- *En Paraguay hay dos lenguas oficiales* ("In Paraguay there are two official languages")
- *En Argentina y Chile hay una cordillera* ("In Argentina and Chile there is a mountain range")

As you can see, the number of the noun doesn't matter, the verb is always *hay*. At this point, we should also note that we can use this verb with quantifiers, such as numbers, without any article (if the noun is in the plural) or with indefinite articles. However, we can't use *hay* with definite articles. For example, we can't say *En España hay las naranjas* or *En Argentina y Chile hay la cordillera*.

Expressing Location: *Estar*

Now it's time to learn an irregular verb. Actually, this isn't the first one we've seen. If you remember the conjugations of *ser* and *tener* correctly, then you'll realize that those were irregular verbs too!

Speaking of *ser*... Remember that we said that it was the verb "to be"? Well, there are two verbs that have the meaning of the verb "to be" in Spanish. The other one is *estar*. You may be wondering how that's possible. In Spanish, *ser* and *estar* aren't synonyms, they are used for different things, but they can be translated into English as the same verb in both cases.

Ser is used for permanent or long-lasting states. For example, we've already used it to describe ourselves. We use the verb *ser* in sentences like *Soy Carlos* because Carlos is always Carlos—it's a permanent state. However, we use *estar* for temporary states. For example, we can say *Estoy feliz* ("I'm happy") because it is something that is happening right now, but it could definitely change in the immediate future, so it's not a permanent state.

Let's look at the conjugation of *estar* now!

	Estar
(yo)	est<u>oy</u>
(tú)	est<u>ás</u>
(él / ella / usted)	est<u>á</u>
(nosotros / nosotras)	est<u>amos</u>
(vosotros / vosotras)	est<u>áis</u>
(ellos / ellas / ustedes)	est<u>án</u>

As you can see, the root stays the same in this irregular verb (thankfully!) and the endings are a bit different from the endings of regular verbs, but not completely different. The main differences, actually, are in the accent marks and in the first person singular form.

We can also use this verb, as mentioned in the title of this section, to express location. Following an example from the previous section, we can say *La cordillera de los Andes está en Argentina y Chile* ("The Andes mountain range is in Argentina and Chile"). With this verb, we say that something (in this case, the Andes mountain range) is located somewhere. Let's look at a few more examples:

- *Las ruinas de Machu Picchu están en Perú* ("The Machu Picchu ruins are in Peru").
- *El templo de Kukulcán está en Cancún* ("The Kukulcan temple is in Cancun").
- *Las cataratas del Iguazú están en Argentina y Brasil* ("The Iguazu falls are in Argentina and Brazil").
- *La torre de la Giralda está en Sevilla* ("The Giralda tower is in Seville").

As you can see, we use the plural when the noun is plural, like *ruinas* and *cataratas*, but we use the singular when the noun is singular, like *templo* and *torre*.

Talking About the Weather

There are many ways to talk about the weather. Two of those ways use the verbs *está* and *hay*, which we've seen before. Let's look at some examples:

- Está soleado ("It's sunny")
- Hay sol ("There's sun")
- Está ventoso ("It's windy")
- Hay viento ("There's wind")

As you can see, we can say almost the same things with these two verbs. And, in both cases, we always use the verbs in the third person singular: *está* and *hay*. We use *está* with adjectives, while we use *hay* with nouns.

Now, let's see other examples so that you can talk about the weather to make small talk in an elevator, with a receptionist, or even to plan what you will do on your trip! You will find some adjectives and nouns in the following table that you can use with *está* and *hay*, along with their pronunciation and translation.

Noun or Adjective	Pronunciation	Translation
sol	sohl	sun
soleado	soh-leh-AH-doh	sunny
nubes	NOO-behs	clouds
nublado	noo-BLAH-doh	cloudy
viento	bee-EHN-toh	wind
ventoso	behn-TOH-soh	windy
lluvia	joo-BEE-ah	rain
lluvioso	joo-bee-OH-soh	rainy
nieve	nee-EH-beh	snow
nevoso	neh-BOH-soh	snowy
neblina	neh-BLEE-nah	fog
neblinoso	neh-blee-NOH-soh	foggy
tormenta	tohr-MEHN-tah	storm
tormentoso	tohr-mehn-TOH-soh	stormy

Adjectives to Describe Places

It's adjective-learning time! In this section we'll see a list with many adjectives you can use to describe places and things, along with their pronunciation and translation. Keep in mind that most adjectives will have a feminine and a masculine form, but some of them will use only one form for both genders.

Adjective	Pronunciation	Translation
bonito bonita	boh-NEE-toh boh-NEE-tah	beautiful, nice
turístico turística	too-REES-tee-koh too-REES-tee-kah	touristic
amable	ah-MAH-bleh	kind
grande	GRAHN-deh	big
pequeño pequeña	peh-KEH-nyoh peh-KEH-nyah	small
tradicional	tra-dee-see-oh-NAHL	traditional
hermoso hermosa	ehr-MOH-soh ehr-MOH-sah	beautiful
seco seca	SEH-koh SEH-kah	dry
agradable	ah-grah-DAH-ble	pleasant
largo larga	LAHR-goh LAHR-gah	long
corto corta	KOHR-toh KOHR-tah	short
frío fría	FREE-oh FREE-ah	cold
caliente	kah-lee-ehn-teh	hot
divertido divertida	dee-behr-TEE-doh dee-behr-TEE-dah	fun
perfecto perfecta	pehr-FEHK-toh pehr-FEHK-tah	perfect

feo fea	FEH-oh FEH-ah	ugly
horrible	oh-rree-bleh	awful, horrible
redondo redonda	rreh-DOHN-doh rreh-DOHN-dah	round
cuadrado cuadrada	koo-ah-DRAH-doh koo-ah-DRAH-dah	square
nuevo nueva	noo-EH-boh noo-EH-bah	new
viejo vieja	bee-EH-hoh bee-EH-hah	old
antiguo antigua	ahn-TEE-goo-oh ahn-TEE-goo-ah	ancient
pintoresco pintoresca	peen-toh-REHS-koh peen-toh-REHS-kah	picturesque
claro clara	KLAH-roh KLAH-rah	light, clear
oscuro oscura	ohs-KOO-roh ohs-KOO-rah	dark

You may have realized that the adjectives ending in -e or in consonant are generally invariable, while the ones ending in -a are generally feminine and the ones ending in -o are generally masculine.

You should also keep in mind that this table only includes the feminine and masculine singular forms, and not the plural forms. This means that, if we have a plural noun, we will have to pluralize the adjectives just like we saw earlier in this chapter.

Colors

Colors can be both nouns or adjectives. As nouns, they are all masculine. However, when they are adjectives, they change in order to agree with the gender and number of the noun. However, some of them have only one form for the masculine and feminine.

Let's have a look at the nouns, the adjectives in the feminine and masculine forms, and their pronunciation and translation!

Noun	Adjective	Pronunciation	Translation
el rojo	rojo roja	RROH-hoh RROH-hah	red
el azul	azul	ah-ZOOL	blue
el amarillo	amarillo amarilla	ah-mah-REE-joh ah-mah-REE-jah	yellow
el verde	verde	BEHR-deh	green
el naranja	naranja	nah-RAHN-hah	orange
el violeta	violeta	bee-oh-LEH-tah	violet
el púrpura	púrpura	POOR-poo-rah	purple
el rosa	rosa	RROH-sah	pink
el marrón	marrón	mah-RROHN	brown
el negro	negro negra	NEH-groh NEH-grah	black
el blanco	blanco blanca	BLAHN-koh BLAHN-kah	white
el gris	gris	grees	gray
el celeste	celeste	seh-LEHS-teh	light blue

Now that we've learned the colors, we should note that, when they are modified by adjectives like *claro* and *oscuro* (which we saw in the previous table), both the adjective *claro* or *oscuro* and the color adjective remain in their masculine singular form, despite the gender and number of the noun. For example: *Hay unas cortinas rojo oscuro* ("There are some dark red curtains").

Describing Places with *Ser*

Now it's finally time to put together everything we've seen in this chapter in order to learn how to describe places.

To describe a place, we can use the verb *ser* with adjectives or nouns in the following ways:

- *Ser* + adjective
    - *Uruguay <u>es</u> <u>hermoso</u>* ("Uruguay is beautiful").
    - *El río <u>es</u> <u>celeste</u>* ("The river is light blue").
    - *Las ciudades españolas <u>son</u> <u>pintorescas</u>* ("Spanish cities are picturesque").
    - *La mesa <u>es</u> <u>marrón</u>* ("The table is brown").
- *Ser* + noun + adjective
    - Uruguay <u>es</u> <u>un país</u> <u>hermoso</u> ("Uruguay is a beautiful country").
    - *El río <u>es</u> <u>un cuerpo de agua</u> <u>celeste</u>* ("The river is a light blue body of water").
    - *Las ciudades españolas <u>son</u> <u>lugares</u> <u>pintorescos</u>* ("Spanish cities are picturesque places").
    - *La mesa <u>es</u> <u>una madera</u> <u>marrón</u>* ("The table is a brown piece of wood").

As you can see, these two sentence structures are similar and we can say the same things with each of them. These structures can be used either to describe or to define as well.

We should note that, in the second structure (*ser* + noun + adjective), the adjective needs to agree with the noun that precedes it. That's why we say *Las ciudades españolas son <u>lugares pintorescos</u>*, and not *Las ciudades españolas son lugares pintorescas*. However, in the first structure, the adjective needs to agree with the first noun, the main noun: <u>*Las ciudades españolas* son *pintorescas*</u>.

Key Takeaways

This was a rather long chapter, but we've covered a lot and reached its end! I hope you're not tired yet and have learned a lot.

In this chapter, we've dealt with:

- Indefinite articles (which are used to introduce a noun)
    - *un, una, unos, unas*
- Definite articles (which are used to refer to a noun that has been introduced)
    - *el, la, los, las*
- Neuter article *lo* (which is used to turn adjectives and adverbs into nouns)
- Some nouns that we might want to describe when we're in a new place
- Plural forms and how to form them
- The present indicative
    - Its uses
    - Its regular conjugations with *-ar, -er*, and *-ir*
- How to express existence with *hay*

- How to express location with *estar*
- How to talk about the weather with *hay* + noun and *está* + adjective
- Some adjectives to describe places
- The colors as nouns and adjectives
- How to describe places and things with *ser* + adjective and *ser* + noun + adjective

We've finally made it to the end of this chapter but, of course, we first need to practice everything we've learned!

Before you go, let me tell you a bit about our next chapter. In it, we will learn everything you will need to go out shopping at a store in a Spanish-speaking country: vocabulary, demonstratives, some questions, quantifiers and some irregular verbs. Head over there once you're done with the exercises!

Exercises

1. Fill in the gaps with a definite or indefinite article (all of the sentences make up one text):

    a. En mi casa hay .... habitación.

    b. En .... habitación hay cuatro sillas.

    c. .... sillas son rojas.

    d. En .... habitación también hay .... armario.

    e. .... armario es negro.

2. Which of the following things doesn't belong in a living room?

    a. Río

    b. Espejo

    c. Ventana

    d. Silla

    e. Mesa

3. Can you pluralize the noun *hotel*? What about the adjective *amable*?

4. Can you match the following conjugations of the regular verb *saltar* ("to jump") in the present indicative with the pronouns *yo, tú, él, nosotras, vosotros,* and *ellas*?

    a. Saltamos

    b. Salta

    c. Saltas

    d. Saltáis

    e. Salto

    f. Saltan

5. How would you translate the sentence "In the lake there are fishes" into Spanish?

    a. En el lago hay los peces.

    b. En el lago están peces.

c. En el lago hay peces.

d. En el lago estás peces.

6. What are the two Spanish verbs that can be translated as the verb to be?

    a. Hay

    b. Estar

    c. Tener

    d. Hablar

    e. Ser

7. How would you translate the sentence "The hotel is on the beach"?

    a. El hotel hay en la playa.

    b. El hotel está la playa.

    c. El hotel están en el playa.

    d. El hotel está en la playa.

8. Which of the following structures is used to talk about the weather? (More than one option can be right).

    a. *Está* + adjective

    b. *Está* + noun

    c. *Hay* + adjective

    d. *Hay* + noun

9. Which of the following adjectives <u>cannot be used</u> to describe a window in Spanish?

    a. Grande

    b. Azul

    c. Roja

    d. Oscuro

10. Can you write sentences using the adjectives that we can use from the previous exercise to talk about a window? Use the structures *ser* + adjective or *ser* + noun + adjective.

Answer Key

    a. una

    b. la

    c. Las

    d. la, un

    e. El

2. a. río

3. hoteles, amables

    a. saltamos → nosotras

    b. salta → él

    c. saltas → tú

    d. saltáis → vosotros

    e. salto → yo

    f. saltan → ellas

4. c. En el lago hay peces.

5. b. Estar and e. Ser

6. d. El hotel está en la playa.

7. a. *Está* + adjective and d. *Hay* + noun

8. d. Oscuro because, in Spanish, *ventana* is a feminine noun.

9. Some of the sentences might be:

    a. La ventana es grande.

    b. La ventana es una ventana grande.

    c. La ventana es azul.

    d. La ventana es una ventana azul.

    e. La ventana es roja

    f. La ventana es una ventana roja

Chapter 4: This or That?

❧

Cuando comienzan a vernos como esto, como aquello, comienzan a no vernos.

- Antonio Porchia

Welcome to our fourth chapter! How are you doing so far? I hope you're mostly enjoying our time together and learning a lot! This chapter will be really useful for the future, when you're shopping in a Spanish-speaking country, so mark it down to have useful phrases on hand for your future shopping sprees. We will not only be dealing with different phrases and questions to use at a store but we will also see some grammatical structures and questions to identify objects at a store and some vocabulary.

Ready? Get set! Learn!

Clothes and Vocabulary Related to Buying

This time, we're going to mix things up a bit and start with the vocabulary so that we can use it throughout the chapter in our example sentences. How does that sound?

In the following table, you will find many pieces of clothing and shopping items along with their respective articles, their pronunciation and their translation.

Word	Pronunciation	Translation
la ropa	RROH-pah	clothes
la camiseta	kah-mee-SEH-tah	T-shirt
la camisa	kah-MEE-saah	shirt
la chaqueta	chah-KEH-tah	jacket
el vestido	behs-TEE-doh	dress
el chaleco	chah-LEH-koh	vest
la falda	FAHL-dah	skirt
el pantalón los pantalones	pahn-tah-LOHN pahn-tah-LOH-nehs	pants
el traje	TRAH-heh	suit
la cartera	kahr-TEH-rah	bag

164

la mochila	moh-CHEE-lah	backpack
las medias	meh-DEE-ahs	socks
los calcetines	kahl-seh-tee-nehs	socks
las botas	BOH-tahs	boots
los zapatos	zah-PAH-tohs	shoes
el sombrero	sohm-BREH-roh	hat
el abrigo	ah-BREE-goh	coat
el pañuelo	pah-nyoo-EH-loh	kerchief
la blusa	BLOO-sah	blouse
la bufanda	boo-FAHN-dah	scarf
la ropa interior	RROH-pah een-teh-ree-OHR	underwear
el cinturón	seen-too-ROHN	belt
la tienda	tee-EHN-dah	store
el precio	preh-SEE-oh	price
el efectivo	eh-fehk-TEE-boh	cash
la tarjeta de crédito	tahr-HEH-tah deh KREH-dee-toh	credit card
la tarjeta de débito	tahr-HEH-tah deh DEH-bee-toh	debit card
el recibo	rreh-see-boh	receipt
el cajero	kah-HEH-roh	cashier
el descuento	dehs-koo-EHN-toh	discount

Demonstratives

It seems that now is a good time to start learning about demonstratives. In English, we have four demonstratives: "this", "that", "these", and "those". Like the personal pronouns we've seen before, demonstratives are pronouns that are used in the place of nouns. However, these pronouns are used to point or signal at people or things.

While "this", "that", "these", and "those" only take into account two levels of distance from the speaker and the number (singular or plural), we have to worry about three levels of distance, gender, and number in Spanish. This makes demonstratives amount to 15 in Spanish... Seems like a lot, right? Let's have a look at a table that will make everything clearer.

	Masculine		Feminine		Neuter
	Singular	Plural	Singular	Plural	Singular
Close to the speaker	este	estos	esta	estas	esto
Close to the addressee	ese	eso	esa	esas	eso
Far from both	aquel	aquellos	aquella	aquellas	aquello

As you can see, the three levels of distance depend on where the object is. If it is closer to the speaker than the addressee, we use the demonstratives from the first row. If it is closer to the addressee than the speaker, we use the demonstratives from the second row. Finally, if it is far from both the speaker and the addressee, we use the demonstratives from the last row.

I guess by now you already understand that we use masculine pronouns with masculine nouns and feminine pronouns with feminine nouns. Of course, in this case, the noun we're talking about is the object or person we're pointing or signaling at. But what are the neuter demonstratives used for? Well, these demonstratives stay the same regardless of gender and number, and they are usually used to make general statements, to talk about abstract ideas or to talk about unknown nouns because we don't know their gender.

Let's see some examples with a few dialogues:

- Masculine demonstratives:

• *¿Quieres probarte este abrigo?* ("Do you want to try on this coat?")

○ *No quiero probarme ese, me gustaría probar aquel.* ("I don't want to try that one, I'd like to try that other one").

• *Estos abrigos son más caros que aquellos.* ("These coats are more expensive than those").

- Feminine demonstratives:

• *¿Quieres probarte esta falda?* ("Do you want to try on this skirt?")

○ *No quiero probarme esa, me gustaría probar aquella.* ("I don't want to try that one, I'd like to try that other one").

• *Estas faldas son más caras que aquellas.* ("These skirts are more expensive than those").

- Neuter demonstratives:

- *¿Qué es <u>esto</u>?* ("What's this?")

○ *<u>Eso</u> es una bufanda.* ("That's a scarf").

- *¿Y <u>aquello</u>?* ("And that?")

○ *<u>Aquello</u> también es una bufanda.* ("That's also a scarf").

Definite Article + Adjective

Another way to talk about a noun without saying its name is to use the structure definite article + adjective. First, let's see some examples:

- *¿Qué <u>cartera</u> llevo? ¿<u>La nueva</u> o <u>la vieja</u>?* ("Which bag should I take? The red one or the black one?")

- *Me gusta este <u>pantalón</u>, pero también me gusta <u>el verde</u>.* ("I like these pants, but I also like the green one").

- *¿Te gustan estas <u>medias</u>? ¿O prefieres <u>las largas</u>?* ("Do you like these socks? Or do you prefer the long ones?")

- *¿Quieres estos <u>zapatos</u> o <u>los marrones</u>?* ("Do you want these shoes or the brown ones?")

As you can see, the gender and number of the article needs to be the same as the gender and number of the noun it refers back to. This helps us easily understand which object or person we're talking about because it agrees in gender and number. What about the adjective? Well, we need to choose an adjective that accurately describes the object or person so that we can identify it. Colors are a good option. We can also say whether it's old or new, etc. Make sure to use an adjective that will make it easier for your addressee to know which object or person you're talking about!

Questions to Identify an Object

We've actually already seen some questions to identify objects in the examples of the two previous objects, but let's talk about them properly now.

First, let's see the structure *qué* + noun. This structure can be used to ask about objects and things. Let's look at one of the examples we've seen before:

- *¿<u>Qué</u> <u>cartera</u> llevo?* ("Which bag should I take?")

In this example, we used the interrogative adjective *qué* and the noun *cartera* to ask someone which one to take. As we can see, a verb follows the *qué* + noun structure. This verb can vary depending on what we want to ask. For example:

- *¿Qué cartera <u>uso</u>?* ("Which bag should I use?")

- *¿Qué cartera <u>compro</u>?* ("Which bag should I buy?")

- *¿Qué cartera <u>prefieres</u>?* ("Which bag do you prefer?")

When we already know what we're talking about, we can also use the interrogative adjectives *cuál* or *cuáles*. Unlike *qué,* which remains unchanged regardless of the number, *cuál* and *cuáles* do change depending on the number: *cuál* is the singular form and *cuáles* is the plural form.

Let's see an example using *qué* as well:

- *¿Qué <u>cartera</u> llevo?* ("Which bag should I take?")
- *Depende, ¿<u>cuál</u> es la más pequeña?* ("It depends, which is the smallest?")

Now, let's see an example in the plural:

- *¿Qué <u>zapatos</u> quieres?* ("Which shoes do you want?")
- *No sé. ¿<u>Cuáles</u> son más lindos?* ("Which do you like best?")

After *cuál* or *cuáles*, we can have the verb *ser* (of course, conjugated in the right person and number), like in the examples above. But we can also have other verbs depending on what we want to say. For example:

- *¿Estos dulces son gratis? ¿Cuáles <u>puedo</u> probar?* (Are these sweets for free? Which ones can I try?)
- *¿Has visto estas chaquetas? ¿Cuál <u>te gusta</u> más?* (Have you seen these jackets? Which one do you like best?)

Expressing Likes, Dislikes and Preferences

Likes and Dislikes

We will be talking about two Spanish verbs in this chapter: *gustar* and *preferir*. *Gustar* could be translated as "to like" and *preferir* could be translated as "to prefer".

Gustar is a bit difficult to learn, but it is a verb that we use a lot. Though in English the verb "to like" is pretty straightforward, *gustar* requires a pronoun that signals who the person who likes something is. Unfortunately, the pronouns that *gustar* requires aren't ones we've seen so far. This verb requires the pronouns *me, te, le, nos, os,* and *les*. These pronouns are the ones that replace the indirect object of a sentence, that is to say, the person who receives or is affected by the direct object (which is the thing or person that receives or is affected by the action).

You will find the indirect object pronoun of each person and number in the following chart and what the actual indirect object would look like:

	Pronoun	Indirect Object
First-person singular	*me*	*a mí*
Second-person singular	*te*	*a ti*
Third-person singular	*le*	*a él / a ella / a usted*
First-person plural	*nos*	*a nosotros / a nosotras*
Second-person plural	*os*	*a vosotros / a vosotras*
Third-person plural	*les*	*a ellos / a ellas / a ustedes*

But why does the verb *gustar* require a pronoun and doesn't simply use the indirect object in full? Well, the indirect object can actually be duplicated with the verb *gustar*. This means that the indirect object can appear both in full and through the pronoun as they both refer to the same indirect object. However, this verb should always be accompanied by the indirect object pronoun.

In the following table, you will find the structure of sentences when we use the verb *gustar*. You will find that, in this case, the verb *gustar* doesn't have the usual 6 conjugations but only a singular form used with singular nouns and a plural form used with plural nouns.

Let's have a look at it and we'll explain it all afterwards!

Indirect object	Negation	Pronoun	Verb	Quantifier	Direct object
(a mí)	(no)	me	gusta gustan	(mucho)	**singular nouns** el cine **verbs** ir al cine **plural nouns** las películas de acción
(a ti)		te			
(a él/ella)		le			
(a nosotros/nosotras)		nos			
(a vosotros/vosotras)		os			
(a ellos/ellas/ustedes)		les			

As you may already know, the elements in parentheses are optional. As we said, the indirect object in full is optional, but the indirect object pronoun isn't. The negation adverb *no* is also optional because it depends on whether you want to say that you like or dislike something. Then, we have the verb, which, as we said, only has a singular form and a plural form. After that, we could include the quantifier *mucho*, which means *a lot* and is optional. Finally, a sentence about our likes or dislikes should include the direct object of the sentences, that is, the thing we like or dislike. With singular nouns and verbs (always in the infinitive), we use the singular verb *gusta*, and with plural nouns we use the plural verb *gustan*.

Let's see some examples:

- *A mí me gusta la falda negra* ("I like the black skirt")
- *A ti no te gusta el sombrero azul* ("You don't like the blue hat")
- *A Carla le gustan los pantalones verdes* ("Carla likes green pants")
- *Nos gusta ir de compras* ("We like going shopping")
- *¿Os gustan estas medias?* ("Do you like these socks?")

169

- *¿Les gusta este vestido?* ("Do you like this dress?")

Preferences

After what we've just seen with the verb *gustar*, the verb *preferir* will seem like a piece of cake.

Preferir is an irregular verb, but that's all there is to it, really. We use it to talk about preferences and it should always have a direct object.

Let's have a look at the present indicative conjugations of *preferir*:

Pronoun	Preferir
(yo)	prefiero
(tú)	prefieres
(él/ella/usted)	prefiere
(nosotros/nosotras)	preferimos
(vosotros/vosotras)	preferís
(ellos/ellas/ustedes)	prefieren

This verb is irregular in all of its conjugations except for the first and second person plural. To make sentences with it, we simply say the subject (which is optional) + the verb + the direct object + *a* + the object we are comparing the direct object with. For example, while we say "I prefer pants to skirts" in English, we say "Prefiero los pantalones a las faldas" in Spanish. Of course, if someone were to ask us something like *¿Te gusta este vestido?* ("Do you like this dress?"), we could answer *No, prefiero la blusa* ("No, I prefer the blouse") as well, without the *a* and the object we are comparing the direct object with because we already know that it's the dress.

Now, let's see some examples

- *Prefiero usar botas a zapatos* ("I prefer to wear boots to shoes")
- *¿Prefieres estas medias o aquellas?* ("Do you prefer these socks or those ones?")
- *Él prefiere la chaqueta roja, pero nosotras preferimos la azul* ("He prefers the red jacket, but we prefer the blue one")
- *¿Vosotras preferís España o Francia?* ("Do you prefer Spain or France?")
- *Marcos y Juana prefieren el cinturón a la bufanda* ("Marcos and Juana prefer the belt to the scarf")

At the Store

Now it's time to learn some questions and phrases that will be handy at the store! As we've already said, we advise you to put a bookmark or a flag in this section because it contains very helpful phrases!

In case you decide to take this book into the store with you, we have decided to make an easy-to-follow guide so that you can find exactly what you're looking for when you need it. So, the following lists contain the question in English, and then its equivalent(s) in Spanish along with its pronunciation. Plus, this section will be divided into subsections so that you can quickly find the question you want to ask. Lastly, you will also find subsections with some questions that people might ask you and how to answer them!

Let's start!

Questions To Ask Before Purchasing

- "How much is this?"
    - *¿Cuánto sale esto?*: koo-AHN-toh SAH-leh EHS-toh
    - *¿Cuánto vale esto?*: koo-AHN-toh BAH-leh EHS-toh
    - *¿Cuánto cuesta esto?*: koo-AHN-toh koo-EHS-tah EHS-toh
- "Can I try it on?"
    - *¿Puedo probármelo?*: poo-EH-doh proh-BAHR-meh-loh
- "Does this look good?"
    - *¿Esto se ve bien?*: EHS-toh seh beh bee-EHN
- "Do you have a bigger/smaller size?"
    - *¿Tienes una talla más grande/pequeña?*: tee-EH-nehs OO-nah TAH-jah mahs GRAHN-deh/peh-KEH-nyah
- "Do you have this in my size?"
    - *¿Lo tienes en mi talla?*: loh tee-EH-nehs ehn mee TAH-jah
- "Do you have this in another color?"
    - *¿Tienes esto en otro color?*: tee-EH-nehs EHS-toh ehn OH-troh koh-LOHR
    - *¿Lo/la tienes en otro color?*: loh/lah tee-EH-nehs ehn OH-troh koh-LOHR

Questions You Might Be Asked Before Purchasing

- "Can I help you?"
    - *¿Puedo ayudarte?*: poo-EH-doh ah-JOO-dahr-teh
    - *¿Puedo ayudarte en algo?*: poo-EH-doh ah-JOO-dahr-teh
    - *¿Necesitas ayuda?*: neh-seh-see-tahs ah-JOO-dah
    - Possible answers
        - "Yes, can you help me find...?" + item

- *Sí, ¿podrías ayudarme a encontrar...?*: see poh-DREE-ahs ah-joo-DAHR-meh ah ehn-KOHN-trahr
  - ■ "Yes, I'm looking for..." + item
    - *Sí, estoy buscando...*: see ehs-TO-ee boos-KAHN-doh
  - ■ "No, I'm good. Thank you."
    - *No, gracias. Estoy bien*: Noh grah-SEE-ahs ehs-TO-ee bee-EHN
  - ■ "No, thanks. I'm just looking."
    - *No, gracias. Estoy mirando*: Noh grah-SEE-ahs ehs-TOO-ee mee-RAHN-doh
- "What color would you like?"
  - ○ *¿Qué color te gustaría?*: keh koh-LOHR teh goos-tah-REE-ah
  - ○ *¿De qué color lo quieres?*: deh keh koh-LOHR loh kee-EH-rehs
  - ○ Possible answers:
    - ■ "I'd like it in..." + color
      - *Lo quiero en...*: loh kee-EH-roh ehn
      - *Me gustaria en...*: meh goos-tah-REE-ah ehn
- "What size would you like?"
  - ○ *¿Qué talla te gustaría?*: keh TAH-jah teh goos-tah-REE-ah
  - ○ *¿En qué talla lo quieres?*: ehn keh TAH-jah loh kee-EH-rehs
  - ○ Possible answers: Go to the possible answers for "What color would you like?" and follow the phrases with the size instead of the color.
- "How does it fit?"
  - ○ *¿Cómo te queda?*: KOH-moh teh KEH-dah
  - ○ Possible answers:
    - ■ "It's great!"
      - *¡Me queda bien!*: meh KEH-dah bee-EHN
      - *Es perfecto*: ehs pehr-FEHK-toh
      - *Me va muy bien*: meh bah moo-EE bee-EHN
    - ■ "It's too small/big"
      - *Me queda grande/chico*: meh KEH-dah GRAHN-deh/CHEE-koh
      - *Es demasiado grande/chico*: ehs deh-mah-see-AH-doh GRAHN-deh/CHEE-koh
    - ■ "I don't like how it looks on me"
      - *No me gusta cómo me queda*: noh meh GOOS-tah KOH-moh meh KEH-dah
- "How about this one?"

- ○ *¿Qué tal este/esta?:* keh tahl EHS-teh/EHS-tah
- ○ Possible answers
  - ■ "I like this one better"
    - • *Este me gusta más*: EHS-teh meh GOOS-tah mahs
  - ■ "I don't like it either"
    - • *Este tampoco me gusta*: EHS-teh tahm-POH-koh meh GOOS-tah
  - ■ "I prefer this one"
    - • *Prefiero este/esta*: preh-fee-EH-roh EHS-teh/EHS-tah
  - ■ "I prefer the previous one"
    - • *Prefiero el anterior*: preh-fee-EH-roh ehl ahn-TEH-ree-ohr

Questions To Ask At Check Out

- • "Do you take credit cards?"
  - ○ *¿Aceptan tarjeta de crédito?*: ah-SEHP-tahn tahr-HEH-tah deh KRE-dee-toh
- • "Can I change it?"
  - ○ *¿Puedo cambiarlo?*: poo-EH-doh kam-bee-AHR-loh
  - ○ *¿Tiene cambio?*: tee-EH-neh KAHM-bee-oh
- • "How long do I have to change it?"
  - ○ *¿Cuánto tiempo tengo para cambiarlo?*: koo-AHN-toh tee-EHM-poh TEHN-goh PAH-rah kahm-BEE-ahr-loh
- • "Can I return it?"
  - ○ *¿Puedo devolverlo?*: poo-EH-doh deh-bohl-BEHR-loh
- • "It's a gift. Can you wrap it?"
  - ○ *Es un regalo. ¿Puedes envolverlo?*: ehs oon rreh-GAH-loh poo-EH-dehs ehn-bohl-BEHR-loh

Questions You Might Be Asked At Check Out

- • "How do you wish to pay?"
  - ○ *¿Cómo quieres pagar?*: KOH-mo kee-eh-rehs pah-GAHR
  - ○ *¿Cómo pagará?*: KOH-mo pah-gah-RAH
  - ○ Possible answers:
    - ■ "In cash"
      - • *En efectivo*: ehn eh-fehk-TEE-boh
    - ■ "With a credit/debit card"
      - • *Con tarjeta de crédito/débito*: kohn tar-HEH-tah deh KRE-dee-toh/DEH-bee-toh

- "Do you need a bag?"
  - *¿Necesita una bolsa?*: neh-seh-SEE-tah OO-nah BOHL-sah
  - Possible answers:
    - Yes, thank you.
      - *Sí, muchas gracias*: see MOO-chahs GRAH-see-ahs

Key Takeaways

We've talked about many things in this chapter, but we've essentially covered all the basics for you to go shopping in a Spanish-speaking country. Here's a summary of everything we've seen:

- A list of vocabulary on clothes and nouns related to shopping
- The 15 Spanish demonstrative pronouns: *este, ese, aquel, estos, eso, aquellos, esta, esa, aquella, estas, esas, aquellas, esto, eso,* and *aquello* which are used to point or signal at people or things.
- The structure definite article + adjective, which can be used to identify a noun by one of its characteristics.
- Questions with *qué* + noun + verb to identify an object.
- Questions with *cuál* or *cuáles* to identify an object when we already know what we're talking about.
- How to express likes and dislikes with the verb *gustar*
  - This verb requires an indirect object pronoun and a direct object.
  - It can also include the indirect object in full, the negative adverb *no*, and the quantifier *mucho*.
  - We use the conjugation *gusta* with singular nouns and verbs in the infinitive
  - We use the conjugation *gustan* with plural nouns
- How to express preferences with the verb *preferir*
  - The irregular conjugation of *preferir*
  - The structure (subject) + *preferir* + direct object + *a* + object we are comparing the direct object with
  - The structure (subject) + *preferir* + direct object.
- Some questions to ask during the whole shopping process
- Some questions you might get asked during the shopping process and how to answer them

I hope this chapter was useful, but there's still a lot more to come! In the next chapter we will be focusing on how to ask for directions, and so we will talk about the prepositions and adverbs of place and many other resources that will help you get everywhere you want in a Spanish-speaking country. See you there!

Exercises

1. What is the gender of the following nouns?

    a. Falda

    b. Pantalón

    c. Traje

    d. Medias

    e. Cinturón

2. What is the English translation of each of the previous pieces of clothing?

3. What are the three distances that the Spanish demonstratives take into account?

4. What are the neuter demonstratives used for?

    a. To talk about adjectives and adverbs.

    b. To talk about verbs.

    c. To talk about unknown things.

5. Choose the right demonstrative for each gap:

    a. .... pantalones son bonitos.

        i. Este

        ii. Estos

        iii. Esta

        iv. Estas

        v. Esto

    b. ¿Qué es ....?

        i. Aquel

        ii. Aquellos

        iii. Aquella

        iv. Aquellas

        v. Aquello

    c. .... cartera es roja.

        i. Ese

        ii. Eso

        iii. Esa

        iv. Esas

        v. Esao

    d. ¿Te gusta .... sombrero?

        i. Aquel

175

        ii.   Aquellos

        iii. Aquella

        iv.   Aquellas

        v.   Aquello

6. Look at the following sentences that contain the structure article + adjective and determine which element they are referring to.

    a. Me gustan mucho <u>los nuevos</u>.

        i.   Camiseta

        ii.   Zapatos

        iii. Traje

        iv.   Carteras

    b. ¿Quieres <u>la nueva o la vieja</u>?

        i.   Camiseta

        ii.   Zapatos

        iii. Traje

        iv.   Carteras

    c. Quiero llevar <u>las marrones</u>.

        i.   Camiseta

        ii.   Zapatos

        iii. Traje

        iv.   Carteras

    d. ¿Te gusta <u>el gris o el negro</u>?

        i.   Camiseta

        ii.   Zapatos

        iii. Traje

        iv.   Carteras

7. Choose between *qué, cuál* and *cuáles* to complete these questions.

    a. ¿........... abrigo te gusta más?

    b. No sé cuál llevar. ¿........... te gusta más a ti?

    c. ¿........... medias usa Juan? ¿........... crees que son?

    d. Mira esas mochilas. ¿........... es más pequeña?

8. Complete the following sentences with *gusta* or *gustan*.

    a. A Carlos le .... comprar.

    b. No me .... las botas.

    c. ¡Nos .... tu sombrero!

d. Me .... mucho los descuentos.

e. A ti no te .... comprar ropa.

9. Complete the following sentences with the right conjugation of *preferir*.

a. ¿(tú)........... decir "medias" o "calcetines"?

b. (nosotros)........... usar botas a usar zapatillas.

c. (ella) .... la cartera negra. ¿Y tú?

d. ¿Vosotros .... llevar traje?

10. Choose the right translation to the following Spanish sentences:

a. *¿Cuánto cuesta esto?*

    i. Do you have it in another color?

    ii. How much is this?

    iii. Does this look good?

b. *¿Tienes una talla más pequeña?*

    i. Do you have a bigger size?

    ii. Do you have it in another color?

    iii. Do you have a smaller size?

c. *¿De qué color lo quieres?*

    i. What color would you like?

    ii. No, thanks, I'm just looking.

    iii. What size would you like?

d. *Es un regalo. ¿Puedes envolverlo?*

    i. Can I change it?

    ii. Can I return it?

    iii. It's a gift. Can you wrap it?

Answer Key

    a. Feminine

    b. Masculine

    c. Masculine

    d. Feminine

    e. Masculine

    f. Skirt

    g. Pants

    h. Suit

    i. Socks

    j. Belt

2. closeness to the speaker, closeness to the addressee and distance from both.

3. c. to talk about unknown things

    a. ii. Estos

    b. v. Aquello

    c. iii. Esa

    d. i. Aquel

    e. ii. Zapatos

    f. i. Camiseta

    g. iv. Carteras

    h. iii. Traje

    i. Qué

    j. Cuál

    k. Qué, Cuáles

    l. ¿Cuál

    m. Gusta

    n. Gustan

    o. Gusta

    p. Gustan

    q. Gusta

    r. Prefieres

    s. Preferimos

    t. prefiere

    u. Preferís

v.   ii. How much is this?

w.   iii. Do you have a smaller size?

x.   i. What color would you like?

y.   iii. It's a gift. Can you wrap it?

Chapter 5: It's Just Around the Corner

✵

La vida es como un viaje sin meta. Lo que cuenta es el camino.

- Isabel Allende

We've arrived at chapter 5! This means we're halfway there! How are you feeling about that? I hope you feel like you're learning a lot–because you are!

In this chapter, our goal is to learn how to ask for directions to get to a place and how to answer if someone asks us for directions! In order to achieve this goal, we will be learning a lot of new vocabulary, prepositions, and many useful verbs and phrases. This is another chapter that will be useful to take with you when you're traveling, so we encourage you to pay attention and bookmark it so that you can find it when you need it.

Let's learn how to **not** get lost in a new city!

Places to Visit

Like in the previous chapter, we will also start with the vocabulary. In this case, we will learn the names of places that you might want to know how to get to while on a trip! As usual, you will find the noun with its corresponding article, pronunciation, and translation in the following chart.

Place	Pronunciation	Translation
el museo	moo-SEH-oh	museum
la plaza	PLAH-zah	square
el parque	PAHR-keh	park
la biblioteca	bee-blee-oh-TEH-kah	library
el banco	BAHN-koh	bank
la estación	ehs-tah-see-OHN	station
el aeropuerto	ah-eh-roh-poo-EHR-toh	airport
la universidad	oo-nee-behr-SEE-dahd	university
la catedral	kah-TEH-drahl	cathedral
la iglesia	ee-GLEH-see-ah	church

el restaurante	rrehs-tah-oo-RAHN-teh	restaurant
la farmacia	fahr-MAH-see-ah	pharmacy
el supermercado	soo-pehr-mehr-KAH-doh	supermarket
el cine	see-neh	movie theater
el hospital	ohs-PEE-tahl	hospital
el ayuntamiento	ah-joon-tah-mee-ehn-toh	city hall
la escuela	ehs-koo-EH-lah	school
el bar	bahr	bar
la calle	KAH-jeh	street
la cafetería	kah-feh-teh-REE-ah	coffee shop
el estadio	ehs-TAH-dee-oh	stadium

We also saw some other places you can visit in chapter 3, which we didn't include here. Remember to check them out!

Means of Transportation

To get to the places we've just seen, we need a means of transportation, right? Here's a list of possible means of transportation with their articles, their pronunciation, and their translation:

Transportation	Pronunciation	Translation
el pie	pee-EH	foot
la bicicleta	bee-see-KLEH-tah	bicycle
el coche	KOH-cheh	car
el carro	KAH-rroh	car
la moto	MOH-toh	motorcycle
el autobús	ah-oo-toh-BOOS	bus

el tren	trehn	train
el subterráneo	soob-teh-RRAH-neh-oh	subway
el avión	ah-bee-OHN	plane
el helicóptero	eh-lee-KOHP-teh-roh	helicopter
el barco	BAHR-koh	ship

To talk about how to use these means of transportation, we usually use the preposition *en* (which we will talk a bit more about in the next section). For example, we say *Voy en carro* ("I go by car") or *Voy en autobús* ("I go by bus"). However, there is one exception: we don't say *Voy en pie*, we say *Voy a pie* ("I go on foot").

Prepositions and Adverbs of Place

As promised, we will now talk about prepositions and adverbs of place. Prepositions and adverbs of place are helpful to indicate where something is in relation to another object or to simply indicate the location or direction of something.

In the following table you will find the preposition or adverb, its pronunciation and its translation, as usual. We will also add a fourth column where you will find an example.

Preposition / Adverb	Pronunciation	Translation	Example
en	ehn	in, inside of, on top of	*La fuente está en la plaza.* "The fountain is in the square"
encima de	ehn-SEE-mah deh	on top of	*La estatua está encima del edificio.* "The statue is on top of the building"
dentro de	DEHN-troh deh	inside of	*La gente está dentro de la iglesia.* "The people are inside the church"
fuera de	foo-EH-rah deh	outside of	*El señor está fuera de la cafetería.*

			"The man is outside the coffee shop"
delante de	deh-LAHN-teh deh	in front of	*Estoy <u>delante de</u> la biblioteca.* "I'm in front of the library"
detrás de	deh-TRAHS deh	behind	*La estatua está <u>detrás</u> del árbol.* "The statue is behind the tree"
al lado de	ahl LAH-doh deh	next to	*El supermercado está <u>al lado</u> de la biblioteca.* "The supermarket is next to the library"
entre	EHN-treh	between	*El museo está <u>entre</u> el banco y la estación.* "The museum is between the bank and the station"
enfrente de	ehn-FREHN-teh deh	in front of	*El museo <u>está</u> <u>enfrente del</u> aeropuerto.* "The museum is in front of the airport"
frente a	FREHN-teh ah	opposite	*La escuela está <u>frente al</u> cine.* "The school is opposite the movie theater"
alrededor de	ahl-rreh-deh-DOHR deh	around	*La gente está <u>alrededor</u> de la plaza.* "The people are around the square"
cerca de	SEHR-kah deh	near	*El cine está <u>cerca de</u> la farmacia.* "The movie theater is near the pharmacy"
lejos de	LEH-hohs deh	far	*La farmacia está <u>lejos de</u> la universidad.* "The pharmacy is far from the university"

debajo de	deh-BAH-hoh deh	under	*La mujer está <u>debajo del</u> árbol.* "The woman is under the tree"
junto a	HOON-toh ah	next to	*El hospital está <u>junto al</u> supermercado.* "The hospital is next to the supermarket"
sobre	SOH-breh	on	*La universidad está <u>sobre la</u> calle Independencia.* "The university is on Independencia street"
aquí	ah-kee	here	*La catedral está <u>aquí</u>.* "The cathedral is here"
allí	ah jcc	thcrc	*El bar está <u>allí</u>.* "The bar is there"

As you can see from the examples, with all of these prepositions and adverbs of place you will find the verb *estar*, because it is the one that we use to express location, remember?

Before we move on to some grammar, let's clarify something you may or may not have noticed from the examples. As you can see, some of the adverbs of place are accompanied by the preposition *de* or the preposition *a*. And you may have noticed that in the examples sometimes these prepositions became *del* and *al*. This happens only when the following adjective is a masculine one and so it is preceded by the article *el*. *Del* and *al* are contractions of *de + el* and *a + el*, and they are the only two contractions that exist in Spanish.

Verbs *Ir* and *Querer*

When we're talking about wanting to go somewhere, there are two verbs we absolutely need: *ir*, which means "to go", and *querer* which means "to want". Both of these verbs are irregular, which means that we need to learn their conjugations and we will also see some examples using them.

Here are the conjugations of *ir* and *querer*.

Pronoun	Ir	Querer
(yo)	voy	qu<u>ie</u>ro
(tú)	vas	qu<u>ie</u>res
(él/ella/usted)	va	qu<u>ie</u>re

(nosotros/nosotras)	vamos	queremos
(vosotros/vosotras)	váis	queréis
(ellos/ellas/ustedes)	van	qui_e_ren

As you can see, the verb *ir* changes a lot! But the endings of the conjugations are similar to those of a regular verb ending in *-ar*, except for the first person singular, which has an ending similar to that of the verb *ser*.

The verb *querer* doesn't change that much, does it? The root of the verb doesn't change for the first and second person plural, but it does for the rest of the persons and numbers. And the change isn't too radical, either: we simply add an *i* between the *u* and the *e*.

Let's see some examples:

- *Hoy voy al museo* ("Today I go to the museum")
- *Carlos va al gimnasio todos los días* ("Carlos goes to the gym every day")
- *Quiero una entrada para el museo, por favor* ("I want one ticket for the museum, please")
- *¿Quieres un chocolate?* ("Do you want a chocolate?")

And what if we wanted to say "I want to go to the museum"? Well, then, just like in English, the second verb (in this case, "to go") needs to be in the infinitive. So we say: *Quiero ir al museo*. This is what we will probably say before asking for directions, right? So let's go to the main objective of this chapter.

Asking for Directions

We're finally ready to tackle our main objective! Now it's time to ask how to get to places. Like in the previous chapter, we will first see the phrases and questions in English, and then their Spanish counterparts along with their pronunciations.

- "Excuse me"
  - *Disculpe*: dees-KOOL-peh
  - *Perdone*: pehr-DOH-neh
- "How do I get to...?"
  - *¿Cómo llego a...?*: KOH-moh JEH-goh ah
  - *¿Cómo voy a...?*: KOH-moh BOH-ee ah
  - *¿Podría decirme cómo llegar/ir a...?* (more polite): poh-DREE-ah deh-SEER-meh KOH-moh jeh-GAHR/eer ah
- "Where is...?"
  - *¿Dónde está...?*: DOHN-deh ehs-TAH
- "Could you show me the way?"
  - *¿Podría indicarme el camino?*: poh-DREE-ah een-dee-KAHR-meh ehl kah-MEE-noh
- "Is... nearby?"

- o *¿... está cerca?*: ehs-TAH SEHR-kah

- o *¿Hay algún/alguna.... cerca?*: AH-ee al-GOON/al-GOO-nah ... SEHR-kah

- o *¿Sabe si hay algún/alguna... por aquí?"*: SAH-beh see AH-ee ahl-GOON/ahl-GOO-nah ... pohr ah-KEE

- "Is... on this street?"

  - o *¿... está en esta calle?*: ehs-TAH ehn EHS-tah CAH-jeh

  - o *¿Hay algún/alguna... en esta calle?*: AH-ee al-GOON/al-GOO-nah ... ehn EHS-tah CAH-jeh

Giving Directions

Now, how do we answer if people ask us any of the previous questions? Or how do we understand people's answers if we ask these questions? To do that, we will need more than just the vocabulary we've learned. We will also need to know some important phrases used to give directions.

We'll see the English version, then the Spanish translation and the pronunciation of all phrases in the following list:

- "You have to go straight"

  - o *Tienes que caminar derecho*: tee-EH-nehs keh kah-mee-NAHR deh-REH-choh

  - o *Tienes que ir recto*: tee-EH-nehs keh eer REHK-toh

- "You have to continue onwards"

  - o *Tienes que seguir recto*: tee-EH-nehs keh seh-GEER RREK-toh

  - o *Tienes que continuar derecho*: tee-EH-nehs keh kohn-tee-noo-AHR deh-REH-choh

- "Turn left/right"

  - o *Gira a la izquierda/derecha*: HEE-rah ah lah eez-kee-EHR-dah/deh-REH-chah

  - o *Dobla a la izquierda/derecha*: DOH-blah ah lah eez-kee-EHR-dah/deh-REH-chah

- "Cross the street"

  - o *Cruza la calle*: CROO-zah lah KAH-jeh

- "It's... blocks away"

  - o *Está a... calles*: ehs-TAH ah ... KAH-jehs

- "It's around the corner"

  - o *Está a la vuelta de la esquina*: ehs-TAH ah lah boo-EHL-tah deh lah es-KEE-nah

- "It's a bit far away"

  - o *Está un poco lejos*: ehs-TAH oon POH-koh LEH-hohs

- "You need to take the train/bus to..." + destination

  - o *Tienes que tomar el tren/autobús hasta...*: tee-EH-nehs keh toh-MAHR ehl trehn/ah-oo-toh-BOOS AHS-tah

Key Takeaways

In this chapter, we've focused on learning how to ask for directions and how to answer if someone else asks us for them. To do this, we've learned:

- Some places to visit
- Some means of transportation
    - We also mentioned that to talk about means of transportation we usually use the preposition *en*, except when we're talking about going on foot, we use the preposition *a*
- The prepositions and adverbs of place
    - We've also mentioned that there are two contractions in Spanish: *del* and *al*, which are formed by *de + el* and *a + el* respectively
- The present indicative conjugations of the verbs *ir* and *querer*
- How to ask for directions
- How to give directions

And just like that, we're halfway done with this book! But we're not done yet, because we will talk a bit about our families, what their traits are, and what they look like in the following chapter. It will be fun!

First, though, make sure you practice everything we've learned in this chapter to make sure we're on the right track!

Exercises

1. What does *ayuntamiento* mean in Spanish?
    a. Hospital
    b. Catedral
    c. City hall
    d. Street

2. How do we say "square" in Spanish?
    a. Plaza
    b. Banco
    c. Parque
    d. Calle

3. True or False: *carro* and *coche* both mean train.

4. In Spanish, is an airplane a feminine or masculine word?

5. How would you say "I go to the museum on foot"?
    a. Voy al museo en pie.
    b. Voy al museo en el pie.
    c. Voy al museo a pie.
    d. Voy al museo al pie.

6. How would you say "I go to the library by bike"?

    a. Voy al banco en autobús.

    b. Voy al bar a subterráneo.

    c. Voy al cine a barco.

    d. Voy a la biblioteca en bicicleta.

7. Can you translate these prepositions and adverbs of place into Spanish?

    a. In front of

    b. Behind of

    c. Under

    d. On top of

8. What happens when I want to put two verbs together, for example, to say "I <u>want</u> <u>to go</u> to the bank"?

    a. Both verbs go in the present: *quiero voy*.

    b. The first verb goes in the infinitive and the second in the present: *querer voy*.

    c. The first verb goes in the present and the second in the infinitive: *quiero ir*.

    d. Both verbs go in the infinitive: *querer ir*.

9. How would you ask if there is a pharmacy nearby?

    a. ¿Hay alguna farmacia cerca?

    b. ¿Cómo llego al farmacia?

    c. ¿Podría indicarme el camino?

    d. ¿Dónde está la farmacia?

10. If you're told *dobla a la derecha*, what should you do?

    a. Cross the street

    b. Turn right

    c. Turn left

    d. Continue onwards

Answer Key

1. c. City hall

2. a. Plaza

3. False. *Carro* and *coche* mean "car"

4. Masculine

5. c. Voy al museo a pie.

6. d. Voy a la biblioteca en bicicleta.

    a. In front of: En frente de

    b. Behind of: Detrás de

    c. Under: Debajo de

    d. On top of: Encima de

7. c. The first verb goes in the present and the second in the infinitive: *quiero ir*.

8. a. ¿Hay alguna farmacia cerca?

9. b. Turn right

Chapter 6: My Family is...

✐

Es hermoso que los padres lleguen a ser amigos de sus hijos, librándoles de todo temor, pero inspirándoles un gran respeto.

- José Ingenieros

Welcome to chapter 6! We're getting closer and closer to the finish line. We started this book over 15 days ago and it's time to focus on the next three days. In this chapter, we will be talking about family members, possessives, appearances, abilities, attributes, and defects. I think we will have a lot of fun talking about our family members, don't you? Then, without further ado, let's get to it!

Family Members

It's about time we learned how to talk about our family members, right? How else are you going to tell people that your siblings are annoying or that you have many cousins? Well, it's time to focus on them.

In the following table, as usual, you will find the feminine and masculine ways to call your family members, the pronunciation, and the translation.

Noun	Pronunciation	Translation
madre	MAH-dreh	mother
padre	PAH-dreh	father
mamá	mah-MAH	mom
papá	pah-PAH	dad
hijo	EE-hoh	son
hija	EE-hah	daughter
esposo	ehs-POH-soh	husband
esposa	ehs-POH-sah	wife
novio	noh-BEE-oh	boyfriend
novia	noh-BEE-ah	girlfriend
hermano	ehr-MAH-noh	brother
hermana	ehr-MAH-nah	sister

abuelo abuela	ah-boo-EH-loh ah-boo-EH-lah	grandfather grandmother
nieto nieta	nee-EH-toh nee-EH-tah	grandson granddaughter
primo prima	PREE-moh PREE-mah	cousin
tío tía	TEE-oh TEE-ah	uncle aunt
sobrino sobrina	soh-BREE-noh soh-BREE-nah	nephew niece
suegro suegra	soo-EH-groh soo-EH-grah	father-in-law mother-in-law
yerno nuera	JEHR-noh noo-EH-rah	son-in-law daughter-in-law
cuñado cuñada	koo-NYAH-doh koo-NYAH-dah	brother-in-law sister-in-law
padrastro madrastra	pah-DRAHS-troh mah-DRAHS-trah	stepfather stepmother
hermanastro hermanastra	ehr-mah-NAHS-troh ehr-mah-NAHS-trah	stepbrother stepsister
hijastro hijastra	ee-HAHS-troh ee-HAHS-trah	stepson stepdaughter
medio hermano media hermana	meh-DEE-oh ehr-MAH-noh meh-DEE-ah ehr-MAH-nah	half-brother half-sister

Remember that, when we're talking about people and we want to talk in general about a group that includes both men and women, we refer to the whole group using the plural form of the masculine. Which is why, in Spanish, "parents" are *padres* and "siblings" are *hermanos*.

Besides our family members, we might also want to talk about people close to us, so here's a short table with some of them:

Noun	Pronunciation	Translation
amigo amiga	ah-MEE-goh ah-MEE-gah	friend
compañero compañera	kohm-pah-NYEH-roh kohm-pah-NYEH-rah	colleague, partner
socio socia	SOH-see-oh SOH-see-ah	business partner
padrino madrina	pah-DREE-noh mah-DREE-nah	godfather godmother
ahijado ahijada	ah-ee-HAH-doh ah-ee-HAH-dah	godson goddaughter

Let's look at a few example sentences using these words so that you can see how they are used in a sentence:

- Tengo tres <u>hermanos</u> en total. Dos <u>hermanas</u> y un <u>hermano</u>. ("I have three siblings in all. Two sisters and one brother")
- El <u>socio</u> de mi <u>esposo</u> es el <u>padrino</u> de nuestro <u>hijo</u>. ("My husband's business partner is our son's godfather")
- La <u>madre</u> de mi mejor <u>amigo</u> y mi <u>padre</u> se casaron. Ahora, mi mejor <u>amigo</u> es mi <u>medio hermano</u>. ("My best friend's mother and my father got married. Now, my best friend is my half-brother")
- Mi <u>tía</u> Julia tuvo una <u>hija</u>. Es mi única <u>prima</u>. ("My aunt Julia had a daughter. She's my only cousin").

Possessives

In English, we use possessives to talk about family members so that we can identify whose brother, sister, mother, father, etc. we're talking about. And, in Spanish, we do the same thing.

As you can tell by their name and what we've just said, possessives are used to talk about belonging, ownership, and possession. And, in Spanish, they always need to agree in gender and number with the noun they're referring to.

While English has, for example, *my* and *mine*, Spanish also has two types of possessives: possessive adjectives and possessive pronouns. The possessive adjectives are the ones that go before the noun and the possessive pronouns are the ones that go in the position of the noun. In other words, possessive pronouns replace the noun in the sentence.

To determine which possessive to use, we need to take into account the gender and number of the object as well as the person and number of the person who possesses the object in question.

Let's take a look at two tables with the possessive adjectives and the possessive pronouns:

Possessive Adjectives

Person who possesses the object	Object			
	Singular		Plural	
	Masculine	Feminine	Masculine	Feminine
yo	mi		mis	
tú	tu		tus	
él / ella / usted	su		sus	
nosotros / nosotras	nuestro	nuestra	nuestros	nuestras
vosotros / vosotras	vuestro	vuestra	vuestros	vuestras
ellos / ellas / ustedes	su		sus	

We can see in the table above that only the first and second person plural have both a feminine and masculine form, while the other possessive adjectives are neuter. Moreover, we can also note that the third person singular and plural possessive adjectives are exactly the same.

Possessive Pronouns

The possessive pronouns are always preceded by a definite article (*el, la, los, las*) that also agrees in gender and number with the object. That's why, in the following table, you will see the possessive pronoun with the definite article.

Person who possesses the object	Object			
	Singular		Plural	
	Masculine	Feminine	Masculine	Feminine
yo	el mío	la mía	los míos	las mías

tú	el tuyo	la tuya	los tuyos	las tuyas
él / ella / usted	el suyo	la suya	los suyos	las suyas
nosotros / nosotras	el nuestro	la nuestra	los nuestros	las nuestras
vosotros / vosotras	el vuestro	la vuestra	los vuestros	las vuestras
ellos / ellas / ustedes	el suyo	la suya	los suyos	las suyas

Unlike possessive adjectives, possessive pronouns do have a masculine and feminine form in all of the persons and numbers. However, as you can see, one thing they have in common is that the possessive pronouns for the third person singular and plural are also exactly the same. This can sometimes make it a bit difficult to understand who the object belongs to, but we can usually tell from context.

Now, let's see some examples using both the possessive adjectives and pronouns.

- *Mi hermano tiene 10 años y el suyo tiene 11 años ¿Y el tuyo?* ("My brother is 10 years old and his is 11. What about yours?")
  - In this sentence, the first possessive is an adjective because it comes before the noun *hermano*. However, the second and third ones are pronouns because they are used instead of *su hermano* and *tu hermano*.

- *Esas no son sus tías, son las nuestras. Las suyas son aquellas.* ("Those aren't her aunts, those are ours. Hers are those other ones").
  - The first possessive in this example is an adjective that refers to *tías*, so it is a plural adjective. Then, we have the possessive pronouns *las nuestras* and *las suyas* which also refer to *tías* and so they are in the feminine plural form.

- *¡Vuestra madre está aquí! La suya también, pero la mía no.* ("Your mother is here! Theirs is too, but mine isn't")
  - Here, we first talk about the mother of the two people or more we are addressing, so we use the possessive adjective *vuestra*. Then, we refer to the mother of two people or more who we are talking about, so we use the possessive pronoun *la suya*, and then we talk about ours, so we use the possessive pronoun *la mía*.

As you can see, we first use the possessive adjective with the noun to establish what we're talking about. Afterwards, if we want to use the same noun, even if it doesn't refer to the exact same object, we don't repeat the noun. Instead, we use the possessive pronouns to refer to it, and we can change the pronoun depending on whose object we're talking about.

Describing People

When we talk about our family members, we might want to describe them so that others can recognize them or even just to talk about them. Of course, we will need to use the things we've already learned, like how to say their names, how old they are, and what they do for a living. But there are other things we might want to say about them as well, like their appearance and some of their virtues and flaws.

Talking About Appearances

We will learn some adjectives used to describe people's appearances in this section. We'll start with some adjectives used to describe people's appearances in general:

Adjective	Pronunciation	Translation
alto alta	AHL-toh AHL-tah	tall
bajo baja	BAH-hoh BAH-hah	short
delgado delgada	dehl-GAH-doh dehl-GAH-dah	lean
corpulento corpulenta	kohr-poo-LEHN-toh kohr-poo-LEHN-tah	stout
grande	GRAHN-de	large
menudo menuda	meh-noo-doh meh-noo-dah	small
musculoso musculosa	moos-koo-LOH-soh moos-koo-LOH-sah	muscular
pelirrojo pelirroja	peh-lee-RROH-hoh peh-lee-RROH-hah	redhead
rubio rubia	roo-BEE-oh roo-BEE-ah	blonde
teñido teñida	teh-NY-doh ten-NY-dah	dyed hair
viejo vieja	bee-EH-hoh bee-EH-hah	old
joven	HOH-behn	young
pequeño	peh-KEH-nyo	little

pequeña	peh-KEH-nya	

At this point, we should note that we generally use the verb *ser* with these adjectives because we're generally talking about a permanent state. However, if something has changed in the way people look or if the state isn't permanent, we can use the verb *estar*. For example, if we say *Juana está alta* ("Juana is tall"), we mean to say that she's grown since the last time we've seen her. This is something that the English verb "to be" can't express on its own, so we usually use a comparative to say something like "Juana is taller than the last time I've seen her". We can compare the uses of *ser* and *estar* with another example, we can say: *Juana es pelirroja, pero ahora está teñida* ("Juana has red hair, but now she has dyed hair"). If we use *es*, we mean that she inherently has red hair, it is her permanent state. However, if we use *está*, we mean that she has dyed her hair now, but that this isn't always the case.

We can also have adjectives that are used specifically to describe certain parts of a person's body. For example, the eyes and the hair.

To talk about the eyes, we say *Tiene los ojos...* ("He/She has ... eyes") and we can finish this sentence with the color of the person's eyes. For example: *Laura tiene los ojos azules* ("Laura has blue eyes").

If we want to talk about someone's hair, however, we would need to say *Tiene el cabello...* ("He/She has ... hair") and then add an adjective from the following list:

castaño	kahs-TAH-nyoh	brown
canoso	kah-NOH-soh	gray
lacio	lah-SEE-oh	straight
rizado	rree-ZAH-doh	curly
ondulado	ohn-doo-LAH-doh	wavy
brillante	bree-JAHN-teh	shiny
corto	KOHR-toh	short
largo	LAHR-goh	long

Let's see some example sentences describing family members!

- Mi prima Susana es <u>joven</u>, <u>baja</u>, tiene el pelo <u>corto</u> y <u>castaño</u> y los ojos <u>marrones</u>. ("My cousin Susana is young, short, has short and brown hair, and brown eyes")

- Ernesto, mi padre, es <u>viejo</u> y tiene el pelo <u>canoso</u>, pero es muy <u>musculoso</u>. ("Ernesto, my father, is old and gray-haired, but he is muscular")

- Mi sobrina Juliana es <u>pequeña</u>, tiene 8 años, pero está <u>alta</u> y <u>delgada</u>. ("My niece Juliana is little, she's 8 years old, but she is tall and lean").

Talking About Personality

We can also talk about the personality of the people closest to us when we don't want to focus on their appearance. To do this, we would need to learn some other adjectives, which you will find in the table below!

Adjective	Pronunciation	Translation
inteligente	een-teh-lee-HEHN-teh	intelligent
puntual	poon-too-AHL	on time
honesto honesta	oh-NEHS-toh oh-NEHS-tah	honest
responsable	rrehs-pohn-SAH-bleh	responsible
amable	ah-MAH-bleh	kind
limpio limpia	LEEM-pee-oh LEEM-pee-ah	clean
desordenado desordenada	dehs-ohr-deh-NAH-doh dehs-ohr-deh-NAH-dah	untidy
paciente	pah-see-EHN-teh	patient
optimista	ohp-tee-MEES-tah	optimist
pesimista	peh-see-MEES-tah	pessimist
realista	rreh-ah-LEES-tah	realist
leal	leh-AHL	loyal
alegre	ah-LEH-greh	joyful
simpático simpática	seem-PAH-tee-koh seem-PAH-tee-kah	nice
generoso generosa	heh-neh-ROH-soh heh-neh-ROH-sah	generous
egoísta	eh-goh-EES-tah	selfish

atento	ah-TEHN-tah	thoughtful
atenta	ah-TEHN-toh	
valiente	bah-lee-EHN-teh	brave
malhumorado	mahl-oo-moh-RAH-doh	moody
malhumorada	mahl-oo-moh-RAH-dah	
cobarde	koh-BAHR-deh	cowardly
divertido	dee-behr-TEE-doh	fun
divertida	dee-behr-TEE-dah	
bueno	boo-EH-noh	good
buena	boo-EH-bah	
malo	MAH-loh	bad
mala	mah-LAH	

As you know by now, some adjectives we've seen in the previous tables remain unchanged regardless of gender, which is why you see only one form in the first column.

Now, let's see some examples using these adjectives:

- Mi novio es <u>malhumorado</u>, pero también es <u>divertido</u> y <u>amable</u>. ("My boyfriend is moody, but he's also fun and kind")

- Mi abuela Carla es <u>simpática</u>, pero también es <u>egoísta</u>. ("My grandmother Carla is nice, but she is also selfish").

- Mi hijo Pablo es <u>inteligente</u> y <u>responsable</u>. ("My son Pablo is intelligent and responsible").

Quantifiers Muy, Bastante, and Un Poco

With so many ways to describe people, we might want to use quantifiers. For example, we might want to say that our father is <u>very</u> tall or <u>a bit</u> pessimistic. So, in this last section, we will talk about the quantifiers *muy, bastante* and *un poco*.

Muy means "very", *bastante* means "quite" or "rather" and *un poco* means "a little". Using them is very easy. We simply put them before the adjectives we want to quantify to say how tall, short, good, bad, etc., a person is. Let's modify some of the examples we've seen before to add *muy, bastante* and *un poco*:

- Ernesto, mi padre, es <u>un poco</u> viejo y tiene el pelo <u>bastante</u> canoso, pero es <u>muy</u> musculoso. ("Ernesto, my father, is a bit old and rather gray-haired, but he is very muscular")

- Mi sobrina Juliana es <u>bastante</u> pequeña, tiene 8 años, pero está <u>muy</u> alta y delgada. ("My niece Juliana is quite little, she's 8 years old, but she is very tall and lean").

- Mi abuela Carla es <u>bastante</u> simpática, pero también es <u>un poco</u> egoísta. ("My grandmother Carla is quite nice, but she is also a bit selfish").

- Mi hijo Pablo es <u>bastante</u> inteligente y <u>muy</u> responsable. ("My son Pablo is quite intelligent and very responsible").

Key Takeaways

We've just finished chapter 6 and we're doing great, don't you think? We saw a lot of vocabulary in this chapter. Let's review everything we've dealt with:

- A list of family members, which also included people close to us such as friends and colleagues

- The possessives, which we use to identify whose family member we're talking about. They need to agree in gender and number with the object and in person with the person who possesses the object. There are two kinds:

  o Possessive adjectives, which go before the noun

  o Possessive pronouns, which replace the noun in the sentence and are always preceded by a definite article

- Adjectives to talk about appearances

  o And adjectives to talk about people's hair

- Adjectives to describe people's personalities

- Quantifiers *muy, bastante,* and *un poco,* which mean *very, quite* and *a little* respectively and precede the adjectives in the sentence

Now we're going to head over to the exercises, but before that, let me tell you about what's in store for you after you've finished them. In chapter 7, we will see another use of the present indicative: talking about habits. For this, we will cover a lot of vocabulary related to time. See you there soon!

Exercises

1. Can you translate the following family members into Spanish?

   a. Sister

   b. Husband

   c. Aunt

   d. Nephew

   e. Grandmother

   f. Father-in-law

2. If I have four nephews and three nieces, I have *siete*...

   a. Tías

   b. Tíos

   c. Sobrinas

   d. Sobrinos

3. What factors do we need to take into account to determine which possessive to use? (More than one option can be right)

   a. Gender of the person who possesses.

   b. Number of the person who possesses.

   c. Person of the person who possesses.

   d. Gender of the object.

   e. Number of the object.

   f. Person of the object.

4. Where do possessive adjectives go in the sentence?

   a. Before the subject pronoun.

   b. In the place of the subject pronoun.

   c. Before the object.

   d. After the object.

   e. In the place of the object.

5. Where do possessive pronouns go in the sentence?

   a. Before the subject pronoun.

   b. In the place of the subject pronoun.

   c. Before the object.

   d. After the object.

   e. In the place of the object.

6. Are the following possessive adjectives or possessive pronouns?

   a. Esta es <u>mi</u> mamá.

   b. Es más baja que <u>la tuya</u>.

   c. <u>La tuya</u> es más alta.

   d. <u>Tu</u> papá es joven.

   e. <u>El mío</u> es más viejo.

7. Marta is young, small, blonde, and muscular. Which of the following Spanish adjectives can be used to describe her?

   a. Rubio

   b. Menudo

   c. Alta

   d. Musculosa

   e. Pelirrojo

   f. Teñida

   g. Joven

h. Pequeño

8. Do the following sentences reflect a permanent state (P) or a temporary state (T)?

    a. Malena es grande.

    b. Pablo es pelirrojo.

    c. Laura está delgada.

    d. Fernando está rubio.

    e. Mario es bajo.

    f. Luis está viejo.

9. All of the following personality traits belong to Guillermo. Are they positive (P) or negative (N)?

    a. Egoísta

    b. Paciente

    c. Alegre

    d. Malhumorado

    e. Limpio

    f. Pesimista

10. Using the previous personality traits, write sentences using *muy* or *un poco* in the right position so that Guillermo is portrayed in the best light possible.

Answer Key

    a. Hermana

    b. Esposo

    c. Tía

    d. Sobrino

    e. Abuela

    f. Suegro

2. d. Sobrinos

3. b. Number of the person who possesses.
   c. Person of the person who possesses.
   d. Gender of the object.
   e. Number of the object.

4. c. Before the object.

5. e. In the place of the object.

    a. Possessive adjective

    b. Possessive pronoun

    c. Possessive pronoun

    d. Possessive adjective

    e. Possessive pronoun

6. d. Musculosa
   g. Joven

    a. P

    b. P

    c. T

    d. T

    e. P

    f. T

    g. N

    h. P

    i. P

    j. N

    k. P

    l. N

    m. Guillermo es un poco egoísta.

    n. Guillermo es muy paciente.

    o. Guillermo es muy alegre.

p. Guillermo es un poco malhumorado.

q. Guillermo es muy limpio.

r. Guillermo es un poco pesimista.

Chapter 7: Every Morning...

❧

Uno tiene en sus manos el color de su día... Rutina o estallido.

- Mario Benedetti

In this chapter, we will talk about another one of the uses of the present indicative that we have talked about but haven't seen in depth yet: talking about habits and routines. Just like the present simple in English, the present indicative is the Spanish tense used to talk about these things. Besides learning this use of the present indicative, we will also learn the days of the week, the time, some verbs of frequency and more!

Let's dive into it!

Days of the Week

We will start this chapter off with the days of the week because, in order to tell people about your routine, you will most definitely need to tell them which day you do what. Right?

Let's see them in a chart alongside their pronunciation and translation.

Day of the week	Pronunciation	Translation
el lunes	LOO-nehs	Monday
el martes	MAHR-tehs	Tuesday
el miércoles	mee-EHR-koh-lehs	Wednesday
el jueves	hoo-EH-behs	Thursday
el viernes	bee-EHR-nehs	Friday
el sábado	SAH-bah-doh	Saturday
el domingo	doh-MEEN-goh	sunday
el fin de semana	feen deh seh-MAH-nah	weekend

Time of the Day

Besides the day of the week, you might want to share approximately at which time of day you do what, right?

In the following table, you will find the times of the day with their pronunciation and translation.

Time of the Day	Pronunciation	Translation
la mañana	mah-NYA-nah	morning
el mediodía	meh-dee-oh-DEE-ah	midday
la tarde	TAHR-deh	afternoon
la noche	NOH-cheh	night

While we can just say "Monday mornings..." in English, we can't simply put the day of the week with the time of the day in Spanish. For example, we can't say *Lunes mañana*. Instead, we use the definite article before the day of the week and then the preposition *por* and the corresponding definite article before the time of the day. For example: *El lunes por la mañana...*

There is one exception, though. We never say *por el mediodía*. Instead, we say *al mediodía* when we want to say that something happens at noon.

Telling the Time

If we want to be more specific about the time at which we usually do something, then we need to know how to tell the time.

First, let's learn how to ask what time it is. To do this in Spanish, we ask *¿Qué hora es?*

- To say "o'clock" in Spanish, we say *en punto*. For example: *Son las dos en punto* ("It's two o'clock")

- To say the exact time, we simply say the number of the hour and the number of the minutes joined by *y*: *Son las cuatro y dieciocho* ("It's four eighteen")

- In Spanish we also divide the hours in quarters. To do this, we use the word *cuarto*, which means exactly "quarter". For example: *Son las doce y cuarto* ("It's a quarter past twelve").

- And, of course, we also divide the hours in half using the word "media". For example: *Son las nueve y media* ("It's half past nine").

- In English, if, for example, it's 06:40, we can say "It's six forty" or "It's twenty to seven". The same happens in Spanish, but to say how much time there is to the next hour, we use the word *menos*. Following the English example, then, we can say either *Son las seis y cuarenta* or *Son las siete menos veinte*.

- And, of course, if it's 7:45, we use the word *cuarto* again with *menos*: *Son las ocho menos cuarto*.

We can add *de la mañana* ("in the morning"), *de la tarde* ("in the afternoon") or *de la noche* ("at night") to any of these times to specify.

As you've seen, we use the verb *ser* to tell the current time. However, if we're talking about at what time we do something, then we wouldn't use the verb *ser*. Instead, we would simply use the preposition *a* before the article and the time, just like we use the preposition "at" in English. For example: *A las siete y media* ("At half past seven"). This last one is actually the form we will use to talk about habits and routines.

Expressing Frequency

There are many ways in which we can express different frequencies.

We can simply use the plural form of the weekdays to say what we do that day. For example: *Los martes...* or *Los sábados...* Note that, in Spanish, the plural form of the weekdays (and not the days of the weekend) is exactly the same as the singular form because they end in -*s*. However, the days of the weekend end in a vowel and so we need to add an -*s* to them: *sábados* and *domingos*.

We can also express frequency with the days of the week and the times of the day. Just like we say "every Thursday" or "every morning" in English, we say *todos los jueves...* or *todas las mañanas...* in Spanish. We can also say *todos los días* ("everyday") and *todos los meses* ("every month").

We can also use the words *semana* ("week") and *mes* ("month") to say how many times a week or a month we do something. For example: *Una vez a la semana* ("Once a week") or *Tres veces al mes* ("Three times a month").

And, of course, we can also use adverbs of frequency. Here's a list with a few of them with their pronunciation and translation:

Adverb of Frequency	Pronunciation	Translation
siempre	see-EHM-preh	always
casi siempre	KAH-see see-EHM-preh	almost always
normalmente	nohr-MAHL-mehn-teh	normally
usualmente	oo-soo-AHL-mehn-teh	usually
a menudo	ah meh-NOO-doh	often
a veces	ah BEH-sehs	sometimes
casi nunca	KAH-see NOON-kah	almost never
nunca	NOON-kah	never

Reflexive Verbs

I think that was enough vocabulary about time and frequency! It's time to talk about the verbs we can use to talk about our routines. The thing about these verbs is that some of them are reflexive. This means that the action affects the same subject that is doing it. One example of this are the Spanish verbs *bañarse* or *vestirse,* which mean "to have a bath" and "to get dressed." They are reflexive because one bathes oneself and dresses oneself.

As you can see, *bañarse* and *vestirse* don't look like normal infinitive verbs because those end in *-ar, -er* or *-ir,* like we've seen before, but these end in *-se.* This is because *se* is a Spanish reflexive pronoun and we need reflexive pronouns to use these verbs. Let's use *bañarse* as an example to see how to conjugate these verbs:

(Subject Pronoun)	Reflexive Pronoun	Verb
(yo)	me	bañ<u>o</u>
(tú)	te	bañ<u>as</u>
(él / ella / usted)	se	bañ<u>a</u>
(nosotros / nosotras)	nos	bañ<u>amos</u>
(vosotros / vosotras)	os	bañ<u>áis</u>
(ellos / ellas / ustedes)	se	bañ<u>an</u>

As you can see, we first write the reflexive pronoun and then conjugate the verb. *Bañarse* is a regular verb, so it is conjugated in the same way as any regular verb ending in *-ar.*

I don't know if you've noticed, but we've actually seen a verb just like this one before. Do you remember? *Llamarse* is a reflexive verb because when we say *Me llamo...,* we are talking about how we call ourselves.

And though we've said many of the verbs we use to talk about routines are reflexive, we've only talked about *bañarse* and *vestirse.* Let's take a look at a few more that use the same reflexive pronouns.

- *despertarse*: to wake up
- *levantarse*: to get up
- *acostarse*: to lay down/go to bed
- *ducharse*: to shower
- *afeitarse*: to shave
- *cepillarse (los dientes)*: to brush (one's teeth)
- *peinarse*: to comb
- *lavarse (la cara)*: to wash (one's face)
- *maquillarse*: to put makeup on

- *quedarse*: to stay

- *ponerse*: to put on/wear

- *vestirse*: to dress

- *sentarse*: to sit down

Some of these verbs are irregular, which means that, though the pronouns will stay the same, the verbs won't follow the conjugation of regular verbs like *bañarse*. However, do not fret! We will talk about all of the irregular verbs on this list and their irregularities in the following section.

Present Indicative of Irregular Verbs

Some Spanish irregular verbs in the present indicative can actually be grouped, and that's what we will talk about in this section.

We are going to talk about four different groups of irregular verbs. But before we do that, we should note that none of the verbs belonging to any of these groups is irregular in the first and second person plural.

First, we have verbs that are only irregular in the first person singular (*yo*), but are regular in the rest. These verbs usually suffer a change from one consonant to *g*. Like *ponerse* which changes to *me pongo*.

Then, we have verbs that change from an *o* in the infinitive form to *ue* in the present indicative. Like *acostarse* which changes from to *me acuesto, te acuestas, se acuesta, se acuestan*.

We also have verbs like *despertarse* and *sentarse* which change from *e* in the infinitive to *ie* in the present indicative: *me despierto, te despiertas, se despierta, se despiertan*, and *me siento, te sientas, se sienta, se sientan*.

And, finally, similarly to the previous irregular verbs, we have verbs that change from *e* in the infinitive to *i* in the present indicative. One of these verbs is *vestirse*, which changes to *me visto, te vistes, se viste,* and *se visten*.

Talking About Habits

As we've been saying, we use the present indicative to talk about habits and routines, so it's time for us to put together everything we've seen in this chapter to talk about habits and routines.

To signal that what we're talking about is a routine or a habit, we first need to set it in time. We can do this with any of the expressions we've learned when we talked about expressing frequency. Let's see some examples of phrases we can use to start talking about our habits and routines:

- *Todos los días...* ("Everyday...")

- *Los miércoles a la tarde...* ("On Wednesday afternoons...")

- *Una vez al mes...* ("Once a month...")

- *Los fines de semana a las 11 de la mañana...* ("On weekends at 11 in the morning...")

- *Normalmente...* ("Normally")

After we've established a time or a frequency that signals that we're talking about a habit or routine, we will add the verb, which may or may not be reflexive, of course, in the present indicative. Let's continue the previous examples to make full sentences:

- *Todos los días me cepillo los dientes.* ("Everyday I brush my teeth")

- *Los miércoles a la tarde juego al fútbol.* ("On Wednesday afternoons I play football")
- *Una vez al mes como comida chatarra.* ("Once a month I eat junk food")
- *Los fines de semana a las 11 de la mañana me levanto.* ("On weekends at 11 in the morning I get up")
- *Normalmente me despierto temprano.* ("Normally I wake up early")

Just like in English, we can also change the order of the elements in the sentence, as long as we keep the different parts separate and don't mix them up.

For example, instead of following the pattern frequency/time + verb, we could use the pattern verb + frequency/time. For example: *Me cepillo los dientes todos los días* ("I brush my teeth every day") or *Me despierto temprano normalmente* ("I wake up early normally").

We could also put the day of the week first and then add the time of day or the hour at the end of the sentence. For example: *Los miércoles juego al fútbol a la tarde* (On wednesdays I play football in the afternoon") or *Los fines de semana me levanto a las 11 de la mañana* ("On weekends I get up at 11 in the morning").

Key Takeaways

We've successfully finished another 3 days and another chapter! Congratulations are in order!

We've talked about habits and routines in this seventh chapter. And, to do so, we've touched on all of the following topics:

- Days of the week: *lunes, martes, miércoles, jueves, viernes, sábado,* and *domingo*
- Times of the day: *mañana, mediodía, tarde, noche*
- Telling the time: *en punto, y cuarto, y media, menos cuarto, menos veinte.*
- Expressing frequency
  - With the plural form of the days of the week
  - With the word *todos* or *todas* and the day of the week or time of the day.
  - With *una vez, dos veces, tres veces,* etc. + *a la semana, al mes,* etc.
  - With adverbs of frequency: *siempre, casi siempre, normalmente, usualmente, a menudo, a veces, casi nunca,* and *nunca*
- Reflexive verbs with their reflexive pronouns and their conjugations
- Four groups of irregular verbs:
  - Consonant → *g* (only in the first person singular)
  - *o → ue*
  - *e → ie*
  - *e → i*
- Patterns to talk about habits and routines:
  - Time/frequency + verb
  - Verb + time/frequence

○ Day + verb + hour/time of day

It's time to put all of this knowledge into practice! We will now get to the exercises (and don't forget to check your answers with the answer key!). And then, in the following chapter, we will learn everything we need to go to a restaurant and order!

Exercises

1. What day comes after *viernes*?
    a. Martes
    b. Domingo
    c. Sábado
    d. Jueves

2. Are all days of the week feminine or masculine words?

3. When do you usually eat lunch?
    a. A la mediodía.
    b. Al mediodía.
    c. Por el mediodía.
    d. Por la mediodía.

4. How do we ask what time it is in Spanish?
    a. ¿Qué hora es?
    b. ¿A qué hora es?
    c. ¿Qué horas son?
    d. ¿A qué horas son?

5. How do we say "It's a half past eight" in Spanish?
    a. Son las ocho y medio.
    b. Es las media y ocho.
    c. Son las ocho y media.
    d. Es las ocho y media.

6. How would you say the following hour in Spanish: 03:45?
    a. Son las tres y cuarto.
    b. Son las cuatro y cuarto.
    c. Son las cuatro menos cuarto.
    d. Son las tres menos cuarto.

7. Can you translate the following phrases used to express frequency into Spanish?
    a. On Mondays
    b. Every morning

    c. Once a month

    d. Often

8. What are reflexive verbs?

    a. Verbs that affect someone else.

    b. Verbs that affect the subject.

    c. Verbs that affect the speaker.

9. Fill in the gaps in the following text with the first person singular present indicative conjugation of the verbs in brackets to learn about Andrea's routine.
Todos los días .... (despertarse) a las 8 de la mañana, ... (bañarse), ... (cepillarse) los dientes, ... (vestirse) y desayuno. Luego voy a trabajar. Los lunes y miércoles juego al fútbol y los martes y jueves voy a la universidad. Los viernes .... (quedarse) en mi casa y .... (acostarse) temprano.
("Everyday I wake up at 8 am, I have a bath, I brush my teeth, I get dressed and have breakfast. Then I go to work. On Mondays and Wednesdays I play football and on Tuesdays and Thursdays I go to school. On Fridays I stay home and go to bed early")

10. Can you change the order of the following sentences while maintaining the same meaning?

    a. Los viernes a la noche como sushi.

    b. Una vez al mes voy al cine.

    c. A menudo salgo a comer.

    d. Todos los días a las 11 de la noche me acuesto.

Answer Key

1. c. Sábado

2. Masculine

3. b. Al mediodía

4. a. ¿Qué hora es?

5. c. Son las ocho y media.

6. c. Son las cuatro menos cuarto.

    a. Los lunes

    b. Todas las mañanas

    c. Una vez al mes

    d. A menudo

7. b. Verbs that affect the subject

8. me despierto
me baño
me cepillo
me visto
me quedo
me acuesto

    a. Como sushi los viernes a la noche. / Los viernes como sushi a la noche. / A la noche como sushi los viernes.

    b. Voy al cine una vez al mes.

    c. Salgo a comer a menudo.

    d. Todos los días me acuesto a las 11 de la noche. / Me acuesto todos los días a las 11 de la noche. / A las 11 de la noche me acuesto todos los días.

Chapter 8: Let's Grab A Bite

❧

El amor es tan importante como la comida pero no alimenta.

- Gabriel García Márquez

We're on our 22nd day of Spanish learning! How are you feeling about that? You've been doing amazingly so far.

I don't know about you, but one of the things I look forward to the most whenever I'm on a trip is going out to eat at different restaurants, try new and different meals, and learn about the culture through food. So, this is actually one of the chapters that excites me the most in this whole book and one you should probably bookmark for the future. We will see different phrases that might be useful when you're at a restaurant, like phrases for asking about the food and vocabulary to understand the menu.

¡Vayamos a comer!

Useful Phrases At a Restaurant

We'll start with some basic phrases that might come in handy whenever you're at a restaurant. As we've done with other phrases before, we will see the English version first, then the Spanish version with its pronunciation.

Before Sitting Down
- "I want to book a table for…" + number
  - *Quiero reservar una mesa para…*: kee-EH-roh rreh-sehr-BAHR OO-nah MEH-sah PAH-rah
- "A table for…" + number
  - *Una mesa para…*: OO-nah MEH-sah PAH-rah dohs, pohr FAH-bohr
- "I have a reservation for…" + number
  - *Tengo una reserva para tres*: TEHN-goh OO-nah rreh-SEHR-bah PAH-rah trehs

About the Menu
- "What's today's special?"
  - *¿Cuál es el menú del día?*: koo-AHL ehs el meh-NOO dehl DEE-ah
- "What's the restaurant's specialty?"
  - *¿Cuál es la especialidad de la casa?*: koo-AHL ehs lah ehs-peh-see-ah-LEE-dahs deh lah KAH-sah
- "What dish do you recommend?"
  - *¿Qué plato recomiendas?*: keh PLAH-toh rreh-koh-mee-EHN-dahs

213

Information About the Dishes

- "What's in this meal?"
  - *¿Qué lleva este plato?*: keh JEH-bah EHS-teh PLAH-toh
- "I'm allergic to..." + allergy
  - *Soy alérgico/alérgica a...*: SOH-ee ah-LEHR-hee-koh/ah-LEHR-hee-kah ah
- "What's the size of this dish?"
  - *¿De qué tamaño es este plato?*: deh keh tah-MAH-nyoh ehs EHS-teh PLAH-toh

Ordering

- "We're ready to order"
  - *Estamos listos para pedir*: ehs-TAH-mohs LEES-tohs PAH-rah peh-DEER
- "I'd like a..." + dish
  - *Me gustaría un...*: meh goos-tah-REE-ah oon
  - *Quiero un...*: kee-EH-roh oon
- "Do you have...?" + dish
  - *¿Tienes...?*: tee-EH-nehs
- "Can I ask you for...?" + dish
  - *¿Puedo pedirte...?*: poo-EH-doh peh-DEER-teh
- "Can we share this dish?"
  - *¿Podemos compartir este plato?*: poh-DEH-mohs kohm-pahr-TEER EHS-teh PLAH-toh
- "Can I order this to go?"
  - *¿Puedo pedirlo para llevar?*: poo-EH-do peh-DEER-loh PAH-rah JEH-bahr

Before You Go

- "Can you bring the bill, please?"
  - *¿Podrías traer la cuenta, por favor?*: poh-DREE-ahs trah-EHR lah koo-EHN-tah
- "Thank you, everything was great."
  - *Gracias. Todo estuvo estupendo*: GRAH-see-ahs. TOH-doh ehs-TOO-boh ehs-too-PEHN-doh

Food, Meals and Useful Words

Well, now it's time to fill in the blanks of some of the phrases we've just seen, right? We're going to have different tables: one with useful words, one with food, and one with meals so that you know how to say those things before going!

Let's start with the useful words!

Useful Word	Pronunciation	Translation
la comida	koh-MEE-dah	food
el restaurante	rres-tah-oo-RAHN-teh	restaurant
el menú	meh-NOOH	menu
la carta	KAHR-tah	restaurant's menu
el plato	PLAH-toh	dish
el platillo	plah-TEE-joh	dish
el desayuno	deh-sah-JOO-noh	breakfast
el almuerzo	ahl-moo-EHR-soh	lunch
la merienda	meh-ree-EHN-dah	afternoon snack
la cena	SEH-nah	dinner
la entrada	ehn-TRAH-dah	starter
el entrante	ehn-TRAHN-teh	starter
el primer plato	pree-MEHR PLAH-toh	first course
el segundo plato	seh-GOON-doh PLAH-toh	second course
el postre	POHS-treh	dessert
el aperitivo	ah-peh-ree-TEE-boh	appetizer (used mainly in Latin America)
el tenedor	teh-neh-DOHR	fork
el cuchillo	koo-CHEE-joh	knife
la cuchara	koo-CHAH-rah	spoon
los cubiertos	kuo-bee-EHR-tohs	cutlery
el vaso	BAH-soh	glass

la copa	KOH-pah	glass, cup
la servilleta	sehr-bee-JEH-tah	napkin
la cuenta	koo-EHN-tah	bill

Now let's see a list of foods!

Food	Pronunciation	Translation
el pan	pahn	bread
la lechuga	leh-CHOO-gah	lettuce
el tomate	toh-MAH-teh	tomato
el huevo	WEH-boh	egg
la zanahoria	zah-nah-OH-ree-ah	carrot
el pollo	POH-joh	chicken
la banana	bah-NAH-nah	banana (used mainly in Latin America)
el plátano	PLAH-tah-noh	banana (used in Spain)
el cereal	seh-reh-AHL	cereal
el chocolate	choh-koh-LAH-teh	chocolate
la cebolla	seh-BOH-jah	onion
el café	kah-FEH	coffee
la mermelada	mehr-meh-LAH-dah	jam
el jamón	jah-MOHN	ham
el queso	KEH-soh	cheese
la palta	PAHL-tah	avocado (used in Argentina and Chile)

el aguacate	ah-wah-KAH-teh	avocado (used in Spain and most Latin American countries)
la fresa	FREH-sah	strawbery
el durazno	duh-RAHZ-noh	peach (used in Latin America)
el melocotón	meh-loh-koh-TOHN	peach (used in Spain)
la papa	PAH-pah	potato (used in Latin America)
la patata	pah-TAH-tah	potato (used in Spain)
la batata	bah-TAH-tah	sweet potato (used in Latin America)
el arroz	ah-RROHZ	rice
la salchicha	sahl-CHEEH-chah	sausage

Finally, let's see a list of meals!

Meal	Pronunciation	Translation
la sopa	SOH-pah	soup
la ensalada	ehn-sah-LAH-dah	salad
la hamburguesa	ahm-boor-GEH-sah	burger
el perrito caliente	peh-RREE-toh kah-lee-EHN-teh	hot dog
el pancho	PAHN-choh	hot dog (used in Argentina and Uruguay)
el bocadillo	boh-kah-DEE-joh	sandwich
la empanada	ehm-pah-NAH-dah	pie, pastry
el taco	TAH-koh	taco
la tortilla	tohr-TEE-jah	tortilla

los fideos	fee-DEH-ohs	noodles
las papas fritas	PAH-pahs FREE-tahs	French fries
la carne	KAHR-neh	beef
el filete	fee-LEH-teh	steak
el pollo	POH-joh	chicken
el huevo frito	WEH-boh FREE-toh	fried egg
el pescado	pehs-KAH-doh	fish
el cerdo	SEHR-doh	pork
los mariscos	mah-REES-kohs	seafood
los ñoquis	NYOH-kees	gnocchi

Ways of Cooking

There are several ways to cook food: fried, baked, steamed... Let's take a look at a list of a few different cooking methods.

Remember that, in the case of the adjectives, you will need to match them with the gender of their noun. For example, while a *pollo* ("chicken") will be *frito* ("fried"), a *papa* ("potato") will be *frita*.

Way of cooking	Pronunciation	Translation
frito	FREE-toh	fried
cocido	koh-SEE-doh	cooked
crudo	KROO-doh	raw
asado	ah-SAH-doh	roasted, grilled
guisado	guee-SAH-doh	stewed
a las brasas	ah lahs BRAH-sahs	grilled (on a grill)
a la parrilla	ah lah pah-RREE-jah	
a la plancha	ah lah PLAHN-chah	grilled (on a warm metal plank)

al horno	ahl OHR-noh	baked
al vapor	ahl bah-POHR	steamed

Talking About Things We Love

Whenever we talk about food, we usually talk about our likes and dislikes because we all have preferences, right? But we might all simply love chocolate.... We've actually already talked about the verb *gustar* to express likes and dislikes in chapter 4, but now we're going to talk about another verb: *encantar*, which means "to love".

As you may remember, we saw that *gustar* always requires a pronoun which is different from the reflexive pronouns we saw in the previous chapter. Well, *encantar* requires the same pronouns as *gustar* and is usually formed by following the same pattern as the one we used with *gustar*. Let's have a look at it!

Indirect object	Negation	Pronoun	Verb	Quantifier	Direct object
(a mí)	(no)	me	encanta encantan	(mucho)	**singular nouns** el queso **verbs** comer queso **plural nouns** los bocadillos de queso
(a ti)		te			
(a él/ella)		le			
(a nosotros/nosotras)		nos			
(a vosotros/vosotras)		os			
(a ellos/ellas/ustedes)		les			

In this case, however, the negative form *no encantar* doesn't mean to dislike. It means that you don't love it, but you might still not mind it or may even like it a bit.

Let's see a few examples!

- A mí <u>me encanta</u> comer carne, pero <u>no me encanta</u> la carne que sirven aquí.
- A Guillermo <u>no le encanta</u> el queso, pero <u>le encanta</u> la pizza.
- A ellos <u>les encantan</u> los fideos, pero a nosotros <u>nos encantan</u> las hamburguesas.

También and Tampoco

Now, when someone says they like/dislike or love/doesn't love something, we would usually want to say that we agree or disagree, right? That's what *también* and *tampoco* are for! We use *también* to express that we also like something, and we use *tampoco* to express that we also don't like something.

We use them in a similar way to "me too" and "me either" in English! In Spanish, we say *a mí también* or *a mí tampoco*. Let's see some example conversations!

● A mí no me gustan los camarones. ¿Y a ti?

○ No, a mí tampoco.

● A mis padres no les gusta el café, pero a mí me encanta.

○ Sí, a mí también me encanta.

● Juan y Carlos, ¿os gustan las ostras?

○ A mí no me encantan, pero puedo comerlas.

□ A mí tampoco me gustan mucho.

But what if we don't agree with what the person is saying? Then, we simply say *a mí sí* or *a mí no*. Let's see some examples:

● A mí no me gustan los camarones. ¿Y a ti?

○ A mí sí.

● A mis padres no les gusta el café, pero a mí me encanta.

○ A mí no.

● Juan y Carlos, ¿os gustan las ostras?

○ A mí no me encantan, pero puedo comerlas.

□ A mí sí.

Comparatives and Superlatives

We know how to say that we like something and how to say that we love something. But how do we express that we like something more than something else? Or that something is our favorite? To say these things, we use the comparative and superlative forms of adjectives or nouns.

Comparative

In Spanish, we can compare one object in relation to another to show superiority, inferiority or equality, and we can do this with adjectives, nouns, and adverbs.

When we want to express that an object is superior to another one, we use the structure: verb + *más* + adjective/noun + *que* + noun. For example, we can say *Las hamburguesas son más ricas que las pizzas* ("Burgers are tastier than pizzas") or *Esta pizza tiene más queso que aquella* ("This pizza has more cheese than that one").

And when we want to express that an object is inferior to another one, we use a similar structure: verb + *menos* + adjective/noun + *que* + noun. For example, we can say *El pescado es menos rico que el cerdo* ("Fish is less tasty than pork") or *El pancho tiene más carne que los fideos* ("The hot dog has more meat than the noodles").

And, finally, we may want to say that they are equal with the structure: verb + *tan* + adjective + *como* + noun. For example: *Estos mariscos son tan ricos como los ñoquis* ("This seafood is as tasty as the gnocchi") or *Este pollo frito es tan pequeño como una papa frita* ("This fried chicken is as small as a french fry").

There are some exceptions to the use of *más* and *menos* + adjective. Instead of *más/menos* + *bueno/malo*, we also say *mejor* and *peor*. And when we use the adjectives *grande* and *pequeño* to refer to age, we use *mayor* and *menor* instead of *más grande* or *más pequeño*, which we use when we're talking about something's size.

Superlative

When we want to say that something is the best or worst of its kind, we use the following structure: definite article (+ noun) + *más/menos* + adjective (+ *de* + group). Let's see a few examples!

- Estos son los fideos más ricos del mundo. ("These are the world's tastiest noodles")
- Esta es la peor paella de toda España. ("This is the worst paella in Spain")
- La banana es la fruta más rica. ("Bananas are the tastiest fruits")

As you can see in the second example, with *bueno, malo, grande,* and *pequeño,* we also use *mejor, peor, mayor* and *menor* as the superlative form.

Adjectives to Describe Food

To use the comparatives and superlatives we've seen, we need to know some adjectives related to food that we generally use, like *rico,* which we've already seen.

Let's see them in a table in their masculine form with their pronunciation and their translation!

Adjective	Pronunciation	Translation
rico	RREE-koh	tasty
sabroso	sah-BROH-soh	savory
dulce	DOOL-seh	sweet
salado	sah-LAH-doh	salty
amargo	ah-MAHR-goh	bitter
ácido	AH-see-doh	sour
agridulce	ah-gree-DOOL-seh	bittersweet
aceitoso	ah-seh-ee-TOH-soh	oily
asqueroso	ahs-keh-ROH-soh	disgusting

seco	SEH-koh	dry
soso	SOH-soh	bland
frío	FREE-oh	cold
caliente	ka-lee-EHN-teh	hot
empalagoso	ehm-pah-lah-GOH-soh	cloying
exquisito	ehx-kee-SEE-toh	exquisite
maduro	mah-DOO-roh	ripe
bueno	boo-EH-noh	good
delicioso	deh-lee-see-OH-soh	delicious
saludable	sah-loo-DAH-bleh	healthy
quemado	keh-MAH-doh	burnt
picante	pee-KAHN-teh	spicy

Quantifiers

The last thing we'll talk about in this chapter are quantifiers and how we can use them with food and some of the phrases we saw at the beginning of the chapter.

Quantifiers change depending on the gender and number of the noun we want to quantify and always precede that noun. Let's learn about them in the following table:

Quantifier	Pronunciation	Translation
demasiado demasiada	deh-mah-see-AH-doh deh-mah-see-AH-dah	too much
mucho mucha	MOO-choh MOO-chah	a lot
bastante	bahs-TAHN-teh	quite a lot
un poco de	oon POH-koh deh	some

poco poca	POH-koh POH-kah	few
nada de	NAH-dah deh	none of
algún alguna	ahl-GOON ahl-GOO-nah	any
ningún ninguna	neen-GOON neen-GOO-nah	none

Have you noticed that *un poco de* and *poco/poca* are two separate things? Well, with *un poco* (which can only be used with uncountable nouns and doesn't change in gender) we express that there is a bit of something in a positive way, but with *poco/poca* we mean that there is little of something in a negative way. Besides, *un poco de* can only be used with uncountable nouns, while *poco/poca* can be used with countable and uncountable nouns.

While *nada de* can only be used with uncountable nouns, just like *un poco de*, *algún/alguna* and *ningún/ninguna* can only be used with countable nouns.

Let's see all of these quantifiers in action with some example sentences!

- *La hamburguesa tiene <u>demasiada</u> sal* ("The burger has too much salt")
- *Ese plato tiene <u>mucho</u> pollo* ("That dish has a lot of chicken")
- *El bocadillo viene con <u>bastantes</u> papas fritas* ("The sandwich comes with quite a lot of fries")
- *¿Puedo pedirte <u>un poco de</u> pan?* ("Can I ask you for some bread?")
- *Me gustaría una sopa con <u>pocas</u> verduras* ("I'd like a soup with few vegetables")
- *No puedo comer <u>nada de</u> sal* ("I can't eat any salt")
- *¿Tienes <u>algún</u> postre?* ("Do you have any dessert?")
- *Lo siento, no tengo <u>ninguna</u> mermelada* ("I'm sorry, I don't have any jam")

Key Takeaways

And just like that, we're done with chapter 8! We just learned everything we need to know to order at a restaurant in Spanish. Let's recap everything we saw:

- Useful phrases to use at a restaurant
- Lists of useful words, foods and dishes
- Ways of cooking a meal
- Talking about things we love and don't love
- Comparative forms
  - verb + *más* + adjective/noun + *que* + noun

- o   verb + *menos* + adjective/noun + *que* + noun
- o   verb + *tan* + adjective + *como* + noun
- Superlative forms
  - o   definite article (+ noun) + *más* + adjective (+ *de* + group)
  - o   definite article (+ noun) + *menos* + adjective (+ *de* + group)
- Adjectives to describe food
- Quantifiers to use with countable and uncountable nouns:
  - o   demasiado
  - o   mucho
  - o   bastante
  - o   un poco de: only used with uncountable nouns
  - o   poco
  - o   nada de: only used with uncountable nouns
  - o   algún: only used with countable nouns
  - o   ningún: only used with countable nouns

After the exercises, we will start chapter nine, which focuses on abilities! We will see how to say that we can or can't do something and some vocabulary related to it! See you there!

Exercises

1. Which of the next options is not a way of ordering food at a restaurant?
    a. Estamos listos para pedir.
    b. Quiero un...
    c. Tengo una reserva para tres.
    d. Me gustaría un...

2. What is the translation of "dish"?
    a. Carta
    b. Plato
    c. Cuchillo
    d. Tenedor

3. How would you say "I'm allergic to..."?
    a. Soy alérgico por...
    b. Soy alérgico con...
    c. Soy alérgico a...
    d. Soy alérgico de...

4. *Durazno* and *plátano* are...

a. Vegetables

b. Fruits

c. Ways of cooking

d. Fish

5. Choose the right option:

   a. Papa (frito/frita)

   b. Carne (asado/asada)

   c. Fideos (cocidas/cocidos)

   d. Ñoquis (crudos/crudas)

6. Complete the following sentences with the words from the box

queso - casa - jamón - cruda - especialidad - mariscos - hamburguesa

   a. Fui a un restaurante y pedí una ...., pero estaba ....

   b. A mi amigo le encantan los ....

   c. Mi comida favorita es el bocadillo de .... y ....

   d. ¿Cuál es la .... de la ....?

7. Complete the following sentences with the right form of the verb *encantar*. Then, answer the statements according to your own likes and dislikes.

   a. A Juan .... la pizza.

   b. A nosotros no .... comer hamburguesas.

   c. A vosotros .... los fideos.

   d. A mí no .... salir a comer.

   e. A ti .... las papas fritas.

8. Write sentences comparing the following elements based on the given adjectives according to your own opinions. Use the comparative form.

   a. saludable: sopa / ensalada

   b. sabroso: hamburguesa / pizza

   c. aceitoso: pollo frito / huevo frito

   d. delicioso: cerdo / pollo

9. Complete the following sentences with the superlative form of the adjectives in brackets.

   a. Este restaurante es .... (bueno) de la ciudad.

   b. Estos tacos son .... (picante) del mundo.

   c. Este queso es .... (amargo) de todos.

   d. La fresa es la fruta .... (dulce).

10. Rearrange the elements to form coherent sentences:

    a. tiene / bastante / este / cereal / plato

b. el / mucho / sándwich / jamón / tiene

c. ¿ / puedo / un poco de / pedirte / agua / ?

d. hay / no / nada de / café.

Answer Key

1. c. Tengo una reserva para tres.
2. b. Plato
3. c. Soy alérgico a...
4. b. Fruits

    a. Frita

    b. Asada

    c. Cocidos

    d. Crudos

    e. Fui a un restaurante y pedí una hamburguesa, pero estaba cruda.

    f. A mi amigo le encantan los mariscos.

    g. Mi comida favorita es el bocadillo de jamón y queso.

    h. ¿Cuál es la especialidad de la casa?

    i. le encanta → a mí también / a mí no.

    j. nos encanta → a mí tampoco / a mí sí.

    k. os encantan → a mí también / a mí no.

    l. me encanta → a mí tampoco / a mí sí.

    m. te encantan → a mí también / a mí no.

    n. La ensalada es más saludable que la sopa. / La sopa es más saludable que la ensalada.

    o. La hamburguesa es más sabrosa que la pizza. / La pizza es más sabrosa que la hamburguesa.

    p. El pollo frito es más aceitoso que el huevo frito. / El huevo frito es más aceitoso que el pollo frito.

    q. El cerdo es más delicioso que el pollo. / El pollo es más delicioso que el cerdo.

    r. Este restaurante es el mejor de la ciudad.

    s. Estos tacos son los más picantes del mundo.

    t. Este queso es el más amargo de todos.

    u. La fresa es la fruta más dulce.

    v. Este plato tiene bastante cereal.

    w. El sándwich tiene mucho jamón.

    x. ¿Puedo pedirte un poco de agua?

    y. No hay nada de café.

Chapter 9: Can you do it?

⁓

Hay raras habilidades perdidas en el mundo y que son mal empleadas en aquellos que no saben aprovecharse de ellas.

- Miguel de Cervantes Saavedra

We all are good at something. I don't know about you, but I'm pretty sure you have many abilities. Do you like to cook? Write, sing, sculpt, act? Do you play any sports, maybe? A person can have many talents, and there's nothing wrong with showing them off a little bit sometimes! In this chapter, we are going to explore how to talk about abilities and the things you can do.

Talking About Abilities

When you meet someone new, you will surely want to know more about them. Similarly, they will want to know more about you! Then, it's important to know how to talk about abilities.

There are two verbs that we can use to talk about skills or abilities: *saber* ("to know") and *poder* ("can"). Both are irregular verbs which, in this case, means that their root changes depending on the conjugation.

Let's see the conjugation of *saber* and *poder* in the present tense:

Pronoun	Saber	Poder
(yo)	sé	puedo
(tú)	sabes	puedes
(él / ella / usted)	sabe	puede
(nosotros / nosotras)	sabemos	podemos
(vosotros / vosotras)	sabéis	podéis
(ellos / ellas / ustedes)	saben	pueden

Thus, there are two ways of asking someone if they can or know how to do something:

- *¿Puedes...?* ("Can you...?")
- *¿Sabes...?* ("Do you know how to...?")

Now, you need to know how to build sentences with these verbs to talk about your abilities. The good news is that it's very simple: you just have to follow the following formula: Subject + conjugated verb (*saber* or *poder*) + verb in the infinitive.

If you want to say that you can't or don't know how to do something, you just have to add the negation word "no" before the conjugated verb.

Let's see some examples:

- *Sé jugar al fútbol* ("I know how to play football").
- *No sé conducir* ("I don't know how to drive").
- *Él puede cocinar* ("He can cook").
- *María no puede cantar* ("María can't sing").

Adverbs To Grade Our Abilities

You can use some adverbs to add information to the sentence. To talk about abilities, we generally use the following adverbs of manner:

Adverb	Pronunciation	Translation
bien	bee-EHN	well
lentamente	LEHN-tah-mehn-teh	slowly
rápidamente	RAH-pee-dah-mehn-teh	quickly
fácilmente	FAH-seel-mehn-teh	easily
estupendamente	ehs-too-pehn-dah-MEHN-teh	fantastically
brillantemente	bree-jahn-teh-MEHN-teh	brilliantly
mal	mahl	badly
minuciosamente	mee-noo-see-OH-sah-mehn-teh	carefully
regular	rreh-goo-LAHR	regularly
fatal	fah-TAHL	really bad

All of these adverbs can, in turn, be graded with the quantifiers *muy, bastante* and *un poco* which mean "very", "quite" and "a little" respectively and are the same as the ones we've said in chapter 6 that can be used to talk about adjectives. Just like with adjectives, these quantifiers are also placed before the adverbs.

Adverbs of manner are placed at the end of the sentence. Let's see their position in the following chart:

(yo)	(no)	sé/puedo	infinitive verb	adverb
(tú)		sabes/puedes		
(él / ella / usted)		sabe/puede		
(nosotros / nosotras)		sabemos/podemos		
(vosotros / vosotras)		sabéis/podéis		
(ellos / ellas / ustedes)		saben/pueden		

Now, let's have a look at some full sentences to see this formula in action!

- *(Yo) sé bailar tango bastante bien* ("I know how to dance tango pretty well").
- *(Yo) no puedo tocar la guitarra bien* ("I can't play the guitar well").
- *Vosotros sabéis cocinar rápidamente* ("You know how to cook fast").
- *Ella sabe jugar al fútbol estupendamente* ("She know how to play football wonderfully").

Talking About Abilities With *Ser*

But the formula we saw earlier is not the only way to talk about abilities. You can also build sentences with this formula: Subject + *(no)* + conjugation of *ser* + adjective + gerund

In these cases, it is common to use negative adjectives, such as *malo/mala* (which, in this context, means "bad at") or positive adjectives such as *bueno/buena* (which, in this context, means "good at"), but we can also use many others:

- *Fernanda es muy buena jugando al baloncesto* ("Fernanda is very good at playing basketball").
- *Pedro es excelente cocinando* ("Pedro is excellent at cooking").
- *David no es muy rápido limpiando* ("David is not very fast cleaning").
- *Teresa es mala bailando* ("Teresa is bad at dancing").
- *Yo era muy buena patinando* ("I was very good at skating").
- *Mónica es genial escribiendo* ("Mónica is great at writing")
- *Sebastián es excelente dibujando* ("Sebastián is excellent at drawing")
- *Yo soy muy malo dibujando, pero soy bueno tomando fotos* ("I'm very bad at drawing, but I'm really good at taking pictures")
- *Mi abuela era extraordinaria con el piano* ("My grandmother was extraordinary with the piano")

You can also replace the gerund with a preposition, such as *en* ("in") followed by a noun. For example: you could say *Soy bueno en la cocina* ("I'm good in the kitchen") instead of *Soy bueno cocinando* ("I'm good at cooking").

Adjectives To Talk About Abilities

Let's see a list with some adjectives we haven't seen so far that can be used to talk about how good or bad we are at something:

Adjective	Pronunciation	Translation
excelente	ehx-eh-LEHN-teh	excellent
genial	heh-NEE-ahl	great
extraordinario	ehx-trah-ohr-dee-NAH-ree-oh	extraordinary
increíble	een-kreh-EE-bleh	incredible
maravilloso	mah-rah-bee-JOH-soh	marvelous
fantástico	fahn-TAHS-tee-koh	fantastic
rápido	RRAH-pee-doh	fast
lento	LEHN-toh	slow
fatal	fah-TAHL	very bad
horrible	oh-RREE-bleh	awful
pésimo	PEH-see-moh	terrible
desastroso	deh-sahs-TROH-soh	disastrous

As you can see, some of these adjectives are actually very similar to the adverbs we saw before!

Vocabulary: Abilities

Here's a chart with a list of abilities. They are all verbs, and they are all accompanied by their corresponding pronunciation and translation.

Ability	Pronunciation	Translation
cantar	kahn-TAHR	singing
bailar	bah-ee-LAHR	dancing
cocinar	koh-SEE-nahr	cooking

correr	koh-RREHR	running
jugar al fútbol	hooh-GAHR ahl FOOT-bohl	playing football
escribir	ehs-kree-BEER	writing
tomar fotos	toh-MAHR FOH-tohs	taking pictures
dibujar	dee-boo-HAHR	drawing
recitar poesía	reh-see-TAHR poh-eh-SEE-ah	reciting poetry
nadar	nah-DAHR	swimming
andar en bicicleta	ahn-DAHR ehn bee-see-KLEH-tah	riding a bike
conducir	kohn-doo-SEER	driving
actuar	ahk-too-AHR	acting
pintar	peen-TAHR	painting
navegar	nah-beh-GAHR	sailing
coser	koh-SEHR	sewing
tejer	teh-HEHR	weaving
hablar otro idioma	ah-BLAHR OH-troh ee-dee-OH-mah	speaking another language

We have already seen a few ways to talk about our abilities. Now, let's see a full dialogue!

- ¿Qué quieres cenar esta noche? ("What do you want for dinner tonight?")

○ Lo que tú quieras. <u>Yo no soy muy bueno cocinando</u>. ("Whatever you want. I'm not very good at cooking")

- Yo también <u>soy malo en la cocina</u>. Si quieres, podemos ir a un restaurante. ¿<u>Sabes conducir</u>? ("I'm bad at cooking too. If you want, we can go to a restaurant. Do you know how to drive?")

○ Sí, <u>sé conducir bastante bien</u>. ("Yes, I know how to drive pretty well.")

- ¡Genial! Después de cenar, podemos ir a un bar de karaoke. Me gusta mucho cantar. ("Cool! After dinner, we can go to a karaoke bar. I really like singing.")

○ <u>Yo no sé cantar</u>, pero ¡definitivamente <u>puedo intentarlo</u>! ("I don't know how to sing, but I can definitely try it!")

Direct Object Pronouns

The word intentarlo appears in the last sentence of our previous dialogue. This word is actually formed by two words: the verb *intentar* ("to try") and the direct object pronoun *lo*. What do we mean by direct object pronoun? Well, even though we've seen many pronouns so far, we haven't yet talked about the direct object pronouns. These pronouns replace the direct object in the sentence, and they can actually be added at the end of some verbs, like in *intentarlo*. In case you don't know, the direct object is the thing or person who receives the action of the verb.

However, we can't use the pronouns every time we have a direct object. We actually need to use them once the direct object is clear for everyone in the conversation so that they can identify what we're talking about. Of course, the direct object pronouns need to agree in gender, person, and number with the object we're talking about, which helps us identify it too.

These are the direct object pronouns in Spanish.

	Masculine	Feminine
first-person singular	me	
second-person singular	te	
third-person singular	lo	la
first-person plural	nos	
second-person plural	os	
third-person plural	los	las

These pronouns can be added to the end of the verb, like we've seen with *intentarlo*, only when we're using a verb in the infinitive, gerund or imperative, or they can go before the verb and on their own.

Let's see a few examples of the use of the direct object with some dialogues!

- *¿Sabes andar en bicicleta?* ("Do you know how to ride a bike?")

○ *Claro que sé hacerlo.* ("Of course I know how to do it").

- *¿Puedes cantar esta canción?* ("Can you sing this song?")

○ *Lo siento, hoy no la puedo cantar. No me siento bien.* ("I'm sorry, I can't do it. I don't feel good")

- *¡Qué ricas pizzas! ¿Quién las hace?* ("What delicious pizzas! Who makes them?")

○ *¡Las hago yo! Pero Rafael me ayuda a hacerlas.* ("I make them! But Rafael helps me make them")

Take into account that when the direct object is a full action, like in the first example where the direct object is *andar en bicicleta*, we use the third person masculine pronoun *lo*, which is why the example says *hacerlo*.

Key Takeaways

Congratulations! Three more days have passed, and so has a new chapter. We hope it has been very instructive for you! To keep things fresh, what do you think about a quick summary?

- Two verbs that you can use to talk about abilities: *poder* and *saber*
  - *Poder* means "can"
  - *Saber* means "to know"
- The correct structure to talk about your abilities is: subject + *saber/poder* + verb in the infinitive
- You can add adverbs to grade those abilities, and we've seen a list full of them
- Another way of talking about abilities is with the verb *ser* following this structure:
  - Subject + (*no*) + conjugation of *ser* + adjective + gerund. You can also replace the gerund by a noun.
- Vocabulary on abilities
- Direct object pronouns: *me, te lo, la, nos, os, los, las*

We are almost at the end of the road! But, for now, how about we do some exercises on what we've learned in this chapter? Don't forget to check the answer key after!

Oh, and in the next (and last!) chapter, we will be talking about other uses of the present indicative, like talking about the future and talking about motives and duration. Ready to find out what the future holds? See you there!

Exercises

1. Complete the following sentences with the right form of the verb *poder*
   a. Yo .... cocinar muy rico.
   b. Tú .... dibujar cosas increíbles.
   c. Las abuelas de Pedro .... tejer lo que les pidas.
   d. Nosotros .... cantar en tu cumpleaños.

2. Complete the following sentences with the right form of the verb *saber*
   a. Fernando .... conducir.
   b. Jorge y Jimena .... bailar salsa.
   c. Yo .... andar a caballo
   d. ¿Vosotros .... nadar?

3. Complete the following sentences with the verbs *saber* or *poder* in their correct conjugations.
   a. Yo no .... hablar alemán.
   b. Mi tío es mecánico, así que él .... reparar autos.
   c. ¿Tú .... bailar salsa?
   d. Ellos .... nadar.

4. Which one of the following adverbs would you use to talk about an ability?

a. Lejos

   b. Abajo

   c. Rápidamente

   d. Ayer

5. Choose the correct adverb in each sentence:

   a. Juan sabe andar en bicicleta (lentamente/mal).

   b. Pedro no sabe hablar japonés muy (bueno/bien).

   c. Mi hijo todavía no puede caminar (mejor/rápidamente).

   d. Laura puede pintar muy (minuciosamente/regular).

6. Rewrite the following sentences to include the quantifier *muy* in the right position

   a. Puedo nadar rápidamente.

   b. Carola cocina bien.

   c. No puedo correr. Lo hago lentamente.

   d. Mi amiga puede pintar cuadros fácilmente.

7. Choose the correct adjective in each sentence:

   a. Martín es (bueno/buen) cantando.

   b. Sergio es (lentamente/lento) corriendo.

   c. Camila y Sandra son (fantásticas/pésima) tejiendo.

   d. Yo soy bastante (mal/malo) dibujando.

8. Can you translate these abilities into Spanish?

   a. Driving

   b. Painting

   c. Riding a bike

   d. Weaving

9. Write down the correct direct object pronoun in each sentence.

   a. ¿Quieres pizza? ¡Tienes que probar......!

   b. ¿Te gusta la pintura? ...... pinté yo.

   c. ¿Sabes tejer? Siempre quise aprender a hacer......

   d. Tomé muchas fotos ese día. ¿...... quieres ver?

10. Rewrite the following sentences so that the direct object is replaced by its corresponding direct object pronoun.

   a. Escucho canciones españolas.

   b. Mi abuela tejió un abrigo.

   c. Tomo fotos todos los días.

   d. Escribo poemas a mano.

Answer Key

a. puedo

b. puedes

c. pueden

d. podemos

e. sabe

f. saben

g. sé

h. sabéis

i. sé or puedo

j. sabe or puede

k. sabes or puedes

l. saben

2. c. rápidamente

   a. lentamente

   b. bien

   c. rápidamente

   d. minuciosamente

   e. Puedo nadar <u>muy</u> rápidamente.

   f. Carola cocina <u>muy</u> bien.

   g. No puedo correr. Lo hago <u>muy</u> lentamente.

   h. Mi amiga puede pintar cuadros <u>muy</u> fácilmente.

   i. Bueno

   j. Lento

   k. Fantásticas

   l. Malo

   m. Conducir

   n. Pintar

   o. Andar en bicicleta

   p. Tejer

   q. probar<u>la</u>

   r. la

   s. hacer<u>lo</u>

   t. Las

u. Las escucho.

v. Mi abuela lo tejió.

w. Las tomo todos los días.

x. Los escribo a mano.

Chapter 10: Other Uses of the Present Indicative

❦

El futuro es posible imaginarlo y no solo aceptarlo.

- Eduardo Galeano.

Welcome to our last chapter together! Don't celebrate yet, we still have a lot to learn!

In this chapter, we will talk about uses of the present indicative that we haven't seen so far. We will talk about how to use the present to talk about the future, how to talk about the progressive tense, and how to talk about duration and motives. We will also learn the months and seasons so that you can use them to establish the time of your actions. Ready to learn? *¡Vamos!*

The Present to Talk About the Future

There are many possible verb tenses to talk about the future in Spanish. Some conjugations are really complex, but don't worry about that now. There is a way to talk about the future using the present tense, and it's something that Spanish speakers do a lot. Let's see some examples.

- *En abril **voy** a México de vacaciones* ("In April, I'm going to Mexico on vacation").
- *El domingo que viene **jugamos** un importante partido de fútbol* ("Next Sunday we will play an important football game").
- *El martes **tengo** una entrevista de trabajo* ("I have a job interview on Tuesday").
- *Dijeron en el pronóstico que mañana **llueve*** ("They said in the forecast that it will rain tomorrow").

Then, the present tense in Spanish is not only used to talk about an action that is happening in this exact moment. Have you noticed that in English we do exactly the same? We use the present tense to talk about things that will happen in the near future! And just like in English, we use the present in Spanish to talk about the future when we're talking about something that has been agreed upon or scheduled, so we have a high degree of certainty that it will happen.

The Present Progressive

The present progressive in Spanish, also known as "present continuous", is a verb tense that we use to talk about something that is happening at the moment. In other words, it's not something that happens at a specific moment, but something that occurs over a period of time. As you have probably noticed, in English we do the same thing. We conjugate the verb "to be" in the present indicative, and then add the suffix "-ing" to the verbs.

Let's look at a table where we compare examples of the present indicative with the present progressive in Spanish using the verb *cantar* ("to sing").

Pronoun	Present Simple	Present Continuous
(yo)	canto	estoy cantando
(tú)	cantas	estás cantando
(él / ella / usted)	canta	está cantando
(nosotros / nosotras)	cantamos	estamos cantando
(vosotros / vosotras)	cantáis	estáis cantando
(ellos / ellas / ustedes)	cantan	están cantando

Now, how do we create sentences in the present continuous? All you have to do is add the verb *estar* ("to be") conjugated appropriately, followed by the gerund form of the verb. To conjugate the verbs in their gerunds, keep the following in mind:

- Verbs ending in -ar are conjugated with their root + *ando* (for example: *caminando,* "walking")
- Verbs ending in -er and -ir are conjugated with their root + *iendo* (for example, *comiendo,* "eating", and *viviendo,* "to live").

Let's take a look at a dialogue in which two friends meet each other and use the present progressive.

○ Tienes cara de cansado. ¿<u>Estás durmiendo</u> bien? ("You look tired. Are you sleeping well?")

● No mucho. <u>Estoy haciendo</u> un curso de diseño web. Es muy divertido, ¡aunque me <u>están poniendo</u> muchos deberes! ("Not much. I'm doing a web design course. It's really fun, even though I'm getting a lot of homework").

○ ¿Y lo <u>estás cursando</u> de forma presencial o virtual? ("And are you taking it in person or virtually?").

● <u>Estamos asistiendo</u> a la universidad dos veces por semana. El resto de los días, <u>estoy tomando</u> clases virtuales ("It's a hybrid format. We are attending the university twice a week. The other days, I'm taking virtual classes").

Talking About Duration

Desde and *hace* (a preposition and a conjugated form of the verb *hacer*, "to do", respectively) are two Spanish words that you will use a lot when you talk about duration of actions. But, how do you use these two words correctly?

Desde is the translation of "since", and it is used in the exact same way as you would use it in English. That is, it is used to talk about an action that began in the past, but continues to occur in the present. Keep in mind that if there is a verb after the word *desde*, you must include the conjunction *que* in the middle of both words. Let's look at some examples.

- *Desde que soy pequeño me han gustado las películas de vaqueros* ("Since I was little, I have liked cowboy movies").

- *Desde que empecé a hacer deporte, me siento mucho mejor* ("Since I started playing games, I feel much better").

- *Francisco no me ha visitado desde que se mudó a otra ciudad* ("Francisco hasn't visited me since he moved to another city").

- *Desde ahora, voy a estudiar más* ("From now on, I'm going to study more").

On the other hand, *hace* (pronounced as AH-se; remember that, as we saw in chapter one, "H" is a silent letter) is a conjugation of the verb *hacer* ("to do"), but it becomes an adverb when accompanied by a quantified adverbial complement. In this case, *hace* is followed by an amount of time and later by *que* which introduces the thing you've been doing for that time. Let's see a few examples:

- *Hace tres años que bailo tango* ("I've been dancing tango for three years").

- *Hace dos meses que no veo a Bárbara* ("I haven't seen Barbara for two months").

- *Hace diez minutos que mi perro está comiendo* ("My dog's been eating for ten minutes").

- *Hace días que no encuentro mi teléfono* ("I haven't found my phone in days").

- *Hace más de media hora que te estoy esperando* ("I've been waiting for you for more than half an hour").

Now, you can also combine the words *hace* and *desde*, although not always. It only makes sense when the action you are describing continues in the present. You must say *desde hace* + an amount of time. Let's see some examples. Underneath them, you will see the same sentences but using only the verb *hace*; in those cases, youw need to add the conjunction *que* after the amount of time.

- *Estudio alemán desde hace dos meses* ("I have been studying German for two months").

    o *Hace dos meses que estudio alemán.*

- *Está lloviendo desde hace tres días* ("It has been raining for three days").

    o *Hace tres días que está lloviendo.*

- *Desde hace tres semanas no visito a mi abuela* ("I haven't visited my grandmother for three weeks").

    o *Hace tres semanas que no visito a mi abuela.*

Months and Seasons

Knowing how to say the months and the seasons in Spanish is essential to talk about current and future actions. Let's see a table with the months of the year (by the way: unlike in English, first letters of months in Spanish are not capitalized).

Month	Pronunciation	Translation
enero	eh-NEH-roh	January
febrero	feh-BREH-roh	February
marzo	MAHR-zoh	March

abril	ah-BREEL	April
mayo	MAH-joh	May
junio	HOO-nee-oh	June
julio	HOO-lee-oh	July
agosto	ah-GOHS-toh	August
septiembre	sehp-tee-EHM-breh	September
octubre	ohk-TOO-breh	October
noviembre	noh-BEE-ehm-breh	November
diciembre	dee-see-EHM-breh	December

Next, we will see some example sentences with the months in Spanish.

- *El cumpleaños de mi madre es en <u>abril</u>* ("My mother's birthday is in April").
- *Las clases comienzan en <u>marzo</u> y terminan en <u>diciembre</u>* ("Classes start in March and end in December").
- *<u>Enero</u> suele ser un mes caluroso en el hemisferio sur* ("January is usually a hot month in the southern hemisphere").
- *Navidad se festeja el 25 de <u>diciembre</u>* ("Christmas is celebrated on December 25").

Now, let's see the seasons:

Season	Pronunciation	Translation
invierno	een-bee-EHR-noh	winter
primavera	pree-mah-BEH-rah	spring
verano	beh-RAH-noh	summer
otoño	oh-TOH-nyoh	autumn

Now, let's have a look at this conversation between two online friends who talk about the months and the seasons:

○ ¿Cuándo es tu cumpleaños? ("When is your birthday?")

● El 10 de <u>enero</u> ("On January 10")

○ ¡Ah, en <u>invierno</u>! ("Oh! In winter!")

● No, en <u>verano</u>. Yo soy de Paraguay. Cuando en el hemisferio norte es invierno, en el hemisferio sur es verano y viceversa ("No, in summer. I'm from Paraguay. When it is winter in the northern hemisphere, it is summer in the southern hemisphere and vice versa")

○ ¿Quieres decir que en <u>julio</u> hace frío? ("Do you mean it is cold in July?")

● ¡Muchísimo! ("Very much!")

Talking About Motives and Motivation

Throughout this book, we've talked about different wh-questions, though perhaps you haven't noticed because they were scattered throughout the book. Let's review them:

- *Quién* ("who")
- *Qué* ("what")
- *Cuándo* ("when")
- *Dónde* ("where")
- *Cómo* ("how")

As you can see, all of them have an accent mark and they should always carry it, otherwise we would be talking about a different word! So, whenever you need to ask a question, you should always remember to use the accent mark with these words.

And though we've seen all of those interrogative pronouns, there's one we haven't talked about so far: *por qué* ("why"). We use it to ask people what their motives and motivations are. In English, we would answer with "because…", but in Spanish we usually use the word *porque*, which is similar to *por qué* but written as one word and without the accent mark.

Both to make a question with *por qué* and to answer using *porque*, we simply use the following construction: *por qué/porque* + conjugated verb. You can include extra information after the conjugated verb, such as a noun or a time period. And, of course, questions will also need question marks at the beginning and at the end of the sentence.

Let's see a few examples of questions and answers with some short dialogues:

○ *¿Por qué quieres comer pizza todos los días?* ("Why do you want to eat pizza every day?")

● *Porque me encanta la pizza.* ("Because I love it")

○ *¿Por qué sales a correr de noche en verano?* ("Why do you go running at night in summer?")

● *Porque hace menos calor.* ("Because it's less hot")

○ *¿Por qué estás trabajando un domingo?* ("Why are you working on a Sunday?")

● *Porque tengo que entregar todo mañana.* ("Because I have to hand everything in tomorrow")

Seems easy enough, right? Well, there are two other possible ways to answer a *por qué* question: the first one is to use the preposition *para* followed by the infinitive, and the second one is to use the preposition *por* followed by a noun. Let's see some example dialogues using both *para* and *por*.

○ *¿Por qué viajas a España en marzo?* ("Why do you travel to Spain in March?")

● *Para visitar a mi tía.* ("To visit my aunt")

○ *¿Por qué hablas español?* ("Why do you speak Spanish?")

- *Para hablar con mi abuela.* ("To talk with my grandmother")
- ○ *¿Por qué quieres ir a la playa?* ("Why do you want to go to the beach?")
- *Por el mar y las olas* ("Because of the sea and the waves")
- ○ *¿Por qué viajas tanto?* ("Why do you travel so much")
- *Por trabajo* ("For work")

Key Takeaways

We've made it all through our last chapter! Congratulations! You've successfully finished this book and, though you may have started it with doubts and insecurities, I hope that you've come out the other side feeling more confident and ready to put your Spanish to practice! Of course, that's what we will be doing in the following exercises!

But before we head to the exercises, let's recap our final chapter, where we talked about…

- Using the present indicative to talk about things that have been agreed upon or scheduled
- The present progressive, which is used to talk about things happening at the time of speaking and is formed with *ser* + the gerund form of the verb
- Duration of actions with *desde* and *hace*
    - ○ With *desde* we need to add *que* if it's followed by a verb
    - ○ With *hace* we also need to add *que* but, in this case, it should go after the entire phrase that begins with *hace* and is followed by an amount of time (like *hace un mes, hace dos años, hace tres semanas,* etc.)
    - ○ We can also have the two of them together when we are describing an action that continues in the present. We write *desde hace* + amount of time
- The months and seasons
- Motives and motivation with *por qué, porque, por,* and *para.*
    - ○ Asking with *por qué* + conjugated verb
    - ○ And answer with:
        - ■ *porque* + conjugated verb
        - ■ *para* + infinitive
        - ■ *por* + noun

Exercises

1. Complete the following sentences with the conjugated verbs in the box:

> *viajamos - junto - corre - caso*

   a. En noviembre me ………… con mi esposo.

   b. El viernes me ………… con mis amigos a jugar al básquet.

   c. El próximo verano mi familia y yo ………… a la playa.

    d. El próximo sábado mi primo .... una maratón.

2. Complete the sentences with the present continuous:

    a. Yo (estudio) .... Medicina.

    b. Mi hermana (nada) .... en la piscina.

    c. ¿Vosotros (dormís) .... bien?

    d. Mis amigos y yo siempre nos (reímos) ....

3. How would you translate "We are eating" into Spanish?

    a. Está comiendo.

    b. Estamos comiendo.

    c. Estáis comiendo.

    d. Están comiendo.

4. Order the sentences correctly.

    a. un / no / viajo / hace / año / que

    b. días / que / hace / tres / está / lloviendo

    c. no / años / desde / viajo / hace / cinco

    d. juego / desde / tres / meses / hace / tenis

5. Can you translate the seasons into Spanish?

    a. Winter

    b. Spring

    c. Summer

    d. Autumn

6. Write the following months in Spanish:

    a. February

    b. April

    c. August

    d. October

7. How would you translate the sentence "In the southern hemisphere, July is winter"?

    a. En el hemisferio sur, en junio es otoño.

    b. En el hemisferio sur, en agosto es primavera.

    c. En el hemisferio sur, en julio es invierno.

    d. En el hemisferio norte, en julio es otoño.

8. Complete the following dialogue with *por qué* and *porque*.
A. ¿ .... sabes bailar?
B. .... estudio desde hace muchos años.
A. ¿Y .... decidiste estudiar baile?
B. ¡............ me encanta la música!

9. Which one of the next sentences is right?

    a. Viajo a Perú el mes que viene por visitar las ruinas de Machu Picchu.

    b. Viajo a Perú el mes que viene porque visitar las ruinas de Machu Picchu.

    c. Viajo a Perú el mes que viene para visitar las ruinas de Machu Picchu.

    d. Viajo a Perú el mes que viene para que visitar las ruinas de Machu Picchu.

10. Now, what about using all the things we learned in the last three days? Complete the next dialogue with the correct words. Use the box below.

> *hace - desde - enero - invierno - porque - para - por qué*

A. ¿Viajas este ....?
B. Sí. Voy a Argentina .... visitar la Patagonia. .... años que vacaciono allí.
A. ¡Qué bonito! No conozco la Patagonia. Yo me voy de vacaciones al Caribe el próximo mes. Voy al Caribe cada año........... que soy una niña.
B. ¿........... vas al Caribe?
A. ¡........... me encanta el mar, claro! ¿Te gustaría venir conmigo?
B. Me encantaría, pero no puedo. ¡Mis vacaciones son en ....!

Answer Key

1.
- a. En noviembre me caso con mi esposo.
- b. El viernes me junto con mis amigos a jugar al básquet.
- c. El próximo verano mi familia y yo viajamos a la playa.
- d. El próximo sábado mi primo corre una maratón.

2.
- a. estoy estudiando
- b. está nadando
- c. estáis durmiendo
- d. estamos riendo

3. b. estamos comiendo

4.
- a. Hace un año que no viajo.
- b. Hace tres días que está lloviendo.
- c. No viajo desde hace cinco años.
- d. Juego tenis desde hace tres meses.

5.
- a. Invierno
- b. Primavera
- c. Verano
- d. Otoño

6.
- a. Febrero
- b. Abril
- c. Agosto
- d. Octubre

7. c. En el hemisferio sur, en julio es invierno.

8.
- A. Por qué
- B. Porque
- C. por qué
- D. Porque

9. c. Viajo a Perú el mes que viene para visitar las ruinas de Machu Picchu.

10.
- A. ¿Viajas este invierno?
- B. Sí. Voy a Argentina para visitar la Patagonia. Hace años que vacaciono allí.
- A. ¡Qué bonito! No conozco la Patagonia. Yo me voy de vacaciones al Caribe el próximo mes. Voy al caribe cada año desde que soy una niña.
- B. ¿Por qué vas al Caribe?
- A. ¡Porque me encanta el mar, claro! ¿Te gustaría venir conmigo?
- B. Me encantaría, pero no puedo. ¡Mis vacaciones son en enero!

Conclusion

You opened this book hoping you would find a simple way to learn Spanish, a way that didn't overcomplicate things and allowed you to focus on learning and taking everything in at your own pace, and I'm sure you've found it here. And now you're done and you've learned a lot along the way. *¡Felicitaciones!*

Shall we make a quick recap of the most important things from every chapter?

In chapter 1, we saw the Spanish alphabet, the name of the letters, and the sounds each letter makes. We also learned different ways of saying "hello" and "goodbye", some useful phrases and the numbers up to 100.

Chapter 2, "Who are you?", focused on foundational things that we would need to know throughout the entire book, like the subject pronouns and the gender and number of words. We also learned some questions to get to know someone new and the answers to those questions so that you know how to answer them if someone asks you. We also saw the present indicative conjugations of the verbs *ser, tener,* and *llamarse*. We closed the chapter with a list of countries and nationalities and jobs and professions.

In chapter 3, we saw the nine different Spanish definite and indefinite articles, some nouns we might want to describe when on a trip, how to form the plurals of nouns and adjectives, and some adjectives and colors used to describe places. We also talked about the present indicative, the regular conjugations with -ar, -er, and -ir, how to express existence with *hay,* location with *estar,* and describe places with *ser,* and how to talk about the weather.

In the fourth chapter, we focused on learning how to shop in Spanish. To do that, we saw a lot of vocabulary related to clothes and shopping and methods to identify objects, such as the demonstratives, the structure definite article + adjective, and some questions. Finally, we saw how to express likes, dislikes and preferences, and some phrases and questions that would be useful at a store.

In chapter 5, we talked about places to visit, means of transportation, prepositions and adverbs of place, and the conjugations of *ir* and *querer* in order to learn how to ask for directions and give them.

We started the second half of our book talking about family members, the possessives and describing people's appearances and personalities. We also learned that we can use the quantifiers *muy, bastante,* and *un poco* to modify the adjectives to describe people.

In chapter 7, we focused on how to use the present indicative to talk about habits. To do this, we saw the days of the week, parts of the day, and the hours. We also learned to express frequency and some reflexive verbs. Finally, we learned some regularities in four groups of irregular verbs in the present indicative.

In chapter 8, we learned what to do at a restaurant with some useful phrases and then we saw a lot of vocabulary related to food, meals, and ways of cooking them. We also learned to talk about things we love with *encantar,* and how to agree or disagree when someone says they love or like something. Then, we moved on to adjectives to describe food and some comparatives and superlatives, as well as some quantifiers to use with countable and uncountable nouns.

Chapter 9 focused on talking about abilities with the verbs *saber*, *poder,* and *ser* + adjective. To do that, we learned the present simple conjugations of *saber* and *poder*, a list of abilities, some adverbs and adjectives to grade our abilities and the direct object pronouns.

We finally got to chapter 10, where we talked about uses of the present indicative we hadn't seen so far. We started learning about how to talk about the future with the present indicative and the present progressive with the structure *estar* + gerund. We also learned how to talk about duration with *desde, hace,* and *desde hace* and talked about months and seasons so that you can use them to explain the duration of an action. We finished the chapter (and the book!) talking about motives and motivations by asking with *por qué* and answering with *porque, para,* and *por*.

Well, that's the end of our journey together! And what now? Well, you should go out and practice! Whether you practice on a trip or with Spanish-speaking friends, you're now prepared to go out into the world and put all your knowledge into practice. And if you loved this book and want to learn a whole lot more, you can check out our intermediate level book, ***Learn Intermediate Spanish for Adults Workbook: Go from Spanish Beginner to Intermediate in 30 Days!*** I believe that you will enjoy it and learn a lot from it!

Whatever you do from now on, I hope this book has helped you learn and practice the beautiful Spanish language. I hope you want to continue practicing your Spanish everywhere you go! You have at least 20 countries where Spanish is the official language, so that's at least 20 countries to visit!

It's time to say *adiós* for now. Keep up the good work and keep on learning Spanish! I hope to see you again soon! *¡Nos vemos!*

Complete Spanish Phrasebook
+ Digital Spanish Flashcards Download

Scan QR code above to claim your free bonuses

OR

visit exploretowin.com/vipbonus

Ready To Start Speaking Spanish?

**Inside this Complete Spanish Phrasebook
+ digital Spanish flashcards combo you'll:**

✓ **Say what you want:** learn the most common words and phrases used in Spanish, so you can express yourself clearly, the first time!

✓ **Avoid awkward fumbling:** explore core Spanish grammar principles to avoid situations where you're left blank, not knowing what to say.

✓ **Improved recall:** Confidently express yourself in Spanish by learning high-frequency verbs & conjugations - taught through fun flashcards!

Scan QR code above to claim your free bonuses

OR

visit exploretowin.com/vipbonus

BOOK 3

Learn Spanish with Short Stories for Adult Beginners

Shortcut Your Spanish Fluency!
(Fun & Easy Reads)

Explore to Win

Book 3 description

Discover Spanish grammar naturally as you read stories, expand your vocabulary, and grow fluent fast!

If you've recently started learning Spanish, you probably noticed the lack of reading material online. Or maybe you found some, but they're for kids, or simply boring. That's why we've brought you *Learning Spanish with Short Stories for Adult Beginners*.

Take your Spanish to the next level with our high-quality short stories designed specifically for adults. With our book, you'll work on more than your reading. You'll learn rich vocabulary and understand how to use new Spanish structures in any given context, as the stories get progressively more challenging as you go on.

Learning a new language is hard enough as it is. Let's make it much, much simpler.

In *Learning Spanish with Short Stories for Adult Beginners* you will discover:

- Engaging stories
- Rich vocabulary and useful everyday phrases
- Stories tailored around a particular structure to challenge your Spanish every time
- Specific verb conjugations within the stories
- The present and present progressive tenses simplified
- Descriptions of weather, people, and places
- Tips and tricks on how to get the best from our stories
- Helpful glossaries
- A summary of every story
- Exercises to put your reading skills to the test
- Answer keys for every exercise set

You don't have to struggle all on your own. Our stories are easy to follow and will help you in this journey every step of the way.

This incredible book was written by Spanish linguists, which means they have a deep understanding of the Spanish language, while also being able to teach you the language and phrases spoken in real life.

If you're ready to start your Spanish journey, then scroll up and click "add to cart" NOW!

Introduction

YYYYYY

You know Spanish is one of the most spoken languages in the world, right? That it is one of the official languages of over 20 countries, which means that being able to speak it can open a door or two for you? And we're not only talking about professional opportunities here, but also the chance of communicating with its many speakers and experiencing a variety of rich cultures.

So, if you've recently added learning Spanish to your bucket list, then buying this book was the right call. After countless hours online, you're probably tired of finding nothing but stories for children, or worse: no reading material at all. *Learn Spanish with Short stories for Adult Beginners* delivers high-quality short stories with exercises specifically designed for you, our very much adult reader. Learning a new language is daunting enough on its own. Let's not make it more complicated than it has to be.

Our short stories are carefully tailored to beginner learners, with vocabulary and structures that get progressively harder as you go on. However, we won't cover concepts that might be too hard for you, and all vocabulary that may seem complicated will be explained in the glossary at the end of each story. Through this method, you will feel a sense of achievement as you notice your Spanish language skills constantly improving.

So, whether you're a true beginner who can barely say "hola", or a more trained learner who's looking for new entertaining material to read, *Learn Spanish with Short stories for Adult Beginners* is the right book for you.

How to use this book

You will notice each story in our book follows the same structure:

Short story in Spanish

A summary in Spanish

A summary in English

A glossary with Spanish words and phrases and their English translation

Quizzes to test your understanding of the story

Answers to check your work

We suggest you follow these tips to get the most out of our stories:

1) **Read the story all the way through**. Don't worry about trying to understand every single word right away. Follow the plot of the story as much as you can, and use the context to fill in those mental gaps you may have.

2) **Take a moment to reflect on the plot of the story**. Think about how much you were able to understand on your own. If it helps, write down in English what you think the story was about.

3) **Read the Spanish summary**. See if the idea of the story is the same you had in your head. If the Spanish summary seems too complicated at first, try reading the English one. And don't worry, even if it feels hard at first, it will get easier as you train your mind.

4) **Read the story once again**. This time, try focusing on the details you may have missed on your first read.

5) **Review the glossary**. Make sure you understand the words in the list. If you're unsure of the meaning of any of the words, go back to the story to put them in context. This will help you fully grasp the meaning of the more complicated phrases or expressions.

6) **Test yourself**. Answer the quizzes to make sure you understood the story from beginning to end.

7) **Check your answers**. Make sure your answers are similar or the same as the ones at the end of the chapter. Don't worry if you don't get all the answers right, though. Making mistakes isn't failing. If you made a mistake, review that part of the story. You'll have a better understanding of both the story as a whole and the concept, phrase or structure that you didn't get the first time around.

8) **Congratulate yourself**. Think about how much you understood on your own, even if it wasn't much at first. Remember that the key to learning a new language is to practice. The more you read and train your brain, the better you will get at this.

9) **Go to the next story**. Once you've gotten everything you could out of the story, go to the next one! Remember that each story has its own set of structures and vocabulary that gets progressively more challenging. The more you read, the closer you will be to your goal of mastering the Spanish language.

Chapter 1: El nuevo trabajo – The new job

El trabajo más productivo es el que sale de las manos de un hombre contento.

- Victor Pauchet

Hoy es el **primer día** de Luis en su nuevo trabajo en la empresa Future Technologies. Luis **llega a** la oficina **a tiempo**. **Está muy nervioso** pero sus **compañeros de trabajo lo reciben con los brazos abiertos**.

–**Mucho gusto**, ¿**cómo te llamas**?

–Mucho gusto, **me llamo** Luis.

–**Bienvenido**, Luis.

Carolina, **la jefa de Luis**, lo acompaña **en todo momento**. Le da un tour del edificio, pasan por la cafetería, la recepción, **el área de descanso**. Ahí **conoce** a otros **desarrolladores web como él** y **se presenta nuevamente**.

–Mucho gusto, Luis –dice un hombre alto.

–¿**Cuáles son sus nombres**?

–**Mi nombre es** Carlos y **ella se llama** Lucía.

–**Un placer** –dice Luis. **Al otro lado de la mesa** Luis ve a más personas conversando. –¿**Quiénes son ellos**?

–Ellos son Javier, Mario y Ana. Son muy **amables y conversadores** –dice Lucía.

–¿Cuál es tu **apellido**, Luis? –pregunta Carlos.

–Alvarado.

–¿**Cómo se deletrea** Alvarado?

–A - L - V - A - R - A - D - O.

–¿Y **de dónde eres**?

–**Soy de** Medellín. ¿Ustedes de dónde son?

–Nosotros somos de acá, de Bogotá –responde Lucía.

Luego de tomar una taza de café con Carlos y Lucía, Luis va a su **lugar de trabajo**. La oficina es **grande, luminosa**, y **hay varios escritorios** de madera. Lucía trabaja en **la misma** oficina que Luis. Su escritorio **está adornado con** algunas plantas y **retratos** de su familia. Lucía **le cuenta a Luis que su hijo tiene siete años** y **va en segundo grado de primaria**.

–¿**A qué se dedica tu esposo**? –pregunta Luis.

–**Mi esposo es ingeniero** y **trabaja en** esta misma compañía. ¿Tienes hijos?

–Sí, **tengo un niño y una niña**.

–¿**Cuántos años tienen tus hijos**?

–Mi hijo tiene tres años y **mi hija tiene dos**.

El resto de la mañana es **bastante tranquila**. Luis **almuerza** con sus compañeros y **se adapta a la perfección** a su nuevo trabajo. **Al final del día**, Luis **se despide** de Lucía y **se va** a casa.

Resumen

Un hombre llamado Luis empieza su primer día en un nuevo trabajo en una empresa llamada Future Technologies. Su jefa, Carolina, le muestra el edificio y terminan en el área de descanso, donde conoce a dos desarrolladores web, Lucía y Carlos. Conversa un rato con sus nuevos compañeros de trabajo y luego se va a su lugar de trabajo. Ahí comparte un poco más de su vida con Lucía. Se adapta muy bien a su nuevo trabajo y al final del día, se va a casa.

Summary

A man named Luis starts his first day at a new job at a company called Future Technologies. His boss, Carolina, shows him around the building and they end up in the break room, where he meets two web developers, Lucía and Carlos. He makes small talk with his new coworkers and then he goes to his workspace. There, he shares a bit more about his life with Lucía. He adapts really well to his new job, and at the end of the day, he goes home.

Glosario – Glossary

Primer día: first day

Llega a: he arrives to

A tiempo: on time

Está muy nervioso: he is very nervous

Compañeros de trabajo: coworkers

Lo reciben con los brazos abiertos: they welcome him with open arms

Mucho gusto: nice to meet you

¿Cómo te llamas?: what's your name?

(Yo) me llamo: my name is

Bienvenido: welcome

La jefa de Luis: Luis's boss

En todo momento: at all times

El área de descanso: the break room

Conoce: he meets

Desarrolladores web: web developers

Como él: like him

Se presenta: he introduces himself

Nuevamente: again

¿Cuáles son sus nombres?: what are your names?

Mi nombre es: my name is

Ella se llama: her name is

¿Quiénes son ellos?: who are they?

Amables y conversadores: kind and talkative

Apellido: last name

¿Cómo se deletrea...?: how do you spell...?

¿De dónde eres?: where are you from?

(Yo) soy de: I am from

Lugar de trabajo: workspace

Grande y luminosa: big and well-lit

Hay varios escritorios: there are several desks

La misma: the same

Está adornado con: it is decorated with

Retratos: pictures

Le cuenta a Luis que: she tells Luis that

Su hijo tiene siete años: her son is seven years old

Va en segundo grado de primaria: he is in the second grade of elementary school

¿A qué se dedica tu esposo?: what does your husband do?

Mi esposo es ingeniero: my husband is an engineer

Trabaja en: he works at

¿Tienes hijos?: do you have any children?

Tengo un niño y una niña: I have a boy and a girl

¿Cuántos años tienen tus hijos?: how old are your children?

Mi hija tiene dos: my daughter is two

Bastante tranquila: pretty calm

Almuerza: he has lunch

Se adapta a la perfección: he adapts perfectly

Al final del día: at the end of the day

Se despide de: he says goodbye to

Se va: he leaves

Ejercicio 1

Contesta las siguientes preguntas – answer the following questions

1- **¿Cómo se siente Luis?** – how's Luis feeling?

_____

2- **¿Cómo se llama la jefa de Luis?** – what's Luis's boss name?

_____

3- **¿A qué se dedica Luis?** – what does Luis do?

_____

4- **¿Cómo son Javier, Mario y Ana?** – what are Javier, Mario and Ana like?

_____

5- **¿Cuál es el apellido de Luis?** – what's Luis's last name?

_____

6- **¿De dónde son Carlos y Lucía?** – where are Carlos and Lucía from?

_____

7- **¿Cómo es la oficina de Luis?** – what is Luis's office like?

_____

8- **¿Cuántos años tiene el hijo de Lucía?** – how old is Lucía's son?

_____

9- **¿Dónde trabaja el esposo de Lucía?** – where does Lucía's husband work at?

_____

10- **¿Cuántos hijos tiene Luis?** – how many children does Luis have?

_____

Ejercicio 2

Elige entre "verdadero" o "falso" – choose "true" or "false"

1- **Luis llega tarde a su primer día de trabajo.** – Luis arrives late to his first day at work.

_____

2- **Carolina es amiga de Luis.** – Carolina is Luis's friend.

_____

3- **Luis conoce a Lucía en la cafetería.** – Luis meets Lucía in the cafeteria.

_____

4- **Luis es de Medellín.** – Luis is from Medellín.

_____

5- **Carlos es de Barranquilla.** – Carlos is from Barranquilla.

_____

6- **El escritorio de Luis es de madera.** – Luis' desk is made of wood.

7- **Lucía solo tiene libros en su escritorio.** – Lucía only has books on her desk.

8- **El hijo de Lucía va en segundo grado.** – Lucía's son is in second grade.

9- **Luis tiene tres hijos.** – Luis has three children.

10- **El esposo de Lucía es ingeniero.** – Lucía's husband is an engineer.

Respuestas – Answers

Ejercicio 1

1- Luis está nervioso.

2- La jefa de Luis se llama Carolina.

3- Luis es desarrollador web.

4- Javier, Mario y Ana son amables y conversadores.

5- El apellido de Luis es Alvarado.

6- Carlos y Lucía son de Bogotá.

7- La oficina de Luis es grande y luminosa.

8- El hijo de Lucía tiene siete años.

9- El esposo de Lucía trabaja en la misma empresa que ella.

10- Luis tiene dos hijos.

Ejercicio 2

1- Falso

2- Falso

3- Falso

4- Verdadero

5- Falso

6- Verdadero

7- Falso

8- Verdadero

9- Falso

10- Verdadero

Puntos clave – Key takeaways

- To say our name in Spanish, we use the verb *llamar* reflexively with the reflexive pronoun *se*.
- The reflexive pronoun *se* has five different conjugations (*me, te, se, nos, se*).
- One of the uses of the verb *ser* is to talk about where we're from.
- The verb *ser* has five different conjugations (*soy, eres, es, somos, son*).
- One of the uses of the verb tener is to talk about our age.
- The verb tener has five different conjugations (*tengo, tienes, tiene, tenemos, tienen*).
- To talk about our job, we use the verb *dedicar* reflexively with the reflexive pronoun *se*.

In the next chapter, you will learn how to use the verb *estar*, how to tell time, and some parts of the house.

Chapter 2: ¿Dónde está Carlos? – Where's Carlos?

❧

Una madre, nunca está sola en sus pensamientos. Una madre siempre piensa dos veces, una en sí misma y otra en su niño.

- Sophia Loren

Marisol llega a casa luego de **un largo día en el trabajo**. Va a **la cocina** y **saluda** a su hija Anabel. **Le pregunta por su hermano** Carlos.

–**Quizás está en el jardín** –dice Anabel.

Marisol **se acerca al jardín** pero **Carlos no está allí**.

–**Tal vez** está en su **cuarto** –dice Anabel.

Marisol va al cuarto de Carlos pero **no hay nadie**. Marisol **revisa el baño**, **la sala**, **el comedor**, **incluso va al balcón**, donde están las plantas. **No sabe dónde está su hijo** Carlos y **está muy preocupada**.

–Anabel, **¿dónde está tu hermano**?

–**No sé**, mamá.

–**¿Qué hora es?**

Anabel dice que **son las 7 p.m. Marisol piensa que Carlos está con su mejor amigo**, José, **así que llama a casa de José**. El padre de José contesta el teléfono.

–**Aló**, **buenas tardes**.

–Buenas tardes, soy Marisol, **la mamá de Carlos**. ¿**De casualidad** mi hijo está en su casa **jugando con José**?

–Hola, Marisol. No, Carlos no está aquí.

–Estoy muy preocupada. Carlos **sale de la escuela a las 3 de la tarde**. **A esta hora** él siempre está en la casa.

–**¿Tienes el número de sus otros amigos**?

–Carlos tiene **pocos** amigos. Su mejor amigo es José.

–Le voy a preguntar a José por Carlos. **Dame un minuto.**

Marisol **espera junto al teléfono**. Piensa en **el horario** de su hijo. **Los martes** Carlos tiene **clases de matemáticas de 8 de la mañana a 10 de la mañana**. De 10 a.m. al **mediodía** tiene **clases de educación física**. Del mediodía a 1 p.m. es su **hora de almuerzo**. Por último, de 1 p.m. a 3 p.m. tiene su **clase de arte**. Carlos siempre llega a casa **antes de las 4 p.m.**

—Marisol, **anota** el número de otro amigo de Carlos —dice el papá de José. —Tal vez Carlos está con él.

Marisol anota el número en un papel y llama **inmediatamente**.

—Aló, ¿David?

—Buenas tardes, no. Soy Marisol, la madre de Carlos, un amigo de David.

—¿Mi hijo está con **usted**?

—No, **de hecho** llamo **para preguntar si** mi hijo Carlos está en su casa.

—No, Marisol, no sabemos dónde está nuestro hijo **tampoco**.

—**¿Y si están juntos? ¿Sabe dónde pueden estar?**

—No sé, pero **voy a salir a buscarlos** en **el parque** cerca de la casa.

—Es una buena idea. Voy a ir con usted.

Marisol va a **la parada de autobús**. **Son las 7 y media**. Toma el autobús 35 que **la deja a una cuadra** del Parque Simón Bolívar. Ahí **se encuentra con la mamá de David**, el amiguito de Carlos. **En su rostro** ve que **la mujer está tan estresada y preocupada como ella**. Marisol ve la hora en su reloj, **son las 8 en punto**.

—Mira, Marisol —dice la mamá de David.

El parque es inmenso. **Algunas mujeres hacen yoga** y **otros pasean a sus perros**. David y Carlos **corren detrás de un perrito** y **sonríen**. Marisol y la mamá de David **se apresuran y abrazan** a sus hijos. Los niños **están sorprendidos**, y luego **arrepentidos**. Dicen que **olvidaron la hora** y como es verano **aún está soleado**. Marisol se despide de David y su mamá. Junto a su hijo **toma un autobús de vuelta a casa**. **Marisol está feliz de tener a su hijo en sus brazos**, pero cuando llegan a casa **le dice que está castigado. Está muy molesta. Aliviada**, pero molesta. Carlos **la entiende** y **le pide disculpas. Marisol le da un beso en la mejilla** y un largo abrazo. Mira el reloj. **Falta un cuarto para las 9**, ya **es hora de cenar**. Cuando **son 20 pasadas las 10**, Carlos **se cepilla los dientes** y **va a la cama porque está cansado. Marisol le lee una historia para dormir** y le desea dulces sueños.

Resumen

Una mujer llamada Marisol vuelve a casa luego de un largo día de trabajo y se da cuenta de que su hijo, Carlos, no está en la casa. Ella se preocupa y llama a los amigos de su hijo para saber dónde está. La madre de otro niño le dice que su hijo tampoco ha llegado a casa y juntas van al parque a buscar a sus hijos. Por suerte, los niños están en el parque jugando. Marisol vuelve a casa con su hijo y lo castiga por lo que hizo. Al final, ella le lee una historia para dormir a Carlos y le desea dulces sueños.

Summary

A woman named Marisol comes back home after a long day of work and realizes that her son, Carlos, is not home. She gets worried and calls her son's friends to find out where he is. Another boy's mom tells her that her son is not home either and they both go to the park to go look for their sons. Luckily, the kids are at the park playing around. Marisol goes back home with her son and grounds him for what he did. At the end, she reads Carlos a bedtime story and wishes him sweet dreams.

Glosario – Glossary

Un largo día en el trabajo: a long day of work

La cocina: the kitchen

Le pregunta por su hermano: she asks her for her brother

Quizás está en el jardín: maybe he is in the garden

Se acerca al jardín: she approaches the garden

Carlos no está ahí: Carlos is not there

Tal vez: maybe

Cuarto: bedroom

No hay nadie: there is no one (there)

Revisa el baño: she checks the bathroom

La sala: the living room

El comedor: the dining room

Incluso va al balcón: she even goes to the balcony

No sabe dónde está su hijo: she doesn't know where her son is

Está muy preocupada: she is very worried

¿Dónde está tu hermano?: where is your brother?

(Yo) no sé: I don't know

¿Qué hora es?: what time is it?

Son las 7 p.m.: it is 7 p.m.

Marisol piensa que Carlos está con su mejor amigo: Marisol thinks that Carlos is with his best friend

Así que llama a casa de José: so she calls Jose's house

El padre de José contesta el teléfono: José's dad picks up the phone

Aló, buenas tardes: hi, good afternoon

La mamá de Carlos: Carlos's mom

De casualidad: by any chance

Jugando con José: playing with José

Sale de la escuela a las 3 de la tarde: he leaves school at 3 in the afternoon

A esta hora: at this time

¿Tienes el número de sus otros amigos?: do you have the number of his other friends?

Pocos: few

Dame un minuto: give me a minute

Espera junto al teléfono: she waits by the phone

El horario: the schedule

Los martes: on Tuesdays

Clases de matemáticas: math classes

De 8 de la mañana a 10 de la mañana: from 8 in the morning to 10 in the morning

Mediodía: noon

Clases de educación física: physical education classes

Hora de almuerzo: lunch break

Clase de arte: art class

Antes de las 4 p.m.: before 4 p.m.

Anota: write down

Inmediatamente: immediately

Usted: you (formal)

De hecho: in fact

Para preguntar: to ask

Tampoco: neither

¿Y si están juntos?: what if they are together?

¿Sabe dónde pueden estar?: do you know where they might be?

Voy a salir a buscarlos: I'm going to go out to look for them

El parque: the park

La parada de autobús: the bus stop

Son las 7 y media: it is half past 7

La deja a una cuadra de...: it leaves her a block from...

Se encuentra con la mamá de David: she meets David's mom

En su rostro: in her face

La mujer está tan estresada y preocupada como ella: the woman is as stressed and worried as her

Son las 8 en punto: it is 8 o'clock

Algunas mujeres hacen yoga: some women do yoga

Otros pasean a sus perros: others walk their dogs

Corren detrás de un perrito: they run after a little dog

Sonríen: they smile

Se apresuran: they hurry up

Abrazan: they hug

Están sorprendidos: they are surprised

Arrepentidos: remorseful

Olvidaron la hora: they lost track of time

Aún está soleado: it is still sunny

Toma un autobús de vuelta a casa: she takes a bus back home

Marisol está feliz: Marisol is happy

De tener a su hijo en sus brazos: about having her son in her arms

Le dice que está castigado: she tells him he is grounded

Está muy molesta: she is very upset

Aliviada: relieved

La entiende: he understands her

Le pide disculpas: he apologizes

Marisol le da un beso en la mejilla: Marisol gives him a kiss on his cheek

Falta un cuarto para las 9: it is a quarter to 9

Es hora de cenar: it is time for dinner

Son 20 pasadas las 10: it is 20 past 10

Se cepilla los dientes: he brushes his teeth

Va a la cama porque está cansado: he goes to bed because he is tired

Marisol le lee una historia para dormir: Marisol reads him a bedtime story

Le desea dulces sueños: she wishes him sweet dreams

Ejercicio 1

Contesta las siguientes preguntas – answer the following questions

1- **¿Dónde está Anabel?** – where's Anabel?

_____

2- **¿Cómo se siente Marisol al no encontrar a su hijo?** – how does Marisol feel upon not finding her son?

_____

3- **¿A quién llama Marisol primero?** – who does Marisol call first?

_____

4- **¿Quién contesta el teléfono?** – who answers the phone?

_____

5- **¿A qué hora Carlos tiene clases de matemáticas?** – what time does Carlos have math class?

_____

6- **¿A quién llama Marisol después?** – who does Marisol call afterwards?

7- **¿A dónde va Marisol a buscar a su hijo?** – where does Marisol go look for her son?

8- **¿Qué hace Carlos cuando Marisol lo encuentra?** – what is Carlos doing when Marisol finds him?

9- **¿Cuáles son las consecuencias por lo que Carlos hizo?** – what are the consequences for what Carlos did?

10- **¿Qué hace Carlos antes de ir a la cama?** – what does Carlos do before going to bed?

Ejercicio 2

Elige entre "verdadero" o "falso" – choose "true" or "false"

1- **Marisol estuvo en la casa todo el día.** – Marisol was home all day.

2- **Carlos está en casa de José.** – Carlos is at José's place.

3- **Carlos tiene clases de matemáticas los martes en la tarde.** – Carlos has math class on Tuesday afternoon.

4- **Carlos siempre llega a casa antes de las 4 p.m.** – Carlos always gets home before 4 p.m.

5- **Marisol toma el autobús 35.** – Marisol takes the bus 35.

6- **A Marisol le toma una hora llegar al parque.** – It takes Marisol one hour to get to the park.

7- **Carlos lee un libro en el parque.** – Carlos is reading a book at the park.

8- **Marisol toma un taxi a casa.** – Marisol takes a taxi home.

9- **Marisol llega a casa a un cuarto para las 9.** – Marisol gets home at a quarter to 9.

10- **Carlos va a la cama antes de las 10 p.m.** – Carlos goes to bed before 10 p.m.

Respuestas – Answers

Ejercicio 1

1- Anabel está en la cocina.

2- Marisol está muy preocupada.

3- Marisol llama a José, el amigo de Carlos.

4- El padre de José contesta el teléfono.

5- Carlos tiene clases de matemáticas de 10 a.m. al mediodía.

6- Marisol llama a David, otro amigo de Carlos.

7- Marisol va al parque a buscar a Carlos.

8- Carlos corre detrás de un perrito.

9- Marisol castiga a Carlos por lo que hizo.

10- Carlos se cepilla los dientes antes de ir a la cama.

Ejercicio 2

1- Falso

2- Falso

3- Falso

4- Verdadero

5- Verdadero

6- Falso

7- Falso

8- Falso

9- Verdadero

10- Falso

Puntos clave – Key takeaways

- One of the uses of the verb *estar* is to talk about where someone or something is.
- The verb *ser* has five different conjugations (*estoy, estás, está, estamos, están*).
- *Aló* is the Spanish phrase we use to answer the phone.
- When the time is 1 a.m. or 1 p.m., we say "es la una". With any other time, we say "son las..."

In the next chapter, you will learn vocabulary about relatives, some professions, and adjectives to describe certain feelings.

Chapter 3: El regalo – The present

Los regalos se hacen para el placer de quien los da, no para el mérito de quien los recibe.

- Carlos Ruiz Zafón

Hoy es **la boda** de Rosa, **la prima de Cristina**. Después de **la ceremonia en la iglesia** La Paz de Cristo, todos **los invitados** van a **una quinta alquilada** muy hermosa. **Además de** muchos amigos de **los novios**, **la familia** de Rosa está presente. Cristina ve a su **abuela** luego de cinco años. **Su abuelo no pudo asistir** porque **está enfermo**. Cristina **conversa** un poco con sus primos pero **está distraída, hablando** con su **novio** por teléfono. El novio de Cristina es **el encargado de encontrar el regalo** perfecto para Rosa. Cristina sabe que es mucha **responsabilidad** para su novio, pero **él insistió**. Ahora ella cree que **fue** un error. **Las tiendas** cierran a las 6 de la tarde los **sábados**. Encontrar un regalo puede ser difícil.

La tía de Cristina le da ideas para regalos. Le dice que algún **electrodoméstico sería** un buen regalo para una pareja de recién casados. **Le enseña** fotos de **licuadoras, microondas, batidoras** y **un juego de ollas. El esposo** de su amiga le sugiere comprar **un tostador. La madrina** de Cristina llega un poco tarde a la fiesta, pero tiene varios regalos en sus manos. Ella es **periodista** y **viaja** constantemente. Siempre que vuelve le regala un perfume nuevo a Cristina. **El primo** de Cristina, **un abogado** con **más deudas que dinero**, trae un regalo modesto. Cristina intenta **distraerse. Se toma fotos con su sobrina** y juega un rato con su **sobrino**. También **charla con su tío**, un **profesor de filosofía** que es muy **parlanchín**. Hablan sobre **la vida y el amor** por un largo rato.

Cristina llama a su novio.

—¿Dónde estás?

—Estoy en **el centro comercial** —responde su novio.

—**Por favor, apresúrate**.

Cristina **prueba unos postres de chocolate** exquisitos y **le pregunta al mesero cómo se llaman**. Su novio **no contesta los mensajes** y Cristina está estresada. **Se siente culpable** porque no **compró** el regalo de su prima con más tiempo. Ella siempre **deja todo para último minuto**.

El nuevo esposo de su prima conversa con ella un momento. **Es doctor** y le cuenta que la semana siguiente tiene varias **cirugías**. Por ahora **está de vacaciones** y está disfrutando de la fiesta. Rosa le pregunta a Cristina **si todo está bien**. Le dice que **parece** algo preocupada. Le muestra **unos zarcillos costosos que le regaló su padrino**, y Cristina **se siente peor**. Piensa que **lo mejor es**

irse de la fiesta **antes de pasar un momento vergonzoso**. Pero cuando **se preparan para cortar el pastel**, llega el novio de Cristina. **Está muy apenado por tardarse tanto,** pero cree que **encontró el regalo ideal** para la novia: **un reloj de oro** muy hermoso. Cristina **al fin está relajada** y **puede divertirse, bailar, comer y tomar**. Toma muchas fotos. **Quiere recordar el día con mucho cariño**.

Resumen

Cristina asiste a la boda de su prima, Rosa. Ahí se encuentra con varios miembros de su familia que tenía tiempo sin ver. Intenta disfrutar de la fiesta, pero está estresada porque aún no ha encontrado el regalo de bodas para su prima. Su novio está buscando el regalo perfecto justo en ese momento. Cristina habla con los invitados, se toma fotos y prueba distintos postres. Justo cuando Cristina piensa en irse de la fiesta, afortunadamente, su novio llega a tiempo con el regalo y ya los dos pueden disfrutar del resto de la noche con tranquilidad.

Summary

Cristina attends her cousin's wedding. There, she sees some of her relatives that she hadn't seen in a while. She tries to enjoy the party, but she's stressed because she still hasn't found her cousin's wedding gift. Her boyfriend is looking for her wedding gift at that very moment. Cristina talks to the guests, takes pictures, and tries different desserts. Just when Cristina is thinking about leaving the party, fortunately, her boyfriend arrives right on time with the wedding gift and then the two of them can enjoy the rest of the night with peace of mind.

Glosario – Glossary

La boda: the wedding

La prima de Cristina: Cristina's cousin (female)

Le ceremonia en la iglesia: the ceremony at the church

Los invitados: the guests

Una quinta alquilada: a rented villa

Además de: aside from

Los novios: the groom and bride

La familia: the family

Abuela: grandmother

Su abuelo no pudo asistir: her grandfather couldn't come

Está enfermo: he is sick

Conversa: she converses

Está distraída: she is distracted

Hablando: talking

Novio: boyfriend

El encargado de encontrar el regalo: the one in charge of finding the gift

Responsabilidad: responsibility

Él insistió: he insisted

Fue: it was

Las tiendas: the stores

Sábados: Saturdays

La tía: the aunt

Electrodoméstico: appliance

Sería: it would be

Le enseña: she shows her

Licuadoras: blenders

Microondas: microwaves

Batidoras: mixers

Un juego de ollas: a set of pans

El esposo: the husband

Un tostador: a toaster

La madrina: the godmother

Periodista: journalist

Viaja: she travels

El primo: the cousin (male)

Un abogado: a lawyer

Más deudas que dinero: more debt than money

Distraerse: keep herself entertained

Se toma fotos con su sobrina: she takes pictures with her niece

Sobrino: nephew

Charla con su tío: she talks to her uncle

Profesor de filosofía: philosophy professor

Parlanchín: talkative

La vida y el amor: life and love

El centro comercial: the mall

Por favor, apresúrate: please, hurry up

Prueba unos postres de chocolate: she tries some chocolate desserts

Le pregunta al mesero cómo se llaman: she asks the waiter what they are called

No contesta los mensajes: he is not answering her texts

Se siente culpable: she feels guilty

Compró: she bought

Deja todo para último minuto: she leaves everything for the last minute

El nuevo esposo de su prima: her cousin's new husband

Es doctor: he is a doctor

Cirugías: surgeries

Está de vacaciones: he is on vacation

Si todo está bien: if everything is okay

Parece: she seems

Unos zarcillos costosos que le regaló su padrino: some expensive earrings that her godfather gave her

Se siente peor: she feels worse

Lo mejor es irse: the best thing to do is leave

Antes de pasar un momento vergonzoso: before going through an embarrassing moment

Se preparan para cortar el pastel: they are getting ready to cut the cake

Está muy apenado por tardarse tanto: he is very sorry for taking so long

Encontró el regalo ideal: he found the perfect gift

Un reloj de oro: a gold watch

Al fin está relajada: she is relaxed at last

Puede divertirse: she can have fun

Bailar, comer y tomar: to dance, to eat, to drink

Quiere recordar el día con cariño: she wants to remember the day fondly

Ejercicio 1

Contesta las siguientes preguntas – answer the following questions

1- **¿Cómo se llama la iglesia?** – what's the name of the church?

_____

2- **¿Por qué el abuelo de Cristina no pudo asistir a la boda?** – why couldn't Cristina's grandpa attend the wedding?

_____

3- **¿Quién busca el regalo de bodas para Rosa?** – who is looking for Rosa's wedding gift?

_____

4- **¿A qué hora cierran las tiendas los sábados?** – what time do stores close on Saturdays?

_____

5- **¿Qué le regala su madrina cuando vuelve de viaje?** – what does her godmother give her when she's back from her trips?

_____

6- **¿A qué se dedica el tío de Cristina?** – what does Cristina's uncle do?

7- ¿Dónde está el novio de Cristina cuando ella lo llama? – where's Cristina's boyfriend when she calls him?

8- ¿Qué le pregunta Cristina al mesero? – what does Cristina ask the waiter?

9- ¿Por qué Cristina se siente culpable? – why does Cristina feel guilty?

10- ¿Cuál es el regalo? – what is the present?

Ejercicio 2

Elige entre "verdadero" o "falso" – choose "true" or "false"

1- **La prima de Cristina se llama Rosa.** – Cristina's cousin is called Rosa.

2- **La fiesta es en casa de la novia.** – The party is at the bride's place.

3- **Cristina no ve a su abuela desde hace tres años.** – Cristina hasn't seen her grandma in three years.

4- **Su tía le sugiere que compre un celular como regalo.** – Her aunt suggests she buy a phone as a gift.

5- **El primo de Cristina es un abogado con mucho dinero.** – Cristina's cousin is a wealthy lawyer.

6- **Cristina habla con su tío sobre política.** – Cristina talks to her uncle about politics.

7- **Cristina prueba varios postres de chocolate.** – Cristina tries several chocolate desserts.

8- **El esposo de Rosa es periodista.** – Rosa's husband is a journalist.

9- **Cristina piensa en irse.** – Cristina thinks about leaving.

10- **Cristina se divierte el resto de la noche.** – Cristina has fun the rest of the evening.

Respuestas – Answers

Ejercicio 1

1- La iglesia se llama La Paz de Cristo.

2- El abuelo de Cristina no pudo asistir a la boda porque está enfermo.

3- El novio de Cristina busca el regalo de bodas para Rosa.

4- Las tiendas cierran a las 6 de la tarde los sábados.

5- La madrina de Cristina siempre le regala un perfume nuevo cuando vuelve de viaje.

6- El tío de Cristina es profesor de filosofía.

7- El novio de Cristina está en el centro comercial cuando ella lo llama.

8- Cristina le pregunta al mesero cómo se llaman los postres de chocolate.

9- Cristina se siente culpable porque no compró el reloj con más tiempo.

10- El regalo es un reloj de oro.

Ejercicio 2

1- Verdadero

2- Falso

3- Falso

4- Falso

5- Falso

6- Falso

7- Verdadero

8- Falso

9- Verdadero

10- Verdadero

Puntos clave – Key takeaways

- *La prima de Cristina* is closely translated as "the cousin of Cristina". There's no construction similar to "Cristina's cousin" in Spanish.

- Most professions in Spanish have a masculine and a femenine form (*abogado, abogada*).

- Most adjectives in Spanish have a masculine and a femenine form (*preocupado, preocupada*).

- We usually use the verb *estar* with adjectives that describe feelings.

In the next chapter, you will learn some vocabulary about groceries, how to talk about prices, how to use the verb *haber*, and some partitives in Spanish.

Chapter 4: Las compras – The grocery shopping

❧

La persona que nunca ha cometido un error nunca ha hecho nada nuevo.

- Albert Einstein

Omar **suele hacer las compras los domingos**, ya que es mejor porque **no hay tanta gente. Escucha música mientras selecciona qué comprar. Nunca hace una lista**, así que **a menudo se le olvidan algunos artículos.** Se acerca a **la sección de frutas** y **escoge un par de manzanas.** También **hay peras y bananas. No hay fresas ni arándanos, lo cual es una pena** porque las fresas **son sus favoritas.** Omar **prepara batidos de frutas casi todos los días** y por eso necesita comprar muchas frutas. En **la sección de verduras** hay **tomates jugosos.** También **hay papas, cebollas, pepinos y lechuga.** Hay algunas **zanahorias** pero **están podridas.** Omar le pregunta a **uno de los trabajadores del supermercado** si hay más zanahorias y él **le pide que espere un momento.**

Omar **se pregunta qué más le falta. Aún no busca la leche ni los cereales** ni **el pan.** Él recuerda que el pan aquí es **un poco caro.** Hay **otro lugar** cerca de su casa donde el pan es **más económico,** y a veces hay **buenos descuentos** o **promociones de dos artículos por el precio de uno.** El chico le da a Omar un par de zanahorias **en muy buen estado** y él continúa haciendo sus compras.

Los muslos de pollo están a mitad de precio así que **él se lleva 2 kilos.** Él **ya tiene salmón en su casa** y por eso no compra.

Omar **se encuentra a su vecina.**

–¿**Tú también** compras los domingos? **¿Te falta algo más?**

–No, **creo que solo me falta la pasta y el arroz** –responde Omar.

–**¿Vas a preparar algún platillo especial?**

–No, nada en especial. **¿Y tú?**

–Estoy comprando **los ingredientes** para **el pastel de cumpleaños** de mi hermana. Mañana es su cumpleaños. **Estás invitado.**

–**Gracias**, ¿a qué hora es la fiesta?

–A las 8 de la noche. **Es solo una reunión pequeña.**

–**Bien**, **nos vemos mañana**.

Hay **dos estantes** con mucho arroz. Él solo necesita **un paquete de 1 kilo**. Toma un paquete y dos paquetes de 1 kilo de pasta, luego se acerca a **la caja** para pagar.

–**¿Eso es todo?** –pregunta el cajero.

–Sí, **por favor**.

–Perfecto, **son 3.500 pesos**.

–**¿Aceptan tarjeta de crédito?**

–Sí, también aceptamos **tarjeta de débito y efectivo**.

En ese momento, Omar se da cuenta que su tarjeta **no está en su bolsillo. Le pide disculpas al cajero** y llama a su novia.

–Creo que **olvidé** mi tarjeta de crédito en la casa.

–**¿En serio?** Yo estoy en casa de mi mamá y **no puedo buscarla**.

–**Sí, lo sé**.

–Bueno, **otro día** haces las compras.

–**No, tranquila, hoy hago todo**.

Omar **está enojado consigo mismo. Se siente como estúpido. Toma un taxi hasta su casa** que **le cobra 200 pesos** y busca su tarjeta. **Pasan algunos minutos** y **no la encuentra**. No está en **la mesa de noche como él pensaba**, tampoco está en **la mesa del comedor**. Encuentra la tarjeta **encima del refrigerador, lo cual es extraño**. En **media hora** ya está de vuelta en el supermercado. El cajero tiene su **carrito con comida** a su lado. Omar **paga todo** y se va a casa con **las bolsas** de comida.

Resumen

Omar va al supermercado a hacer las compras un domingo. Agarra algunas frutas y verduras mientras intenta recordar qué le falta en casa. Se encuentra a una vecina y conversan por unos minutos. Cuando se dirige a la caja, se da cuenta de que no tiene su tarjeta de débito en el bolsillo y que probablemente la dejó en casa. Con mucha pena, toma un taxi a casa, busca la tarjeta y se devuelve al supermercado para finalmente pagar por sus compras.

Summary

Omar goes to the supermarket to get some groceries on a Sunday. He picks up some fruits and vegetables as he tries to remember what he needs at home. He runs into a neighbor and talks to her for a few minutes. When he gets to the cash register, he realizes he doesn't have his credit card in his pocket, and he probably left it at home. Feeling embarrassed, he takes a taxi home, looks for his card and returns to the supermarket to finally pay for his groceries.

Glosario – Glossary

Suele hacer las compras: he usually goes grocery shopping

Los domingos: on Sundays

No hay tanta gente: there isn't that many people

Escucha música: he listens to music

Mientras selecciona qué comprar: as he selects what to buy

Nunca hace una lista: he never makes a list

A menudo olvida algunos artículos: he often forgets some items

La sección de frutas: the fruit section

Escoge un par de manzanas: he chooses a couple of apples

Hay peras y bananas: there are pears and bananas

No hay fresas ni arándanos: there aren't any strawberries or cranberries

Lo cual es una pena: which is a pity

Son sus favoritas: they are his favorite

Prepara batidos de fruta: he makes smoothies

Casi todos los días: almost every day

La sección de verduras: the vegetable section

Tomates jugosos: juicy tomatoes

Hay papas, cebollas, pepinos y lechuga: there are potatoes, onions, cucumbers, and lettuce

Zanahorias: carrots

Están podridas: they are rotten

Uno de los trabajadores del supermercado: one of the employees of the supermarket

Le pide que espere un minuto: he asks him to wait a minute

Se pregunta qué más le falta: he wonders what else he's missing

Aún no busca la leche ni los cereales: he still hasn't looked for milk or cereals

El pan: the bread

Un poco caro: a bit expensive

Otro lugar: another place

Más económico: cheaper

Buenos descuentos: good discounts

Promociones de dos artículos por el precio de uno: special offers of two items for the price of one

En buen estado: in good shape

Los muslos de pollo: the chicken thighs

Están a mitad de precio: they are half off

Él se lleva 2 kilos: he takes 2 kilograms

Ya tiene salmón en su casa: he already has salmon at home

Se encuentra a su vecina: he runs into his neighbor

Tú también: you too

¿Te falta algo más?: do you need anything else?

Creo que: I think that

Solo me falta la pasta y el arroz: I'm only missing pasta and rice

¿Vas a preparer un plato especial?: Are you going to make a special dish?

¿Y tú?: and you?

Los ingredientes: the ingredients

El pastel de cumpleaños: birthday cake

Estás invitado: you are invited

Gracias: thank you

Es solo una reunión pequeña: it is just a little get-together

Bien, nos vemos mañana: good, see you tomorrow

Dos estantes: two shelves

Un paquete de 1 kilo: a package of 1 kilogram

La caja: the cash register

¿Eso es todo?: is that all?

Por favor: please

Son 3.500 pesos: it is 3,500 pesos

¿Aceptan tarjeta de crédito?: do you take credit cards?

Tarjeta de débito y efectivo: debit card and cash

En ese momento: in that moment

No está en su bolsillo: it is not in his pocket

Le pide disculpas a el cajero: he apologizes to the cashier

(Yo) olvidé: I forgot

¿En serio?: really?

No puedo buscarla: I can't look for it

Sí, lo sé: yes, I know

Otro día: another day

No, tranquila: No, don't worry

Hoy hago todo: I will get it all done today

Está enojado consigo mismo: he is angry at himself

Se siente como estúpido: he feels stupid

Toma un taxi hasta su casa: he takes a taxi home

Le cobra 200 pesos: he charges him 200 pesos

Pasan algunos minutos: a few minutes go by

No la encuentra: he can't find it

La mesa de noche: the nightstand

Como él pensaba: as he thought

La mesa del comedor: the dining table

Encima del refrigerador: on the fridge

Lo cual es extraño: which is weird

Media hora: half an hour

Carrito con comida: shopping cart with food

Paga todo: he pays for everything

Las bolsas: the bags

Ejercicio 1

Contesta las siguientes preguntas – answer the following questions

1- **¿Por qué Omar hace las compras los domingos?** – why does Omar do the grocery shopping on Sundays?

_____

2- **¿Cuál es la fruta favorita de Omar?** – what 's Omar' s favorite fruit?

_____

3- **¿Qué verduras hay en la sección de verduras?** – what vegetables are there in the vegetable section?

_____

4- **¿Por qué Omar no compra pan ahí?** – why doesn't Omar buy bread there?

_____

5- **¿Cuántos kilos de muslo de pollo compra Omar?** – how many kilograms of chicken thighs does Omar buy?

_____

6- **¿Qué compra su vecina?** – what is his neighbor buying?

_____

7- **¿A qué hora es la fiesta de la hermana de la vecina?** – what time is his neighbor's sister's party?

_____

8- **¿Por qué Omar no puede pagar su comida?** – why can't Omar pay for his food?

_____

9- **¿Cuánto le cobra el taxi a casa?** – how much is the taxi home?

_____

10- **¿Dónde está la tarjeta de crédito?** – where is his credit card?

Ejercicio 2

Elige entre "verdadero" o "falso" – choose "true" or "false"

1- **Omar nunca olvida ningún artículo.** – Omar never forgets any items.

2- **No hay bananas en la sección de frutas.** – There are no bananas in the fruit section.

3- **Las zanahorias están podridas.** – The carrots are rotten.

4- **Omar compra 1 kilo de salmón.** – Omar buys 1 kilogram of salmon.

5- **Omar rechaza la invitación de su vecina.** – Omar turns down his neighbor's invitation.

6- **Omar compra 2 kilos de pasta.** – Omar buys 2 kilograms of pasta.

7- **El total de Omar es 4.000 pesos.** – Omar's total is 4,000 pesos.

8- **Omar toma un taxi a casa.** – Omar takes a taxi home.

9- **Omar tiene que buscar los artículos de nuevo.** – Omar has to look for the food items again.

10- **Omar paga en efectivo.** – Omar pays in cash.

Respuestas – Answers

Ejercicio 1

1- Omar hace las compras los domingos porque no hay tanta gente.

2- La fresa es la fruta favorita de Omar.

3- En la sección de verduras hay tomates, papas, cebollas, pepinos, lechuga y zanahorias.

4- Omar no compra pan ahí porque es un poco caro.

5- Omar compra 2 kilos de muslo de pollo.

6- La vecina de Omar compra los ingredientes para el pastel de cumpleaños de su hermana.

7- La fiesta de la hermana de la vecina es a las 8 de la noche.

8- Omar no puede pagar su comida porque no tiene su tarjeta de crédito.

9- El taxi a casa le cobra 200 pesos.

10- La tarjeta de crédito está encima del refrigerador.

Ejercicio 2

1- Falso

2- Falso

3- Verdadero

4- Falso

5- Falso

6- Verdadero

7- Falso

8- Verdadero

9- Falso

10- Falso

Puntos clave – Key takeaways

- When we talk about prices, we say *son* followed by the price, "*son 100 pesos*".
- The verb *soler* is often translated as the adverb usually, and it's always followed by another verb.
- *Hay* can be translated as either "there is" or "there are".

In the next chapter, you will learn some vocabulary about school supplies, colors, how to use plural nouns, and how to ask and give personal information.

Chapter 5: De vuelta a clases – Back to classes

❧

Una buena madre vale por cien maestros.

- George Herbert

El hijo de Marisol **empieza las clases en un par de días**. Este año **está en segundo grado**. Marisol **le pide a su hermana que la acompañe** a una tienda a comprar algunas cosas para su hijo. Escoge unos nuevos **cuadernos**, unos muy hermosos. **Está segura de que su hijo va a estar feliz con** los cuadernos de **super héroes**. **Su color favorito es el rojo**, así que compra uno rojo, también uno **amarillo**, uno **azul** y uno **verde**. Todos con **colores** lindos. **Por desgracia**, Marisol **no consigue todos los libros** de su hijo en esta tienda. Solo puede comprar el libro de **historia** y el libro de **matemáticas**.

Le preocupa un poco porque **las tiendas cierran** en una hora, pero **espera encontrar el resto de los útiles escolares** pronto. En una tienda de **computadoras y celulares** pregunta **el precio** de algunos artículos. Hay una computadora muy **moderna** que **quiere comprar** pero **no tiene suficiente dinero**. Ve un celular **a buen precio** y piensa en su hijo. **Él está creciendo** y **necesita** un celular **para comunicarse**. Marisol **decide comprarlo** con la tarjeta de crédito.

–Necesito **algunos datos para finalizar su compra**.

–**Está bien**, no hay problema –responde Marisol.

–**¿Cuál es su número de teléfono?**

–Mi número de teléfono es 0 11 25184567.

–Muy bien, **¿cuál es su correo electrónico?**

–**Marisol@gmail.com**

–**Por último, ¿cuál es su estado civil?**

–¿En verdad necesita **esa información**?

–Sí, es una de las **preguntas estándares**.

–**Okey, estoy soltera.**

–**Aquí tiene, que disfrute su compra.**

Marisol y su hermana **salen** de la tienda y se apresuran a buscar **las cosas que les faltan**. En media hora cierran las tiendas.

−Esas preguntas **fueron muy extrañas, ¿no te parece?** −pregunta Marisol.

−Sí, **no entiendo por qué necesita saber si estás casada o no**.

Marisol busca en los estantes de libros en otra tienda. Hay libros de **castellano y literatura** de **primer grado** hasta **sexto grado**. Marisol agarra el libro de segundo grado y también compra los libros de **física y química** para Anabel, **su hija mayor**.

−¿Te falta **lápiz y borra**? −pregunta su hermana.

−Sí, **agarra una caja de lápices y dos borras**.

−**Mira esta cartuchera. Está muy linda**.

−Sí, es linda. **¿Cuánto cuesta?**

−600 pesos.

−Está bien. También **necesito comprar una caja de colores**.

Marisol **gasta** casi 3000 pesos en todos los artículos. El hombre **le entrega** las cosas y ellas se van.

−**¿Qué te falta?** −pregunta su hermana.

−Solo falta **el uniforme, la camisa blanca** y **el pantalón azul oscuro**.

Cuando llegan a **la tienda donde venden ropa escolar, las puertas están cerradas**.

−**¿Ya cerraron?**

−Sí, **ya cerramos por hoy** −dice **el dueño de la tienda**.

−Tengo que comprar el uniforme de mi hijo.

−**Disculpe, vuelva mañana**.

Marisol y su hermana **toman el tren** a su casa. Marisol **se siente un poco desanimada** porque no compró el uniforme de su hijo.

−**No te preocupes**, lo compras mañana −dice su hermana.

−Mañana no puedo, **estoy ocupada todo el día** en la oficina.

−**Yo sé que encontrarás una manera de hacerlo**.

−**Eso espero**.

−¿La computadora es para Anabel?

−Sí, este año estudia **computación** y necesita **una mejor computadora**.

−Pero esas computadoras **están carísimas**.

−Sí, **tengo que pensarlo. Puedo pedir un préstamo en el banco**.

Antes de ir a casa, Marisol toma una taza de café en casa de su hermana. El esposo de su hermana la saluda y **le pregunta cómo están sus hijos**. Cuando Marisol le habla sobre el uniforme de su hijo Carlos, **él se ofrece a comprar** el uniforme porque **tiene el día libre**. Marisol le agradece y se siente más aliviada. Habla con ellos **por casi una hora** y luego se va a casa **a descansar**.

Resumen

Marisol va a varias tiendas a comprar los útiles escolares de sus hijos en compañía de su hermana. Compra cuadernos, libros, lápices, cartucheras y otros artículos, incluso un celular para su hijo más pequeño. Tiene muy poco tiempo así que se apresura yendo de tienda en tienda. Por desgracia, la tienda de uniformes escolares está cerrada cuando llega y no puede comprar la camisa blanca y el pantalón azul oscuro que su hijo necesita. Algo desanimada, se detiene en casa de su hermana a tomar café. Luego de hablar con el esposo de su hermana, él se ofrece a comprar el uniforme de su hijo, resolviendo su problema.

Summary

Marisol goes to a few stores to get her kids' school supplies along with her sister. She buys notebooks, books, pencils, pencil cases and other items, even a phone for her younger son. She has very little time so she has to hurry as she makes her way from store to store. Unfortunately, the uniform store is already closed when she gets there so she can't buy the white shirt and dark blue pants her son needs. Feeling a bit down, she stops at her sister's for some coffee. After talking to her sister's husband, he offers to buy her son's uniform, solving her problems.

Glosario – Glossary

Empieza las clases: he starts classes

En un par de días: in a couple of days

Está en segundo grado: he is in second grade

Le pide a su hermana que la acompañe: she asks her sister to come with her

Cuadernos: notebooks

Está segura de que su hijo va a estar feliz con: she is sure her son is going to be happy with

Super héroes: he never makes a list

Su color favorito es el rojo: his favorite color is red

Amarillo, azul y verde: yellow, blue, and green

Por desgracia: unfortunately

No consigue todos los libros: she can't find all the books

Historia: history

Matemáticas: math

Le preocupa: it worries her

Las tiendas cierran: the stores close

Espera encontrar el resto de los útiles escolares: she hopes to find the rest of the school supplies

Computadoras y celulares: computers and cell phones

El precio: the price

Moderna: modern

Quiere comprar: she wants to buy

No tiene suficiente dinero: she doesn't have enough money

A buen precio: at a good price

Él está creciendo: he is growing up

Necesita: he needs

Para comunicarse: to keep in touch

Decide comprarlo: she decides to buy it

Algunos datos para finalizar su compra: some information to complete your purchase

Está bien: that's okay

¿Cuál es su número de teléfono?: what's your phone number?

¿Cuál es su correo electrónico?: what's your email address?

(@) arroba: at

(.) punto: dot

Por último: lastly

¿Cuál es su estado civil?: what's your marital status?

Esa información: that information

Preguntas estándares: standard questions

Okey: okay

Estoy soltera: I am single

Aquí tiene: here you go

Que disfrute su compra: enjoy your purchase

Salen: they leave

Las cosas que les faltan: the rest of the things they need

Fueron muy extrañas: they were very strange

¿No te parece?: don't you think?

No entiendo por qué: I don't understand why

Necesita saber si estás casada o no: he needs to know if you're married or not

Castellano y literatura: Spanish and literature

Primer grado: first grade

Sexto grado: sixth grade

Física y química: physics and chemistry

Su hija mayor: her eldest daughter

Lápiz y borra: a pencil and an eraser

Agarra: take

Una caja de lápices: a box of pencils

Dos borras: two erasers

285

Mira esta cartuchera: look at this pencil case

Está muy linda: it is really pretty

¿Cuánto cuesta?: how much does it cost?

Necesito comprar una caja de colores: I need to buy a box of colored pencils

Gasta: she spends

Le entrega: he gives her

¿Qué te falta?: what else do you need?

El uniforme: the uniform

La camisa blanca: the white shirt

El pantalón azul oscuro: the dark blue pants

La tienda donde venden ropa escolar: the store where they sell school uniforms

Las puertas están cerradas: the doors are closed

¿Ya cerraron?: are you closed?

Ya cerramos por hoy: we are closed for the day

El dueño de la tienda: the store's owner

Disculpe, vuelva mañana: I'm sorry, come back tomorrow

Toman el tren: they take the train

Se siente un poco desanimada: she feels a bit down

No te preocupes: don't worry

Estoy ocupada todo el día: I will be busy all day

Yo sé que encontrarás una manera de hacerlo: I know you will find a way to do it

Eso espero: I hope so

Computación: IT

Una mejor computadora: a better computer

Están carísimas: they are extremely expensive

Tengo que pensarlo: I have to think about it

Puedo pedir un préstamo en el banco: I can get a loan from the bank

Le pregunta cómo están sus hijos: he asks her how her kids are

Él se ofrece a comprar: he offers to buy

Tiene el día libre: he has the day off

Por casi una hora: for almost an hour

A descansar: to rest

Ejercicio 1

Contesta las siguientes preguntas – answer the following questions

1- **¿Quién acompaña a Marisol?** – who is accompanying Marisol?

_____

2- **¿De qué colores son los cuadernos que compra Marisol?** – what color are the notebooks Marisol buys?

_____

3- **¿Qué libros compra en la primera tienda?** – what books does she buy in the first store?

_____

4- **¿Por qué Marisol no compra la computadora?** – why doesn't Marisol buy the computer?

_____

5- **¿Marisol está casada?** – Is Marisol married?

_____

6- **¿Qué piensa Marisol de las preguntas del empleado de la tienda?** – what does Marisol think about the store employee's questions?

_____

7- **¿Qué libros compra Marisol para su hija?** – what books does Marisol buy for her daughter?

_____

8- **¿Por qué Marisol no puede comprar el uniforme de su hijo?** – why can't Marisol buy her son's uniform?

_____

9- **¿Por qué Anabel necesita una nueva computadora?** – why does Anabel need a new computer?

_____

10- **¿Quién se ofrece a comprar el uniforme?** – who offers to buy the uniform?

_____

Ejercicio 2

Elige entre "verdadero" o "falso" – choose "true" or "false"

1- **El hijo de Marisol está en tercer grado.** – Marisol's son is in third grade.

_____

2- **El color favorito del hijo de Marisol es el rojo.** – Marisol's son's favorite color is red.

_____

3- **Las tiendas cierran en dos horas.** – The stores close in two hours.

_____

4- **Marisol se compra un celular para sí misma.** – Marisol buys a phone for herself.

5- **Marisol está soltera.** – Marisol is single.

6- **Marisol gasta casi 3.000 pesos en una de las tiendas.** – Marisol spends almost 3,000 pesos in one of the stores.

7- **Marisol tiene que comprar una camisa azul.** – Marisol has to buy a blue shirt.

8- **Marisol toma un autobús a casa.** – Marisol takes the bus home.

9- **Marisol considera pedir un préstamo al banco.** – Marisol is considering getting a loan from the bank.

10- **Marisol se toma un café en casa de su hermana.** – Marisol has a coffee at her sister's.

Respuestas – Answers

Ejercicio 1

1- La hermana de Marisol la acompaña.

2- Marisol compra un cuaderno rojo, uno amarillo, uno azul y uno verde.

3- Marisol compra el libro de historia y el de matemáticas.

4- Marisol no compra la computadora porque no tiene suficiente dinero.

5- No, Marisol está soltera.

6- Marisol piensa que las preguntas del empleado de la tienda son extrañas.

7- Marisol compra un libro de física y uno de química para su hija.

8- Marisol no puede comprar el uniforme de su hijo porque cuando llega a la tienda ya está cerrada.

9- Anabel necesita una nueva computadora porque este año estudia computación.

10- El esposo de la hermana de Marisol se ofrece a comprar el uniforme.

Ejercicio 2

1- Falso

2- Verdadero

3- Falso

4- Falso

5- Verdadero

6- Verdadero

7- Falso

8- Falso

9- Verdadero

10- Verdadero

Puntos clave – Key takeaways

- Most adjectives in Spanish have a singular and a plural form (*lindo, lindos*).
- Nouns that end in a vowel can be turned into plural by adding an *s* (*cuaderno = cuadernos*).
- Nouns that end in a consonant can be turned into plural by adding *es* (*color = colores*).
- *¿Cuánto cuesta?* or *¿Cuánto es?* are questions to ask about prices.

In the next chapter, you will learn how to use the verb *gustar*, some adjectives to describe both appearance and personality, and how to make comparisons between two people.

Chapter 6: La cita – The date

No hay ningún instinto como el del corazón.

- Lord Byron

Daniela está soltera y **a Cristina le encanta presentarle chicos nuevos**. Aunque son muy **buenas amigas**, Cristina **no sabe muy bien qué tipo de hombres le gustan a Daniela**, y **por eso las citas** siempre son **un completo desastre. Para evitar esos momentos incómodos**, Daniela **descargó una aplicación de citas** llamada **Cupido para encontrar** a **un chico que a ella le parezca interesante**. Ella **no sabe si quiere una relación** o **algo más casual. De momento, la idea es divertirse**.

Cristina y Daniela **se juntan** para ver los distintos **perfiles de los chicos** y ven **algunos más interesantes que otros**. Hay muchos perfiles **con pocas fotos**, otros **sin ninguna descripción ni información sobre el posible candidato**. Ellas **descartan** este tipo de perfiles inmediatamente. A Daniela le gustan **los hombres que se toman el tiempo para al menos describirse un poco**. También encuentran algunos chicos muy **apuestos y encantadores. Entre esos** chicos, **hay dos que a Daniela le encantan**: uno es un chico llamado Juan y el otro se llama Sebastián.

Juan es abogado, **lo cual no le gusta a Cristina** porque piensa que **significa que Juan es aburrido**. Pero a Daniela le gusta que Juan **tenga un lado creativo**. Juan **dice que le gusta cantar y escribir poemas. Parece que** Juan es un chico **sensible, lo cual es bueno para Daniela**. Juan dice que es un chico **introvertido**, que **prefiere quedarse en casa viendo una película que salir a un bar a tomar**. A Daniela le gusta ver películas en casa, pero también **le gusta salir** y **le gustaría** salir con Juan **de vez en cuando**, entonces **no sabe si sus personalidades son compatibles**.

Sebastián es dos años menor que Daniela y **estudia economía. Por el momento** no trabaja y **sus padres lo ayudan económicamente**. Daniela prefiere a hombres que son **independientes**, pero Sebastián tiene **otras cualidades buenas**. Le gusta mucho cocinar y parece muy **atento**. También le gusta salir a **explorar nuevos lugares**, tiene muchas fotos en **montañas**, diferentes **playas, andando en bicicleta**. A Daniela le gustan las **actividades al aire libre** y le parece que sus personalidades **pueden ser** compatibles.

Juan es **cinco años mayor que** Sebastián, y también es **más alto**. Sebastián es **más musculoso que** Juan y también es **más extrovertido y directo**. Sebastián parece **menos maduro que** Juan, pero **Sebastián es tan educado como Juan**. Daniela cree que Juan es **más apuesto** que Sebastián, pero Juan **coquetea mejor** que Sebastián.

Sebastián **vive más lejos** que Juan, lo cual puede ser un problema si Daniela quiere **hacer planes con él**. A Juan **le gustan los animales** y a Sebastián no, y Daniela tiene un **gato** así que **quizás eso sea** un problema.

Daniela está muy **indecisa**.

–**¿Quién te gusta más?** –pregunta Cristina.

–**La verdad**, no sé. **Ambos** tienen buenas y **malas** cualidades.

–**A ti te gustan** los chicos **graciosos. ¿Quién es más gracioso?**

–Creo que Sebastián es más gracioso que Juan.

–¿Juan es **más atractivo** que Sebastián?

–Ambos son muy lindos.

–¿Quién es **más respetuoso**?

–Creo que Juan.

–**¿Quién es menos atento?**

–Creo que Sebastián.

–¿Juan es **más listo** que Sebastián?

–No, creo que Sebastián es **tan inteligente como** Juan. Es una decisión muy difícil.

En los siguientes días, Daniela tiene una cita con los dos chicos. El jueves Daniela **va al cine** con Juan, y el sábado va a un bar con Sebastián. El domingo en la mañana, Daniela ve a Cristina y **le cuenta todo**.

–¿Ya sabes quién te gusta más? –pregunta Cristina.

–**Estoy más confundida que nunca** –responde Daniela.

–¿Por qué?

–Creo que **los dos me gustan igual**. Juan es muy **caballeroso**, y también **es buen besador**. Sebastián **es bueno bailando** y **la paso muy bien con él**, y **se nota que tiene un lado sensible. ¿Qué hago?**

–**Pues, conócelos un poco mejor**, y **con el tiempo decide qué vas a hacer**. De momento, **disfruta de su compañía. No tienes que apresurarte**.

–**Tienes toda la razón, es muy temprano para tomar una decisión**. Gracias por tus **consejos**.

Resumen

Daniela está buscando conocer chicos interesantes, así que descarga una aplicación de citas llamada Cupido. Su amiga Cristina le ayuda a revisar los perfiles de muchos chicos y a escoger los mejores para tener una cita. Entre tantos perfiles, encuentran a dos chicos que parecen prometedores: Juan y Sebastián. Daniela y Cristina hablan sobre los atributos de ambos chicos y si creen que serían compatibles con Daniela. Más tarde esa semana, Daniela tiene una cita con cada uno de los chicos, y al final ella decide que quiere ir conociéndolos sin prisa.

Summary

Daniela is looking to meet interesting guys so she downloads a dating app called Cupid. Her friend Cristina helps her check the profiles and choose the best ones to go on a date with. Among all the profiles, they find two guys that seem promising: Juan and Sebastián. Daniela and Cristina talk about the attributes of both guys and whether they think they would be a good match with Daniela. Later that week, Daniela has a date with each of the guys, and in the end she decides she wants to get to know them in no rush.

Glosario – Glossary

A Cristina le encanta presentarle chicos nuevos: Cristina loves to introduce new guys to her

Buenas amigas: good friends

No sabe muy bien: she doesn't know that well

Qué tipo de hombres le gustan a Daniela: what type of men Daniela likes

Por eso: that's why

Las citas: the dates

Un completo desastre: a total disaster

Para evitar: to avoid

Esos momentos incómodos: those awkward moments

Descargó una aplicación de citas: she downloaded a dating app

Cupido: Cupid

Para encontrar: to find

Un chico que a ella le parezca interesante: a guy she finds interesting

No sabe si quiere: she doesn't know if she wants

Una relación: a relationship

Algo más casual: something more casual

De momento: for the time being

La idea es divertirse: the idea is to have fun

Se juntan: they get together

Los perfiles de los chicos: the guys' profiles

Algunos más interesantes que otros: some more interesting than others

Con pocas fotos: with few pictures

Sin ninguna descripción ni información: with no description or information

Sobre el posible candidato: about the possible candidate

Descartan: they rule out

Los hombres que se toman el tiempo: the men who take the time

Para al menos describirse un poco: to at least describe themselves a bit

Apuestos y encantadores: handsome and charming

Entre esos: among those

Hay dos que a Daniela le encantan: there are two that Daniela loves

Lo cual no le gusta a Cristina: which Cristina doesn't like

Significa que: it means

Juan es aburrido: Juan is boring

Tiene un lado creativo: he has a creative side

Dice que le gusta cantar y escribir poemas: he says he likes to sing and to write poems

Parece que: it seems that

Sensible: tender

Lo cual es bueno para Daniela: which is good for Daniela

Introvertido: introverted

Prefiere: he prefers

Quedarse en casa viendo una película: to stay home watching a movie

Que salir a un bar a tomar: rather than going out to a bar to drink

Le gusta salir: she likes to go out

Le gustaría: she would like

De vez en cuando: once in a while

No sabe si: she doesn't know if

Sus personalidades son compatibles: their personalities are compatible

Sebastián es dos años menor que Daniela: Sebastián is two years younger than Daniela

Estudia economía: he studies economics

Por el momento: for the moment

Sus padres lo ayudan: his parents help him

Económicamente: financially

Independientes: independent

Otras cualidades buenas: other good qualities

Atento: thoughtful

Explorar nuevos lugares: to explore new places

Montañas: mountains

Playas: beaches

Manejando bicicleta: riding a bike

Actividades al aire libre: outdoor activities

Pueden ser: they might be

Cinco años mayor que: five years older than

Más alto: taller

Más musculoso que: more muscular than

Más extrovertido y directo: more extroverted and direct

Menos maduro que: less mature than

Sebastián es tan educado como Juan: Sebastián is as polite as Juan

Más apuesto: more handsome

Coquetea mejor: he flirts better

Vive más lejos: he lives farther

Hacer planes con él: to make plans with him

Le gustan los animales: he likes animals

Gatos: cats

Quizás eso sea: that might be

Indecisa: indecisive

¿Quién te gusta más?: who do you like more?

La verdad: honestly

Ambos: they both

Malas: bad

A ti te gustan: you like

Graciosos: funny

¿Quién es más gracioso?: who is funnier?

Más atractivo: more attractive

Más respetuoso: more respectful

¿Quién es menos atento?: who is less thoughtful?

Más listo: smarter

Tan inteligente como: as smart as

En los siguientes días: in the following days

Va al cine: she goes to the movies

Le cuenta todo: she tells her everything

Estoy más confundida que nunca: I'm more confused than ever before

Los dos me gustan igual: I like them both the same

Caballeroso: chivalrous

Es buen besador: he is a good kisser

Es bueno bailando: he is a great dancer

La paso muy bien con él: I have a great time with him

Se nota que tiene un lado sensible: you can tell he has a sensitive side

¿Qué hago?: what should I do?

Pues, conócelos un poco mejor: Well, get to know them a little better

Con el tiempo: with time

Decide qué vas a hacer: decide what you're going to do

Disfruta de su compañía: enjoy their company

No tienes que apresurarte: you don't have to rush

Tienes toda la razón: you're totally right

Es muy temprano: it's too early

Para tomar una decisión: to make a decision

Consejos: advice

Ejercicio 1

Contesta las siguientes preguntas – answer the following questions

1- **¿Por qué sus citas son tan malas?** – why are her dates so bad?

_____

2- **¿Qué es Cupido?** – what is Cupid?

_____

3- **¿Qué busca Daniela ahora?** – what is Daniela looking for right now?

_____

4- **¿Qué tipo de perfiles no le gustan a Daniela?** – what kinds of profiles doesn't Daniela like?

_____

5- **¿Por qué a Cristina no le gusta que Juan sea abogado?** – why doesn't Cristina like Juan being a lawyer?

_____

6- **¿Cuál es el lado creativo de Juan?** – what is Juan's creative side?

_____

7- **¿Juan es sociable?** – is Juan sociable?

_____

8- **¿Cómo paga sus cuentas Sebastián?** – how does Sebastián pay his bills?

_____

9- **¿Por qué Daniela piensa que ella y Sebastián son compatibles?** – why does Daniela think that she and Sebastián are compatible?

_____

10- **¿Qué piensa hacer Daniela al final?** – what is Daniela considering in the end?

Ejercicio 2

Elige entre "verdadero" o "falso" – choose "true" or "false"

1- **Daniela y Cristina son primas.** – Daniela and Cristina are cousins.

2- **A Daniela le gusta el lado creativo de Juan.** – Daniela likes Juan's creative side.

3- **Sebastián es menor que Daniela.** – Sebastián is younger than Daniela.

4- **Sebastián es más alto que Juan.** – Sebastián is taller than Juan.

5- **A Juan no le gustan los animales.** – Juan doesn't like animals.

6- **Juan es más atento que Sebastián.** – Juan is more thoughtful than Sebastián.

7- **Daniela va al cine con Juan.** – Daniela goes to the movies with Juan.

8- **Daniela ve a Cristina el sábado a la noche.** – Daniela meets Cristina on Saturday night.

9- **Sebastián es bueno bailando.** – Sebastián is a good dancer.

10- **Daniela comienza una relación con Juan.** – Daniela starts a relationship with Juan.

Respuestas – Answers

Ejercicio 1

1- Las citas de Daniela son malas porque su amiga no sabe el tipo de hombre que le gusta.

2- Cupido es una aplicación de citas.

3- Por ahora, Daniela busca divertirse.

4- A Daniela no le gustan los perfiles sin fotos o con poca información.

5- A Cristina no le gusta que Juan sea abogado porque piensa que puede ser aburrido.

6- El lado creativo de Juan es que le gusta cantar y escribir.

7- No, Juan es un poco introvertido.

8- Los padres de Sebastián lo ayudan económicamente.

9- Daniela piensa que ella y Sebastián son compatibles porque a ambos les gustan las actividades al aire libre.

10- Daniela piensa conocer mejor a Juan y a Sebastián, sin apresurarse.

Ejercicio 2

1- Falso

2- Verdadero

3- Verdadero

4- Falso

5- Falso

6- Verdadero

7- Verdadero

8- Falso

9- Verdadero

10- Falso

Puntos clave – Key takeaways

- The verb *gustar* is very particular. *Me gusta el café* can be closely translated as "coffee pleases me".

- When we use verbs like *gustar*, we have to switch the structure of the sentence around. Though *me gusta el café* means "I like coffee", here *el café* is the subject of the sentence, unlike in English where "coffee" is the object of the sentence.

- *Gustar* is preceded by the correct objective pronoun (*me, te, le, nos, les*).

- To make comparisons we use *más* an adjective and *que*, (*Yo soy más alto que tú* = I'm taller than you)

In the next chapter, you will learn vocabulary about parts of the house, adverbs of place, and how to talk about possession.

Chapter 7: El gatito – The kitten

El tiempo pasado en compañía de gatos no es tiempo malgastado.

- Sigmund Freud

Daniela vive en una casa **antigua** en Belgrano, un **barrio algo costoso** en la ciudad de Buenos Aires. A ella le gustaría vivir **sola**, pero, **por desgracia,** necesita a sus dos **compañeras de piso** para **compartir los gastos del alquiler. Ella y Raquel se llevan muy bien.** Tienen algunas **cosas en común** y a menudo **hablan sobre su día** o **alguna otra cosa que tengan en mente.** Raquel es muy **trabajadora y ordenada**, y también es **servicial.** Ayuda con **la limpieza de la casa** y en ocasiones **le prepara el almuerzo o la cena** a Daniela.

Martina es **un caso diferente. Constantemente está de muy mal humor**, y **casi nunca** ayuda con las cosas de la casa. Su **habitación** siempre es un desastre y no es **considerada** ni con Daniela ni con Raquel. A veces **incluso es maleducada,** ya que **ignora a Daniela** cuando **le hace alguna pregunta. Tanto Daniela como Raquel odian a Martina.**

Daniela **adoptó un gatito** recientemente. A Raquel **le gustó la idea de una mascota,** y Martina **no dio su opinión.** El gatito es hermoso, **de pelaje negro y ojos marrones.** A menudo **llora mucho porque quiere comida** o porque **quiere dormir. Eso es lo que hace** el gatito **todo el día.** Duerme, come y llora. También **le gusta esconderse en lugares extraños.**

El gatito está desaparecido desde esta mañana.

–No te voy a ayudar a buscarlo. Es tu gato, no el mío –dijo Martina.

Daniela **no le hace caso** y **sigue buscando al gato.**

–¿Está **detrás del mueble?** –pregunta Raquel.

–No, ahí no está –responde Daniela.

Busca **debajo de la cama** pero solo ve unos **tacones rojos.**

–¿De quién son estos tacones? –pregunta Daniela.

–Son míos –responde Raquel.

Entre la cama y la mesa de noche, Daniela encuentra unos **audífonos blancos.**

–¿Estos audífonos son **tuyos**, Raquel?

–No, no son míos. ¿Y Martina? Tal vez son **suyos**.

–Sí, **supongo que son de ella**.

Las chicas están preocupadas porque no encuentran al gato **aún. Le sirven un poco de leche** en un plato **para atraerlo**, pero **no funciona**. Siguen buscando en todos los lugares **que se les ocurre** que **el gatito pueda estar. Encima de la nevera** no está, tampoco en el pequeño espacio **junto a la planta de sábila**. Raquel cree que el gatito puede estar **dentro de las cajas vacías** en su cuarto, ya que **le gusta jugar ahí**, pero no lo encuentran.

–¿Qué importa? Adopta** otro gato –dice Martina

Daniela y Raquel ignoran **sus comentarios**.

Daniela **cancela su clase de yoga** para seguir buscando al gatito. **Todavía tiene esperanzas de encontrarlo. A eso de las 8 p.m.**, Daniela **escucha un sonido** y le pregunta a Raquel **si ella también lo escucha**. Las dos **siguen el sonido** hasta el baño, **parece venir del cesto de la ropa sucia. Mueven el cesto** y ven al gatito. Las dos **casi lloran de la emoción**, están muy **contentas** porque al fin **encontraron** al gatito. Piensan que el gato **tiene mucha hambre** así que le dan algo de leche, y, como **se la toma muy rápido**, le dan un poco más. Daniela le prepara una **pequeña camita para que duerma** en el cuarto con ella.

Al día siguiente, Martina le dice a Daniela que tiene algo **para ella**. Le da una bolsa y **dentro de ella** hay **un collar con cascabel** para el gatito.

–¿Y eso que compraste esto?** –pregunta Daniela.

–Bueno, **ayer estaban preocupadas por el estúpido gato** así que **me parece que** ese collar **puede ayudar a que lo encuentren la próxima vez**.

–Es precioso. ¿Dónde lo compraste?** –pregunta Raquel.

–En **la tienda de mascotas** que está **enfrente de mi oficina**.

–Es un lindo detalle**, gracias –dice Daniela.

Daniela y Raquel **están sorprendidas** con **la actitud de Martina hacia el gato desde ese momento**. Tal vez **no es tan mala persona como ellas pensaban**.

Resumen

Daniela adoptó a un gatito recientemente. Por desgracia, el gatito se pierde y Daniela no puede encontrarlo en ningún lado. Raquel, su compañera de piso, la ayuda a buscar al gatito. Su otra compañera, Martina, no ayuda en nada. Es evidente que no le importa el gato, y esto es solo una de las razones por las que Raquel y Daniela odian a Martina. Se la pasan todo el día buscando al gato pero no pueden encontrarlo. No es hasta las 8 de la noche que al fin lo encuentran detrás del cesto de ropa sucia en el baño. Al día siguiente, Martina le compra un collar de cascabel al gato luego de ver lo preocupadas que estaban sus compañeras, lo que hace que Daniela y Raquel cambien un poco su opinión sobre ella.

Summary

Daniela adopted a kitten recently. Unfortunately, the cat is missing and Daniela can't find it anywhere. Raquel, her roommate, helps her look for the kitten. Her other roommate, Martina, doesn't help at all. It's clear she doesn't care about the cat, and this is just one of the reasons why Raquel and Daniela hate

Martina. They spend all day looking for the cat but they can't find it. It's not until 8 at night that they finally find the cat behind the laundry hamper in the bathroom. The next day, Martina buys a collar with a bell for the cat after seeing how worried her roommates were, which makes Daniela and Raquel change their mind about her a little.

Glosario – Glossary

Antigua: ancient

Barrio: neighborhood

Algo costoso: somewhat expensive

Sola: alone

Por desgracia: unfortunately

Compañeras de piso: roommates

Compartir los gastos del alquiler: to share the rent

Ella y Raquel se llevan muy bien: she and Raquel get along pretty well

Cosas en común: things in common

Hablan sobre su día: they talk about their day

Alguna otra cosa que tengan en mente: any other thing they have in mind

Trabajadora y ordenada: hardworking and organized

Servicial: helpful

La limpieza de la casa: the house chores

Le prepara el almuerzo o la cena: she makes lunch or dinner for her

Un caso diferente: a different case

Constantemente: constantly

Está de muy mal humor: she's in a very bad mood

Casi nunca: almost never

Habitación: bedroom

Considerada: considerate

Incluso es maleducada: she's even rude

Ignora a Daniela: she ignores Daniela

Le hace alguna pregunta: she asks her a question

Tanto Daniela como Raquel odian a Martina: both Daniela and Raquel hate Martina

Adoptó un gatito: she adopted a cat

Le gustó la idea de una mascota: she liked the idea of a pet

No dio su opinión: she didn't give her opinion

De pelaje negro: with black fur

Ojos marrones: brown eyes

Llora mucho porque quiere comida: he cries a lot because he wants food

Quiere dormir: he wants to sleep

Eso es lo que hace: that's what he does

Todo el día: all day

Le gusta esconderse en lugàres extraños: he likes to hide in strange places

El gatito está desaparecido desde esta mañana: the kitten has been missing since this morning

No te voy a ayudar a buscarlo: I'm not going to help you look for him

Es tu gato, no el mío: it's your cat, not mine

No le hace caso: she doesn't listen to her

Sigue buscando al gato: she keeps looking for the cat

Detrás del mueble: behind the couch

No, ahí no está: no, he's not there

Debajo de la cama: under the bed

Tacones rojos: red high heels

¿De quién son estos tacones?: whose high heels are these?

Son míos: they're mine

Entre la cama y la mesa de noche: between the bed and the nightstand

Audífonos blancos: white earphones

Tuyos: yours

Suyos: hers

Supongo que son de ella: I guess they're hers

Aún: yet

Le sirven un poco de leche: they pour him some milk

Para atraerlo: to lure him

Que se les ocurre: that they can think of

El gatito pueda estar: the kitten may be

Encima de la nevera: on the refrigerator

Junto a la planta de sábila: next to the aloe vera plant

Dentro de las cajas vacías: inside the empty boxes

Le gusta jugar ahí: he likes to play there

¿Qué importa?: who cares?

Adopta: adopt (imperative)

Sus comentarios: her comments

Cancela su clase de yoga: she cancels her yoga class

Todavía tiene esperanzas de encontrarlo: she still has hopes of finding him

A eso de las 8 p.m.: at around 8 p.m.

Escucha un sonido: she hears a sound

Si ella también lo escucha: if she hears it too

Siguen el sonido: they follow the sound

Parece venir del cesto de la ropa sucia: it seems to be coming from the laundry hamper

Mueven el cesto: they move the hamper

Casi lloran de la emoción: they almost cry out of happiness

Contentas: happy

Encontraron: they found

Tiene mucha hambre: he's very hungry

Se la toma muy rápido: he drinks it very fast

Pequeña camita: little bed

Para que duerma: so that he sleeps

Al día siguiente: the next day

Para ella: for her

Dentro de ella: inside of it

Un collar con cascabel: a collar with a bell

¿Y eso que compraste esto?: how come you bought this?

Ayer: yesterday

Estaban preocupadas por: you were worried about

El estúpido gato: the stupid cat

Me parece que: I think that

Puede ayudar a que lo encuentren: it might help you find him

La próxima vez: next time

Es precioso: it's beautiful

¿Dónde lo compraste?: where did you buy it?

La tienda de mascotas: the pet store

Enfrente de mi oficina: in front of my office

Es un lindo detalle: it's a nice gesture

Están sorprendidas: they are surprised

La actitud de Martina hacia el gato: Martina's attitude towards the cat

Desde ese momento: from that moment

No es tan mala persona: she's not such a bad person

Como ellas pensaban: as they used to think

Ejercicio 1

Contesta las siguientes preguntas – answer the following questions

1- **¿Dónde vive Daniela?** – where does Daniela live?

_____

2- **¿Por qué Daniela no puede vivir sola?** – why can't Daniela live on her own?

_____

3- **¿Cómo es Raquel?** – what is Raquel like?

_____

4- **¿Cómo es Martina?** – what is Martina like?

_____

5- **¿Qué hace el gato todo el día?** – what does the cat do all day?

_____

6- **¿Dónde están los tacones rojos?** – where are the red high heels?

_____

7- **¿De quién son los audífonos blancos?** – who's the owner of the white earphones?

_____

8- **¿Dónde cree Raquel que puede estar el gato?** – where does Raquel think the cat might be?

_____

9- **¿Dónde está el gato?** – where's the cat?

_____

10- **¿Qué compra Martina el día siguiente?** – what does Martina buy the next day?

_____

Ejercicio 2

Elige entre "verdadero" o "falso" – choose "true" or "false"

1- **Daniela vive en un departamento.** – Daniela and Cristina are cousins.

_____

2- **Daniela tiene tres compañeras de piso.** – Daniela has three roommates.

_____

3- **Raquel y Daniela tienen muchas cosas en común.** – Raquel and Daniela have a lot of things in common.

_____

4- **Raquel odia a Martina.** – Raquel hates Martina.

_____

5- **El gato tiene los ojos verdes.** – The cat has green eyes.

6- **El gatito está desaparecido desde anoche.** – The cat's been missing since last night.

7- **Daniela cancela su clase de yoga.** – Daniela cancels her yoga class.

8- **Las chicas casi lloran cuando encuentran al gato.** – The girls almost cry when they find the cat.

9- **Raquel le compra un regalo al gato.** – Raquel buys a gift for the cat.

10- **Daniela cambia de opinión sobre Martina.** – Daniela changes her mind about Martina.

Respuestas – Answers

Ejercicio 1

1- Daniela vive en el barrio de Belgrano, en la ciudad de Buenos Aires.

2- Daniela no puede vivir sola porque necesita a alguien para compartir los gastos del alquiler.

3- Raquel es trabajadora, organizada y servicial.

4- Martina es malhumorada, desconsiderada e incluso maleducada.

5- Lo que el gato hace todo el día es comer, dormir y llorar.

6- Los tacones rojos están debajo de la cama.

7- Los audífonos blancos son de Martina.

8- Raquel cree que el gato puede estar en las cajas vacías en su habitación.

9- El gato está detrás del cesto de ropa sucia en el baño.

10- Martina compra un collar de cascabel para el gato.

Ejercicio 2

1- Falso

2- Falso

3- Verdadero

4- Verdadero

5- Falso

6- Falso

7- Verdadero

8- Verdadero

9- Falso

10- Verdadero

Puntos clave – Key takeaways

- *Mío* and *tuyo* are examples of possessive pronouns.
- Possessive pronouns often substitute the noun that we're referring to. (*Es mío* = it's mine).
- *¿De quién es…?* is a question to ask about possession.
- *Aquí, detrás de, al lado de* are examples of adverbs of place.

In the next chapter, you will learn how to describe someone's appearance in detail and some specific adjectives about personality.

Chapter 8: La alumna nueva – The new student

Ser valiente es ser libre.

- Séneca

Tomás **estudia cine en una universidad muy conocida** de Bogotá. Aunque **apenas está en el primer semestre, ya ha hecho varios amigos** y a menudo se junta con ellos **a almorzar** o **simplemente a hablar en la cafetería después de clases. Esta tarde** no tienen **mucho que hacer,** así que se juntan en la cafetería a tomar **un café** y comer **un pedazo de torta de vainilla.** Hablan un poco sobre **uno de sus profesores, un hombre canoso con las cejas pobladas.** También hablan sobre **la alumna nueva,** Camila. Tomás cree que Camila es muy **bonita.** Tiene **unos ojos penetrantes** y **una personalidad muy misteriosa, es completamente su tipo de chica. Todos parecen estar de acuerdo con él.**

—**¿Está buena?** —pregunta un amigo de Tomás.

—Sí, tiene **las piernas largas** y **unas caderas anchas** —contesta otro chico.

—**¿De qué color tiene los ojos?**

—**Marrón oscuro.**

—**¿Cómo tiene el pelo? ¿Lo tiene liso?**

—**Tiene el cabello largo y enrulado.**

—A mí me encantan **las chicas con rulos** —dice Tomás.

—**¿Es negra o morena?**

—Es morena y **se nota que tiene la piel suave.**

Luis, **otro amigo de Tomás que estudia odontología, se sienta** en la mesa con ellos y **les pregunta de quién hablan.**

—De la nueva alumna, se llama Camila.

—**¿Cómo es?** —pregunta Luis.

—**¿Físicamente?**

—Sí, físicamente.

Los chicos **buscan una foto de la chica** en Instagram y **se la muestran a Luis**.

—Es hermosa. **Se parece a una actriz famosa**.

—**¿Cuál?**

—**No recuerdo su nombre**.

Tomás ve la foto de la chica y **piensa en las otras cosas que le gustan de ella. Tiene los dientes blancos y derechos, una sonrisa preciosa.** Tiene **varios piercings en las orejas**, y **uno en la nariz, sus mejillas son rosadas**.

—**¿Cómo es como persona?** –pregunta Luis.

—**¿Su personalidad?**

—Sí.

—Pues, está estudiando cine, **eso la hace automáticamente bacana**. Aunque yo creo que **es algo tímida**.

—¿Tímida? Yo creo que **ella es todo lo contrario. Participa en clases** a menudo y **habla con todo el mundo**.

—¿Sí? **Yo la veo muy callada**.

—**¿Estamos hablando de la misma persona?**

—**¿Alguien ya la invitó a salir?** –pregunta Luis.

—**Creo que no** –responde Tomás.

—¿Por qué? **¿Es intimidante?**

—**Tiene una mirada bastante intimidante**.

—**¿O es que todos ustedes son unos cobardes?**

—**También es una posibilidad**.

—**Yo no la puedo invitar a salir** porque **si mi novia se entera, me mata. ¿Cuál es tu excusa,** Tomás? –pregunta otro amigo.

—Sí, **¿por qué no la invitas a salir? ¿Tienes novia?**

—No, **no tengo novia** – responde Tomás.

—**¿No quisieras salir con ella?**

—**Obvio** –responde Tomás. –Se nota que **es una persona muy apasionada** y **segura de sí misma. Eso me atrae mucho a ella**.

—Pues **invítala a salir antes de que alguien se te adelante** –dice Luis.

—**¿Y si dice que no?** –pregunta Tomás.

—Bueno, **lo aceptas y sigues con tu vida**. Yo sé que tú eres muy indeciso, pero **no pienses tanto las cosas**.

—**¿A dónde debería llevarla?**

—Al cine, **quizás**.

—Sí, es una buena idea.

–Si no la invitas **pronto**, **la voy a invitar yo** –dice uno de sus amigos.

–**No te creo, a ti te gustan las chicas que son más bajas que tú**, y que tienen **el cabello corto y liso**. También te gustan las chicas **un poco más rellenitas**, ¿no?

–Sí, ese es exactamente mi tipo.

–Lo sé, pero está bien, **mañana la invito a salir**, **lo prometo. Espero que diga que sí**.

–Sí, **seguro dice que sí. Ella cree que eres gracioso. Capaz hasta piense que eres inteligente**.

–**¿Por qué dices eso?**

–**Ella se río de tus chistes** en clases ayer. **¿Lo recuerdas?**

–Sí, **lo recuerdo. Tienes razón.**

–**Apuesto 1.000 pesos a que dice que no** –dice uno de sus amigos.

–**Ay, sí eres malo**.

El día siguiente, a la hora del almuerzo, Tomás invita a Camila al cine a ver **una película de terror**. En ese momento Camila le dice que no puede salir con él porque tiene novio.

Resumen

Tomás estudia cine en una universidad de Bogotá y un día se junta en la cafetería a hablar con sus amigos. Entre las cosas que hablan, discuten un poco sobre su nueva compañera de clases, una chica llamada Camila. Tomás piensa que ella es muy linda y todos sus amigos parecen pensar lo mismo. Mencionan las cosas que a todos les gusta de ella, tanto físicamente como sobre su personalidad. Al final, los chicos animan a Tomás a que invite a Camila a salir, y Tomás promete que lo hará al día siguiente. Tomás se arma de valor y la invita al cine, pero, por desgracia, Camila le dice que no puede salir con él porque tiene novio.

Summary

Tomás studies film at a university in Bogotá and one day he gets together with his friends in the cafeteria to talk. Among the things they talk about, they bring up their new classmate, a girl called Camila. Tomás thinks she's really pretty and everyone else seems to agree with him. They mention the things they like about her, both physically and personality-wise. In the end, the guys encourage Tomás to ask Camila out, and Tomás promises he will do it the next day. Tomás builds up the courage to ask her out to the movies, but unfortunately, Camila says she can't go out with him because she has a boyfriend.

Glosario – Glossary

Estudia cine: he studies film

En una universidad muy conocida: at a well-known university

Apenas está en el primer semestre: he's just in the first semester

Ya ha hecho varios amigos: he's made some friends

A almorzar: to have lunch

Simplemente a hablar: just to talk

En la cafetería: in the cafeteria

Después de clases: after class

Esta tarde: this afternoon

Mucho que hacer: much to do

Un café: a coffee

Un pedazo de torta de vainilla: a piece of vanilla cake

Uno de sus profesores: one of their professors

Un hombre canoso: a gray-haired man

Con las cejas pobladas: with bushy eyebrows

La alumna nueva: the new student

Bonita: pretty

Unos ojos penetrantes: piercing eyes

Una personalidad muy misteriosa: a very mysterious personality

Es completamente su tipo de chica: she's totally his type of girl

Todos parecen estar de acuerdo con él: they all seem to agree with him

¿Está buena?: is she hot?

Las piernas largas: long legs

Unas caderas anchas: broad hips

¿De qué color tiene los ojos?: what color are her eyes?

Marrón oscuro: dark brown

¿Cómo tiene el cabello?: what's her hair like?

¿Lo tiene liso?: is it straight?

Tiene el cabello largo y enrulado: she has long, curly hair

Las chicas con rulos: girls with curly hair

¿Es negra o morena?: is she black or brunette?

Se nota que tiene la piel suave: you can tell she has soft skin

Otro amigo de Tomás que estudia odontología: another friend of Tomás's who studies dentistry

Les pregunta de quién hablan: he asks them who they're talking about

¿Cómo es?: what is she like? / what does she look like?

¿Físicamente?: physically?

Buscan una foto de la chica: they look for a picture of the girl

Se la muestran a Luis: they show it to Luis

Se parece a una actriz famosa: she looks like a famous actress

¿Cuál?: which one?

No recuerdo su nombre: I don't remember her name

Piensa en las otras cosas que le gustan de ella: he thinks about the other things he likes about her

Tiene los dientes blancos y derechos: she has straight, white teeth

Una sonrisa preciosa: a gorgeous smile

Varios piercings en las orejas: several piercings in her ear

En la nariz: in her nose

Sus mejillas son rosadas: her cheeks are pink

¿Cómo es como persona?: what's she like as a person?

¿Su personalidad?: her personality?

Eso la hace: that makes her

Automáticamente bacana: automatically cool

Es algo tímida: she's a little shy

Es todo lo opuesto: she's the exact opposite

Participa en clases: she participates in class

Habla con todo el mundo: she talks to everyone

Yo la veo muy callada: I think she's pretty quiet

¿Estamos hablando de la misma persona?: are we talking about the same person?

¿Alguien ya la invitó a salir?: did anyone ask her out already?

Creo que no: I don't think so

¿Es intimidante?: is she intimidating?

Tiene una mirada bastante intimidante: her eyes are pretty intimidating

¿O es que todos ustedes son cobardes?: or is it that you're all cowards?

También es una posibilidad: that's another possibility

Yo no la puedo invitar a salir: I can't ask her out

Si mi novia se entera, me mata: if my girlfriend finds out, she will kill me

¿Cuál es tu excusa?: what's your excuse?

¿Por qué no la invitas a salir?: why don't you ask her out?

¿Tienes novia?: do you have a girlfriend?

No tengo novia: I don't have a girlfriend

¿No quisieras salir con ella?: they follow the sound

Obvio: it seems to be coming from the hamper

Es una persona apasionada: she's a very passionate person

Segura de sí misma: confident

Eso me atrae mucho a ella: I really like that about her

Invítala a salir: ask her out (imperative)

Antes de que alguien más se te adelante: before someone else does it before you

¿Y si dice que no?: what if she says no?

Lo aceptas: you accept it

Sigues con tu vida: move on with your life

No pienses tanto las cosas: don't overthink things

¿A dónde debería llevarla?: where should I take her?

Quizás: perhaps

Pronto: soon

La voy a invitar yo: I will ask her out

No te creo: I don't believe you

A ti te gustan las chicas que son: you like girls that are

Más bajas que tú: shorter than you

El cabello corto y liso: short, straight hair

Un poco más rellenitas: a little bit chubbier

Mañana la invito a salir: I will ask her out tomorrow

Lo prometo: I promise

Espero que diga que sí: I hope she says yes

Seguro dice que sí: she will probably say yes

Ella cree que eres gracioso: she thinks you're funny

Capaz hasta piense que eres inteligente: she may even think you're smart

¿Por qué dices eso?: what makes you say that?

Ella se rió de tus chistes: she laughed at your jokes

¿Lo recuerdas?: remember?

Lo recuerdo: I remember

Tienes razón: you're right

Apuesto 1.000 pesos a que dice que no: I bet 1,000 pesos she says no

Ay, sí eres malo: you're so mean

Una película de terror: a horror movie

Ejercicio 1

Contesta las siguientes preguntas – answer the following questions

1- **¿Qué semestre de la carrera estudia Tomás?** – what semester of college is Tomás in?

2- **¿Cómo es su profesor?** – what's his professor like?

3- **¿Cómo es el cabello de Camila?** — what does Camila's hair look like?

4- **¿Qué estudia Luis?** — what's Luis studying?

5- **¿Camila es rubia o morena?** — is Camila blonde or brunette?

6- **¿Qué piensa Tomás de su mirada?** — what does Tomás think about the way she looks at others?

7- **¿Tomás tiene novia?** — does Tomás have a girlfriend?

8- **¿Qué le gusta a Tomás de su personalidad?** — what does Tomás like about her personality?

9- **¿Cómo cree Luis que es Tomás?** — what does Luis think of Tomás?

10- **¿Por qué es probable que Camila crea que Tomás es gracioso?** — why is it likely Camila thinks Tomás is funny?

Ejercicio 2

Elige entre "verdadero" o "falso" — choose "true" or "false"

1- **Tomás estudia cine.** — Tomás studies film.

2- **Camila tiene los ojos azules.** — Camila has blue eyes.

3- **A Tomás le gustan las chicas con rulos.** — Tomás likes girls with curly hair.

4- **Camila tiene una linda sonrisa.** — Camila has a nice smile.

5- **Camila tiene un piercing en la ceja.** — Camila has a piercing in her eyebrow.

6- **Uno de ellos ya invitó a Camila a salir.** — One of them already asked Camila out.

7- **Tomás no quiere salir con Camila.** — Tomás doesn't want to go out with Camila.

8- **Tomás va a invitar a Camila al cine.** – Tomás is going to ask Camila out to the movies.

9- **Tomás habla con camila en la mañana.** – Tomás talks to Camila in the morning.

10- **Camila rechaza la invitación de Tomás.** – Camila rejects Tomás's invitation.

Respuestas – Answers

Ejercicio 1

1- Tomás está estudiando el primer semestre de la carrera.

2- El profesor de Tomás es un hombre canoso con las cejas pobladas.

3- El cabello de Camila es largo y enrulado.

4- Luis estudia odontología.

5- Camila es morena.

6- Tomás piensa que la mirada de Camila es intimidante.

7- No, Tomás no tiene novia.

8- A Tomás le gusta que Camila sea una persona apasionada y segura de sí misma.

9- Luis cree que Tomás es indeciso.

10- Porque Camila se ríe de los chistes de Tomás.

Ejercicio 2

1- Verdadero

2- Falso

3- Verdadero

4- Verdadero

5- Falso

6- Falso

7- Falso

8- Verdadero

9- Falso

10- Verdadero

Puntos clave – Key takeaways

- *¿Cómo es?* is a question to ask either about someone's appearance or their personality.
- The verb tener is commonly used to describe a person's appearance.
- When we talk about a body part, it is common to use the definite article (*el, la, los, las*) as in *Ella tiene los ojos marrones*.

In the next chapter, you will learn about reflexive verbs, and how to use adverbs of frequency to describe your daily routine.

Chapter 9: Saliendo a trotar – Going out for a jog

✑

De las dificultades nacen milagros.

- Jean de la Bruyère

Cristina **vive con su novio desde hace un par de meses.** Él **entra muy temprano a su trabajo**, así que **la mayoría del tiempo, él ya no está** cuando ella **se levanta.** Cristina entra a su trabajo a las 9 de la mañana, **lo que le da tiempo de hacer todo con calma. Su alarma suena a las 7 y media** y Cristina **se para de la cama** y **se cepilla los dientes. Se prepara una arepa** y la acompaña **con un café con leche. Ve televisión por unos minutos** y luego **se prepara para salir a trotar. Ella prefiere trotar a esta hora** porque **no hay tanta gente en la calle. Trota a su ritmo, respirando profundamente** y **apreciando el paisaje. El día es bonito, el cielo está despejado** y **hace sol.** Hay **un parque con muchos árboles** en **el vecindario de Cristina** que a ella le encanta porque es hermoso y **siempre hay ardillas escalando los árboles. Ella a veces alimenta a las ardillas** con fresas o bananas.

Antes de irse del parque, Cristina **se detiene un momento a tomar algo de sol** y a **apreciar los sonidos de la naturaleza. Revisa la hora** en su teléfono y **se apresura de vuelta a casa para no llegar tarde a su trabajo. Aún le falta tomar una ducha** y **vestirse.** Cuando **llega a la puerta de su casa, no consigue las llaves.** No está **en sus bolsillos**, ni en **su riñonera.** Quizás **dejó las llaves** en casa, o **las perdió en el parque.**

Un poco **angustiada**, llama a su novio, pero él **no contesta el teléfono.** Tal vez **está en una reunión** importante, o simplemente **está ocupado.** Cristina **no sabe qué hacer**, ya que no quiere ser **irresponsable** y llegar tarde a su trabajo. **Camina de vuelta al parque, al lugar donde se sentó hace unos minutos** y busca las llaves. Hasta revisa en **un arbusto** pero no ve las llaves **en ningún lado.** Vuelve a la puerta de su casa y **su vecina** le pregunta **si todo está bien, le dice que pase a su casa por una taza de café. El cielo se oscurece** un poco y **hace frío**, así que Cristina **acepta. Es mejor que quedarse esperando en la calle.** Cristina **le envía un correo a su jefe explicando la situación, esperando que él entienda.** Cristina **está molesta consigo misma por ser tan despistada** y **perder las llaves.** Su vecina **le dice que no se preocupe, que esas cosas le pasan a todo el mundo.**

Minutos más tarde, el novio de Cristina al fin contesta el teléfono. Le dice que en este momento está **muy ocupado para salir de la oficina**, pero que en una hora **puede** volver a la casa. Cristina **se resigna** y acepta la situación. **Mientras espera, se pone a jugar con el perro** de la vecina, un perro viejo pero muy **juguetón**. **Lanza la pelota** y el perro **la busca** y **la trae de vuelta**. Juega con él hasta que su novio llega. Cristina **corre al baño, se desviste** y se ducha. **Se pone una blusa y una falda** y su novio **le da un aventón** al trabajo. Cristina **se disculpa** con su jefe **por su tardanza** y su jefe le dice que no se preocupe, le dice que **no está molesto con ella** porque ella **siempre llega a la oficina a tiempo. Eso la hace sentir un poco mejor.**

En la noche, **ya sin presión**, Cristina busca sus llaves pero no las encuentra. **Es muy extraño.** Al día siguiente **va al cerrajero** por unas llaves nuevas.

Resumen

Cristina se levanta una mañana, preparada para tener un día normal. Desayuna, ve televisión y sale a trotar un rato al parque cerca de su casa. Cuando vuelve a casa, se da cuenta de que las llaves no están en sus bolsillos. Llama a su novio pero él ya está en el trabajo y no le contesta. Su vecina la invita a esperar en su casa con una taza de café. Se entretiene un rato jugando con el perro de su vecina. Cuando su novio llega, se apresura a ducharse y vestirse para salir al trabajo. Cristina está muy apenada pero su jefe le dice que no se preocupe. Al día siguiente, va al cerrajero por unas llaves nuevas.

Summary

Cristina wakes up one morning, ready to have a normal day. She has breakfast, watches TV, and goes jogging for a while at the park near her house. When she comes back home, she realizes her keys are not in her pockets. She calls her boyfriend, but he's at work so he doesn't pick up the phone. Her neighbor invites her over to her house for a cup of coffee while she waits. She distracts herself playing with her neighbor's dog for a while. When her boyfriend gets home, she rushes to take a shower and get dressed for work. Cristina feels ashamed but her boss tells her not to worry. The next day, she goes to the locksmith for new keys.

Glosario – Glossary

Vive con su novio desde hace un par de meses: she's been living with her boyfriend for a couple of months

Entra muy temprano al trabajo: he starts work pretty early

La mayoría del tiempo: most of the time

Se levanta: she wakes up

Él ya no está: he's already gone

Lo que le da tiempo: which gives her time

De hacer todo con calma: to do everything calmly

Su alarma suena a las 7 y media: her alarm goes off at 7 and half

Se para de la cama: she gets out of bed

Se cepilla los dientes: she brushes her teeth

Se prepara una arepa: she makes herself an arepa

La acompaña con un café con leche: she pairs it with a coffee with milk

Ve televisión por unos minutos: she watches TV for a few minutes

Se prepara para salir a trotar: she gets ready to go jogging

Ella prefiere trotar a esta hora: she prefers to jog at this time

No hay tanta gente en la calle: there aren't that many people on the street

Trota a su ritmo: she jogs at her own pace

Respirando profundamente: breathing deeply

Apreciando el paisaje: taking in the view

El día es bonito: it's a nice day outside

El cielo está despejado: the sky is clear

Hace sol: it's sunny

Un parque con muchos árboles: a park with lots of trees

En el vecindario de Cristina: in Cristina's neighborhood

Siempre hay ardillas: there's always squirrels

Escalando los árboles: climbing the trees

A veces alimenta a las ardillas: she sometimes feeds the squirrels

Se detiene un momento: she stops for a moment

A tomar algo de sol: to take in the sun

Apreciar los sonidos de la naturaleza: to take in the sounds of nature

Revisa la hora: she checks the time

Se apresura de vuelta a casa: she rushes back home

Para no llegar tarde al trabajo: to not be late for work

Aún le falta tomar una ducha: she still has to take a shower

Vestirse: to get dressed

Llega a la puerta de la casa: she gets to her front door

No consigue las llaves: she can't find her keys

En sus bolsillos: in her pockets

Su riñonera: her fanny pack

Dejó las llaves: she left her keys

Las perdió en el parque: she lost them in the park

Angustiada: worried

No contesta el teléfono: he doesn't pick up the phone

Está en una reunión: he's in a meeting

No sabe qué hacer: she doesn't know what to do

Irresponsable: irresponsible

Camina de vuelta al parque: she walks back to the park

Al lugar donde se sentó: to the place where she sat down

Hace unos minutos: a few minutes ago

Un arbusto: a bush

En ningún lado: nowhere

Su vecina: her neighbor (female)

Si todo está bien: if everything is alright

Le dice que pasa a su casa: she invites her into her house

Por una taza de café: for a cup of coffee

El cielo se oscurece: the sky gets dark

Hace frío: it's cold

Acepta: she accepts

Es mejor que: it's better than

Quedarse esperando en la calle: waiting on the street

Le envía un correo a su jefe: she emails her boss

Explicando la situación: explaining the situation

Esperando que él entienda: hoping he will understand

Está molesta consigo misma: she's angry at herself

Por ser tan despistada: for being so absent-minded

Perder las llaves: losing her keys

Le dice que no se preocupe: she tells her not to worry

Que esas cosas le pasan a todo el mundo: that those things happen to everyone

Minutos más tarde: a few minutes later

Muy ocupado para salir de la oficina: too busy to leave the office

Puede: he can

Se resigna: she gives up

Mientras espera: while she waits

Se pone a jugar con el perro: she starts playing with the dog

Juguetón: playful

Lanza la pelota: she throws the ball

La busca: he goes for it

La trae de vuelta: he brings it back

Corre al baño: she runs to the bathroom

Se desviste: she undresses

Se pone una blusa y una falda: she puts on a blouse and a skirt

Le da un aventón: he gives her a ride

Se disculpa: she apologizes

Por su tardanza: for her tardiness

No está molesto con ella: he's not mad at her

Siempre llega a la oficina a tiempo: she always gets to the office on time

Eso la hace sentir mejor: that makes her feel better

Ya sin presión: now without pressure

Es muy extraño: it's very strange

Va al cerrajero: she goes to the locksmith

Ejercicio 1

Contesta las siguientes preguntas – answer the following questions

1- **¿A qué hora se levanta Cristina?** – what time does Cristina wake up?

_____

2- **¿Qué desayuna Cristina?** – what does Cristina have for breakfast?

_____

3- **¿Por qué Cristina prefiere trotar a esa hora?** – why does Cristina prefer to go jogging at that time?

_____

4- **¿Qué animal ve en el parque?** – what animal does she see at the park?

_____

5- **¿Qué hace Cristina antes de irse del parque?** – what does Cristina do before leaving the park?

_____

6- **¿Qué pierde Cristina?** – what does Cristina lose?

_____

7- **¿Por qué Cristina está tan angustiada?** – why is Cristina so worried?

_____

8- **¿Dónde espera Cristina a su novio?** – where does Cristina wait for her boyfriend?

_____

9- **¿Cómo llega Cristina a su trabajo?** – how does Cristina get to work?

_____

10- **¿Por qué el jefe de Cristina no está molesto con ella?** – why is Cristina's boss not mad at her?

_____

Ejercicio 2

Elige entre "verdadero" o "falso" – choose "true" or "false"

1- **Cristina vive con su novio desde hace algunos años.** – Cristina has been living with her boyfriend for a few years.

_____

2- **El novio de Cristina se levanta antes que ella.** – Cristina's boyfriend wakes up before her.

_____

3- **Es una mañana fría.** – It's a cold morning.

_____

4- **El parque queda cerca de su casa.** – The park is near her home.

_____

5- **Cristina a veces alimenta a las ardillas.** – Cristina sometimes feeds the squirrels.

_____

6- **Su vecina le da una taza de café.** – Her neighbor offers her a cup of coffee.

_____

7- **El perro de su vecina la ataca.** – Her neighbor's dog attacks her.

_____

8- **Cristina llama a su jefe para explicarle la situación.** – Cristina calls her boss to explain the situation.

_____

9- **Cristina se pone una blusa y una falda.** – Cristina puts on a blouse and a skirt.

_____

10- **Cristina encuentra las llaves en su cuarto.** – Cristina finds her keys in her room.

_____

Respuestas – Answers

Ejercicio 1

1- Cristina se levanta a las 7 y media.

2- Cristina desayuna una arepa con café con leche.

3- Cristina prefiere trotar a esa hora porque no hay gente en la calle.

4- Cristina ve muchas ardillas en el parque.

5- Antes de irse, Cristina se detiene un momento para tomar sol y apreciar los sonidos de la naturaleza.

6- Cristina pierde sus llaves.

7- Cristina está angustiada porque no quiere llegar tarde a su trabajo.

8- Cristina espera a su novio en la casa de su vecina.

9- El novio de Cristina le da un aventón a su trabajo.

10- El jefe de Cristina no está molesto con ella porque ella siempre llega a tiempo al trabajo.

Ejercicio 2

1- Falso

2- Verdadero

3- Falso

4- Verdadero

5- Verdadero

6- Verdadero

7- Falso

8- Falso

9- Verdadero

10- Falso

Puntos clave – Key takeaways

- Most verbs we use to talk about daily routines are reflexive (*levantarse, cepillarse, bañarse, vestirse*).
- To conjugate a reflexive verb, we put the *se* before the verb and conjugate the verb (*Ella se levanta temprano*).
- *Siempre* and *a veces* are examples of frequency adverbs.
- We can use frequency adverbs to say how often we do things, so it's common to use them when talking about daily routines.

In the next chapter, you will learn more about frequency adverbs and other ways to ask and talk about frequency.

Chapter 10: El show de comedia – The comedy show

❦

La experiencia es simplemente el nombre que le ponemos a nuestros errores.

- Oscar Wilde

Últimamente, Tomás **estudia demasiado**, así que **no ve a sus amigos desde hace más de un mes**. Su amigo Luis **lo invitó a un show de comedia por el centro de Bogotá**. El bar es bonito, con **una decoración playera**, con **colores cálidos** y hasta **un aroma agradable a agua de playa**. Tomás le pide una piña colada al bartender mientras espera a Luis. Tomás **intenta pasarla bien** y **no pensar en todas las cosas que tiene que hacer** para la universidad. Él **usualmente va al gimnasio al menos dos veces a la semana** y **nunca se pierde su show favorito los viernes en la noche**, pero **en estos días** solo estudia y estudia. **Está exhausto**. Luis lo saluda y le pide un mojito al bartender.

–**¿Estás nervioso?** –pregunta Tomás.

–**Muchísimo**.

–**¿Invitaste a alguien más?**

–**Invité a poca gente. No quiero humillarme frente a todos los que me conocen.**

Hacer standup es algo nuevo para Luis, es solo **un pasatiempo. Es normal que esté así de nervioso**. Tomás le habla de otras cosas **para distraerlo**. Le pregunta sobre **un viejo amigo de ellos**.

–**Casi nunca** veo a Pedro –responde Luis.

–**¿Qué tan seguido ves a Ana?**

–**La veo muy a menudo porque** somos vecinos.

–**Ah, cierto**.

El bar se queda en silencio y **encienden las luces** del pequeño **escenario**. Un chico con **un sombrero les da las gracias a todos por venir** esta noche y **presenta al primer comediante** de la noche. Luis **va a ser** el número cuatro.

Los primeros tres comediantes son **más o menos entretenidos**. No todos sus **chistes** son graciosos y **se nota porque nadie se ríe**. La tercera chica parece ser **la más graciosa**. Es una chica

de lentes que habla de **su experiencia saliendo con chicos** y ella **recibe muchos aplausos cuando sale del escenario. Llaman el nombre de Luis** y él **se dirige al escenario**. Dice su primer chiste, **algo sobre ser daltónico** y algunas **personas se ríen. Los siguientes** chistes **no son tan graciosos. Nadie se ríe, e incluso algunos parecen aburridos.** Tomás **siente pena por su amigo** pero **le aplaude para animarlo a que continúe. Absolutamente** nadie se ríe **con los últimos chistes**, pero al menos le aplauden **cuando se baja del escenario.**

Luis **parece bastante avergonzado. Le dice a Tomás que quiere irse** del bar y él **le dice que está bien**. Van a otro bar **cercano**.

—**Sé honesto. Apesto, ¿verdad?** —pregunta Luis.

—No, **estuvo bien para ser tu primera vez**.

—¿De verdad? **Siento que no tengo talento para esto.**

—Sí, **es normal que no seas perfecto. Con el tiempo aprenderás.**

—No sé, **nadie se reía**.

—Tu primer chiste **fue gracioso** y **la gente se rió**. Quizás puedes hacer más chistes **de ese estilo**.

—Sí, **tengo que practicar más y escribir más**. Esta semana **no practiqué lo suficiente**, pero con la universidad **no tengo tiempo de nada**.

—**Te entiendo, yo estoy igual que tú. No hago las cosas que normalmente disfruto. Por ejemplo**, me gusta ir al cine **todos los sábados**. ¿Tú **qué tan a menudo haces lo que te gusta**, como **jugar tenis**?

—Normalmente juego tenis los miércoles y viernes, pero sí, **no tengo mucho tiempo** últimamente. Todos los días **tengo que leer algo** o **hacer algo sobre la carrera**.

—Podemos intentar **hacer algo juntos. Nos puede ayudar a sentirnos más motivados.**

—Es una buena idea. ¿Y si vamos mañana domingo a trotar al parque?

—Sí, vamos, **me gustaría**.

—Genial, ahora **a tomar hasta que olvide lo terrible que me fue** esta noche.

Resumen

Luis, el amigo de Tomás, lo invita a un show de comedia en un bar en el centro de Bogotá. Luis va a ser uno de los comediantes que se presente esta noche, así que está muy nervioso ya que es algo nuevo para él. Ellos conversan un rato mientras toman algunos tragos y luego empieza el show. Luis es el cuarto comediante de la noche, y aunque parece empezar bien, el resto de su rutina no parece causarle risa al público. Luis se siente muy avergonzado y le pide a Tomás irse del bar. En otro bar cercano, hablan sobre lo ocupados que están con la universidad últimamente y deciden juntarse para hacer algunas actividades al aire libre.

Summary

Luis, Tomás's friend, invites him to a comedy show in a bar in downtown Bogotá. Luis is going to be one of the comedians in tonight's show, so he's very nervous since this is something new to him. They talk for some time while they have some cocktails, then the show starts. Luis is the fourth comedian of the night, and though he seems to have a good start, the rest of his routine doesn't make the audience laugh. Luis feels really embarrassed and tells Tomás that they should leave the bar. In another bar nearby, they talk about how busy they have been lately with university schoolwork and decide to get together to do some outdoor activities.

Glosario – Glossary

Ultimamente: lately

Estudia demasiado: he studies too much

No ve a sus amigos desde hace más de un mes: he hasn't seen his friends in over a month

Lo invitó a un show de comedia: he invited him to a comedy show

Por el centro de Bogotá: around downtown Bogotá

Una decoración playera: a beach-style decoration

Colores cálidos: warm colors

Un aroma agradable a agua de playa: a pleasant smell of beach water

Intenta pasarla bien: he tries to have a good time

Y no pensar en todas las cosas que tiene que hacer: and not think about all the things he has to do

Usualmente: he usually

Va al gimnasio: goes to the gym

Al menos: at least

Dos veces a la semana: twice a week

Nunca se pierde su show favorito: he never misses his favorite show

Los viernes en la noche: on Friday nights

En estos días: these days

Está exhausto: he's exhausted

¿Estás nervioso?: are you nervous?

Muchísimo: extremely

¿Invitaste a alguien más?: did you invite anyone else?

Invité a poca gente: I invited few people

No quiero humillarme: I don't want to humiliate myself

Frente a todos los que me conocen: in front of everyone I know

Hacer standup es algo nuevo: doing stand-up is something new

Un pasatiempo: a hobby

Es normal que esté así de nervioso: it's normal for him to be this nervous

Para distraerlo: to distract him

Un viejo amigo de ellos: an old friend of theirs

El bar se queda en silencio: everyone in the bar stays silent

Encienden las luces: they turn on the lights

Escenario: stage

Un sombrero: a hat

Les da las gracias a todos por venir: he thanks everyone for coming

Presenta al primer comediante de la noche: he introduces the first comedian of the night

Va a ser: he's going to be

Los primeros: the first ones

Más o menos entretenidos: more or less entertaining

Chistes: jokes

Se nota porque nadie se ríe: you can tell because no one is laughing

La más graciosa: the funniest

De lentes: with glasses

Su experiencia saliendo con chicos: her experience dating guys

Recibe muchos aplausos: she receives lots of applause

Cuando sale del escenario: when she leaves the stage

Llaman el nombre de Luis: they call Luis's name

Se dirije al escenario: he walks to the stage

Algo sobre ser daltónico: something about being color blind

Personas se ríen: people laugh

Los siguientes: the next ones

No son tan graciosos: aren't that funny

Nadie se ríe: no one laughs

Incluso algunos parecen aburridos: some even seem bored

Siente pena por su amigo: he feels sorry for his friend

Le aplaude para animarlo a que continúe: he claps for him to cheer him on to continue

Absolutamente: absolutely

Con los últimos: with the last ones

Cuando se baja del escenario: when he gets off the stage

Parece bastante avergonzado: he seems pretty embarrassed

Le dice a Tomás que quiere irse: he tells Tomás he wants to leave

Le dice que está bien: he says it's fine

Cercano: nearby

Sé honesto: be honest (imperative)

Apesto, ¿verdad?: I suck, right?

Estuvo bien para ser tu primera vez: it was fine for your first time

Siento que no tengo talento para esto: I feel like I don't have the talent for this

Es normal que no seas perfecto: it's normal not to be perfect

Con el tiempo aprenderás: with time you will learn

Nadie se reía: no one was laughing

Fue gracioso: it was funny

La gente se rió: people were laughing

De ese estilo: of that kind

Tengo que practicar más y escribir más: I have to practice more and write more

No practiqué lo suficiente: I didn't practice enough

No tengo tiempo para nada: I don't have time for anything

Te entiendo: I understand you

Yo estoy igual que tú: I'm the same as you

No hago las cosas que normalmente disfruto: I don't do the things I normally enjoy

Por ejemplo: for example

Todos los sábados: every Saturday

¿Qué tan a menudo haces lo que te gusta?: how often do you do what you enjoy?

Jugar tenis: playing tennis

No tengo mucho tiempo: I don't have much time

Tengo que leer algo: I have to read something

Hacer algo para la carrera: to do something for school (university)

Hacer algo juntos: to do something together

Nos puede ayudar a sentirnos motivados: it can helps us feel motivated

Me gustaría: I would like that

A tomar hasta que olvide lo terrible que me fue: let's drink until I forget how terribly I did

Ejercicio 1

Contesta las siguientes preguntas – answer the following questions

1- ¿Cómo es la decoración del bar? – what's the decoration of the bar like?

_____

2- ¿Qué pide Tomás para tomar? – what does Tomás order to drink?

_____

3- ¿Qué tan seguido Tomás va al gimnasio? – how often does Tomás go to the gym?

_____

4- ¿Por qué Luis no invitó a tanta gente al show? – why didn't Luis invite many people to the show?

5- ¿Cuál es el mejor comediante antes que Luis? – which is the best comedian before Luis?

6- ¿Sobre qué es el primer chiste de Luis? – what's Luis's first joke about?

7- ¿Cómo reacciona el público por los chistes de Luis? – how does the audience react to Luis's jokes?

8- ¿Cómo se siente Luis luego de su turno? – how does Luis feel after his turn?

9- ¿Qué hacen? – what do they do?

10- ¿Qué planean hacer Tomás y Luis? – what do Tomás and Luis plan to do?

Ejercicio 2

Elige entre "verdadero" o "falso" – choose "true" or "false"

1- **Tomás no ve a sus amigos desde hace más de un mes.** – Luis hasn't seen his friends in over a month.

2- **Tomás casi nunca estudia.** – Tomás almost never studies.

3- **Luis pide una cerveza.** – Luis orders a beer.

4- **Luis siempre hace standup.** – Luis always does stand-up.

5- **Luis ve a su amiga Ana muy a menudo.** – Luis sees his friend Ana very often.

6- **Luis es el quinto comediante de la noche.** – Luis is the fifth comedian of the night.

7- **Nadie aplaude a Luis.** – No one claps for Luis.

8- **Tomás le da ánimos a Luis.** – Tomás gives Luis words of encouragement.

9- **Luis está muy ocupado con la universidad.** – Luis is very busy with schoolwork.

10- **Luis no quiere hacer standup nunca más.** – Luis doesn't want to do stand-up ever again.

Respuestas – Answers

Ejercicio 1

1- La decoración del bar es playera, con colores muy cálidos.

2- Tomás pide una piña colada.

3- Tomás va al gimnasio al menos dos veces a la semana.

4- Porque no quiere humillarse frente a todos los que lo conocen.

5- La mejor comediante antes de Luis es una chica de lentes.

6- El primer chiste de Luis es sobre su experiencia siendo daltónico.

7- El público se ríe del primer chiste de Luis, pero no del resto, varios parecen aburridos.

8- Luis se siente muy avergonzado y hasta cree que no tiene talento para la comedia.

9- Luis y Tomás se van del bar porque Luis se siente muy avergonzado y no quiere estar ahí.

10- Luis y Tomás planean salir a trotar al parque mañana domingo.

Ejercicio 2

1- Verdadero

2- Falso

3- Falso

4- Falso

5- Verdadero

6- Falso

7- Falso

8- Verdadero

9- Verdadero

10- Falso

Puntos clave – Key takeaways

- *¿Qué tan seguido...?* and *¿Qué tan a menudo...?* are questions to ask about frequency.
- *Dos veces a la semana* and *Tres veces al día* are more specific ways to talk about frequency than *siempre* or *a veces.*

In the next chapter, you will learn more vocabulary about the city, other ways to use *haber,* and how to ask about quantity.

Chapter 11: De visita en Buenos Aires – Visiting Buenos Aires

---

Un viaje se mide mejor en amigos que en millas.

- Tim Cahill

Sofía viene a Buenos Aires **por primera vez**. Su amiga Daniela vive en la ciudad y **se ofreció a llevarla** a distintos lugares.

Daniela le dice a Sofía que **se puede quedar en su casa**, pero Sofía decide **hospedarse en un hotel**. Ella sabe que Daniela tiene dos compañeras de cuarto y **no quiere ocasionarles ninguna incomodidad**.

Daniela sabe que a Sofía le gusta mucho la historia, así que **planea llevarla** al Cementerio de La Recoleta, **donde algunas personas famosas están enterradas**. En la mañana compran unas medialunas, **que es un tipo de pan dulce típico** en Argentina, y **van a desayunar en** la Plaza del Congreso. El día es **soleado y agradable** y **hay mucha gente a su alrededor desayunando** o **tomando té** y hablando. **Ellas se ponen al día**. Sofía **le cuenta** a Daniela que **pronto se va a mudar a otro país**, quizás Perú, y Daniela le cuenta que también **tiene planes de mudarse**. **Al principio** piensan en **ir caminando al cementerio**, pero **es mejor idea tomar el metro** de la ciudad en la estación de la Avenida Corrientes que **está a solo tres cuadras**. **Abordan el metro** y solo hay un **asiento disponible** que **prefieren cederle a una señora mayor**. Siguen conversando pero **están atentas** de **la estación en la que deben bajarse del metro**, la estación Las Heras.

–**¿Cuántas salidas hay?** –pregunta Sofía.

–**Hay varias salidas** en esta estación.

–**¿Por cuál salimos?**

–**Sígueme**.

Salen de la estación y **siguen su camino al cementerio**. En la entrada del cementerio, en las enormes **rejas de metal**, hay **un grupo de extranjeros hablando en inglés**. Les hacen **un par de preguntas** a Daniela y Sofía y ellas responden **tan bien como pueden**. **Ninguna de las dos habla inglés tan fluido**. El grupo de extranjeros **parece estar esperando a su guía que está un poco atrasado**. Ellas entran al cementerio y **echan un vistazo a su alrededor**. Algunas **capillas** son más modernas que otras, unas **gigantes**, otras pequeñas. Unas parecen **abandonadas**, que **nadie visita en mucho tiempo, lo que a Sofía le parece triste**. Aunque **no hay nadie que la** escuche, Sofía **le pide permiso al espíritu de la persona en la capilla antes de tomar una foto. Junta sus manos como en una oración** y **les da las gracias por permitirle tomar sus fotos**. Ellas **no son las únicas personas** tomando fotos, **especialmente** en **las tumbas de las personas más famosas**, como la tumba de Eva Perón donde hay personas incluso **grabando videos**.

Cuando las chicas **se cansan de caminar** y tomar fotos, van a almorzar unas pizzas en **uno de los lugares favoritos de Daniela**. Sofía le cuenta los planes que tiene, los otros lugares que **quiere visitar** en la ciudad, como **el museo** Malba. Daniela le dice que el museo **no está muy lejos** y que **si quiere la puede llevar**, que ella también **tiene ganas de ver las nuevas exhibiciones** en el museo. Sofía, **encantada**, le dice que sí. **Hablan alrededor de una hora** y toman un autobús hasta Palermo, **donde se encuentra el museo**. Por suerte, **hoy la entrada está a mitad de precio**. A Sofía **le gusta apreciar el arte en silencio** y por un momento **se separa de Daniela**, que **sube al segundo piso** a ver una exhibición distinta. Sofía entra en **una sala enorme** donde exhiben **el trabajo de una fotógrafa chilena** muy **talentosa. Las fotos le parecen bellísimas a Sofía** porque **la conmueven** mucho, y su favorita es una **sobre una relación tóxica**.

Al rato, Sofía y Daniela **se encuentran** en una de las salas.

—**¿Cuántas salas hay en este museo?** —pregunta Sofía.

—No sé, creo que un par.

—**¿Hay más de diez?**

—No, **no hay tantas. Hay pocas,** pero son muy grandes.

Sofía y Daniela **recorren todas las salas** del museo y se van. Sofía le agradece a Daniela **por acompañarla**, y **hacen planes de salir otro día** a un bar **a beber**.

Resumen

Sofía, la amiga de Daniela, viene a Buenos Aires por primera vez y Daniela se ofrece a mostrarle la ciudad. Desayunan medialunas en una plaza y luego visitan el Cementerio de La Recoleta, donde algunas personas famosas están enterradas. Sofía tiene la oportunidad de tomar muchas fotos y aprender sobre el lugar. La última parada es un museo llamado Malba en Palermo, donde Sofía aprecia unas hermosas fotografías de una talentosa fotógrafa. Al final del día, las chicas hacen planes para verse otro día.

Summary

Sofía, Daniela's friend, comes to Buenos Aires for the very first time and Daniela offers to show her the city. They have *medialunas* for breakfast in a square and then they visit the Recoleta Cemetery, where several famous people are buried. Sofía has the opportunity to take loads of pictures and learn about the place. The last stop is a museum called Malba in Palermo, where Sofía sees some beautiful pictures from a talented photographer. At the end of the day, the girls make plans to see each other another day.

Glosario – Glossary

Por primera vez: for the first time

Se ofreció a llevarla: she offered to take her

Se puede quedar en su casa: she can stay at her place

Hospedarse en un hotel: to stay in a hotel

No quiere causarles ninguna incomodidad: she doesn't want to inconvenience them

Planea llevarla a: she plans to take her

Donde algunas personas famosas están enterrada: where some famous people are buried

Que es un tipo de pan dulce: which is a type of pastry

Típico en Argentina: common in Argentina

Van a desayunar en: they go have breakfast in

Soleado y agradable: sunny and nice

Hay mucha gente: there are a lot of people

A su alrededor: around them

Desayunando: having breakfast

Tomando té: drinking tea

Ellas se ponen al día: they catch up

Le cuenta: she tells her

Pronto se va a mudar a otro país: she's going to move to another country soon

Tiene planes de mudarse: she has plans of moving out

Al principio: at the beginning

Ir caminando al cementerio: to walk to the cemetery

Es mejor idea tomar el metro: it's a better idea to take the subway

Está a solo tres cuadras: it's just three blocks away

Abordan el metro: they board the subway

Asiento disponible: seat available

Prefieren cederle a una señora mayor: they prefer to give it up to an older woman

Están atentas: they are alert

La estación en la que deben bajarse del metro: the station in which they have to get off the subway

¿Cuántas salidas hay?: how many exits are there?

Hay varias salidas: there are several exits

¿Por cuál salimos?: which one should we take?

Sígueme: follow me

Siguen su camino al cementerio: they continue their way to the cemetery

Rejas de metal: metal bars

Un grupo de extranjeros: a group of foreigners

Hablando en inglés: speaking English

Un par de preguntas: a couple of questions

Tan bien como pueden: as well as they can

Ninguna de las dos: neither of them

Habla inglés tan fluido: speak English as fluently

Parece estar esperando a su guía: they seem to be waiting for their tour guide

Que está un poco atrasado: who is a little late

Echan un vistazo a su alrededor: they take a look around

Capillas: chapels

Gigantes: huge

Abandonadas: abandoned

Nadie visita en mucho tiempo: no one has visited in a long time

Lo que a Sofía le parece triste: which Sofía finds sad

No hay nadie que la escuche: there's no one who can hear her

Le pide permiso al espíritu de la persona en la capilla: she asks for permission to the spirit of the person in the chapel

Antcs dc tomar una foto: before taking a picture

Junta sus manos como en una oración: she puts her hands together as if in prayer

Les da las gracias: she thanks them

Por permitirle tomar sus fotos: for letting her take her pictures

No son las únicas personas: they're not the only people

Especialmente: especially

Las tumbas de las personas más famosas: the graves of the most famous people

Grabando videos: recording videos

Se cansan de caminar: they get tired of walking

Uno de los lugares favoritos de Daniela: one of Daniela's favorite places

Quiere visitar: she wants to visit

El museo: the museum

No está muy lejos: it's not very far

Si quiere la puede llevar: she can take her there if she wants to

Tiene ganas de ver las nuevas exhibiciones: she wants to see the new exhibitions

Encantada: more than happy

Hablan alrededor de una hora: they talk for about an hour

Donde se encuentra el museo: where the museum is at

Hoy la entrada está a mitad de precio: the ticket is half price today

Le gusta apreciar el arte en silencio: she likes to appreciate art in silence

Se separa de Daniela: she and Daniela split

Sube al segundo piso: she goes up to the second floor

Una sala enorme: a huge room

El trabajo de una fotógrafa chilena: the work of a Chilean photographer

Talentosa: talented

Las fotos le parecen bellísimas a Sofía: Sofía thinks the pictures are really beautiful

La conmueven: they move her

Sobre una relación tóxica: about a toxic relationship

Al rato: later

Se encuentran: they meet

¿Cuántas salas hay en este museo?: how many rooms are there in this museum?

¿Hay más de diez?: are there more than ten?

No hay tantas: there aren't that many

Hay pocas: there are a few

Recorren todas las salas: they go through all the rooms

Por acompañarla: for coming with her

Hacen planes de salir otro día: they make plans to go out another day

A beber: to drink

Ejercicio 1

Contesta las siguientes preguntas – answer the following questions

1- ¿Por qué Sofía no se queda con Daniela? – why isn't Sofía staying with Daniela?

_____

2- ¿Qué desayunan? – what do they have for breakfast?

_____

3- ¿Qué le cuenta Sofía a Daniela? – what does Sofía tell Daniela?

_____

4- ¿Cómo van al cementerio? – how do they go to the cemetery?

_____

5- ¿En qué estación se bajan? – at what station do they get off?

_____

6- ¿A quién se encuentran en la entrada del cementerio? – who do they meet at the entrance of the cemetery?

_____

7- ¿Qué hace Sofía antes de tomar fotos en las capillas? – what does Sofía do before taking pictures in the chapels?

8- ¿Las entradas del museo son costosas? – are the tickets to the museum expensive?

9- ¿Por qué a Sofía le encantan tanto las fotos en el museo? – why does Sofía like the pictures in the museum so much?

10- ¿Qué planean hacer otro día? – what do they plan to do another day?

Ejercicio 2

Elige entre "verdadero" o "falso" – choose "true" or "false"

1- Sofía se hospeda en un hotel. – Sofía is staying in a hotel.

2- Ellas desayunan en una cafetería. – They have breakfast at a coffee shop.

3- Ellas van al cementerio en autobús. – They go to the cemetery by bus.

4- Ellas le ceden su puesto a una señora mayor. – They give up their seat to an older lady.

5- Los extranjeros hablan francés. – The foreigners speak French.

6- Todas las capillas son muy similares. – All the chapels are very similar.

7- El museo queda en Palermo. – The museum is in Palermo.

8- La fotógrafa es argentina. – The photographer is Argentinian.

9- Hay pocas salas en el museo. – There are just a few rooms in the museum.

10- Ellas hacen planes de ir a cenar. – They make plans to go out for dinner.

Respuestas – Answers

Ejercicio 1

1- Sofía no se queda con Daniela porque sabe que ella tiene dos compañeras de cuarto y no quiere causarles incomodidades.

2- Sofía y Daniela desayunan medialunas.

3- Sofía le cuenta a Daniela que piensa mudarse a otro país, quizás Perú.

4- Sofía y Daniela van al cementerio en el metro de la ciudad.

5- Sofía y Daniela se bajan en la estación Las Heras.

6- Sofía y Daniela se encuentran a unos extranjeros en la entrada del cementerio.

7- Sofía les pide permiso a los espíritus en las capillas antes de tomar una foto.

8- No, las entradas del museo están a mitad de precio hoy.

9- A Sofía le encantan las fotos en el museo porque la conmueven mucho.

10- Sofía y Daniela planean salir a un bar a beber otro día.

Ejercicio 2

1- Verdadero

2- Falso

3- Falso

4- Verdadero

5- Falso

6- Falso

7- Verdadero

8- Falso

9- Verdadero

10- Falso

Puntos clave – Key takeaways

- *¿Cuántos...?* and *¿Cuántas...?* are used with countable nouns.
- *¿Cuánto...?* and *¿Cuánta...?* are used with uncountable nouns.
- *Tantas* and *pocas* are examples of quantifiers, which we can use to give an approximate amount of something.

In the next chapter, you will learn how to ask and talk about the weather in detail.

Chapter 12: A la playa – Going to the beach

Un buen viajante no tiene planes.

- Confucio

Tomás y sus amigos **van a ir a la playa** este viernes **aprovechando que es un fin de semana largo.** Todos se levantan muy temprano la mañana del viernes y **se encuentran en la terminal de autobuses** donde un autobús enorme **los espera para llevarlos** a la playa. Luis, el amigo de Tomás, **alquiló el autobús por el día, lo que es un poco caro** pero **es posible pagarlo entre todos.** El autobús **arranca** a las 6 de la mañana **para evitar el tráfico** y **llegar a la playa antes de las 8. Entre Tomás y sus amigos, hay alrededor de dieciséis personas** en el autobús. Algunos son **compañeros de clases,** otros **amigos que estudian otras carreras.** Algunos **toman una siesta** antes de llegar a la playa, otros **empiezan a tomar cervezas** o **comer alguna chuchería.** El viaje a la playa **es tranquilo, no hay mucho tráfico** y **el cielo está despejado. Es un día perfecto** para ir a la playa.

El autobús **los deja cerca de un local donde venden sándwiches y empanadas.** Los chicos desayunan y luego van **al puerto** donde **se montan en unas lanchas** para ir a **la isla donde queda la playa.** Algunos **no quieren montarse en las lanchas** porque **les da miedo caerse al agua,** pero **es la única forma de llegar a la isla. Las olas sacuden el bote** y **unas chicas gritan mientras que otros se ríen** o sacan fotos y videos. **Todos llegan bien a la isla,** aunque Tomás **se siente un poco mareado.** Piensa que desayunar y montarse en la lancha **no fue una buena idea.**

Son aproximadamente las 8 de la mañana y la playa **comienza a llenarse de gente.** Los chicos **dejan sus cosas en un lugar que reservaron** donde hay **sillas playeras** y **paraguas** muy grandes **para cuidarlos del sol.** Todos **se desvisten,** quedándose en shorts o **trajes de baño, se ayudan a colocarse protector solar para no quemarse,** y luego corren al agua. La playa es hermosa, con **arena marrón clara** y **el agua es cristalina,** parece agua de **pecera.** La gente juega en el agua, con las olas, se toman fotos, juegan con **pelotas playeras,** y hasta juegan **excavando hoyos en la arena.**

Un par de horas más tarde, el cielo se nubla un poco. **Hace algo de frío.** Los chicos salen del agua y vuelven al lugar donde están sus cosas. **Hace viento** y a los minutos **comienza a llover.**

–**¿Cuántos grados hace?** –pregunta uno de los chicos.

338

–**Hace 19 grados** –responde Tomás.

–**¿Va a llover todo el día? Yo veo relámpagos.**

–No, yo creo que **es temporal. Tenemos que esperar.**

–Pero **es raro, en un momento hace buen tiempo** y **el cielo está claro**, y **luego el cielo se oscurece de repente**, y **no es temporada de lluvia. ¿Y si hay neblina o comienza a caer granizo?**

–**Estás exagerando, eso no va a pasar.**

Los chicos hablan, beben y **juegan cartas para pasar el rato. Tienen la esperanza de que el tiempo mejore** ya que en la tarde **tienen que volver al autobús que los llevará a casa.** Luis siempre **pierde jugando este tipo de juegos de beber** y **termina borracho primero que los demás.** Se ríe mucho y **dice cosas graciosas.** Quiere ir al agua **a pesar de la lluvia** y los demás **no lo dejan** porque **les parece peligroso.**

–**¿Estás loco? ¿Y si te ahogas?** –dice Tomás.

Todos siguen jugando y **pasándola bien.** A eso de las 2 de la tarde **deja de llover** y **sale el sol.** Los chicos almuerzan **pescado frito** y **esperan a que haga más sol** para ir al agua. Luis **se queda dormido** en una silla **mientras los demás se divierten** en el agua. **Lo despiertan cuando es hora de irse.** Luis **siente un poco de pena por embriagarse** pero cuando se montan en el autobús **ya no es el único ebrio.** Todos siguen tomando y escuchando música **todo el camino de vuelta. El conductor del autobús hace una parada** en una **gasolinera** porque algunos chicos **tienen ganas de vomitar. Les toma un par de horas** llegar a casa porque hay mucho tráfico ya que a esta hora **todos vuelven a casa de la playa. A pesar de todo,** los chicos se divierten mucho y le agradecen a Luis por **organizar la salida** y alquilar el autobús.

Resumen

Tomás y sus amigos se van a la playa en un autobús el viernes en la mañana. El autobús los deja en un puerto donde deben tomar unas lanchas para llegar a la isla. Disfrutan del sol y el agua durante un par de horas hasta que el cielo se oscurece y comienza a llover. Los chicos toman cervezas y juegan cartas para pasar el tiempo. Luis toma mucho y se emborracha. Cuando el cielo se despeja, él se queda dormido en una de las sillas mientras los demás se divierten. En la tarde vuelven al autobús. Varios chicos toman demasiado y tienen que hacer una parada en una gasolinera para que ellos puedan vomitar. A pesar de todo eso, Tomás y sus amigos la pasan muy bien.

Summary

Tomás and his friends go to the beach on a bus on Friday morning. The bus drops them off at the port, where they have to take some boats to get to the island. They enjoy the sun and the water for a couple of hours until the sky goes dark and it starts raining. The guys have some beers and play cards to kill time. Luis drinks a lot and gets drunk. When it stops raining, he falls asleep in one of the chairs while the rest have fun. They get back on the bus in the afternoon. Some of them drink too much and they have to make a stop at a gas station so that they can throw up. In spite of it all, Tomás and his friends have a really good time.

Glosario – Glossary

Van a ir a la playa: they're going to go to the beach

Aprovechando que es un fin de semana largo: taking advantage of the fact that it is a long weekend

Se encuentran en la terminal de autobuses: they meet at the bus terminal

Los espera para llevarlos: it waits for them to take them there

Alquiló el autobús por el día: he rented the bus for the day

Lo que es un poco caro: which is a little expensive

Es posible pagarlo entre todos: it's possible to pay for it together

Arranca: it takes off

Evitar el tráfico: to avoid traffic

Llegar a la playa antes de las 8: to arrive at the beach before 8

Entre Tomás y sus amigos: between Tomás and his friends

Hay alrededor de dieciséis personas: there are around sixteen people

Compañeros de clases: classmates

Amigos que estudian otras carreras: friends that study other majors

Toman una siesta: they take a nap

Empiezan a tomar: they start drinking

Comer chucherías: to eat snacks

Es tranquilo: it's quiet

No hay mucho tráfico: there isn't much traffic

El cielo está despejado: the sky is clear

Es un día perfecto: it's a perfect day

Los deja cerca de un local donde venden sándwiches y empanadas: it drops them off near a place where they sell sandwiches and empanadas

El puerto: the port

Se montan en unas lanchas: they get on some boats

La isla donde queda la playa: the island where the beach is located

No quieren montarse en las lanchas: they don't want to get on the boats

Les da miedo caerse al agua: they're afraid of falling into the water

Es la única forma de llegar a la isla: it's the only way to get to the island

Las olas sacuden el bote: the waves rock the boat

Unas chicas gritan: some girls scream

Mientras otros se ríen: while others laugh

Todos llegan bien a la isla: they all make it to the island just fine

Se siente un poco mareado: he feels a little dizzy

No fue una buena idea: it wasn't a good idea

Comienza a llenarse de gente: it starts to fill up with people

Dejan sus cosas en un lugar que reservaron: they leave their things in a place they reserved

Sillas playeras: beach chairs

Paraguas: umbrellas

Para cuidarlos del sol: to shield them from the sun

Se desvisten: they undress

Trajes de baño: bathing suits

Se ayudan a colocarse protector solar: they help each other put on sunscreen

Para no quemarse: to not get sunburned

Arena marrón clara: light-brown sand

El agua es cristalina: the water is crystal clear

Pecera: fish tank

Pelotas playeras: beach balls

Escavando hoyos en la arena: digging holes in the sand

Un par de horas más tarde: a couple of hours later

El cielo se nubla: it gets cloudy

Hace un poco de frío: it's a little cold

Hace viento: it's windy

Comienza a llover: it starts raining

¿Cuántos grados hace?: what's the temperature?

Hace 19 grados: it's 19 degrees

¿Va a llover todo el día?: is it going to rain all day?

Yo veo relámpagos: I see lightning

Es temporal: it's temporary

Tenemos que esperar: we have to wait

Es raro: it's strange

En un momento hace buen tiempo: one moment the weather's fine

El cielo está claro: the sky is clear

Luego el cielo se oscurece de repente: then the sky gets dark all of a sudden

No es temporada de lluvia: it's not rainy season

¿Y si hay neblina o comienza a caer granizo?: what if there's mist or it starts to hail?

Estás exagerando: you're overreacting

Eso no va a pasar: that's not going to happen

Juegan cartas para pasar el rato: they play with cards to pass the time

Tienen la esperanza de que el tiempo mejore: they have hopes that the weather will improve

Tienen que volver al autobús que los llevará a casa: they have to get back on the bus that will take them home

Pierde jugando este tipo de juegos de beber: he loses playing these kinds of drinking games

Termina borracho primero que los demás: he ends up drunk before anyone else

Dice cosas graciosas: he says funny things

A pesar de la lluvia: despite the rain

No lo dejan: they don't let him

Les parece peligroso: they think it's dangerous

¿Estás loco?: are you insane?

¿Y si te ahogas?: what if you drown?

Pasándola bien: having a good time

Deja de llover: it stops raining

Sale el sol: the sun comes out

Pescado frito: fried fish

Esperan a que haga más sol: they wait for it to be sunnier

Se queda dormido: he falls asleep

Mientras los demás se divierten: while the rest have fun

Lo despiertan cuando es hora de irse: they wake him up when it's time to leave

Siente pena por embriagarse: he feels embarrassed for getting drunk

Ya no es el único ebrio: he's not the only one drunk anymore

Todo el camino de vuelta: all the way back

El conductor del autobús hace una parada: the bus driver makes a stop

Gasolinera: gas station

Tienen ganas de vomitar: they feel like throwing up

Les toma un par de horas: it takes them a couple of hours

Todos vuelven a casa: they're all going back home

A pesar de todo: in spite of everything

Organizar la salida: organizing the trip

Ejercicio 1

Contesta las siguientes preguntas – answer the following questions

1- **¿Por qué van a la playa un viernes en la mañana?** – why are they going to the beach on a Friday morning?

2- ¿A qué hora arranca el autobús? – what time does the bus leave?

3- ¿Cuántas personas hay en el autobús? – how many people are there in the bus?

4- ¿Por qué a algunos les da miedo montarse en las lanchas? – why are some of them afraid of getting on the boat?

5- ¿Cómo es la playa? – what's the beach like?

6- ¿Qué hace la gente alrededor? – what do the people around them do?

7- ¿Por qué los chicos salen del agua? – why do the guys get out of the water?

8- ¿Por qué Luis termina borracho primero? – why does Luis end up drunk first?

9- ¿A qué hora vuelven a entrar al agua? – what time do they get back in the water?

10- ¿Por qué se detienen en una gasolinera? – why do they stop at a gas station?

Ejercicio 2

Elige entre "verdadero" o "falso" – choose "true" or "false"

1- Los chicos se encuentran en casa de Tomás para salir a la playa. – They guys meet at Tomás's house to leave for the beach.

2- Tomás alquila un autobús para que los lleve a la playa. – Tomás rents a bus to take them to the beach.

3- Tomás se marea en la lancha. – Tomás gets seasick on the boat.

4- No hay casi gente en la playa. – There aren't that many people on the beach.

5- Los chicos se meten al agua a pesar de la lluvia. – The guys get in the water despite the rain.

6- Todos almuerzan pescado frito. – Everyone has fried fish for lunch.

7- **Luis se queda dormido en una silla.** – Luis falls asleep on a chair.

8- **Luis vomita en el autobús.** – Luis throws up on the bus.

9- **Hay mucho tráfico en el camino de vuelta a casa.** – There's a lot of traffic on the way back home.

10- **Todos le agradecen a Luis por organizar todo.** – They all say thank you to Luis for organizing everything.

Respuestas – Answers

Ejercicio 1

1- Van a la playa un viernes en la mañana porque aprovechan que es un fin de semana largo.

2- El autobús arranca a las 6 de la mañana.

3- Hay alrededor de 16 personas en el autobús.

4- A algunos les da miedo montarse en las lanchas porque no quieren caer al agua.

5- La playa es hermosa, con arena marrón clara y agua cristalina.

6- La gente alrededor juega en el agua, se toman fotos, juegan con pelotas playeras y hasta excavan huecos en la arena.

7- Los chicos salen del agua porque comienza a hacer frío y a llover.

8- Luis termina borracho primero porque siempre pierde jugando juegos de beber.

9- Los chicos vuelven a entrar al agua a eso de las 2 de la tarde que el clima mejora.

10- Se detienen en una gasolinera porque algunos de los chicos tienen ganas de vomitar.

Ejercicio 2

1- Falso

2- Falso

3- Verdadero

4- Falso

5- Falso

6- Verdadero

7- Verdadero

8- Falso

9- Verdadero

10- Verdadero

Puntos clave – Key takeaways

- The verb *hacer* is used impersonally to talk about weather (*Hace frío* = it's cold).
- *¿Cómo está el clima?* is how you ask about the weather.
- *¿Cómo está la temperatura?*, *¿Cuántos grados hace?* and *¿A cuántos grados estamos?* are ways to ask about the temperature.
- *Hace 20 grados* and *estamos a 20 grados* are ways to answer those questions.

In the next chapter, you will learn vocabulary about the hair, how to use reciprocal pronouns, and other reflexive verbs.

Chapter 13: Un nuevo look – A new look

Por sobre la oreja fina baja lujoso el cabello, lo mismo que una cortina que se levanta hacia el cuello.

- José Martí

Marisol y su hermana **tienen cita hoy en la peluquería** Las Cuatro Rosas **para cortarse el cabello**. Marisol **está un poco aburrida de su cabello** y **quiere probar algo nuevo pero aún no sabe qué**. Ella **espera que en la peluquería se le ocurra algo**. Marisol y su hermana llegan a la peluquería a las 3 de la tarde, justo a tiempo para sus citas, pero **sus peluqueras de confianza** están ocupadas así que **tienen que esperar un rato**. Se sientan en las sillas a esperar. Marisol **le da una ojeada a las revistas de chismes** pero son muy viejas, **de hace más de quince años**, así que prefiere hablar con su hermana.

–**¿Qué te pasó en la mano?** –pregunta Marisol.

–**No es nada. Me quemé** –responde su hermana.

–**¿No te duele?**

–No, ya no.

–**Eres muy descuidada.**

–**Mira quién habla. Tú te cortas todo el tiempo** cuando cocinas.

–Sí, tienes razón.

–Y **cada tanto te caes caminando en la calle.**

–Sí, ya, **yo soy descuidada como tú.**

La peluquera de Marisol **se desocupa** y la lleva al **lavabo de cabello** para **aplicarle champú**. El agua es **tibia** y agradable. La chica **le masajea el cabello** con **movimientos circulares** y Marisol se siente muy relajada. El champú **huele a coco** y a Marisol le encanta, le pregunta a la chica el nombre del champú **para comprarlo**. Después del lavado, la chica **envuelve el cabello de Marisol en una toalla** y la lleva a **su estación para proceder a cortarle el cabello**.

–**¿Qué te quieres hacer en el pelo?** –pregunta la chica.

–**La verdad**, no sé. Quiero algo diferente.

–¿Quieres **un peinado diferente** o quieres **otro color**?

–**Quiero que me cortes las puntas** y quiero otro color. Ya **estoy aburrida del rubio.**

−¿Qué te parece en negro?

−No lo sé.

La chica **le da un catálogo con varios colores** a Marisol **para que se decida qué color quiere**, o si prefiere **el mismo** color. **Mientras tanto**, comienza a **cortarle las puntas** con **una tijera profesional**. La hermana de Marisol se sienta en la silla de al lado y **le da su opinión sobre qué color sería mejor**.

−**¿Sabes qué? Escoge tú un color** −dice Marisol.

−**¿Segura?** −responde la peluquera.

−Sí, **sorpréndeme.**

Marisol **se ve en el espejo** una vez más y, **en su mente, se despide del rubio** en su cabello.

−Yo a veces **me corto el cabello yo misma** −dice la hermana de Marisol.

−**¿Tú misma? ¿Por qué haces eso?** −dice Marisol.

−**Lo hago** cuando tengo las puntas muy **dañadas**, **secas**, y **no tengo tiempo** para ir a la peluquería.

−**Qué locura**.

−Antes **nos cortábamos el cabello la una a la otra. ¿No te acuerdas?**

−**Eso fue hace muchos años.**

−**Tú tenías otra peluquera antes**, ¿no? **¿Qué pasó?**

−**No nos vemos desde que se mudó a Madrid.**

−**Ay, qué mal**. Pero tu nueva peluquera es **excelente.**

−**Así es.**

La chica **le aplica el colorante** a Marisol, luego **le seca el cabello**. **Cuando está listo**, le dice a Marisol que se mire en el espejo. Su cabello es **rojo** ahora.

−**¿Te gusta?** −pregunta la peluquera.

−Me encanta. **Me gusta como me veo pelirroja.**

−**¿Quieres que te haga las uñas también?**

−Sí, **yo no sé pintarme las uñas.**

−**¿Qué pintura quieres?**

−**Rosado,** o quizás rojo **para que combine con el cabello.**

Marisol y su hermana salen de la peluquería **luego de cuatro horas**.

−**¿En serio te gustó?** −pregunta la hermana de Marisol.

−No, **lo odio, me quedó horrible.**

−**¿Por qué no dijiste nada?**

−No sé, **entré en pánico. ¿Se ve muy mal?**

−**Al menos a mí me gusta mi nuevo corte.**

Marisol **se arrepiente de pintarse el cabello**. Ahora **extraña** su color rubio.

Resumen

Marisol y su hermana tienen una cita en la peluquería Las Cuatro Rosas a las 3 de la tarde. Marisol está cansada de tener el cabello rubio, pero no está segura de qué se quiere hacer. Ella espera que en la peluquería se le ocurra algo. Marisol espera un rato a que su peluquera esté desocupada, luego ella le lava el cabello y le corta las puntas. Marisol sigue indecisa sobre el color, así que lo deja en las manos de su peluquera. Marisol le dice a su peluquera que le encantó el nuevo color, pero al salir de la peluquería le dice a su hermana la verdad: odia su nuevo color y se arrepiente de pintarse el cabello de rojo.

Summary

Marisol and her sister have an appointment at the salon *Las Cuatro Rosas* at 3 in the afternoon. Marisol is tired of having blonde hair but she's not sure what she wants. She hopes that she will come up with something at the salon. Marisol waits for her hair stylist to be available, then she washes Marisol's hair and trims her ends. Marisol is still unsure about the color, so she leaves it in her stylist's hands. Marisol tells her stylis that she liked the new color, but when they leave the salon, she tells her sister the truth: she hates the new color and she regrets dying her hair red.

Glosario – Glossary

Tienen una cita hoy en la peluquería: they have an appointment at the hair salón today

Para cortarse el cabello: to get a haircut

Está un poco aburrida de su cabello: she's a little bored of her hair

Quiere probar algo nuevo: she wants to try something new

Pero aún no sabe qué: but she doesn't know what yet

Espera que en la peluquería se le ocurra algo: she hopes she will come up with something at the salon

Sus peluqueras de confianza: the hair stylist they like

Tienen que esperar un rato: they have to wait for a while

Le da una ojeada a: she takes a look at

Las revistas de chismes: the gossip magazines

De hace más de quince años: from more than fifteen years ago

¿Qué te pasó en la mano?: what happened to your hand?

No es nada: it's nothing

Me quemé: I burned myself

¿No te duele?: doesn't it hurt?

Ya no: not anymore

Eres muy descuidada: you're so clumsy

Mira quién habla: look who's talking

Tú te cortas todo el tiempo: you cut yourself all the time

Cada tanto: every now and then

Te caes caminando en la calle: you fall on the street while walking

Yo soy descuidada como tú: I'm clumsy like you

Se desocupa: she is available

Lavabo de cabello: hair basin

Aplicarle champú: to apply shampoo on her hair

Tibia: lukewarm

Le masajea el cabello: she massages her hair

Movimientos circulares: circular movements

Huele a coco: it smells like coconut

Para comprarlo: to buy it

Envuelve el cabello de Marisol en una toalla: she wraps Marisol's hair in a towel

Su estación: her station

Para proceder a cortarle el cabello: to proceed to cut her hair

¿Qué te quieres hacer en el pelo?: what do you want for your hair?

La verdad: honestly

Un peinado diferente: a different hair style

Otro color: another color

Quiero que me cortes las puntas: I want you to trim my ends

Estoy aborrida del rubio: I'm bored of the blonde hair

¿Qué te parece negro?: what do you think about black?

Le da un catálogo de varios colores: she gives her a catalog with several colors

Para que se decida qué color quiere: so she can decide what color she wants

El mismo: the same

Mientras tanto: meanwhile

Cortarle las puntas: to trim her ends

Una tijera profesional: professional scissors

Le da su opinión sobre qué color sería mejor: she tells her which color she thinks will be best

¿Sabes qué?: you know what?

Escoge tú: you choose

¿Segura?: are you sure?

Sorpréndeme: surprise me

Se ve en el espejo: she looks at herself in the mirror

En su mente: in her mind

Se despide del rubio: she says goodbye to the blonde

Me corto el cabello yo misma: I cut my own hair

¿Tú misma?: on your own?

¿Por qué haces eso?: why do you do that?

Lo hago: I do it

Dañadas: damaged

Secas: dry

No tengo tiempo: I don't have time

Qué locura: that's insane

Nos cortábamos el cabello la una a la otra: we used to cut each other's hair

¿No te acuerdas?: don't you remember?

Eso fue hace muchos años: that was many years ago

Tú tenías otra peluquera antes: you used to have another hair stylist

¿Qué pasó?: what happened?

No nos vemos desde que se mudó a Madrid: we haven't seen each other since she moved to Madrid

Ay, qué mal: that's too bad

Excelente: excellent

Así es: that's right

Le aplica el colorante: she applies the hair dye

Le seca el cabello: she blow-dries her hair

Cuando está listo: when it's done

Rojo: red

¿Te gusta?: do you like it?

Me gusta como me veo pelirroja: I like how I look as a readhead

¿Quieres que te haga las uñas también?: do you want me to do your nails too?

Yo no sé pintarme las uñas: I don't know how to do my nails

¿Qué pintura quieres?: what nail polish do you want?

Rosado: pink

Para que combine con el cabello: so it matches my hair

Luego de cuatro horas: after four hours

¿En serio te gustó?: did you really like it?

Lo odio: I hate it

Me quedó horrible: it looks horrible

¿Por qué no dijiste nada?: why didn't you say anything?

Entré en pánico: I panicked

¿Se ve muy mal?: does it look that bad?

Al menos: at least

A mí me gusta mi corte: I like my new haircut

Se arrepiente de pintarse el cabello: she regrets dying her hair

Extraña: she misses

Ejercicio 1

Contesta las siguientes preguntas – answer the following questions

1- **¿Por qué Marisol quiere un nuevo look?** – why does Marisol want a new look?

_____

2- **¿A qué hora es la cita de Marisol en la peluquería?** – what time is Marisol's appointment at the hair salon?

_____

3- **¿Qué tan viejas son las revistas?** – how old are the magazines?

_____

4- **¿Por qué Marisol es descuidada?** – why is Marisol clumsy?

_____

5- **¿A qué huele el champú?** – what does the shampoo smell like?

_____

6- **¿Qué quiere Marisol que le hagan?** – what does Marisol want to get done?

_____

7- **¿Por qué la hermana de Marisol se corta el cabello ella misma?** – why does Marisol's sister cut her own hair?

_____

8- **¿Qué pasó con la peluquera anterior de Marisol?** – what happened to Marisol's previous hair stylist?

_____

9- **¿De qué color le pintan el pelo a Marisol?** – what color do they dye Marisol's hair?

_____

10- **¿Cuánto tiempo pasan en la peluquería?** – how long do they stay at the hair salon?

_____

Ejercicio 2

Elige entre "verdadero" o "falso" – choose "true" or "false"

1- **La peluquería se llama Las Cuatro Hermanas.** – The hair salon is called The Four Sisters.

_____

2- **Marisol se corta el cabello con alguien que no conoce.** – Marisol gets a haircut from someone she doesn't know.

3- **La hermana de Marisol se quemó la mano.** – Marisol's sister burned her hand.

4- **El lavado de cabello es relajante.** – The hair wash is relaxing.

5- **Marisol tiene el cabello negro actuamente.** – Marisol currently has black hair.

6- **La hermana de Marisol escoge un color nuevo para ella.** – Marisol's sister chooses a new color for her.

7- **Marisol se corta el cabello ella misma.** – Marisol cuts her own hair.

8- **A Marisol le encanta el nuevo color.** – Marisol loves the new color.

9- **Marisol también se hace las uñas.** – Marisol also gets her nails done.

10- **A la hermana de Marisol no le gusta su corte.** – Marisol's sister doesn't like her own haircut.

Respuestas – Answers

Ejercicio 1

1- Marisol quiere un nuevo look porque está aburrida de su cabello rubio.

2- La cita de Marisol es a las 3 de la tarde.

3- Las revistas son de hace más de quince años.

4- Marisol es descuidada porque se corta todo el tiempo cuando cocina y también se cae en la calle.

5- El champú huele a coco.

6- Marisol quiere que le corten las puntas del cabello y quiere otro color.

7- La hermana de Marisol se corta el cabello ella misma porque a veces tiene las puntas dañadas y no tiene tiempo de ir a la peluquería.

8- La peluquera anterior de Marisol se mudó a Madrid.

9- A Marisol le pintan el cabello de rojo.

10- Marisol y su hermana pasan cuatro horas en la peluquería.

Ejercicio 2

1- Falso

2- Falso

3- Verdadero

4- Verdadero

5- Falso

6- Falso

7- Falso

8- Falso

9- Verdadero

10- Falso

Puntos clave – Key takeaways

- There are only two reciprocal pronouns (*se, nos*).
- Reciprocal pronouns and reflexive pronouns can be often confused since two of them are the same (se, nos). We need to pay attention to the context to see which they are referring to.
- *Querer* has five different conjugations (*quiero, quieres, quiere, queremos, quieren*).
- *Querer* can be followed by another verb (*¿Qué quieres hacer?* = What do you want to do?).
- *Querer* is one of the most common irregular verbs.

In the next chapter, you will learn more about irregular verbs.

Chapter 14: El escape room – The escape room

❦

El miedo es natural en el prudente, y el saberlo vencer es ser valiente.

- Alonso de Ercilla y Zúñiga

Tomás y sus amigos van a un escape room el sábado a las 6 de la tarde. Tomás está muy emocionado porque **es su primera vez** en un escape room. Su amigo Luis, **por otra parte**, está nervioso porque es un poco **claustrofóbico, pero igual quiere atreverse** y **vivir la aventura. La chica que recibe a Tomás** y sus cuatro amigos **les cuenta** que hay tres salas diferentes **para escoger.** La primera sala **simula un hospital de noche,** la segunda es **una casa embrujada** y la tercera sala, **que es la más difícil, simula un avión que está a punto de estrellar. Después de pensarlo unos minutos,** los chicos deciden probar la tercera sala **porque les gusta el reto. Pagan por sus entradas** y **dejan sus teléfonos, mochilas y carteras** en un locker **afuera de la sala. No saben por qué tienen que hacerlo,** pero **es la única regla que hay.**

Dentro de la sala, la chica **les da las instrucciones.** Les dice que **tienen una hora para salir** de la sala, y **les entrega** un walkie-talkie **para que le pidan pistas si lo necesitan.** También les habla sobre **el botón de emergencia** que **deben presionar en caso de que suceda algo.** La chica cierra la puerta, **el reloj marca una hora** y **comienza la cuenta regresiva. Apagan las luces.** Todos **comienzan a buscar en todos lados, debajo de los asientos, dentro de las maletas.** Solo tienen **una linterna** así que **el proceso es lento y frustrante.** Una chica encuentra **la primera pista** en **un periódico: números subrayados.** Esto le parece **una especie de combinación.** Tomás **introduce** el número en **un teclado** al lado de una puerta y se abre. Pasan a una pequeña habitación con un enorme **mapa** y **fotos en la pared.** La luz roja **hace que sea más fácil ver.**

Luego, Tomás **se da cuenta de que Luis está bastante pálido.**

–**¿Estás bien?** –pregunta Tomás.

–**Me siento mareado, como que me falta el aire** –responde Luis.

–**¿Quieres irte?**

–No, **acabamos de empezar.**

–**¿Seguro?**

–Sí, **no te preocupes.**

Los chicos **siguen resolviendo los acertijos**. Tomás **organiza los números de los asientos en el orden correcto** y **encuentra la contraseña** para **una pequeña caja fuerte**. Dentro de la caja fuerte hay **una llave dorada**. Tomás **la prueba en la única puerta cerrada que queda** pero **no se abre. Cuando está hablando con la chica** en el walkie-talkie, **Luis se desmaya.**

Todos se alarman. Tocan el botón de emergencia y la chica **rápidamente abre la puerta** y salen de la habitación **llevando a Luis por los hombros.** Luis está muy pálido pero **reacciona cuando llaman su nombre. Abre los ojos. Parece no recordar lo que pasó.** Le dan algo de agua y un chocolate **para subirle el nivel de azúcar.**

–¿**Cómo me desmayé?**

–**Desmayándote** –responde Luis.

–**No me acuerdo de nada.**

Después de pasar un poco el susto y **asegurarse de que Luis está bien,** los chicos se van a un café a hablar.

–**Nos mataste del susto** –dice Tomás.

–**Perdón por arruinar la diversión.**

–**No pasa nada. Lo importante es que estás bien. Igual esa sala era muy fácil, me estaba aburriendo. Tú hiciste las cosas más interesantes.**

–**No me hagas reír que me duele un poco la cabeza.**

–**Claro que te duele. Te pegaste en la cabeza con el piso ¿Seguro que no quieres ir al hospital?**

–No, estoy bien. **La próxima vez vamos a un lugar al aire libre.**

Resumen

Tomás y sus amigos deciden pasar un día distinto en un escape room. Tomás en particular está entusiasmado porque es la primera vez que va a uno, mientras que Luis está un poco nervioso por su claustrofobia. Las empleadas los reciben amablemente y les explican todo sobre las salas disponibles y las reglas. Los chicos escogen la tercera sala, una simulación de un avión a punto de estallar. Trabajando en equipo, encuentran diversas pistas y avanzan bastante hasta que Luis se comienza a sentir mal y termina desmayándose. Todos se asustan y lo sacan de la sala, pero al rato Luis se siente mejor y eso es todo lo que importa.

Summary

Tomás and his friend decide to spend a different day at an escape room. Tomás is particularly excited since this is his first time going to one, while Luis is a little nervous because of his claustrophobia. The employees welcome them kindly and explain everything about the rooms available as well as the rules. The guys choose the third room, a simulation of a plane about to explode. Working as a team, they find several clues and get pretty far until Luis starts feeling sick and ends up fainting. They all get scared and take him out of the room, but after a while he feels better and that's all that matters.

Glosario – Glossary

Es su primera vez: it's his first time

Por otra parte: on the other hand

Claustrofóbico: claustrophobic

Pero igual quiere atreverse: but he wants to dare to do it anyway

Vivir la aventura: to live the adventure

La chica que recibe a Tomás: the girl who welcomes Tomás

Les cuenta: tells them

Para escoger: to choose from

Simula un hospital de noche: it simulates a hospital at night

Una casa embrujada: a haunted house

Que es la más difícil: which is the most difficult one

Simula un avión que está a punto de estallar: it simulates a plane that's about to explode

Porque les gusta el reto: because they like a challenge

Pagan por sus entradas: they pay for their tickets

Dejan sus teléfonos, mochilas y carteras: they leave their phones, backpacks and purses

Afuera de la sala: outside of the room

No saben por qué tienen que hacerlo: they don't know why they have to do it

Es la única regla que hay: it's the only rule there is

Dentro de la sala: inside the room

Le da las instrucciones: she gives them instructions

Tienen una hora para salir: they have an hour to get out

Les entrega: she gives them

Para que le pidan pistas si lo necesitan: so they can ask for clues if they need to

El botón de emergencia: the emergency button

Deben presionar en caso de que suceda algo: they must press it if anything goes wrong

El reloj marca una hora: there's one hour on the clock

Comienza la cuenta regresiva: the countdown starts

Apagan las luces: they turn off the lights

Comienzan a buscar en todos lados: they start looking everywhere

Debajo de los asientos: under the seats

Dentro de las maletas: inside the suitcases

Una linterna: a flashlight

El proceso es lento y frustrante: the process is slow and frustrating

La primera pista: the first clue

Un periódico: a newspaper

Números subrayados: highlighted numbers

Una especie de combinación: some kind of combination

Introducir: put

Un teclado: a keyboard

Mapa: map

Fotos en la pared: pictures on the wall

Hace que sea más fácil ver: it makes it easier to see

Se da cuenta de que Luis está pálido: he notices Luis looks pale

¿Estás bien?: are you okay?

Me siento mareado: I feel dizzy

Como que me falta el aire: like I'm out of breath

¿Quieres irte?: do you want to go?

Acabamos de empezar: we just started

¿Seguro?: are you sure?

No te preocupes: don't worry

Siguen resolviendo los acertijos: they keep solving the puzzles

Organiza los números de los asientos en el orden correcto: he puts the seat numbers in the right order

Encuentra la contraseña: he finds the password

Una pequeña caja fuerte: a small safe

Una llave dorada: a golden key

La prueba en la única puerta cerrada que queda: he tries it on the only locked door left

No se abre: it won't open

Cuando está hablando con la chica: when he's talking to the girl

Luis se desmaya: Luis faints

Todos se alarman: they all get alarmed

Tocan el botón de emergencia: they press the emergency button

Rápidamente abre la puerta: she quickly opens the door

Llevando a Luis por los hombros: carrying Luis by the shoulders

Reacciona cuando llaman su nombre: he reacts when they call his name

Abre los ojos: he opens his eyes

No parece recordar lo que pasó: he doesn't seem to remember what happened

Para subirle el nivel de azúcar: to raise his sugar levels

¿Cómo me desmayé?: how did I faint?

Desmayándote: fainting

No me acuerdo: I don't remember anything

Después de pasar el susto: after the scare

Asegurarse de que Luis está bien: making sure Luis is fine

Nos mataste del susto: you scared the life out of us

Perdón por arruinar la diversión: sorry for ruining the fun

No pasa nada: It's okay

Lo importante es que estás bien: What matters is that you're okay.

Igual esa sala era muy fácil: That room was very easy anyway

Me estaba aburriendo: I was getting bored.

Tú hiciste las cosas más interesantes: You made things more interesting.

No me hagas reír: don't make me laugh

Me duele un poco la cabeza: my head hurts a bit

Claro que te duele: of course it hurts

Te pegaste en la cabeza con el piso: you hit your head on the ground

¿Seguro que no quieres ir al hospital?: are you sure you don't want to go to the hospital?

La próxima vez vamos a un lugar al aire libre: next time we'll go someplace outdoors

Ejercicio 1

Contesta las siguientes preguntas – answer the following questions

1- **¿Por qué Luis está nervioso?** – why is Luis nervous?

_____

2- **¿Cuántas salas hay para escoger?** – how many rooms are there to choose from?

_____

3- **¿Cómo es la segunda sala?** – what's the second room like?

_____

4- **¿Cuál es la única regla que hay?** – what's the only rule there is?

_____

5- **¿Cuánto tiempo tienen para salir de la sala?** – how much time do they have to leave the room?

_____

6- **¿Cuál es la primera pista?** – what's the first clue?

_____

7- **¿Qué hay en la nueva habitación?** – what's in the new room?

_____

8- ¿Qué hay en la caja fuerte? – what's in the safe?

9- ¿Qué le pasa a Luis? – what happens to Luis?

10- ¿Por qué a Luis le duele la cabeza? – why does Luis have a headache?

Ejercicio 2

Elige entre "verdadero" o "falso" – choose "true" or "false"

1- Esta es la primera vez de Tomás en un escape room. – This is Tomas's first time in an escape room.

2- Tomás se aparece con seis amigos. – Tomás shows up with six friends.

3- La tercera sala es la más difícil. – The third room is the hardest.

4- Tienen solo una linterna. – They just have one flashlight.

5- Luis encuentra la primera pista. – Luis finds the first clue.

6- La primera pista es un mapa. – The first clue is a map.

7- Luis se siente mareado. – Luis feels dizzy.

8- Luis decide salir de la sala. – Luis decides to leave the room.

9- Los chicos van a un café después. – They go to a café afterwards.

10- Los chicos están molestos con Luis por arruinar su diversión. – They're mad at Luis for ruining their fun.

Respuestas – Answers

Ejercicio 1

1- Luis está nervioso porque es un poco claustrofóbico.

2- Hay tres salas para escoger.

3- La segunda sala es una casa embrujada.

4- La única regla que hay es que deben dejar sus pertenencias en los lockers afuera de la sala.

5- Tienen una hora para salir de la sala.

6- La primera pista es unos números subrayados en un periódico, una especie de combinación.

7- En la nueva habitación hay un enorme mapa y fotos pegadas en la pared.

8- En la caja fuerte hay una llave dorada.

9- Luis se desmaya.

10- A Luis le duele la cabeza porque pegó la cabeza del piso.

Ejercicio 2

1- Verdadero

2- Falso

3- Verdadero

4- Verdadero

5- Falso

6- Falso

7- Verdadero

8- Falso

9- Verdadero

10- Falso

Puntos clave – Key takeaways

- *Hacer* is one of the most common irregular verbs.
- *Hacer* has five different conjugations (*hago, haces, hace, hacemos, hacen*).
- *Hacer* can be followed by another verb (*Me hacer reír* = You make me laugh).
- *Probar* has five different conjugations (*pruebo, pruebas, prueba, probamos, prueban*).
- Irregular verbs can fall into different categories, having small changes when conjugating, or changing completely.

Conclusion

You made it to the end of this book, kudos to you! It wasn't easy, but you put in the work regardless. By reading all the stories and finishing all the exercises compiled in *Learn Spanish with Short Stories for Adult Beginners*, you now have the practice to solidify you as an A1 Spanish learner. All the vocabulary you have learned will aid you in the following steps of your journey. You have learned several ways to greet others and say goodbye, as well as how to express what you do for work, or chat about the hobbies you're passionate about. You can easily talk about numbers, time, days of the week, and colors. You know how to describe someone's appearance in detail or mention traits of their personality. You have the tools to describe the places you visit and talk about the weather there. You can even talk about aspects of your day to day life with ease. You can do all these things now with confidence because you've worked hard for it.

And the best part is, you can always go back to the stories. Any time you're feeling rusty or out of practice, you can review the stories and find comfort while reinforcing what you already know.

Now, we hate to say goodbye, but this doesn't have to end here. By picking up the next book in our series, *Learn Spanish with Short Stories for Adult Beginners 2*, we guarantee more exciting stories that will take your Spanish to the next level. We will be covering more complicated structures from A2, such more irregular verbs in present, as well as the past tenses. The latter, more specifically, tend to be quite challenging for new learners, which is why these stories will be quite valuable in the long run. We hope to see you soon.

BOOK 4

Learn Intermediate Spanish for Adults Workbook:

Go from Spanish Beginner to Intermediate in 30 Days!

Explore to Win

Book 4 description

Are you already familiarized with the Spanish basics but want to take your knowledge to the next level? Do you feel like Spanish courses aren't made for you? Do you need a book that makes Spanish grammar simple and practical?

Well, we have just the thing for you: ***Learn Intermediate Spanish for Adults Workbook: Go from Spanish Beginner to Intermediate in 30 Days!*** is the perfect book for people who already know the Spanish basics and want to get to intermediate at their own pace.

You see, getting to an intermediate level doesn't need to be difficult, and Spanish grammar doesn't need to be explained in an intricate way. It can actually be simple, fun and practical!

In *Learn Intermediate Spanish for Adults Workbook: Go from Spanish Beginner to Intermediate in 30 Days!* you will discover:

- Past, present, and future tenses made easy
- Grammar explanations in simple language
- Tips and tricks to remember conjugations
- Pronunciation guides you can understand and reproduce
- Useful everyday phrases
- Adjectives to describe everything you need
- How to mix different tenses
- How to make hypothesis
- Summaries with key takeaways after every chapter
- Explanation and uses of the subjunctive and the imperative
- Impersonal constructions
- Exercises to practice every topic
- Answer keys for every exercise set

Imagine being able to talk in Spanish with a native speaker without second-guessing yourself? It's time for you to welcome all this language knowledge and practice and to see a new way of learning Spanish: simple and at your own pace.

Even if you think you won't be able to do it on your own, this book is so interactive, simple, and fun, that what you won't be able to do is stop learning Spanish.

This incredible book was written by Spanish linguists, which means they have a deep understanding of the Spanish language, while also being able to teach you the language and phrases spoken in real life.

If you're ready to start your intermediate Spanish journey, then scroll up and click "add to cart" NOW!

Introduction

Do you want to improve your Spanish but language courses are not your cup of tea? Or, do you feel like grammar explanations in a classroom setting are hard to grasp? Well, then you've come to the right place.

Learn Intermediate Spanish for Adults Workbook: Go from Spanish Beginner to Intermediate in 30 Days! will allow you to learn Spanish in an easy and practical way and at your own pace.

As a Spanish beginner, you probably know all the basics for a trip—how to introduce yourself, how to order at a restaurant, how to shop, and, of course, all the essential vocabulary and grammar to do so. But we're here to take you to the next level!

Learning Spanish is not only useful for trips, it is useful for life. You may find Spanish speakers where you live, you may have to use it for work, or you may also want to understand the Spanish books, movies, series, or songs you constantly hear about.

Since Spanish has over 580 million speakers, finding a person you can talk to in Spanish won't be hard. And since you're already familiar with the basics, moving forward will be relatively easy for you.

As an intermediate student, you should be able to:

- Understand and be understood in conversations about simple topics.
- Read and write simple and coherent texts.
- Describe experiences, events, people, and things.
- Give your opinion on any topic.
- Use natural expressions.
- Handle any everyday conversation with a native speaker.
- Talk about your plans for the future.
- Express simple conditions.

And this book will provide you with everything you need to achieve this—easy grammar explanations, vocabulary, exercises, and chapter takeaways to make your Spanish learning easier.

Besides being linguists and knowing Spanish to a T, the authors are also native speakers of Spanish, which means that they know exactly how to use the language in real life. Additionally, they will also be able to teach you how to speak and sound like a true native.

In this 30-day course, grammar topics are taught in a practical and easy-to-understand way. We know how hard and overwhelming learning a whole new set of grammatical rules can be, so we decided to give you all of the content in a clear way that is especially thought for native English speakers.

But simple grammar explanations are not the only thing you will find on these pages. You will also find pronunciation guides to sound like a native, a short summary after each chapter to check that you got all of the important things, and exercises to solidify your new knowledge in practice.

This book can be used in three different ways:

- To study on your own: We know that learning on your own can be difficult, but this book is specially designed to guide you through all of the lectures. Moreover, it includes the solutions to all the exercises so that you can check your understanding as you go.

- To complement your Spanish course: If you are already on a guided study program, you can always use this book to find grammar explanations, vocabulary, expressions, and extra practice!

- For particular situations: You will also be able to use the book as a reference and easily go to the chapter or topic you need. For instance, you may need to find an expression to give your opinion, so all you need to do is go to the chapter on opinions to find it and put it to use.

These pages hold everything you need to continue your Spanish-learning journey and become an intermediate speaker in just 30 days. You'll find everything you ever needed to move on!

Are you ready to find new ways of actually improving your Spanish? Then let's get to it! *¡Vamos!*

Chapter 1: Blast from the past

෴

Recordar un buen momento es sentirse feliz de nuevo.

- Gabriela Mistral

As a Spanish beginner, you already know how to talk about the present. But what do you do if you want to talk about something that happened? You most definitely will need to resort to a past tense!

Did you know that in Spanish there are **many** tenses to talk about the past? Well, in this chapter we will be talking about the past tenses from the indicative mood—the *pretérito perfecto simple*, the *pretérito perfecto compuesto* and the *pretérito imperfecto*—as well as some time markers for the past and verbal phrases. So that you can talk about all the past habits, events, and experiences you want to!

Talking about events in the past

Pretérito perfecto simple

To talk about particular events that started and finished in the past, we use the *pretérito perfecto simple*. When we use this tense, the event we're talking about has no connection whatsoever with the present, it is simply something that happened, an anecdote.

Like every Spanish tense, the *pretérito perfecto simple* needs to agree in person and number with the subject, that is, the person who is doing the action. As you may already know, Spanish verbs can be classified according to their infinitive ending into three groups: verbs ending in -*ar*, verbs ending in -*er* and verbs ending in -*ir*. This classification makes it easier for us to know how to conjugate regular verbs, because if we know what the infinitive ends in, then we can follow a prototype to form the conjugations. Here are three conjugations that you can use as models for the conjugation of regular verbs in the *pretérito perfecto simple*:

	Cantar	Comer	Vivir
yo	cant<u>é</u>	com<u>í</u>	viv<u>í</u>
tú	cant<u>aste</u>	com<u>iste</u>	viv<u>iste</u>
él / ella / usted	cant<u>ó</u>	com<u>ió</u>	viv<u>ió</u>
nosotros / nosotras	cant<u>amos</u>	com<u>imos</u>	viv<u>imos</u>
vosotros / vosotras	cant<u>asteis</u>	com<u>isteis</u>	viv<u>isteis</u>

ellos / ellas / ustedes	cant<u>aron</u>	com<u>ieron</u>	viv<u>ieron</u>

Before we move onto the examples, let's make a few things clear about the table. Despite being next to *él* and *ella*, *usted* is not a third person singular pronoun, but actually the formal version of the second-person singular pronoun. However, to simplify the chart, we've coupled it with *él* and *ella* so that you know that their conjugation is the same. Actually, this is also the case for *ustedes*, which is conjugated in the same way as *ellos* and *ellas*, but is actually a second-person plural form used in most Latin American countries.

Now that that's settled, we can see some simple examples of these three verbs in use so that you understand how to use them:

- *Mi hermana **cantó** en frente de todo el colegio.* ("My sister sang in front of the whole school.")
- *Ayer **comí** una hamburguesa.* ("Yesterday I ate a hamburger.")
- *Vosotros **vivisteis** en la casa cerca del lago, ¿verdad?* ("You lived in the house near the lake, right?")

And now, let's see some examples of conjugations of other regular verbs so that you can see that the endings are the same!

- *En la reunión **hablamos** de nuestros problemas.* ("In the meeting we talked about our problems.")
- ***Corrieron** para llegar a clase a tiempo* ("They ran to get to class on time.")
- *¿Tú **abriste** el frasco de pepinillos?* ("Was it you who opened the pickle jar?")

As you know, Spanish has many irregular verbs, and the *pretérito perfecto simple* is actually the tense with the most irregular verbs out of all the tenses. So, we should definitely see some of them. In the following table, you will find the conjugations of some commonly used irregular verbs:

	Ser/Ir	Estar	Haber	Dar	Venir
yo	fui	estuve	hube	di	vine
tú	fuiste	estuviste	hubiste	diste	viniste
él / ella / usted	fue	estuvo	hubo	dio	vino
nosotros / nosotras	fuimos	estuvimos	hubimos	dimos	vinimos
vosotros/vosotras	fuisteis	estuvisteis	hubisteis	disteis	vinisteis
ellos/ellas/ustedes	fueron	estuvieron	hubieron	dieron	vinieron

Have you noticed that there are actually two verbs in the first example? Well, that's because *ser* and *ir* have the exact same conjugation in the *pretérito perfecto simple*. It's weird, I know, but we understand which one we're talking about depending on the context. The good news is you only need to remember one conjugation, right?

368

And now, let's see all of these verbs in action:

- *Hace una semana **fui** a la montaña.* ("A week ago I went to the mountain.")
- *Tú **fuiste** violinista en una orquesta.* ("You were a violin player in an orchestra.")
- ***Estuvo** enferma toda la semana.* ("She was sick all week.")
- *Cuando **hubimos** terminado de pintar, nos fuimos.* ("When we were done painting, we left.")
- *Le **diste** una linda sorpresa a Lucía, no se lo esperaba.* ("You gave Lucía a nice surprise, she didn't expect it.")
- *Jorge y Luis **vinieron** a España a pasar la Navidad.* ("Jorge and Luis came to Spain for Christmas.")

Talking about past experiences

Pretérito perfecto compuesto

Unlike the *pretérito perfecto simple*, the *pretérito perfecto compuesto* talks about an action that is somehow related to the moment of speaking.

If it helps, you can think of the *pretérito perfecto simple* as the Spanish counterpart of the past simple, and the *pretérito perfecto compuesto* as the Spanish counterpart of the present perfect. As we'll see now, even the form of the *pretérito perfecto compuesto* is similar to that of the English present perfect.

The *pretérito perfecto compuesto* is formed with the present form conjugation of the verb *haber*, which works as an auxiliary, and the participle form of the action verb. Here are some examples of regular verbs we've seen before:

	Cantar	Comer	Vivir
yo	he cantado	he comido	he vivido
tú	has cantado	has comido	has vivido
él / ella / usted	ha cantado	ha comido	ha vivido
nosotros / nosotras	hemos cantado	hemos comido	hemos vivido
vosotros / vosotras	habéis cantado	habéis comido	habéis vivido
ellos / ellas / ustedes	han cantado	han comido	han vivido

Some examples of the *pretérito perfecto compuesto* with these verbs are:

- *¿Tú **has cantado** toda la noche?*
- *Anoche **he comido** unas manzanas buenísimas.*
- *¿Ya **habéis visitado** Madrid?*

369

The participle form doesn't need to agree in person and number with the subject because it is one of three verb forms that always stay the same. In Spanish, the participle is formed by adding -*ado* to the root of verbs ending in -*ar*, and adding -*ido* to the root of verbs ending in -*er* and -*ir*, like we've seen in the table above. However, there are also some irregular participles. Some of the most frequent ones are:

- *abrir → abierto*
- *decir → dicho*
- *ver → visto*
- *poner → puesto*
- *escribir → escrito*
- *hacer → hecho*
- *romper → roto*
- *volver → vuelto*

Some examples with these irregular verbs are:

- *¡Les **he dicho** hace media hora que vayan a dormir!*
- *Este mes le **hemos escrito** una carta a la abuela.*
- *¿Alguna vez **has roto** un plato?*
- *María se fue a trabajar a Canadá y nunca **ha regresado**.*
- *¿**Han visto** las noticias de hoy?*
- *La puerta está entreabierta, ¿la **habéis abierto** vosotras?*

Talking about past habits

Pretérito imperfecto

The *pretérito imperfecto* is the last past tense we will see in this chapter. This tense is used to describe an action that happened in the past with no temporal limits. For example, we can use this tense to talk about things we used to do when we were younger or that used to be a certain way.

Let's see how this tense is conjugated with the three prototype regular verbs we've been using.

	Cantar	Comer	Vivir
yo	cant<u>aba</u>	com<u>ía</u>	viv<u>ía</u>
tú	cant<u>abas</u>	com<u>ías</u>	viv<u>ías</u>
él / ella / usted	cant<u>aba</u>	com<u>ía</u>	viv<u>ía</u>
nosotros / nosotras	cant<u>ábamos</u>	com<u>íamos</u>	viv<u>íamos</u>

| vosotros / vosotras | cant<u>abais</u> | com<u>íais</u> | viv<u>íais</u> |
| ellos / ellas / ustedes | cant<u>aban</u> | com<u>ían</u> | viv<u>ían</u> |

Did you notice that the first and third person singular conjugations are exactly the same? That definitely makes it easier to remember, right? Moreover, the endings of the conjugations for verbs ending in -er and verbs ending in -ir are exactly the same, just like with the *pretérito perfecto simple* and the participle!

Now, let's see some examples of these verbs in use to talk about things that used to happen in the past for a period of time:

- *Cuando era pequeño, **vivía** cerca de un lago.*
- *A los 10 años, ustedes no **comían** vegetales.*
- *De pequeñas, vosotras **cantabais** esa canción todo el día.*

But since these conjugations can be used as prototypes, we can change the root of the verb with another regular verb's root and add the *pretérito imperfecto* ending to them. Let's see some examples!

- *Cuando eras pequeña, tú **amabas** los caramelos.*
- *Antes de la operación, Malena siempre **sentía** dolor en la espalda.*
- *Cuando vivíamos en Madrid, **teníamos** un perro.*

Now, it's time to focus on irregular verbs. The *pretérito imperfecto* doesn't have as many irregular verbs as the *pretérito perfecto simple*. Here are the most frequently used ones:

	Ser	Ver	Ir
yo	era	veía	iba
tú	eras	veías	ibas
él / ella / usted	era	veía	iba
nosotros / nosotras	éramos	veíamos	íbamos
vosotros/vosotras	érais	veíais	íbais
ellos/ellas/ustedes	eran	veían	iban

Now, let's see some examples!

- *Cuando era pequeño, **íbamos** a la playa todos los días.*
- *De niños, vosotros **queríais** todo lo que veíais.*
- *Antes no **éramos** tan amigos, pero ahora sí.*

371

Time markers for the past

There are several words and phrases that trigger the past tenses because they let us know beforehand that what follows is an event in the past.

Time markers for the pretérito perfecto simple

Since the *pretérito perfecto simple* is used to talk about a single event that happened in the past, there are some words and phrases that are generally used with it. Here are some of them and some examples to see them in use:

- *Ayer* ("yesterday"): ***Ayer*** *fuimos al cine con Juan.*
- *Anoche* ("last night"): ***Anoche*** *salí a comer sola.*
- *Anteayer/antier* ("the day before yesterday"): ***Anteayer*** *visitó a su abuela.*
- *El año/mes pasado/anterior* ("last month/year"): ***El año pasado*** *hicieron una fiesta.*
- *La semana pasada/anterior* ("last week"): *¿No os visteis **la semana pasada**?*
- *Hace días/semanas/meses/años* ("days/weeks/months/years ago"): ***Hace tres años*** *hice un viaje por Europa.*
- *El otro día* ("the other day"): ***El otro día*** *vi un pájaro majestuoso.*
- *En + year/month* ("In + year/month"): ***En 1945*** *terminó la Segunda Guerra Mundial.*
- *El + date* ("On + date"): ***El 2 de marzo de 2010**, Julia y Samuel fueron padres.*

Time markers for the pretérito perfecto compuesto

The *pretérito perfecto compuesto* is connected to the time of speaking. Generally, this connection between the past and the present is expressed through a time marker. Some of them are:

- *Hoy* ("today"): ***Hoy*** *no he tenido mucho trabajo.*
- *Esta mañana/semana* ("this morning/week"): ***Esta mañana*** *hemos salido a correr.*
- *Este mes/año* ("this month/year"): ***Este año*** *ha sido muy productivo para la empresa.*
- *Este fin de semana* ("this weekend"): ***Este fin de semana**, Juana y Pablo han ido a España.*
- *Estos días* ("these days"): *¿Has podido disfrutar de la tranquilidad de **estos días**?*
- *Varias veces* ("several times"): *¿Os habéis quebrado la pierna **varias veces**?*
- *Alguna vez* ("ever"): *¿Han ido a patinar sobre hielo **alguna vez**?*
- *Nunca* ("never"): ***Nunca*** *me he subido a un avión.*

Time markers for the pretérito imperfecto

The *pretérito imperfecto* is used to talk about things that used to be in a certain way. Though some time markers we've talked about can be used for the *pretérito imperfecto* as well, there are some that usually trigger this particular tense. Let's see some of them:

- *Cuando era niño/joven/adolescente* ("When I was a kid/young/a teenager"): ***Cuando era joven*** *usaba el pelo largo.*

- *De niño/joven/adolescente* ("When I was a kid/young/a teenager"): ***De niña***, *le encantaban los camiones de juguete.*

- *Cuando tenía + age* ("When I was + age"): ***Cuando tenías 33 años***, *viajabas todos los días en tren.*

- *A los + age* ("At + age"): ***A los 25 años***, *creíamos que la música nueva era horrible.*

- *Antes* ("Before"): ***Antes***, *la gente no comía tanta chatarra.*

- *En esa/aquella época* ("at that time"): ***En aquella época***, *os bañabais solo una vez por semana.*

- *En aquellos tiempos* ("in those times"): ***En aquellos tiempos***, *todo era más fácil.*

- *Entonces* ("then"): ***Entonces***, *Camila y Juan salían juntos.*

Beginning and duration of an action

Now we will see some verbal phrases that are used to mark the beginning, duration, iteration and ending of an action. Verbal phrases, or *perífrasis* in Spanish, are a combination of two verbs: one of them needs to be conjugated according to the time, person and number, and the other is a non-personal form (infinitive, gerund or participle). Sometimes, they are joined with a preposition.

Empezar a + infinitive

This verbal phrase means "to start doing something" and is used to mark the beginning of an action.

- *Ana **empezó a trabajar** hace una semana.*
- *Carlos y yo **empezamos a viajar** después de jubilarnos.*

Acabar de + infinitive

This verbal phrase means "to have just finished doing something" and is used to talk about something that happened recently.

- ***Acabo de salir** de la casa de mi abuela, ¿quieres ver una película?*
- *Juana **acaba de comer** la mejor paella de su vida.*

Terminar de + infinitive

It is used to express the ending of an action.

- *La semana pasada **terminé de leer** dos libros.*
- *Hoy **he terminado de diseñar** el proyecto del edificio.*

Volver a + infinitive

This verbal phrase is used to express the repetition of an action

- *Esta tarde **he vuelto a jugar** al tenis después de cuatro años.*
- *¿**Volvisteis a ver** a tu abuela?*

Dejar de + infinitive

It is used to express the interruption of an action.

- ***Dejaban de jugar** cuando alguien se lastimaba.*
- *¿Por qué **dejaste de pintar**?*

Llevar + gerund

This verbal phrase is used to express the duration of an action.

- ***Llevábamos** más de 2 años **ahorrando** y nos fuimos de viaje.*

- ***Llevo trabajando** en este libro más de 10 años.*

Seguir + gerund

It expresses the continuity of an action.

- *Después de comer, **seguíamos charlando** hasta las 10.*

- *¿**Seguisteis corriendo** toda la tarde?*

Key Takeaways

Now, let's see a short summary of everything we've seen in this chapter before moving on to the exercises.

- The *pretérito perfecto simple* is used to talk about specific events that happened in the past.

- The *pretérito perfecto compuesto* is used to talk about events in the past that are somehow connected to the time of speaking.

- The *pretérito imperfecto* is used to talk about actions that used to happen in the past with no temporal limits, like past habits.

- Time markers for the *pretérito perfecto simple* are:

  - *ayer, anoche, anteayer/antier, el año/mes pasado/anterior, la semana pasada/anterior, hace días/semanas/meses/años, el otro día, en + year/month, el + date.*

- Time markers for the *pretérito perfecto compuesto* are:

  - *hoy, esta mañana/semana, este mes/año, este fin de semana, estos días, varias veces, alguna vez, nunca.*

- Time markers for the *pretérito imperfecto* are:

  - *cuando era niño/joven/adolescente, de niño/joven/adolescente, cuanto tenía + age, a los + age, antes, en esa/aquella época, en aquellos tiempos, entonces.*

- To express the beginning, ending, duration and repetition of an action, we can use the following verbal phrases:

  - *empezar a* + infinitive

  - *acabar de* + infinitive

  - *terminar de* + infinitive

  - *volver a* + infinitive

  - *dejar de* + infinitive

  - *llevar* + gerund

  - *seguir* + gerund

In the following chapter, we will be dealing with a lot of vocabulary to describe people and things. Furthermore, we will see some relative pronouns and clauses that will make your sentences more complex!

Exercises

Now, it's time to practice everything we've seen in this chapter!

1. The *pretérito perfecto simple* is used to talk about:

    a. Past habits.

    b. Particular events in the past.

    c. Past events related to the time of speaking.

2. Complete the following text with the *pretérito perfecto simple* form of the verbs in parentheses.
   En 1992, mi marido y yo .... (ir) a un evento de gala. .... (ser) un evento por el aniversario de una empresa importante en un salón enorme. Yo me .... (poner) un vestido largo color verde y mi marido se .... (poner) un traje con una corbata verde. Esa noche .... (nosotros/bailar) y .... (nosotros/comer) mucho.

La semana pasada, 20 años después, me .... (volver) a poner ese mismo vestido para el casamiento de mi hija.

3. Which of these time markers is not usually used for the *pretérito perfecto simple*?

    a. El otro día

    b. Ayer

    c. En aquellos tiempos

    d. La semana pasada

4. The *pretérito perfecto compuesto* is used to talk about:

    a. Past habits.

    b. Particular events in the past.

    c. Past events related to the time of speaking.

5. Complete the following text with the *pretérito perfecto compuesto* form of the verbs in parentheses.
   ¿Alguna vez .... (estar) muy estresado? Pues, hoy no .... (yo/tener) tiempo para nada. Esta mañana .... (yo/correr) solo 20 minutos porque no tenía tiempo. Luego, ... (yo/ir) a comprar un café y fui a mi casa. Desde allí, ... (yo/trabajar) hasta las 7 de la tarde sin descansar y luego .... (yo/salir) a una cena de negocios. Estos días en el trabajo .... (ser) terribles, nunca .... (yo/estar) tan estresado en mi vida.

6. Which of these time markers is not usually used for the *pretérito perfecto compuesto*?

    a. Este mes

    b. Este fin de semana

    c. Varias veces

    d. La semana pasada

7. The *pretérito imperfecto* is used to talk about:

    a. Past habits.

    b. Particular events in the past.

    c. Past events related to the time of speaking.

8. Complete the following text with the *pretérito imperfecto* form of the verbs in parentheses.
    Cuando mi abuela era niña, las cosas .... (ser) muy diferentes. Los niños .... (jugar) en los patios y las calles. En la playa, las mujeres .... (usar) trajes de baño más conservadores.

Cuando ella tenía mi edad, muchas de sus amigas ya .... (estar) casadas y algunas incluso .... (tener) hijos. En aquellos tiempos, la mayoría de las mujeres no .... (trabajar), ellas se .... (encargar) de la casa y de sus hijos.

9. Which of these time markers is not usually used for the *pretérito imperfecto*?

    a. Hoy

    b. Antes

    c. En aquellos tiempos

    d. De niño

10. Complete the following text with the *pretérito perfecto simple* form of the verbal phrases between parentheses.
    Ayer fuimos de excursión a la montaña con mi familia. .... (empezar) a caminar a las ocho de la mañana, pero luego de una hora nos dimos cuenta de que estábamos yendo por otro camino, así que regresamos al punto de partida y .... (volver) a empezar. Luego de 3 horas de caminata, ... (dejar) de caminar para poder almorzar. Cuando .... (terminar) de comer, ... (seguir) caminando hasta llegar a la cima. Descansamos y luego .... (empezar) a regresar. ¡Fue una linda experiencia!

Answer Key

1. b. Particular events in the past

2. fuimos; Era; puse; puso; bailamos; comimos; volví

3. c. En aquellos tiempos

4. c. Past events related to the time of speaking

5. has estado; he tenido; he corrido; he ido; he trabajado; he salido; han sido; he estado

6. d. La semana pasada

7. a. Past habits

8. eran; jugaban; usaban; estaban; tenían; trabajaba; encargaban

9. a. Hoy

10. Empezamos; volvimos; dejamos; terminamos; seguimos; empezamos.

Chapter 2: Describing people, places, and things

§

Es mucho más difícil describir que opinar. Infinitamente más. En vista de lo cual, todo el mundo opina.

- Josep Pla

Since you are not new to Spanish, you've probably already described many things. I'm sure you've read, heard, and even used the words in this chapter at least a few times. However, in order to improve your Spanish, it's good to delve into the resources we use to describe people, places and things.

Relative pronouns

Relative pronouns (or *pronombres relativos*, in Spanish) are the words we use to introduce information about the person or thing we are talking about. We can either provide information that makes it clear who or what we are referring to, or we can introduce further information about that person or thing. Take a look at these example sentences:

- *Mi hermano **que** vive en Colombia habla muy bien en Español.* ("My brother who lives in Colombia speaks Spanish very well.")
- *Sus hijas, **que** han nacido en Medellín, son bilingües.* ("His daughters, who were born in Medellín, are bilingual.")

Que

Que is the Spanish relative pronoun we use to talk about people, equivalent to English "who", "whom" and "that":

- *Dáselo al hombre **que** llamó ayer.* ("Give it to the guy who phoned yesterday.")
- *Ella es la mujer con **la que** tienes que hablar.* ("She's the lady (whom) you need to talk to.")
- *Él es el muchacho **que** conocí en el partido de fútbol.* ("He's the guy (that) I met at the soccer match.")

As you can see from these examples, we can sometimes omit the relative pronoun in English. It's perfectly correct to say "She's the lady you need to talk to," or "He's the guy I met at the soccer match." However, you can never leave que or any other relative pronoun out in Spanish.

We use "which" and "that" to talk about things in English. Luckily, in Spanish, we also use *que*:

- *Compré el libro **que** me recomendaste.* ("I bought the book (that) you recommended.")
- *Entraron a la casa, **que** estaba vacía.* ("They entered the house, which was empty.")

Once again, English sometimes leaves out the pronoun (you can say "I bought the book you recommended"), but that's not possible in Spanish.

378

El/la/los/las que

Now that we know that we use que both for people and things and that we can never leave the relative pronoun out in Spanish. Let's focus on one of the example sentences:

- *Ella es la mujer con **la que** tienes que hablar.*

Have you noticed that, unlike the other examples, there's a definite article (in this case *la*) before the relative pronoun *que*? This is because the relative pronoun is being used with a preposition (in this case *con*). So, when the relative pronouns are used together with prepositions, we need to use the following combination:

proposition + definite article (*el, la, los* or *las*, depending on the noun that's being replaced) + *que*.

Let's take a look at some examples:

- *La amiga **con la que** fui al cine el sábado llegó tarde.* ("The friend with whom I went to the cinema on Saturday was late.")

- *Esta es la casa **en la que** crecí.* ("This is the house in which I grew up.")

- *Me compré el coche **del que** te hablé.* ("I bought the car that I talked to you about.")

Note that, as it happens in other contexts, when preposition *de* is followed by *el*, they become *del*. Likewise, when *a* is followed by *el*, they become *al*.

Here you have a chart with the correct article depending on the gender and number of the noun they are replacing:

	Masculine noun	Feminine noun
Singular noun	el que	la que
Plural noun	los que	las que

Before moving on to the next relative pronoun, there's one more use of *que* that's worth noting. Let's see some examples first, and then we'll go to the explanation:

- *Siempre viste de amarillo, **lo que** me parece un poco extraño.* ("She is always dressed in yellow, which I find a bit weird.")

- *Mi madre llegó tarde a buscarme, **lo que** me hizo enojar.* ("My mom was late to pick me up, which made me mad.")

In these examples, *lo que* (which is neuter, that is, it doesn't have gender nor number) refers to the whole previous part of the sentence. For example, in the first example, *lo que* doesn't stand for *amarillo*; it's actually replacing *Siempre viste de amarillo*.

El/la cual, los/las cuales

Other relative pronouns that can be used after a preposition and together with an article are *cual* and its plural form *cuales*. They work just like *que*, but they are a bit more formal, so it's more common to run across them while reading. Since they distinguish between singular and plural, they also come in handy when the person or thing that's being referred to is not immediately before the relative pronouns. Let's take a look at some examples.

- *El padre de mi mejor amiga de la infancia, **del cual** no recuerdo el nombre, me saludó por la calle.* ("The father of my childhood best friend, **whose** name I don't remember, said hello to me on the street.")

- *Las pinturas de Leonardo Da Vinci expuestas en el Vaticano, **sobre las cuales** escribí un ensayo, son mis preferidas.* ("The painting by Leonardo Da Vinci on display at the Vatican, **on which** I wrote an essay, are my favorites.")

Depending on the gender and number of the noun they are replacing, you have to choose between these options:

	Masculine noun	Feminine noun
Singular noun	el cual	la cual
Plural noun	los cuales	las cuales

Quien/quienes

There is yet a third relative pronoun: *quien* and its plural form *quienes*. These ones are only used to introduce information about people. Also, they are always separated from the noun to which they refer either by a comma or by a preposition. Let's see some examples from the sections above, but this time with *quien* or *quienes*.

- *La amiga **con quien** fui al cine el sábado llegó tarde.* ("The friend with **whom** I went to the cinema on Saturday was late.")

- *El padre de mi mejor amiga de la infancia, **de quien** no recuerdo el nombre, me saludó por la calle.* ("The father of my childhood best friend, **whose** name I don't remember, said hello to me on the street.") See how in this case, *del cual* is a better option, because with *quien*, the sentence is ambiguous (whose name the narrator doesn't remember? The friend's or the father's?).

- *Sus hijas, **quienes** han nacido en Medellín, son bilingües.* ("His daughters, **who** were born in Medellín, are bilingual.")

Quien and *quienes* are invariable to gender, so the only choice is between singular or plural:

	Masculine noun	Feminine noun
Singular noun	quien	quien
Plural noun	quienes	quienes

Cuyo/cuya/cuyos/cuyas

These words are actually adjectives, but they function as relatives that show possession, similarly to English "whose." Let's see some examples:

- *La persona que me saludó en la calle, **cuyo** nombre no recordaba, era el padre de mi amiga de la infancia.* ("The person who said hi to me in the street, **whose** name I didn't remember, was the father of my childhood friend.")

380

- *Admiro a las autoras **cuyos** libros me transportaron a otro mundo.* ("I admire the authors **whose** books took me to another world.")

Cuyo and its variants *cuya*, *cuyos* and *cuyas* designate the owner of the object they accompany, which is expressed in the main sentence. They agree in gender and number with the thing that's possessed, not with the possessor. If we take the first example, *la persona* is feminine, but *el nombre* is masculine, that's why we use *cuyo*. Take a look at this chart to know when to use which variant.

	Masculine noun (that is possessed)	Feminine noun (that is possessed)
Singular noun (that is possessed)	cuyo	cuya
Plural noun (that is possessed)	cuyos	cuyas

Cuyo is quite formal, so it's more common to come across it in writing. In oral speech, we tend to reformulate the sentence to use another relative pronoun. For instance, the second example could be transformed to:

- *Admiro a las autoras que escribieron libros que me transportaron a otro mundo.* ("I admire the authors who wrote books that took me to another world.")

Relative clauses

We've been talking about relative clauses throughout this chapter without properly naming them. The relative pronouns we have described are the link between a main sentence and a relative clause, which provides additional information about an element in the main clause. Let's take a look at how this works with an example:

- *Mi bicicleta está rota* ("My bike is broken") + *Mi bicicleta es roja* ("My bike is red") = *Mi bicicleta, **que es roja**, está rota.* ("My bike, **which is red,** is broken.")
- *Uno de mis hermanos vive en Alemania* ("One of my brothers lives in Germany") + *Va a venir de visita* ("He is coming to visit") = *Mi hermano **que vive en Alemania** va a venir de visita.* ("My brother **who lives in Germany** is coming to visit.")

There's a sentence that's very similar to the one above, but with a difference in meaning. Let's take a look at it:

- *Mi hermano, **que vive en Alemania**, va a venir de visita.* ("My brother, **who lives in Germany,** is coming to visit.")

In the first sentence, the one without the commas, there is more than one brother and we need to specify which one is coming to visit (the one who lives in Germany). In the second sentence, there is only one brother, and the information between commas (that he lives in Germany), is extra. That's the difference between the two types of relative clauses in Spanish, but don't worry, we'll see each type in detail.

Defining relative clauses

In Spanish, they are called *oraciones de relativo especificativas*. Their function is to identify the thing being described from a group of similar things. Both in English and in Spanish, relative clauses are written without commas. Moreover, the clause cannot be removed from the sentence without a change of meaning. Let's see an example:

- *Los cuadros de Leonardo Da Vinci **que están expuestos en el Vaticano** son mis preferidos.* ("The painting by Leonardo Da Vinci **that are on display at the Vatican** are my favorites.") This means that there are paintings by Leonardo Da Vinci in other places, and that the ones I prefer are the ones in the Vatican.

If we took away the relative clause, the meaning would change completely:

- *Los cuadros de Leonardo Da Vinci son mis preferidos.* ("The painting by Leonardo Da Vinci are my favorites.")

Non-defining relative clauses

These are called *oraciones de relativo explicativas* in Spanish, and they provide additional information about the noun they are describing. This information is not needed to distinguish the noun form others. Moreover, if you remove an *oración de relativo explicativa* from a sentence, the general meaning will stay the same, with a little less detail. Both in Spanish and in English, non-defining relative clauses go between commas.

- *Da Vinci pintó La Gioconda**, que está en el Museo de Louvre,** en el siglo XVI.* ("Da Vinci painted the Mona Lisa, **which is in the Louvre Museum,** in the 16th Century.").

As we can see, saying where the Mona Lisa is on display only adds more detail, but it's not essential to know which Mona Lisa we are talking about (because there's only one).

Adjectives

In this chapter we've been talking about the pronouns and clauses we use to describe something or someone, to say something more about them, whether it's an opinion or an objective fact. Now, we'll focus on another tool we have to do this, which is also the most common one, by the way. Let's take some time to talk about adjectives.

We'll start with a quick review. Adjectives are words that describe nouns (people, things, places, feeling or concepts). They usually describe quality (*lindo, grande, sincero*); quantity (*muchos, uno, dos, tres, décimo*); location (*eso, esto, aquellas*); possession (*mi, su, nuestro*); and origin (*europeo, colombiano, renacentista*).

Spanish adjectives have the same functions as English ones. However, as you already know, the two languages are different, so you have to take into account the grammatical differences.

Syntactical differences:

I know that "syntax" sounds like a difficult concept, but it actually isn't. Think of it as the way in which a language orders the different types of words to create sentences that make sense. Talking about the way in which the language orders adjectives and nouns, we can say that, in English, the adjective usually comes before the noun. For example, we say:

- "I bought a **red jacket**. A **nice, tall, and blonde store clerk** helped me."

If we translated that into Spanish, we would have:

- *Me compré una **chaqueta roja**. Me ayudó un **empleado amable, alto y rubio**.*

As you can see, in Spanish, we put the adjectives after the nouns they are describing. You can use this as a rule of thumb. However, as with all rules, there are some exceptions. And, since you're not new to Spanish, it's time to study them.

First exception: Demonstrative and Possessive Adjectives

Demonstratives like *ese, este, aquel* and their feminine and plural forms come before the nouns they describe. For example:

- ***Esa camisa** te queda chica.* ("That shirt is too small for you.")
- ***Este pincel** está roto.* ("This paint brush is broken.")

The same can be said of possessives like *tu, mi, su* and *nuestro*:

- ***Mi hermana** es muy menuda.* ("My sister is very small.")
- *Hace meses que no vemos a **nuestro padre**.* ("We haven't seen our father in months.")

Second exception: Limiting Adjectives

These are the adjectives that define the number, quantity or amount of a noun. They are always placed before it:

- *Compramos **ocho manzanas**.* ("We bought eight apples.")
- *Había **mucho viento**.* ("It was very windy.")
- *No nos vemos desde hace **bastante tiempo**.* ("We haven't seen each other in a long time.")

Third exception: Essential Qualities

There are some adjectives that don't describe or give new information about a noun. Instead, they emphasize an essential quality of the noun they are modifying. These adjectives tend to go before the noun:

- *La **blanca nieve** cubría la pradera.* ("The white snow covered the prairie.")
- *Esparció la **dulce miel** por la rodaja de pan.* ("She spread the sweet honey in the slice of bread.")

As you can see in the example above, the adjective *blanca* is not adding any new information on the noun *nieve*, its function is to highlight a quality of the snow.

Fourth exception: Change of Meaning

The last exception is made up by a group of adjectives that have different meanings depending on whether they are placed before or after the noun. Let's see them in action:

- *Mi madre es una **alta ejecutiva** en una compañía internacional.* ("My mother is a high-class executive in an international company.")
- *Yo soy un **hombre alto**.* ("I'm a tall man.")
- *Me regaló un **vestido muy bonito**.* ("She gave me a very nice dress.")
- *En **bonito lío** te has metido.* ("You've put yourself in quite a mess.")

Can you grasp the difference in meaning between these sets of sentences? We could say that, after the noun, the adjective is more objective and descriptive. When it's placed before the noun, the meaning is more subjective or expressive.

Here's a list with some other adjectives that experience a change in meaning depending on where they are placed:

Adjective	Pronunciation	Meaning when placed before the noun	Meaning when placed after the noun
antiguo	ahn-TEE-goo-oh	old, former, ancient	antique
bajo	BAH-hoh	of low quality	short
cierto	see-EHR-toh	certain	true, right
diferente	dee-feh-REHN-teh	various	different
dulce	DOOL-seh	good, nice	sweet
grande	GRAHN-deh	great	big
mismo	MEES-moh	same	himself/herself
nuevo	noo-EH-boh	another, newly acquired	new, newly made
pobre	POH-breh	unfortunate	poor
puro	POO-roh	sheer	pure
raro	RRAH-roh	rare	strange
simple	SEEM-pleh	mere	simple, modest
solo	SOH-loh	one, only	lonely, alone
único	OO-nee-koh	only	unique
viejo	vee-EH-hoh	former	old

Morphological differences:

Morphology is another difficult word, you might think. But don't worry, I have a simple definition for this one as well. Morphology studies the way words are formed in a language.

In Spanish, to know how to form an adjective, we need to look at the noun that it is modifying. As you already know, Spanish nouns have not only number but also gender. And adjectives do as well. Since they have to agree with the nouns they are modifying in gender and number, almost all adjectives have four forms:

- The masculine, singular form ending in -O (*feo*)
- The feminine, singular form ending in -A (*fea*)
- The masculine, plural form ending in -OS (*feos*)
- The feminine, plural form ending in -AS (*feas*)

However, there're also some invariable adjectives, which stay the same regardless of the gender of the noun they are modifying. Thus, they have only two forms, one singular and one plural. Let's take a look at some examples:

- *Eran una pareja **feliz**.* ("They were a happy couple.")
- *Los niños estaban **felices** de ver a su padre.* ("The children were happy to see their father.")
- *Mañana tengo un día **difícil** en el trabajo.* ("Tomorrow I have a hard day at work.")
- *¡Qué **difícil** fue la prueba de Matemáticas!* ("The Math test was really hard!")

As you can see in the list of invariable adjectives below, they tend to end in -E, -A or a consonant.

Invariable adjective	Pronunciation	Translation
caliente	kah-LEE-ehn-teh	hot
débil	DEH-beel	weak
difícil	dee-FEE-seel	hard, difficult
dulce	DOOL-seh	sweet
enorme	eh-NOHR-meh	huge
fácil	FAH-seel	easy
familiar	fah-mee-lee-AHR	familiar
feliz	feh-LEES	happy
fuerte	foo-EHR-teh	strong
genial	heh-NEE-ahl	awesome
grande	GRAHN-deh	big

gris	grees	grey
importante	eem-pohr-TAHN-teh	important
imposible	eem-poh-SEE-bleh	impossible
increíble	een-kreh-EE-bleh	unbelievable
joven	hoh-BEHN	young
naranja	nah-RAHN-hah	orange
picante	pee-KAHN-teh	spicy
pobre	POH-breh	poor
rosa	RROH-sah	pink
simple	SEEM-pleh	simple
suave	soo-AH-beh	soft
torpe	TOHR-peh	clumsy
triste	TREES-teh	sad
valiente	bah-lee-EHN-teh	brave
verde	BEHR-deh	green
violeta	bee-oh-LEH-tah	purple

To finish this section on Spanish adjectives, let me mention one last morphological change this type of words can have. As a way of emphasizing, we can add -ÍSIMO (for masculine adjectives) or –ÍSIMA (for feminine adjectives) as a suffix. It's a different way of saying muy ("very"). Let's take a look at some examples:

- *La comida en ese restaurante es **buenísima**.* ("The food at that restaurant is **so good**.")
- *Sí, pero el lugar es **carísimo**.* ("Yes, but the place is **very expensive**.")

Key Takeaways

Let's review the most important concepts of this chapter.

Relative pronouns are the words we use to introduce information about the person or thing we are talking about:

- *Que* is the Spanish relative pronoun we use to talk about people, equivalent to English "who", "whom" and "that".

- When the relative pronouns are used together with prepositions, we need to use the following combination: proposition + definite article (*el, la, los* or *las*, depending on the noun that's being replaced) + *que*.

- We use *lo que* to refer to the whole previous part of the sentence.

- Other relative pronouns that can be used after a preposition and together with an article are *cual* and its plural form *cuales*. They work just like *que*, but they are more formal.

- *Quien* and its plural form *quienes* are only used to introduce information about people. They are always separated from the noun to which they refer either by a comma or by a preposition.

- *Cuyo, cuya, cuyos* and *cuyas* designate the owner of the object they accompany, which is expressed in the main sentence. They agree in gender and number with the thing that's possessed, not with the possessor.

Relative pronouns are the link between a main sentence and a **relative clause**, which provides additional information about an element in the main clause. There are two types of relative clauses.

- Defining relative clauses identify the thing being described from a group of similar things. These clauses are written without commas.

- Non-defining relative clauses provide additional information about the noun they are describing. This information is not needed to distinguish the noun form others. If they are removed from a sentence, the general meaning will stay the same. These clauses go between commas.

Adjectives are words that describe nouns.

- They usually describe quality, quantity, location, possession, and origin.

- They come after the nouns they are describing, except in these cases:
  - Demonstratives (*ese, este, aquel* and their feminine and plural forms) and possessives (*tu, mi, su*, etc.) come before the nouns they describe.
  - Limiting adjectives, the ones that define the number, quantity or amount of a noun, are always placed before the noun.
  - Some adjectives emphasize an essential quality of the noun they are modifying, without providing any new information. These adjectives tend to go before the noun.
  - Some adjectives have different meanings depending on whether they are placed before or after the noun.

- Since they have to agree with the nouns they are modifying in gender and number, almost all adjectives have four endings (-O, -A, -OS and -AS).

- There are also some invariable adjectives, which stay the same regardless of the gender of the noun they are modifying. Thus, they have only two forms: one singular and one plural.

- We can add -ÍSIMO or -ÍSIMA to an adjective as a different way of saying *muy* ("very").

In the next chapter, we'll delve into one of the most intimidating Spanish subjects: the subjunctive mood. But don't fear! We'll make it simple and entertaining for you. Before moving on, let's see how much you've learned so far!

Exercises

1. Complete using the correct relative pronoun (que, quien, quienes)
   a. La convocatoria va dirigida a .... nacieron entre 1980 y 1985.
   b. Trajeron las cosas .... les había pedido.
   c. Quiero llevarle un regalo a .... me ayudó a conseguir trabajo.

2. Complete using the correct definite article (la, el, las, los)
   a. Las mujeres con .... que me encontré son compañeras de trabajo.
   b. Este es el barrio en .... que se crió mi papá.
   c. Allí está la heladería de .... que te hablé.
   d. Tengo amigos a .... que veo poco.

3. Choose the correct one.
   Cuyo, cuya, cuyos and cuyas:
   a. agree in gender and number with the thing that's possessed.
   b. agree in gender and number with the possessor.
   c. agree with the relative pronoun.

4. Complete with "defining" or "non-defining":
   a. .... relative clauses identify the thing being described from a group of similar things.
   b. .... relative clauses are written without commas.
   c. .... relative clauses cannot be removed from the sentence without a change of meaning.
   d. .... relative clauses provide additional information about the noun they are describing.
   e. The information .... relative clauses provide is not needed to distinguish the noun form others.
   f. If you remove a .... relative clauses from a sentence, the general meaning will stay the same.
   g. .... relative clauses go between commas.

5. Put the commas where you believe they are needed:
   a. La Estatua de la Libertad que está en Nueva York mide 93 metros.
   b. El presidente de Francia Emmanuel Macron llegó a la ciudad el lunes por la noche.
   c. Los niños que vinieron anoche son los hijos de mi hermana.
   d. La famosa fuente romana que se llama Fontana de Trevi se construyó en el siglo XVI.

6. Which of the following statements about adjectives is not true?
   a. They usually describe quality, quantity, location, possession and origin.
   b. Spanish adjectives, like English ones, are placed before the noun.
   c. Spanish adjectives have the same functions as English ones.

7. Put the adjectives in parentheses in the correct place (before or after the noun).
   a. La ...... camisa ...... te queda muy bien. (roja)
   b. Mi marido me pidió que compre ...... bananas ...... porque va a cocinar una torta. (cuatro)
   c. Hace ...... tiempo ...... que no veo a Julio. (mucho)
   d. Le gusta cocinar, por eso busca una casa que tenga una ...... cocina ...... (grande)

8. Complete the blank cells of the following table:

Adjective	Meaning when placed before the noun	Meaning when placed after the noun
	good, nice	sweet
mismo	same	
cierto		true, right
diferente	various	
solo		lonely, alone

9. Complete with -O, -A, -OS or -AS:
   a. Feminine, plural adjectives end in ...
   b. Masculine, singular adjectives end in ...
   c. Feminine, singular adjectives end in ...
   d. Masculine, plural adjectives end in ...

10. Complete the missing cells of the following table.

Masculine singular	Feminine singular	Masculine plural	Feminine Plural
		bonitos	
imposible			
		familiares	
			cuadradas

389

Answer Key

1. a. quienes
    b. que
    c. quien

2. a. las
    b. el
    c. la
    d. los

3.
    a.

4.
    a. defining
    b. defining
    c. defining
    d. non-defining
    e. non-defining
    f. non-defining
    g. non-defining

5.
    a. La Estatua de la Libertad, que está en Nueva York, mide 93 metros.
    b. El presidente de Francia, Emmanuel Macron, llegó a la ciudad el lunes por la noche.
    c. Los niños que vinieron anoche son los hijos de mi hermana.
    d. La famosa fuente romana, que se llama Fontana de Trevi, se construyó en el siglo XVI.

6. b.

7. a. La camisa roja te queda muy bien.
    b. Mi marido me pidió que compre cuatro bananas porque va a cocinar una torta.
    c. Hace mucho tiempo que no veo a Julio.
    d. Le gusta cocinar, por eso busca una casa que tenga una cocina grande.

Adjective	Meaning when placed before the noun	Meaning when placed after the noun
dulce	good, nice	sweet
mismo	same	himself, herself
cierto	certain	true, right
diferente	various	different
solo	one, only	lonely, alone

8. a. -AS
   b. -O
   c. -A
   d. -OS

9.

Masculine singular	Feminine singular	Masculine plural	Feminine Plural
bonito	bonita	bonitos	bonitas
imposible	imposible	imposibles	imposibles
familiar	familiar	familiares	familiares
cuadrado	cuadrada	cuadrados	cuadradas

Chapter 3: Present Subjunctive in Use

En verdad hay sentimientos que es mejor que se queden en lo platónico; y es mejor recordarlos así, irreales, inacabados, porque eso es lo que los hace perfecto.

- Gabriel García Márquez

In this chapter, we will be talking about the subjunctive mood. So far, we've only talked about the indicative mood, which is used for real situations. Now, we will enter the realm of unreal situations, which is what the subjunctive mood is used for.

In English, this mood isn't expressed through tenses but through the use of modals. In Spanish, there are three subjunctive mood tenses: *presente del subjuntivo, futuro del subjuntivo* and *pretérito imperfecto del subjuntivo*. In this chapter, we'll be dealing with the present subjunctive and its uses.

Presente del subjuntivo

The present subjunctive can be used to express possibility, desire, impressions and hypothetical situations and giving opinions and recommendations.

Of course, in Spanish, this tense needs to be conjugated to agree in person and number with the subject. Here's how the prototype verbs we've been using are conjugated in the present subjunctive.

	Cantar	Comer	Vivir
yo	cante	coma	viva
tú	cantes	comas	vivas
él / ella / usted	cante	coma	viva
nosotros / nosotras	cantemos	comamos	vivamos
vosotros / vosotras	cantéis	comáis	viváis
ellos / ellas / ustedes	canten	coman	vivan

If you take a look at the chart above, you will see that the present subjunctive endings of infinitive verbs ending in *-er* and *-ir* are exactly the same, which makes it easier to remember. However, there's another trick to remembering this conjugation: if we compare these conjugations with the present indicative conjugations, you might see that it is as if the conjugations for verbs ending in *-ar* and the conjugations for verbs ending in *-er* have been swapped!

Take a look at the following chart to see what I mean:

	Cantar		Comer	
	presente de indicativo	presente de subjuntivo	presente de indicativo	presente de subjuntivo
yo	canto	cant<u>e</u>	como	com<u>a</u>
tú	cant<u>as</u>	cant<u>es</u>	com<u>es</u>	com<u>as</u>
él / ella / usted	cant<u>a</u>	cant<u>e</u>	com<u>e</u>	com<u>a</u>
nosotros / nosotras	cant<u>amos</u>	cant<u>emos</u>	com<u>emos</u>	com<u>amos</u>
vosotros / vosotras	cant<u>áis</u>	cant<u>éis</u>	com<u>éis</u>	com<u>áis</u>
ellos / ellas / ustedes	cant<u>an</u>	cant<u>en</u>	com<u>en</u>	com<u>an</u>

Can you see now that the endings for present indicative verbs ending in -*ar* are now the endings for present subjunctive verbs ending in -*er* and -*ir*? And that the endings for present indicative verbs ending in -*er* are now the endings for present subjunctive verbs ending in -*ar*? I hope this trick makes it easier for you to remember these regular conjugations!

Let's see these verbs in use!

- *Espero que **vivas** una vida larga y feliz.*
- *Quiero que **coman** todo lo que tienen en el plato.*
- *Ojalá que **cantemos** mejor que nunca.*

As these are only prototypes of regular verbs, we can also apply these endings to form the present subjunctive of other regular verbs, so let's see some examples!

- *¿Quieres que **hablemos** de lo que te sucede?*
- *Tal vez **partamos** a horario esta vez.*
- *Quiero que **lean** el libro hasta la página 30.*

However, and as you might already imagine, there are also irregular verbs in the present subjunctive. In the following table, there are a few of them:

	Ser	Ir	Poder	Pedir	Hacer
yo	sea	vaya	pueda	pida	haga
tú	seas	vayas	puedas	pidas	hagas

él / ella / usted	sea	vaya	pueda	pida	haga
nosotros / nosotras	seamos	vayamos	podamos	pidamos	hagamos
vosotros / vosotras	seáis	vayáis	podáis	pidáis	hagáis
ellos / ellas / ustedes	sean	vayan	puedan	pidan	hagan

Here are some examples using these irregular verbs:

- *Aunque **podamos** salir, no creo que sea una buena idea.*
- *Espero que **vayáis** a la boda de Pedro y Luz.*
- *Dudo que Juan **haga** todo hoy, dijo que estaba muy ocupado.*
- *No me **pidas** que me case contigo si no me amas.*
- *Ojalá sus nuevos compañeros no **sean** malos con ella, es una niña muy sensible.*

Maybe you didn't notice, but some irregularities in the present subjunctive are similar to those in the present indicative, only with a different ending.

First, we have verbs like *poder* which, in the present indicative and in the present subjunctive, undergo a vocalic change in the first, second a third-person singular and in the third person plural. In this case, *poder* goes from O to UE. And the same happens with verbs like *querer*, which go from E to IE, and verbs like *jugar*, which go from U to UE, and maintain this irregularity in the present subjunctive. Here's a table to illustrate this:

	Poder		Querer		Jugar	
	presente de indicativo	presente de subjuntivo	presente de indicativo	presente de subjuntivo	presente de indicativo	presente de subjuntivo
yo	puedo	pueda	quiero	quiera	juego	juegue
tú	puedes	puedas	quieres	quieras	juegas	juegues
él / ella / usted	puede	pueda	quiere	quiera	juega	juegue
nosotros / nosotras	podemos	podamos	queremos	queramos	jugamos	juguemos
vosotros / vosotras	podéis	podáis	queréis	queráis	jugáis	juguéis
ellos / ellas / ustedes	pueden	puedan	quieren	quieran	juegan	jueguen

394

Let's compare the present indicative and subjunctive with some examples:

- Indicative: ***Puedo*** *ir a comprar el pan si* **quieres**.
- Subjunctive: *Aunque* **pueda** *comprar el pan, no creo que* **quieras** *que lo haga.*
- Subjunctive: *Me pone nerviosa que los niños* ***jueguen*** *con esas cosas.*
- Indicative: *Mis niños no* ***juegan*** *con esas cosas.*

Moreover, some verbs like *hacer* that present an irregularity in the first person of the present indicative (*hago*) have the same irregularity in the present indicative, only in every person. This also applies to other verbs like *pedir*, which undergoes a vocalic change like we've seen before (but this time from E to I). In this case, this irregularity is maintained in all present subjunctive conjugations, including the first and second-person plural. Here's a table that compares the present indicative and the present subjunctive of these two verbs.

	Hacer		Pedir	
	presente de indicativo	presente de subjuntivo	presente de indicativo	presente de subjuntivo
yo	hago	haga	pido	pida
tú	haces	hagas	pides	pidas
él / ella / usted	hace	haga	pide	pida
nosotros / nosotras	hacemos	hagamos	pedimos	pidamos
vosotros/vosotras	hacéis	hagáis	pedís	pidáis
ellos/ellas/ustedes	hacen	hagan	piden	pidan

Let's compare the present indicative and subjunctive forms of these verbs:

- Indicative: Cuando **haces** eso, me haces enojar.
- Subjunctive: Me enoja que **hagas** eso.
- Indicative: ¿**Pedimos** una pizza?
- Subjunctive: ¿Quieres que **pidamos** una pizza?

Here's a list of other verbs with these irregularities in the present indicative and the present subjunctive with some examples:

- *tener → tengo - tenga*
  - *Ojalá que* ***tengas*** *dinero porque lo vamos a necesitar.*
- *poner → pongo - ponga*

- ○ *¿Te molesta que **ponga** los pies encima de la mesa?*
- *salir → salgo - salga*
  - ○ *Cuando **salga** la próxima película estaré emocionadísimo.*
- *decir → digo - diga*
  - ○ *Necesitamos que **digas** la verdad.*
- *venir → vengo - venga*
  - ○ *Aunque **venga**, no lo dejaré entrar.*
- *conocer → conozco - conozca*
  - ○ *No creo que **conozcas** a Carlos, es nuevo.*
- *seguir → sigo - siga*
  - ○ *Quiero que sigas trabajando en la empresa.*

Uses of the present subjunctive

As we've already mentioned, the present subjunctive can be used to express possibility, desire, impressions and hypothetical situations and giving opinions and recommendations. But now, it's time to see how to use it for each of these things.

Expressing desire

We use the subjunctive to express desire when we want someone different from the subject of the main clause to do something.

For example, we can express our desire for someone else to do something: *Deseo que Juan **llegue** temprano a casa* ("I wish Juan would get home early"). In this example, the first person is the one who wishes something, but the wish is about Juan, a third-person.

However, if we wanted to say "I wish to get home early", we would not use the subjunctive but the infinitive because the person who wishes and the person the wish is about are the same: *Deseo **llegar** temprano a casa.*

Another example could be: *Queremos que **vengas** a cenar con nosotros.* ("We want you to come have dinner with us"). In this example, the subject of the main clause is *nosotros*, but the person who *nosotros* wants to do the action is an implicit *tú*.

To express desire and trigger the subjunctive mood, we can use phrases such as these ones:

- *Ojalá que* ("to wish…"): *Ojalá que te **vaya** bien hoy.*
- *Esperar que* ("to hope…"): *Espero que te **guste** el regalo.*
- *Desear que* ("to wish…"): *Deseo que **tengas** un feliz cumpleaños.*
- *Querer que* ("to want…"): *Quiero que me **envíes** los papeles mañana.*

Expressing necessity

Expressing necessity with the subjunctive works similarly to expressing desire. In this case, there are also two different subjects. Compare these two sentences:

- *Necesitamos **cambiar** el horario de la reunión.*
- *Necesito que **cambies** el horario de la reunión.*

In the first one, we use the infinitive and the same subject: the first-person plural is the one speaking and the one who needs to change the time of the meeting. However, in the second sentence we use *que* and the subjunctive and two different subjects: a first-person singular is the one who needs a second-person singular to change the time of the meeting.

Stating an opinion or perception

When giving opinions, we should use the present indicative with affirmative phrases, like *Creo que a Ana le **gusta** la pizza*, but the present subjunctive with negative phrases, like *No creo que a Ana le **guste** la pizza.*

In this case, the subjects of the sentence can be the same or different. For example, if we've never tried it before, we can say *No creo que me **guste** la pizza.*

However, we need to take into account that, if the subordinate clause is the one that is negative, then we should use the indicative mood. For example: *Creo que a Ana no le **gusta** la pizza.*

- *No creer que* ("to don't think…"): *No creo que **vaya** a la fiesta de hoy.*
- *No pensar que* ("to don't think…"): *No pienso que **tengas** razón.*
- *No estar convencido/a de que* ("to not be sure that…"): *Juan no está convencido de que **sea** una buena idea.*

Expressing interests and feelings

To express interests and feelings, we can use expressions such as *encantar*. Even though we can use verbs such as *encantar* with singular nouns, plural nouns and infinitive verbs, we can also use them with *que* + subjunctive. For example: *Me encanta que vengas a verme.*

We should bear in mind that, just like when expressing necessity or desire with the subjunctive, our interests and feelings are about someone else doing something. That is to say that there are two subjects in the same sentences: one who has feelings or interests and one who provokes them.

Other verbs we can use in this way are:

- *dar miedo* ("to find scary"): *Nos da miedo que **apagues** las luces.*
- *dar pereza* ("to be lazy"): *Les da pereza que Juan no los **lleve** a la clase.*
- *entusiasmar* ("to find exciting"): *¿Os entusiasma que **sea** mejor alumna?*
- *fascinar* ("to find fascinating"): *Me fascina que mi hermano **dirija** películas.*
- *gustar* ("to like"): *Le gusta que su novio le **regale** bombones.*
- *importar* ("to care"): *Te importa que tu hija **haga** bien la tarea.*
- *interesar* ("to find interesting"): *Le interesa que las camareras **estén** cómodas.*
- *irritar* ("to find irritating"): *Me irrita que mi suegra no me **llame** por mi nombre.*
- *molestar* ("to find annoying"): *A Juana le molesta que **toques** el piano tan temprano.*
- *poner nervioso* ("to feel nervous"): *A nosotros nos pone nerviosos que Juana no nos **cuente** la historia completa.*
- *poner triste* ("to feel sad"): *Me pone triste que mi perro **pueda** morir.*

Remember that it is necessary to use the personal pronouns *me, te, le, nos, os,* or *les* with every one of these verbs. These personal pronouns need to agree with the subject of the main sentence and not the thing or person that provokes the feeling or interest.

Expressing doubt and probability

Using the subjunctive, we can also express doubt and probability when we are merely hypothesizing and we are not at all certain whether what we are saying is true or not. For example: *Seguramente* **esté** *en su casa.*

We can also use the indicative for sentences like this one to express that something may or may not happen, but we are almost certain that it's true. For example: *Seguramente está en su casa.*

There are some phrases that we can use to express doubt using the subjunctive. Here are a few of them:

- *Dudar que* ("to doubt that"): *Dudo que Juan* **vuelva** *a la fiesta.*
- *Tal vez* ("maybe"): *Tal vez* **vaya** *a saludarlos más tarde.*
- *Quizás* ("maybe"): *Quizás* **pueda** *ir a la reunión de mañana.*
- *Probablemente* ("probably"): *Probablemente* **corramos** *en el torneo de mañana.*
- *Posiblemente* ("possibly"): *Posiblemente* **veáis** *una película esta noche.*
- *Seguramente* ("surely"): *Seguramente* **estén** *viajando.*

Giving advice and orders and asking someone to do something

We can also give advice and ask someone to do something using the subjunctive.

To give advice, we can use the following verbs:

- *Aconsejar* ("advice"): *Te aconsejo que te* **acuestes** *temprano.*
- *Recomendar* ("recommend"): *Te recomiendo que* **dejes** *de tomar alcohol.*

To give orders, we can use the following verbs:

- *Prohibir que* ("to prohibit"): *Le prohibo que* **mire** *más de dos horas diarias de televisión.*
- *Ordenar que* ("to give an order"): *Te ordeno que* **limpies** *todas las mesas.*
- *Exigir que* ("to demand"): *Exijo que* **llames** *al gerente.*

Finally, to ask someone to do something, we can use the following verbs:

- *Pedir que* ("to ask"): *Juana me pidió que la* **acompañe** *al médico.*

Expressing purpose

In this case, the subjunctive is also used when there are two different subjects in the same sentence, whereas we can use the infinitive when the two subjects coincide. For example, compare the following sentences:

- *Vamos al concierto para* **disfrutar**.
- *Vamos al concierto para que* **disfrutes**.

In the first one, the people who went to the concert and who had to enjoy it are the same. However, in the second sentence, there is a first person plural who went to the concert, but only one of them was the one who had to enjoy it.

To express purpose, we can use the following words or phrases:

- *Para* ("to"): *Vamos en auto para que Camila no se **maree**.*

- *Con el objetivo de que* ("with the purpose of"): *Tomamos exámenes con el objetivo de que los alumnos **sean** evaluados.*

- *Con la intención de que* ("with the intention of"): *Jugamos a las cartas con la intención de que nuestros hijos se **diviertan**.*

- *Con el fin de que* ("with the purpose of"): *Me cepillo el cabello todas las mañanas con el fin de que no se **encrespe**.*

Other words and phrases that trigger the subjunctive

Some words and phrases need to be followed by the subjunctive in some cases. Here are a few of those words with their meanings along with an example.

- *a no ser que* ("unless"): *Quiero que vengas, a no ser que **tengas** otros planes.*

- *a pesar de que* ("despite"): *A pesar de que te **vayas**, siempre te voy a querer.*

- *antes de que* ("before"): *Ve a buscarla antes que **sea** tarde.*

- *aunque* ("although"): *Aunque no lo **digas**, sé que la amas.*

- *con tal de que* ("as long as"): *Haría cualquier cosa con tal de que se **vayan**.*

- *cuando* ("when"): *Cuando **tengas** frío, ponte el abrigo.*

- *después de que* ("after"): *Iré a verte después de que me **llames**.*

- *en el caso que* ("in case that"): *Os llamaré en caso de que los **necesite**.*

- *hasta que* ("until"): *Te veré en el hospital hasta que **estés** mejor.*

- *sin que* ("without"): *Sin que te **ofendas**, creo que debes dejar de hacer eso.*

- *tan pronto como* ("as soon as"): *Tan pronto como ella te **escuche** llegar, se emocionará.*

Key Takeaways

In this chapter we've talked about the **present subjunctive** in Spanish.

- The subjunctive is one of the Spanish language's three moods (indicative, subjunctive and imperative).

- The subjunctive is used to talk about unreal situations. This can include:

  o Expressing desire.

  o Expressing necessity.

  o Stating an opinion or perception.

  o Expressing interests or feelings.

  o Expressing doubt and probability.

- o Giving advice and orders, and asking someone to do something.
- o Expressing purpose.
- There are also words and phrases that trigger the subjunctive:
  - o *a no ser que*
  - o *a pesar de que*
  - o *antes de que*
  - o *aunque*
  - o *con tal de que*
  - o *cuando*
  - o *después de que*
  - o *en el caso que*
  - o *hasta que*
  - o *sin que*
  - o *tan pronto como*

In the following chapter, we will be dealing with another past tense and everything we need to narrate good anecdotes. But first, it's time for some exercises on everything we've covered in this chapter!

Exercises

1. Which of the following is **not** a use of the subjunctive:
   a. Expressing desire
   b. Expressing interests and feelings
   c. Expressing necessity
   d. Expressing quantity

2. Can you complete this table with the present subjunctive form of these verbs?

	Sentir	Salir	Decir
yo	sienta	....	diga
tú	....	salgas	....
él / ella / usted	....	salga	diga
nosotros / nosotras	sintamos	....	....
vosotros / vosotras	....	salgáis	....
ellos / ellas / ustedes	sientan	....	digan

3. What is the present subjunctive used for in the following sentences?
   a. ¡Exijo que me devuelvan mi dinero!
   b. Seguramente Camila se quede a dormir en mi casa.

    c. Necesitamos que vengas cuanto antes.

    d. Espero que estés muy bien.

    e. No creo que sea una buena idea salir con nieve.

4. How would you express desire using the subjunctive?

    a. Deseo que tienes un buen día.

    b. Ojalá que tengas un buen día.

    c. Necesito tener un buen día.

5. How would you give advice using the subjunctive?

    a. Recomiendo dejar de hacer eso.

    b. Te prohibo que dejes de hacer eso.

    c. Te aconsejo que dejes de hacer eso.

6. Fill in the gaps with the present subjunctive form of the verbs in parentheses.

    a. Iremos a la playa para que mi perro .... (tocar) el mar por primera vez.

    b. Me da miedo que Helena y José .... (tener) problemas para llegar.

    c. Necesito que .... (tú/ir) a comprar una torta de cumpleaños.

    d. Posiblemente vosotros .... (salir) mañana a la mañana.

7. Complete the following text with the present subjunctive form of the verbs in parentheses.
Tengo ganas de que mi familia y yo .... (viajar) a Japón el próximo verano. Para
eso, necesito que todos .... (ahorrar) mucho dinero, así que me da miedo que no
.... (llegar) a conseguir todo. Ojalá .... (poder) hacerlo, pero es un poco
difícil. Iremos para que mis hijos .... (conocer) a mi hermana, que vive allí desde
hace algunos años. Cuando .... (estar) allí, mi hermano nos ayudará con el idioma,
así que no creo que .... (tener) problemas con eso. ¡Espero que todo ....
(salir) bien!

8. Complete the following sentences with either the present indicative or the present subjunctive
forms of the verbs in parentheses.

    a. Quiero que .... (tú/venir) a mi casa hoy.

    b. ¿......................... (tú/venir) a mi casa hoy?

    c. La biblioteca no .... (tener) el libro que necesito.

    d. Espero que la biblioteca .... (tener) el libro que necesito.

    e. Creo que .... (yo/ir) a jugar al fútbol a la tarde.

    f. No creo que Iván .... (ir) a jugar al fútbol a la tarde.

    g. Posiblemente Juan .... (hacer) sus quehaceres mañana.

    h. Nunca .... (hacer) mis quehaceres por la mañana.

9. Complete the following sentences with the phrases from the box. They are only used once each.

> sin que - cuando - a no ser que -

> con tal de que - después de que - aunque

    a. No podrás ir a la fiesta .... hagas tu tarea.

    b. ¡Mira! He sacado la basura .... me lo hayas pedido.

    c. Siempre estaré para ayudar, ... sea difícil.

    d. Haré todo lo que quieras .... me dejes en paz.

    e. .... vayas a la casa de Sandra, salúdala de mi parte.

    f. Solo haré lo que me pides .... te vayas.

10. Complete the following sentences with the phrases from the box. They are only used once each.

> antes de que - hasta que - tan pronto como -
>
> en el caso que - a pesar de que

    a. .... no hayas hecho nada, puedes ir a jugar.

    b. No puede salir de la casa .... te laves las manos.

    c. .... tengas que hacer algo, no te preocupes por venir.

    d. Iré a verte .... llegue a la ciudad.

    e. Debemos limpiar esa herida .... se infecte.

Answer Key

1. d. Expressing quantity

2.

	Sentir	Salir	Decir
yo	sienta	<u>salga</u>	diga
tú	<u>sientas</u>	salgas	<u>digas</u>
él / ella / usted	<u>sienta</u>	salga	diga
nosotros / nosotras	sintamos	<u>salgamos</u>	<u>digamos</u>
vosotros / vosotras	<u>sintáis</u>	salgáis	<u>digáis</u>
ellos / ellas / ustedes	sientan	<u>salgan</u>	digan

3.

    a. Asking someone to do something

    b. Expressing probability

    c. Expressing necessity

    d. Expressing desire

    e. Stating an opinion

4. b. Ojalá que tengas un buen día.

5. c. Te aconsejo que dejes de hacer eso.

6.

    a. toque

    b. tengan

    c. vayas

    d. salgáis

7. viajemos; ahorremos; lleguemos; podamos; conozcan; estemos; tengamos, salga

8.

    a. vengas (subjunctive)

    b. vienes (indicative)

    c. tiene (indicative)

    d. tenga (subjunctive)

    e. voy (indicative)

    f. vaya (subjunctive)

    g. haga (subjunctive)

    h. hago (indicative)

9.

a. a menos que

b. sin que

c. aunque

d. con tal de que

e. Cuando

f. después de que

10.

a. A pesar de que

b. hasta que

c. En el caso que

d. tan pronto como

e. antes de que

Chapter 4: Anecdotes

⌘

Cuando alcanzas mi edad, te das cuenta de que no podrías haber hecho las cosas mucho mejor o mucho peor de lo que las hiciste en primer lugar.

- Jorge Luis Borges

We will be learning to narrate anecdotes in this chapter. To do this, we will be learning to use the *pretérito pluscuamperfecto* in order to combine it with some resources that will help us use different past tenses in our narrations. That way, our anecdotes will be full of details and we will be able to recount exactly what happened.

Let get to it!

Pretérito pluscuamperfecto

In the first chapter of this book, we've seen three different past tenses from the indicative, but now it's time to learn a fourth one—the *pretérito pluscuamperfecto*. This tense is used to talk about a past action that took place before another past action, which is why sometimes we also refer to it as the past of the past. We can also use it to say that it is the first time we're doing something because we've never done it before and to express that an action happened immediately after another one. Let's see some examples:

- Pablo y Susana **habían caminado** cinco kilómetros para llegar.
- Juana está de viaje por Europa, nunca antes **había ido**.
- Marcos y Lorena se casaron en mayo y en agosto ya **habían tenido** su primer hijo.

If it makes it easier, we could say that the *pretérito pluscuamperfecto* is used in a similar way to the English past perfect. And this is also true for its form and conjugation! Just like the *pretérito perfecto compuesto*, the *pretérito pluscuamperfecto* is formed by the verb *haber* as an auxiliary and the participle form of the action verb. However, for the *pretérito pluscuamperfecto,* the verb *haber* needs to be conjugated in the *pretérito imperfecto* instead of the present. Look at the following chart to see the *pretérito pluscuamperfecto* form of the regular verbs we've been working with:

	Cantar	Comer	Vivir
yo	había cantado	había comido	había vivido
tú	habías cantado	habías comido	habías vivido
él / ella / usted	había cantado	había comido	había vivido
nosotros / nosotras	habíamos cantado	habíamos comido	habíamos vivido

| vosotros / vosotras | habíais cantado | habíais comido | habíais vivido |
| ellos / ellas / ustedes | habían cantado | habían comido | habían vivido |

Let's see a few examples with these verbs:

- Daniela nos invitó a cenar con ellos, pero ya **habíamos comido** antes de llegar.
- Malena recordaba ese escenario, **había cantado** allí con el coro de su escuela cuando era pequeña.
- Vosotros **habíais vivido** tres años en Madrid antes de mudaros a Barcelona, ¿verdad?

Luckily, the irregular verbs in this case are the same as the irregular participles we've seen for the *pretérito imperfecto*.

After all, the name of this past tense is harder than its conjugation, right?

Combining past tenses

Now we're going to see how to use all the past tenses we've seen so far to narrate an anecdote.

First of all, in any anecdote we need to set the scene or put our audience in context. To do this, we usually use the *pretérito imperfecto*. For example, we can say:

1. ***Eran*** *las 6 de la mañana y no podía dormir...*
2. ***Había*** *mucha gente en el aeropuerto...*
3. ***Estaba*** *paseando al perro....*

However, you should note that the context is not enough when we're telling an anecdote. When combining past tenses, you always need to use the *pretérito imperfecto* to describe some main events that happen in the situation. When telling an anecdote of a particular event in the past, we use the *pretérito perfecto simple*. For example, following the previous examples, we can say:

1. *Eran las 6 de la mañana y no podía dormir. De pronto,* ***oí*** *un ruido muy extraño afuera de mi puerta.*
2. *Había mucha gente en el aeropuerto, así que* ***estuve*** *mucho tiempo en la fila hasta que me* ***atendieron.***
3. *Estaba paseando al perro cuando* ***vi*** *un oso cerca del agua.*

You should know that the differences in use between the uses of the *pretérito imperfecto* and the *pretérito perfecto simple* are unrelated to the duration of the actions. Instead, you should focus on how you want to present the action and what its function inside the anecdote is. Let's compare these two examples:

- *Como ayer* ***nevaba,*** *no* ***pude*** *ir.* (In this sentence, the fact that it was snowing is merely a circumstance that prevented me from going somewhere)
- *Ayer* ***nevó*** *toda la tarde y no* ***pude*** *ir.* (In this sentence, we present the snow and not being able to go as two events at the same level, and we also express the duration of the snow)

We can also mention some events that happened before the ones in *pretérito perfecto simple* that may be useful to explain something else. For this, we use the *pretérito pluscuamperfecto*. Following the previous examples, we can say:

1. *Eran las 6 de la mañana y no podía dormir. De pronto, oí un ruido muy extraño afuera de mi puerta. No era la primera vez que **había oído** un ruido como ese.*

2. *Había mucha gente en el aeropuerto, así que estuve mucho tiempo en la fila hasta que me atendieron. La persona que me atendió me preguntó por qué **había hecho** esa fila ya que, en realidad, debía hacer la fila de al lado.*

3. *Estaba paseando al perro cuando vi un oso cerca del agua. Cuando era pequeño, me **habían dicho** que si me sucedía algo así, debía quedarme quieto, así que hice eso.*

Though it is not always the case, you can finish your anecdote using the *pretérito perfecto compuesto* to say something that is linked with the time of speaking. For example:

1. *Eran las 6 de la mañana y no podía dormir. De pronto, oí un ruido muy extraño afuera de mi puerta. No era la primera vez que había oído un ruido como ese. Hoy, cuando me desperté, **he vuelto** a oírlo.*

2. *Había mucha gente en el aeropuerto, así que estuve mucho tiempo en la fila hasta que me atendieron. La persona que me atendió me preguntó por qué había hecho esa fila ya que, en realidad, debía hacer la fila de al lado. Ese día la chica me dejó pasar igual, pero esta mañana **he vuelto** al aeropuerto e hice la fila correcta.*

3. *Estaba paseando al perro cuando vi un oso cerca del agua. Cuando era pequeño, me habían dicho que si me sucedía algo así, debía quedarme quieto, así que hice eso. Y este fin de semana, me **ha pasado** lo mismo, ¿puedes creerlo?*

Moreover, the *pretérito perfecto compuesto* could be used to talk about the main events of the anecdote, just like the *pretérito perfecto simple*. However, you should always keep in mind that the events need to have some kind of connection with the present if we use the *pretérito perfecto compuesto*.

1. ***Hoy** no **he podido** dormir nada.*

2. ***Este mes he ido** al aeropuerto unas 3 veces.*

3. *Esta mañana estaba paseando al perro y **he visto** un oso cerca del agua.*

Resources to narrate anecdotes

In order to tell a good anecdote, we need to learn some resources that will make our stories more interesting and appealing. Let's see some of them!

Starting an anecdote

First things first, we need to learn how to start narrating anecdotes, right? Well, to do this, we can use several phrases such as:

- *Resulta que* ("so, it turns out that"): ***Resulta que** estaba en Barcelona cuando...*

- *Una vez* ("once"): ***Una vez** estaba caminando cuando...*

- *Un día* ("one day"): ***Un día** encontré dinero en el piso.*

407

- *Una noche* ("one night"): ***Una noche*** *soñé contigo.*

- *Hace unos meses* ("a few months ago"): ***Hace unos meses*** *vi a tu hermano.*

- *El otro día* ("the other day"): ***El otro día*** *fui al cine...*

- *Ayer* ("yesterday"): ***Ayer*** *mis padres fueron al museo.*

- *El mes pasado* ("last month"): ***El mes pasado*** *tenía mucha comezón.*

- *No sabes lo que me pasó* ("You won't believe what happened to me"): ***No sabes lo que me pasó***, *íbamos caminando por la calle cuando...*

Connectors of order

To present our anecdote in an orderly manner, we can use connectors of order

- *En primer lugar* ("in the first place"): ***En primer lugar***, *fui a la tienda. En segundo lugar, fui a la farmacia.*

- *Para comenzar* ("to begin with"): ***Para comenzar***, *hicimos una fogata.*

- *Luego* ("afterwards"): ***Luego*** *fuimos a la casa de Juan.*

- *Después* ("after"): ***Después*** *de caminar, fuimos a la playa.*

- *Más tarde* ("later"): ***Más tarde*** *tomamos un té y conversamos.*

Add new or similar ideas

We might also want to add some events or ideas to our anecdotes, and to do this we can use the following words and phrases.

- *Igualmente* ("likewise", "anyway"): *Laura y Sandra no querían ir a la fiesta, pero* ***igualmente*** *fueron.*

- *Otra vez* ("again"): *Cuando la vi, llevaba puesto ese vestido* ***otra vez***.

- *De nuevo* ("again"): *Fui a Barcelona* ***de nuevo*** *este verano.*

- *También* ("too"): *¿Habéis estado en Madrid en 2005? ¡Yo también!*

Limit or contradict an idea

We can also limit or contradict an idea we are talking about in our anecdotes:

- *Aunque* ("although"): ***Aunque*** *te parezca una tontería, para mí era importante.*

- *Pero* ("but"): *Tenía miedo,* ***pero*** *salí a investigar.*

- *A pesar de* ("in spite of"): ***A pesar de*** *que quería comer chocolate, dije que no.*

- *Sin embargo* ("However"): *Me preparé y salí de mi casa.* ***Sin embargo***, *me arrepentí al instante.*

Connectors of cause and consequence

To present causes and consequences, we can use the following words and phrases:

- *Como* ("as"): ***Como*** *estaba perdido, llegué tarde a la fiesta.*

- *Porque* ("because"): *Estaba en mi casa **porque** ese día no trabajaba.*

- *Así que* ("so"): *No tenía dinero, **así que** no fui al restaurante.*

- *De modo que* ("so"): *La turbina había fallado, **de modo que** tuvimos que esperar a que arreglaran el avión.*

- *Por eso* ("that's why"): *Clara estaba ocupada, **por eso** no vino.*

- *Entonces* ("so"): *Estaba enfermo, **entonces** no vistió a su abuela.*

Temporal references to tell an anecdote

We should also know how to present different temporal references to make our anecdote move forwards and backwards in time:

- *Aquel día* ("that day"): ***Aquel día,** fui a verla y le llevé un ramo de flores.*

- *Aquella mañana* ("that morning"): ***Aquella mañana,** nos encontramos en el banco.*

- *Al año siguiente* ("the next year"): ***Al año siguiente,** nos volvimos a ver.*

- *A la semana siguiente* ("the next week"): ***A la semana siguiente**, el problema se había solucionado.*

- *El mes anterior* ("the previous month"): ***El mes anterior**, Juan había hecho el mismo trámite que yo.*

- *La noche anterior* ("the previous night"): ***La noche anterior,** nos habían dado una clase sobre eso.*

Ending an anecdote

Finally, when our anecdote has come to an end, we need to add a connector to end it. Some connectors you could use are:

- *Al final* ("in the end"): ***Al final**, ninguno de ellos recordaba nada.*

- *Total, que* ("so"): ***Total, que** hicimos todo y nos divertimos mucho.*

- *Al fin y al cabo* ("after all"): ***Al fin y al cabo**, todo lo que habíamos hecho no era necesario.*

- *Después de todo* ("after all"): ***Después de todo**, Andrés pudo comer todo.*

Listening to anecdotes

Listening to anecdotes, especially at first, is just as important as narrating the anecdote itself. Of course, we are not talking about how to use your ears, but about how to react when somebody is telling you about something that happened to them.

To show interest when someone is talking to us, we can ask questions to learn more details. For example:

Phrase	Pronunciation	Translation
¿Y qué hiciste?	ee kee ee-SEES-teh	And what did you do?

¿Y qué te dijo?	ee keh teh DEE-hoh	And did he/she say?
¿Cómo terminó?	KOH-mo tehr-mee-NOH	How did it end?
¿Qué pasó?	keh pah-SOH	What happened?

We can also agree with what the other person is stating. To do this, we can say:

Word	Pronunciation	Translation
Claro	KLAH-roh	Sure
Lógico	LOH-hee-koh	Of course
Normal	NOHR-mal	Right
Ya	Shah	Right
Obviamente	oh-bee-ah-MEN-teh	Obviously

Moreover, in Spanish, we can use some interjections to express the feelings the anecdote makes us feel. We can use phrases such as:

Phrase	Pronunciation	Translation
¡No!	noh	¡No!
¿En serio?	ehn seh-REE-oh	Really?
¿De verdad?	deh BEHR-dahd	¿Seriously?
¿Ah, sí?	ah see	Really?
¡No lo puedo creer!	noh loh poo-EH-doh kreh-EHR	I can't believe it!
¡Qué mala suerte!	keh MAH-lah SOO-ehr-teh	How unlucky!
¡Qué buena suerte!	keh BOO-eh-nah SOO-ehr-teh	How lucky!
¡No me digas!	noh meh DEE-gahs	Really?
¡Qué rabia!	keh RRAH-bee-ah	That's enraging!

¡Qué extraño!	keh ehx-TRAH-nyoh	How strange!
¡Qué mal!	keh mahl	How bad!
¡Qué bien!	keh bee-ehn	How good!

Key Takeaways

Here's a list of topics we've covered throughout this chapter on **anecdotes**:

- The *pretérito pluscuamperfecto* is used to talk about an action in the past that took place before another action in the past.

- We can combine the *pretérito pluscuamperfecto* with the *pretérito perfecto simple*, *pretérito perfecto compuesto* and the *pretérito imperfecto* to tell anecdotes:

  - We use the *pretérito imperfecto* to talk about the circumstances surrounding the anecdote.

  - We use the *pretérito perfecto simple* or the *pretérito perfecto compuesto* to talk about the main events of the anecdote. We can only use the *pretérito perfecto compuesto*, however, if the event is somehow related to the time of speaking.

  - We can also use the *pretérito pluscuamperfecto* to talk about an action or event that happened before the action or event in the *pretérito perfecto simple*.

  - We can also use the *pretérito perfecto compuesto* at the end of the anecdote to relate the resolution of the anecdote to the present.

- To tell an anecdote, we can also use some connectors:

  - To start:
    - *Resulta que*
    - *Una vez*
    - *Un día*
    - *Una noche*
    - *Hace unos meses*
    - *El otro día*
    - *Ayer*
    - *El mes pasado*
    - *No sabes lo que me pasó*

  - To order:
    - *En primer lugar*
    - *Para comenzar*
    - *Luego*
    - *Después*

- ■ *Más tarde*
  - ○ To add new or similar ideas:
    - ■ *Igualmente*
    - ■ *Otra vez*
    - ■ *De nuevo*
    - ■ *También*
  - ○ To limit or contradict an idea
    - ■ *Aunque*
    - ■ *Pero*
    - ■ *A pesar de*
    - ■ *Sin embargo*
  - ○ To express cause and consequence
    - ■ *Como*
    - ■ *Porque*
    - ■ *Así que*
    - ■ *De modo que*
    - ■ *Por eso*
    - ■ *Entonces*
  - ○ To express temporal reference
    - ■ *Aquel día*
    - ■ *Aquella mañana*
    - ■ *Al año siguiente*
    - ■ *A la semana siguiente*
    - ■ *El mes anterior*
    - ■ *La noche anterior*
  - ○ To finish
    - ■ *Al final*
    - ■ *Total, que*
    - ■ *Al fin y al cabo*
    - ■ *Después de todo*
- We can also use some words and expressions to react to an anecdote
  - ○ To show interest
    - ■ *¿Y qué hiciste?*
    - ■ *¿Y qué te dijo?*
    - ■ *¿Cómo terminó?*

- ■ *¿Qué pasó?*
  - ○ To agree with what the other person is saying
    - ■ *Claro*
    - ■ *Lógico*
    - ■ *Normal*
    - ■ *Ya*
    - ■ *Obviamente*
  - ○ To express feelings
    - ■ *¡No!*
    - ■ *¿En serio?*
    - ■ *¿De verdad?*
    - ■ *¿Ah, sí?*
    - ■ *¡No lo puedo creer!*
    - ■ *¡Qué mala suerte!*
    - ■ *¡Qué buena suerte!*
    - ■ *¡No me digas!*
    - ■ *¡Qué rabia!*
    - ■ *¡Qué extraño!*
    - ■ *¿Qué mal!*
    - ■ *¡Qué bien!*

We've covered a lot in this chapter, but wait until you see what awaits you in the following chapter: hypotheses about the future. You will learn about the future and conditional tenses in Spanish. Are you ready?

Exercises

1. To form the *pretérito pluscuamperfecto*, which tense should the verb *haber* be conjugated in?
   a. presente
   b. pretérito perfecto simple
   c. pretérito imperfecto

2. Can you conjugate the following verbs in their correct *pretérito pluscuamperfecto form?*
   a. yo/cansar:
   b. él/dormir:
   c. nosotros/correr:
   d. vosotros/armar:
   e. ella/sentir:

f. tú/beber:

g. nosotras/saltar:

h. ustedes/mentir:

3. Complete the following sentences with the *pretérito pluscuamperfecto* form of the verbs in parentheses.

    a. Mi dentista me dijo que .... (ir) al supermercado el día anterior.

    b. En la reunión, mis padres comieron muchísimo porque no .... (comer) nada en todo el día.

    c. Ayer, sacamos pasajes para ir a México porque no .... (visitar) ese país.

    d. ¿Jamás .... (tú/ver) un pez de ese tamaño?

    e. Ayer llovió toda la tarde, pero el día anterior .... (hacer) mucho calor.

4. Complete the anecdote with either the *pretérito perfecto simple,* the *pretérito perfecto compuesto,* the *pretérito imperfecto or* the *pretérito pluscuamperfecto* form of the verbs in parentheses.
Mercedes .... (caminar) por la playa cuando .... (encontrarse) con León. Era la primera vez que .... (verse) en mucho tiempo y nunca .... (encontrarse) fuera del trabajo, así que ambos .... (estar) sorprendidos. .... (conversar) por unos minutos y luego .... (quedar) para tomar un café. Hoy .... (reunirse) a tomar ese café y Mercedes .... (descubrir) que León le gusta mucho.

5. Complete the anecdote with the right form of the verbs in parentheses.
No sabes lo que me .... (pasar). El sábado .... (tener) que ir al médico. .... (ir) por última vez hace 3 años, así que necesitaba ir. .... (salir) temprano para no llegar tarde, pero .... (llegar) 20 minutos antes, así que me .... (sentar) a esperar. En la sala de espera, ... (haber) solo dos personas más: una señora y Pablo, nuestro amigo de la infancia. .... (hablar) de todo lo que .... (hacer) estos últimos años y nos .... (reír) mucho. Hoy .... (volver) a verlo y me .... (decir) que le gustaría verte.

6. Complete the following sentences with the phrases from the box. They are only used once each.

> resulta que - otra vez - como - la noche anterior - aquel día

    a. Vi a Milagros .... ayer por la tarde.

    b. .... la había visto a Paula dos veces.

    c. Pablo había tenido un accidente .... al accidente de Helena.

    d. .... no me gusta el queso, no comí la pizza.

    e. .... Pedro y Lucía se casan este fin de semana.

7. Put the following sentences in order so that they form one text.

    a. Sin embargo, más tarde la vi comer patatas fritas.

    b. Al final, me confesó que me había mentido.

    c. En la fiesta, Marta me dijo que no le gustaban las patatas fritas.

d. Como la vi comer patatas fritas de nuevo, la confronté.

e. Ella me dijo que nunca me había dicho eso.

8. Complete the following anecdote with the phrases from the box. They are only used once each.

> pero - al final - igualmente - para comenzar - después - por eso

Fuimos a comer a un restaurante con mi mamá y todo salió mal. ...., nos tuvimos que sentar al lado del baño. .... tardaron muchísimo en atendernos. ...., nos explicaron que tenían algunos problemas en la cocina, ... los entendimos y nos quedamos a esperar, ... cuando llegó la comida no estaba nada rica. .... decidimos no volver jamás.

9. In these conversations, what would you say to the people telling the anecdotes?

a. • Tuve que ir al médico porque no podía mover el cuello.
    ○ ....
    • Me dijo que descansara.

b. • No podrás creerlo.
    ○ ....
    • Juan casi come manteca en lugar de queso.

c. • Ayer se me averió el auto en la autopista
    ○ ....
    • Llamé al mecánico.

d. • Anoche Luisa y Gonzalo se pelearon.
    ○ ....
    • No lo sé, no quise preguntarles.

10. Complete the conversations with the phrases from the box. They are only used once each.

> ¿En serio? - ¡Qué mala suerte! - ¡Qué extraño! - ¡No lo puedo creer!

a. • Ayer la vi a Ana en la calle. ¡Está muy linda!
    ○ ....

b. • Mi hija es amiga de la estrella de rock que tanto amas.
    ○ ....

c. • No solo tuve que quedarme en mi casa hoy, sino que además no tuve luz en todo el día.
    ○ ....

d. • Me pareció ver algo verde en el cielo.
    ○ ....

Answer Key

1. c. pretérito imperfecto
2.
   a. había cansado
   b. había dormido
   c. habíamos corrido
   d. habíais armado
   e. había sentido
   f. habías bebido
   g. habíamos saltado
   h. habían mentido
3.
   a. había ido
   b. habían comido
   c. habíamos visitado
   d. habías visto
   e. había hecho
4. caminaba, se encontró, se veían, se habían encontrado, estaban, Conversaron, quedaron, se han reunido, ha descubierto
5. pasó, tenía, Había ido, Salí, llegué, senté, había, Hablamos, habíamos hecho, reímos, he vuelto, dijo
6.
   a. otra vez
   b. Aquel día
   c. la noche anterior
   d. Como
   e. Resulta que
7. Order of the sentences: 1) c. 2) a. 3) d. 4) e. 5) b.
8. Para comenzar; Después; Igualmente; por eso; pero; Al final
9.
   a. ¿Y qué te dijo?
   b. ¿Qué pasó?
   c. ¿Y qué hiciste?
   d. ¿Cómo terminó?
10.

a. ¿En serio?

b. ¡No lo puedo creer!

c. ¡Qué mala suerte!

d. ¡Qué extraño!

Chapter 5: Hypotheses

❧

Procuremos más ser padres de nuestro porvenir que hijos de nuestro pasado.

- Miguel de Unamuno

What do you think the earth will look like in the year 2500? Do you believe we'll be driving flying cars a few decades from now? And what about you? What are your plans for the future? Where do you see yourself in five years? And in ten? We have different resources to talk about all these things and to make hypotheses about the future. Let's take a look at them!

Futuro simple

The simple future is a common tool to make hypotheses about the present and predictions about the future. You've probably used this tense plenty of times to talk about the future in sentences like the following ones:

- Mañana **iremos** al cine.

- Me **pasará** a buscar mi esposa para llevarme al aeropuerto.

- La cena **estará** lista a las ocho. No llegues tarde.

These are things that will happen or that will be true in the future.

However, the future tense has another use. Let's take a close look at these examples:

- Sofía se fue sin saludar. **Estará** apurada.

- -No encuentro las llaves de casa. -Las **tendrás** en el otro bolso, no te preocupes.

- -Llamé para pedir cita en el dentista, pero no me atendió nadie. -**Será** porque es domingo.

Can you grasp the difference in the meaning of "**estará**" between (a) *La cena **estará** lista a las ocho*, and (b) *Sofía se fue sin saludar. **Estará** apurada*? In (a), we are using the simple future tense to talk about something that will happen in the future. We can translate that sentence like this: "Dinner **will be** ready at eight."

In (b), on the other hand, we are using the simple future to hypothesize about the present. A possible translation of that sentence is: "Sofía left without saying goodbye. She **is probably** in a hurry." So, we are not saying that Sofía will be in a hurry in the future, we are guessing that she is in a hurry now, in the present.

Here are some more examples of how we use these verbs in the simple future to make hypotheses about the present:

- -Nunca la oímos cantar. -**Cantará** mal y le **dará** vergüenza.

- Se fueron sin probar un bocado, pero imagino que **comerán** al llegar a su casa.

- No quiso que lo llevara a su casa. **Vivirá** cerca.

Now, let's take a look at the three model conjugations that you already know and that you can use as a model for the conjugation of regular verbs in the *futuro simple*:

	Cantar	Comer	Vivir
yo	cantar<u>é</u>	comer<u>é</u>	vivir<u>é</u>
tú	cantar<u>ás</u>	comer<u>ás</u>	vivir<u>ás</u>
él / ella / usted	cantar<u>á</u>	comer<u>á</u>	vivir<u>á</u>
nosotros / nosotras	cantar<u>emos</u>	comer<u>emos</u>	vivir<u>emos</u>
vosotros / vosotras	cantar<u>éis</u>	comer<u>éis</u>	vivir<u>éis</u>
ellos / ellas / ustedes	cantar<u>án</u>	comer<u>án</u>	vivir<u>án</u>

Did you notice any difference between this chart and the ones you saw before? The conjugation of the *futuro simple* varies in two ways from the tenses we've seen so far.

On the one hand, we don't drop the -AR, -ER and -IR endings of the infinitive to form the *futuro simple*. We've said that in the verb *cantar*, for instance, *cant-* is the root and *-ar* is the ending. To form the present simple in the first person, we drop the infinitive ending and we ad *-o*: *yo canto*. However, as you can see in the chart above, to form the *futuro simple*, **we add the ending without modifying the infinitive**. So, we have *cantar* and, to form the first person singular of the simple future, we just add *-é*: *yo cantaré*.

On the other hand, the endings of the *futuro simple* are the same for the first, second and third conjugations. If we take the second row of the table above, the one dedicated to the second person singular *tú*, we have *cantar*, *comer* and *vivir* + *-ás*: *cantarás*, *comerás* and *vivirás*. So, it doesn't matter which conjugation the verb belongs to, all we need to do is to add the corresponding ending:

yo		+ <u>é</u>
tú		+ <u>ás</u>
él / ella / usted		+ <u>á</u>
nosotros / nosotras	infinitive of the verb	+ <u>emos</u>
vosotros / vosotras		+ <u>éis</u>
ellos / ellas / ustedes		+ <u>án</u>

Pretty simple, right?

Another thing you might like about this tense is that there aren't many irregular verbs. We can divide the irregularities into three groups:

419

- *tener, salir, valer, poner* and *venir*. To conjugate these verbs in the *futuro simple*, we don't use the infinitive as it is. We change the vowel of the infinitive ending (the *e* or the *i*) into a *d* before adding the *futuro simple* ending. Thus, with *salir*, for example, we change the *i* for a *d* and we have *saldr-*, and to that new root, we add the corresponding ending (-é, -ás, -á, -emos, -éis, -án).

- *poder, caber*, querer, *haber* and *saber*. In this group, the vowel of the infinitive ending (the *e*) simply goes away. For example with *saber*, we drop the *e* and we get *sabr-*, and to that new root, we add the corresponding ending to form the *futuro simple*.

- *hacer* and *decir*. These two verbs change their root and then take the ending of the *futuro simple*.

Here are some of the irregular verbs:

	Tener	Poder	Decir→dir-	Hacer→har-
yo	ten<u>dré</u>	po<u>dré</u>	di<u>ré</u>	ha<u>ré</u>
tú	ten<u>drás</u>	po<u>drás</u>	di<u>rás</u>	ha<u>rás</u>
él / ella / usted	ten<u>drá</u>	po<u>drá</u>	di<u>rá</u>	ha<u>rá</u>
nosotros / nosotras	ten<u>dremos</u>	po<u>dremos</u>	di<u>remos</u>	har<u>emos</u>
vosotros / vosotras	ten<u>dréis</u>	po<u>dréis</u>	di<u>réis</u>	ha<u>réis</u>
ellos / ellas / ustedes	ten<u>drán</u>	po<u>drán</u>	di<u>rán</u>	ha<u>rán</u>

Let's see examples of some of these conjugations in use:

- Mira, todo el mundo anda desabrigado. **Hará** calor.
- Mi hijo me avisó que ya está camino a casa. **Habrá salido** temprano de la escuela.
- Me escribió Clara para pedirme que le lleve un abrigo. **Tendrá** frío.
- Me llamaron mis padres, pero no llegué a atender. **Querrán** invitarme a cenar.

Before going into the next section, let me tell you how reflexive verbs behave in the *futuro simple*. With this tense, the reflexive pronoun (*me, te, se, nos, os* or *se*) is always placed before the verb:

- **Se irán** de vacaciones el mes que viene.
- No le gusta el barrio, por eso **se mudará**.

Condicional simple

Another way to talk about something hypothetical that might be true in the present or the future is by using the simple conditional tense:

- ¡Qué frío! Me **tomaría** un chocolate caliente.
- **Iría** a visitarte si tuviera tiempo.

How to form the simple conditional

But, before going into this and other uses of the conditional tense, let's take a look at how we form this verb conjugation. By now, you are probably used to the chart of regular verbs:

	Cantar	Comer	Vivir
yo	cantaría	comería	viviría
tú	cantarías	comerías	vivirías
él / ella / usted	cantaría	comería	viviría
nosotros / nosotras	cantaríamos	comeríamos	viviríamos
vosotros / vosotras	cantaríais	comeríais	viviríais
ellos / ellas / ustedes	cantarían	comerían	vivirían

As you can see, this chart is similar to the one of the *futuro simple*. Just like in that tense, to form the *condicional simple* we don't drop the -AR, -ER and -IR endings of the infinitive. What we do is **add the ending without modifying the infinitive**. So, we have *cantar* and, to form the first person singular of the conditional, we just add *-ía: yo cantaría*.

And again, the endings of the *condicional simple* are the same for the three conjugations. If we take the first row of the table above, the one dedicated to the first person singular *yo*, we have *cantar, comer* and *vivir* + *-ía: cantaría, comería* and *vivirás*. No matter the conjugation, we just add the corresponding ending:

yo		+ ía
tú		+ ías
él / ella / usted		+ ía
nosotros / nosotras	infinitive of the verb	+ íamos
vosotros / vosotras		+ íais
ellos / ellas / ustedes		+ ían

Just like in the *futuro simple*, in this tense there aren't many irregular verbs. We have the same three groups as above:

- *tener, salir, valer, poner* and *venir*. First, we have to change the vowel of the infinitive ending (the *e* or the *i*) into a *d*. Then, we just add the conditional ending.

- *poder, caber, querer, haber* and *saber*. First, we drop the vowel of the infinitive ending (the *e*). Then, we add the corresponding ending to form the conditional.
- *hacer* and *decir*. First we change the root. Then, we add the ending of the *condicional simple*.

Here are some of the irregular verbs:

	Tener	Poder	Decir→dir-	Hacer→har-
yo	ten<u>dría</u>	po<u>dría</u>	diría	haría
tú	ten<u>drías</u>	po<u>drías</u>	dirías	harías
él / ella / usted	ten<u>dría</u>	po<u>dría</u>	diría	haría
nosotros / nosotras	ten<u>dríamos</u>	po<u>dríamos</u>	diríamos	haríamos
vosotros / vosotras	ten<u>dríais</u>	po<u>dríais</u>	diríais	haríais
ellos / ellas / ustedes	ten<u>drían</u>	po<u>drían</u>	dirían	harían

In this tense, reflexive verbs behave just like the *futuro simple*: the reflexive pronoun goes before the verb:

- **Se irían** de vacaciones si pudieran.
- No me gusta el barrio. Te juro que **me mudaría**.

Uses of the simple conditional

Now that we know how to form it, let's delve into the different uses of the *condicional simple* in Spanish!

1. We've already mentioned that it's used to make assumptions and hypotheses:
    - **Deberían** estar por llegar.
    - **Llegaría** mañana si todo sale bien.

2. We also use this tense to make assumptions about the past and to hypothesize about the past:
    - María casi no abrió la boca ayer en la cena. **Estaría** cansada.
    - Hoy a la mañana no vi al encargado de mi edificio. Se **sentiría** mal.

3. The conditional is used to talk about the future of the past:
    - El lunes me dijo que **vendría** al día siguiente.
    - Cuando empecé el trabajo final de la materia, pensé que me **llevaría** un mes.

4. In the present, we can use the conditional to express a wish:
    - ¡Me **encantaría** que vinieras!
    - Tengo tanta hambre que me **comería** una pizza entera.

5. We also use this tense to make suggestions:

   ○ **Deberías** salir ahora si quieres llegar a tiempo.

   ○ Yo que tú, lo **llamaría** para disculparme.

6. The conditional is used as an indication of politeness. We use it for formal invitations and for polite requests:

   ○ ¿Les **gustaría** venir a cenar el viernes?

   ○ ¿**Podrían** traer un postre?

Condicional compuesto

How to form the compound conditional

Just like the other compound tenses we've seen so far, the *condicional compuesto* is formed with the verb *haber* as an auxiliary plus the participle form of the main verb. For this tense, *haber* needs to be conjugated in the conditional. Here's a chart for you to see how the *condicional compuesto* is formed:

yo	habría	
tú	habrías	
él / ella / usted	habría	+ the participle of the verb
nosotros / nosotras	habríamos	
vosotros / vosotras	habríais	
ellos / ellas / ustedes	habrían	

Uses of the compound conditional

We use this tense when we want to talk about things that were supposed to happen or could have happened in the past, but, for some reason, they didn't take place. Let's see some examples:

- Si me lo hubieras pedido, **habría ido**.

In this case, the speaker is saying that going was a possibility. In other words, they could have gone, but nobody asked them to.

- De haber salido en hora, **habríamos llegado** a tiempo.

In this other example, something was supposed to happen. They were supposed to arrive at a specific time, but, since they didn't leave on time, they were late.

423

Oraciones condicionales

Throughout this chapter, we've been using a set of structures that are very common both in English and in Spanish without properly talking about them: the *oraciones condicionales* ("conditional sentences").

In the present, we use *oraciones condicionales* to express the possibility with which something is going to happen if a particular condition is met. However, these sentences can also be used to talk about the past and future.

A very distinguishable characteristic of these sentences is that they are made up of two clauses, one of them starting with conditional *si* or an equivalent. There are four types of conditional sentences in Spanish. Let's see each one of them!

1. Verbs of both clauses in the present

This is the structure we use to express that, when something occurs, there's a second action that takes place as a result. Both common sense truths and more specific situations can take this type of conditional sentence. As you can tell by the title, this structure is formed with two verbs in the present, in the following way:

si + presente simple + presente simple

- Si pones la mano en el fuego, te quemas.
- Si tengo tiempo, miro la televisión.

2. Conditional clause in the present and result clause in the future

We use conditional sentences to talk about real possibilities in the future that are tied to present conditions. The future action will take place if the present action is carried out. We form it in the following way:

si + presente simple + futuro

- Si termino de trabajar temprano, iré a cenar con mis amigas.
- Si estudiamos para el examen, lo aprobaremos.

3. Conditional clause in the past of the subjunctive and result clause in the conditional

This type of conditional sentence is used to talk about hypothetical situations that we already know are not real. They're formed like this:

si + pretérito del subjuntivo + condicional simple

- Si viviera cerca, te visitaría más seguido. (I don't live close by, so I can't visit you more often.)
- Si tuviéramos dinero, nos iríamos de vacaciones. (We don't have money, so we are not going on holiday.)

4. Conditional clause in the pluperfect subjunctive and result in the compound conditional

This last type of conditional sentence is used to talk about hypothetical situations in the past. They're formed in following manner:

si + pluscuamperfecto del subjuntivo + condicional compuesto

- Si ella hubiera estudiado, habría aprobado el examen. (She didn't study and, thus, she didn't pass the exam.)

- Si mi madre me lo hubiera pedido, la habría pasado a buscar por el aeropuerto. (My mother didn't ask, so I didn't pick her up from the airport).

Expressing certainty, doubt and uncertainty

As we've already mentioned in Chapter 3, after a main clause with a verb that expresses doubt or uncertainty from the speaker, we use the subjunctive:

- **Es posible** (*uncertainty*) que me **tenga** (*subjunctive*) que ir temprano hoy.
- **Quizás** (*uncertainty*) **se adelante** (*subjunctive*) mi vuelo.

So, uncertainty is expressed by a phrase or a verb in the main clause plus a subordinate clause in the subjunctive mood.

After some expressions, we need to use *que* before the subjunctive:

Phrase	Pronunciation	Translation
es posible que	ehs poh-SEE-bleh keh	it's possible that
es imposible que	ehs im-poh-SEE-bleh keh	it's impossible that
puede ser que	POO-eh-de sehr keh	it could be that
es fácil que	ehs FAH-seel keh	it's easy that
es difícil que	ehs dee-FEE-seel keh	it's difficult that
es probable que	ehs proh-BAH-bleh keh	it's likely that
es improbable que	ehs im-pro-BAH-bleh keh	it's unlikely that
no creer que	noh KREH-ehr keh	not to believe that

Let's look at a few examples of these expressions in use:

- Es imposible que ganen el partido.
- Es probable que lleguemos tarde.
- No creo que venga de nuevo.

However, there's another set of expression after which we don't need *que* before the subjunctive:

Phrase	Pronunciation	Translation
quizás	kee-ZAHS	maybe
quizá	kee-ZAH	maybe

425

tal vez	tahl vehz	perhaps
a lo mejor	ah loh meh-HOHR	perhaps
posiblemente	poh-see-bleh-MEHN-teh	possibly

Here are a couple of examples:

- **Tal vez** lo compremos mañana.
- **Quizás** Clara esté ocupada.
- **Tal vez** nos veamos ahí.

It's worth noting that we can sometimes express doubt or uncertainty without using the subjunctive. This is the case with these verbs and expressions:

Phrase or verb	Pronunciation	Translation
creer	kreh-EHR	to believe
parecer que	pah-REH-seh keh	to seem like
pensar	pehn-SAHR	to think

Let's see them in use:

- **Creo** que están en camino.
- Me **parece que** estoy resfriada.
- **Pienso** que es muy interesante.

While doubt and uncertainty almost always require the subjunctive, certainty requires the indicative. These are some of the verbs and expressions we use to talk when we have no doubts about what we are saying:

Phrase	Pronunciation	Translation
saber	sah-BEHR	to know
es verdad	ehs behr-DAHD	it's true
es cierto	ehs see-EHR-toh	it's true
seguro que	seh-GOO-roh keh	surely
es evidente	ehs eh-vee-DEHN-teh	it's evident

es obvio	ehs oh-BEE-oh	it's obvious
no dudar de	noh doo-DAHR deh	not to doubt that
no negar que	noh neh-GAHR keh	not to deny that

Below, you can see a few examples of these expressions in use:

- **Sé** que estás ahí.
- **Es verdad** que tengo miedo.
- **Es cierto** que está nublado.
- Pero **seguro que** más tarde sale el sol.
- **Es evidente** que estas enojada.
- **Es obvio** que Nadia se quiere marchar.

Key Takeaways

Now, it's time for our short review of the chapter before putting everything you've learned into practice.

Futuro simple

- **Uses**:
  - To talk about the future.
  - To make hypotheses about the present and predictions about the future.
- **Form:**
  - To conjugate the regular verbs in *futuro simple*, we add an ending to the infinitive, without modifying it. The endings of the *futuro simple* are the same for the first, second and third conjugations.
  - Irregular verbs can be divided into three groups: With *tener, salir, valer, poner* and *venir*, we change the vowel of the infinitive into a *d* and we add the *futuro simple* ending. With *poder, caber, querer, haber* and *saber,* we drop the vowel of the infinitive ending and we add the corresponding ending. *hacer* and *decir* change their root and then take the ending of the *futuro simple.*
  - In the *futuro simple*, the reflexive pronoun always comes before the verb:

Condicional simple

- **Form**: The simple conditional is formed like the simple future, but with its own endings:
- **Uses:**
  - To make assumptions and hypotheses about the future.
  - To make assumptions and hypothesize about the past.
  - To talk about the future of the past.
  - To express a wish in the present.

- To make suggestions in the present.
- For formal invitations and polite requests.

Condicional compuesto

- **Form**: the compound conditional is formed with the verb *haber* conjugated in the conditional as an auxiliary plus the participle form of the main verb.
- **Uses**: We use it when we want to talk about things that were supposed to happen or could have happened in the past but didn't take place.

Oraciones condicionales

- They can be used to talk about the present, the past and the future.
- They are made up of two clauses, one of them starting with conditional *si* or an equivalent and the other one showing a result or consequence.
  - Type 1. **si + presente simple + presente simple**. Used to express that, when something occurs, there's a second action that takes place as a result.
  - Type 2. **si + presente simple + future**. Used to talk about real possibilities in the future that are tied to present conditions.
  - Type 3. **si + pretérito del subjuntivo + condicional simple**. Used to talk about hypothetical situations that we already know that are not real.
  - Type 4. **si + pluscuamperfecto del subjuntivo + condicional compuesto**. Used to talk about hypothetical situations in the past.

Expressing certainty, doubt and uncertainty

- Uncertainty is expressed by a phrase or a verb in the main clause plus a subordinate clause in the subjunctive mood.
  - After some expressions of doubt and uncertainty, we need to use *que* before the subjunctive. There's a set of expressions after which we don't need *que*.
  - With certain verbs and expressions we can express doubt or uncertainty without using the subjunctive.
- Certainty requires the indicative.

We've certainly covered quite a lot of topics. Let's check what you've learned before going to the next chapter, where we'll cover all you need to know about impersonal sentences!

Exercises

1. Can you complete this table with the *futuro simple* form of these verbs?

	Hablar	Salir	Caber
yo	....	saldré	....
tú	hablarás	....	....
él / ella / usted	....	....	cabrá
nosotros / nosotras	....	saldremos	....

vosotros / vosotras	....	....	cabréis
ellos / ellas / ustedes	hablarán	....	....

2. Complete the following text with the *futuro simple* form of the verbs in parentheses.
El mes que viene, ... (irse) de vacaciones con mis amigas a Málaga. ....
(ser) la primera vez que vaciono sin mi familia. El avión .... (despegar) a las nueve
de la mañana. .... (llegar) a Málaga cerca del mediodía. Mis amigas y yo
.... (tomar) un taxi al hotel. .... (nosotras/alojarse) en un lugar cerca del
centro. Después de dejar nuestras maletas, ... (nosotras/irse) directo a la playa.
.... (nosotras/bañarse) mucho en el mar y .... (nosotras/comer) cosas
ricas.

3. Choose the one that doesn't apply. The *futuro simple* is used:

   a. To talk about the future.

   b. To make hypotheses about the present.

   c. To refer to the past.

4. Are the following instances of the *futuro simple* referring to the future or making hypotheses about the present? Use F for future and P for present.

   a. El encargo **estará** listo mañana por la tarde.

   b. No son ni las 9 y Malena ya se fue a acostar. **Estará** cansada.

   c. No veo mi bolso por ningún lado. **Estará** en el coche.

   d. Mis padres **querrán** verte cuando llegues.

   e. Mañana **serán** dos semanas desde la última vez que la vi.

   f. Llamó tu padre. **Querrá** saber cómo estás.

   g. Fui a la tienda y estaba cerrada. **Será** porque es feriado.

5. Can you complete this table with the *condicional simple* form of these verbs?

	Mover	Querer	Hacer
yo	movería	....	....
tú	....	....	harías
él / ella / usted	....	querría	....
nosotros / nosotras	moveríamos	....	....
vosotros / vosotras	....	querríais	....
ellos / ellas / ustedes	....	....	harían

6. Choose the one that doesn't apply. The *condicional simple* is used:

   a. To make assumptions and hypotheses about the future.

   b. To make assumptions and hypothesize about the past.

   c. To talk about things that could have happened in the past but didn't.

d. To express a wish in the present.

e. To make suggestions in the present.

f. For formal invitations and polite requests.

7. The following sentences belong to the type 1 *oraciones condicionales*. Complete with the correct form of the verb in parentheses.

  a. Si .... (tú/venir), te..................... (yo/esperar).

  b. Si .... (salir) el sol, ... (secarse) la ropa.

  c. Si .... (tú/tener) hambre, te .... (yo/preparar) algo de comer.

8. The following sentences belong to the type 2 *oraciones condicionales*. Complete with the correct form of the verb in parentheses.

  a. Si .... (despejarse) el cielo, ... (yo/ir) a la playa.

  b. Si .... (yo/terminar) temprano, te .... (yo/pasar) a buscar.

  c. Si lo .... (ellos/llamar) del nuevo trabajo, ... (él/renunciar) al que tiene ahora.

9. Use the *condicional compuesto* of the verbs in parentheses to complete the following sentences.

  a. Si me lo hubieras pedido, te .... (acompañar).

  b. Si hubieran sabido que era más barato así, ... (pagar) en efectivo.

  c. Si hubierais tomado el camino que os dije, ... (llegar) en horario.

  d. Si se hubiera quedado dormida, Malena .... (perder) el avión.

10. Choose between the two options in parentheses to complete the following sentences.

  a. Es posible que .... (tenga/tengo) que ir a París el mes que viene.

  b. Es verdad que la ciudad me .... (agrade/agrada).

  c. A lo mejor .... (va/vaya) mi compañero y no yo.

  d. Aunque seguro esta vez me .... (toca/toque) a mí.

Answer Key

1.

	Hablar	Salir	Caber
yo	<u>hablaré</u>	saldré	<u>cabré</u>
tú	hablarás	<u>saldrás</u>	<u>cabrás</u>
él / ella / usted	<u>hablará</u>	<u>saldrá</u>	cabrá
nosotros / nosotras	<u>hablaremos</u>	saldremos	<u>cabremos</u>
vosotros / vosotras	<u>hablaréis</u>	<u>saldréis</u>	cabréis
ellos / ellas / ustedes	hablarán	<u>saldrán</u>	<u>cabrán</u>

2. me iré; será; despegará; Llegaremos; tomaremos; Nos alojaremos; nos iremos; Nos bañaremos; comeremos.

3. c.

4.
    a. F
    b. P.
    c. P.
    d. F.
    e. F.
    f. P.
    g. P.

5.

	Mover	Querer	Hacer
yo	movería	<u>querría</u>	<u>haría</u>
tú	<u>moverías</u>	<u>querrías</u>	harías
él / ella / usted	<u>movería</u>	querría	<u>haría</u>
nosotros / nosotras	moveríamos	<u>querríamos</u>	<u>haríamos</u>
vosotros / vosotras	<u>moveríais</u>	querríais	<u>haríais</u>
ellos / ellas / ustedes	<u>moverían</u>	<u>querrían</u>	harían

6. c.

7.
    a. vienes; espero.
    b. sale; se seca.
    c. tienes; preparo.

8.

     a. se despeja; iré.

     b. termino; pasaré.

     c. llaman; renunciará.

9.

     a. habría acompañado.

     b. habrían pagado.

     c. habrías llegado.

     d. habría perdido.

10.

     a. tenga.

     b. agrada.

     c. va.

     d. toca.

Chapter 6: Nothing personal

⸎

Estoy colmado de imprecisos deseos, de una vaguedad que es como neblina, y adentrándose en todo mi ser, lo torna casi aéreo, impersonal y alado.

- Roberto Arlt

Sometimes, we don't want to specify who is doing an action. It can be because we don't know it, because we're generalizing, because it isn't relevant, because it is obvious, or because we simply don't want to. In Spanish, of course, we have the option of not having an overt subject and simply omit it, but this is not exactly an impersonal form. That is because, even though the subject isn't overt, it is still present in the conjugation of the verb or in the gender and number of articles, pronouns, and adjectives.

In this chapter, we will be dealing with different ways to make sentences that don't mention the subject, hide it or bring the attention to another part of the sentences so that the subject isn't perceived as responsible for the action.

Impersonal constructions

Verb in the third-person plural

When we don't know who is doing the action, we use a third-person plural for the action verb and we always omit the pronoun. For example, if we hear that someone is knocking the door but don't know who it is, we can say ***Tocan** la puerta, ¿puedes abrir?* ("Someone is knocking the door, can you get it?"). It may be only one person who is knocking, but we use the third-person plural to show that we don't know who it is.

Keep in mind that we could also express that we don't know who is doing the action using a grammatical subject like *alguien* with the third-person singular (*Alguien toca la puerta*), but this one would not be an impersonal sentence.

We could also use the third-person plural to express that the person who does the action is not relevant in that context or if we don't want to disclose who they are. For example, if we say *En la televisión **dijeron** que la policía atrapó a los ladrones* ("On the TV they said that the police caught the thieves"), we might know the name of the TV anchors who said that, but we decide that we want to focus on the fact and not the person who said it.

An example of the third-person plural being used when we don't want to disclose the person who does the action is *Me **dijeron** que quieres decirme algo* ("Somebody told me you want to tell me something"). In this sentence, we use the third person plural because we don't want the other person to know who told us, even though we definitely know.

Verbs in the third-person singular/plural

We can also use verbs in the third person singular or plural for impersonal sentences. In this case, there are several set phrases that use them. We may be able to use the singular or plural form of the verbs, depending on the context.

Let's see some of these phrases.

Está + weather

When we talk about the weather, we should always use the verb *estar* in the third-person singular. For example, we can say **Está lloviendo** ("It's raining") or **Está nublado** ("It's cloudy").

Está prohibido/permitido

In this case, we use the phrases *está prohibido* ("It is forbidden") or *está permitido* ("It is allowed") in the singular when we are talking about a singular noun. For example, **Está permitida** *la venta de alcohol hasta las 21* ("Alcohol sale is allowed until 9 p.m.") or when we are talking about an action. For example, **Está prohibido** *pisar el césped* ("Stepping on the grass is forbidden").

However, we use the verb *estar* in the third-person plural when we are talking about plural nouns. For example, **Están prohibidas** *las ventas telefónicas* ("Phone sales are forbidden").

Note that the words *prohibido* and *permitido* need to agree in gender and number with the object that is forbidden or allowed, or in the masculine form if we are talking about an action.

Here's a table that sums all of this up:

Está	prohibido/a permitido/a	singular nouns
Está	prohibido permitido	verbs in the infinitive
Están	prohibidos/as permitidos/as	plural nouns

Es + adjective + infinitive

We can also use the verb *ser* with an adjective in a similar way to *estar* + *prohibido/permitido*. In this case, to make impersonal sentences we use the verb *ser* in the third-person singular (*es*) with a verb in the infinitive verbs. We should also take into account that the adjective needs to be in the masculine to agree with the infinitive verb. For example, we could say: **Es obligatorio** *hacer todas las tareas* ("Doing all the assignments is compulsory").

Other adjectives that are used with this structure are:

Adjective	Pronunciation	Translation
normal	nohr-MAL	normal
habitual	ah-bee-too-AHL	usual
frecuente	freh-koo-EHN-teh	frequent

raro	RRAH-roh	rare
conveniente	kohn-beh-nee-EHN-teh	convenient
recomendable	rreh-koh-mehn-DAH-bleh	advisable
mejor	meh-HOHR	better
peor	peh-OHR	worse
fácil	FAH-seel	easy
difícil	dee-FEE-seel	hard
útil	OO-teel	useful
inútil	ee-NOO-teel	unuseful
importante	eem-pohr-TAHN-teh	important

Hay que + infinitive

We can also use the structure *hay que* + infinitive to talk about something that is necessary in a general and impersonal way. For example, we can use say ***Hay que*** *estudiar mucho para aprobar el examen* ("Studying a lot is necessary to pass the test").

Have you noticed that here the third-person singular conjugation of *haber* is *hay* and not *ha*? In this structure, the form *hay* which is actually the third-person impersonal conjugation of *haber*. This structure is used to make statements about nobody in particular and doesn't have a subject.

Resulta/parece que

As we've seen before, we can use *resulta que* and *parece que* to start anecdotes. Both of them are impersonal phrases that refer to nothing in particular. In this case, we should always use them in the third-person singular.

Verb in the second-person singular

To make impersonal sentences, we could also use the second-person singular to generalize, especially in informal spoken language. For example, *Con este clima, te* puedes *caer en cualquier momento* ("With this weather, you could slip and fall at any time").

This form is commonly used with the conjunction *si*. For example, we could say *En este país,* **si no ganas** *mucho dinero, no puedes tener tu propia casa* ("In this country, if you don't earn a lot of money, you can't own a house").

Use of the pronoun se

Another resource to make impersonal sentences is the structure *se* + verb in the 3rd person (singular or plural). This structure is used when we know who does the action but don't want to say it or don't want the attention to fall into the subject but the object.

Se + verb in the third-person singular

The impersonal construction with *se* + third-person singular elides the subject completely, generally because it is obvious, and puts the focus on the action. Here's an example: *En Estados Unidos, **se cena muy temprano*** ("In the United States, people have dinner very early"). In this sentence, the subject is *las personas* ("people"), which is obvious, so it is omitted.

Furthermore, notice that the subject *personas* is a third-person subject, but, still, the verb should be conjugated in the third-person singular. In fact, the subject cannot be added to the previous example sentence (with its corresponding third-person plural conjugation) without there being a change in meaning. For example, if we said *En Estados Unidos las personas se cenan muy temprano*, it would mean that they have themselves or each other for dinner very early, which doesn't make any sense.

We should also mention that when the verb is reflexive (that is, when the infinitive form of the verb already has the pronoun *se*) we cannot use this construction. For example, we cannot say *En Estados Unidos se levanta temprano* to talk about people in general, we can only use it to talk about one specific person. Instead, we should always introduce a collective or diffuse subject to explain that we are talking about people in general. For example, we can say *En Estados Unidos **la gente se levanta** temprano*.

Se + verb in the third-person singular/plural + object

Despite what we've just said about the third-person plural with the pronoun *se* and a third-person subject, there are certain cases in which we can use the third-person singular or plural. We can add an object to the construction we've seen before. For example, *En ese restaurante **se come una paella increíble***.

The thing is that, when the object is included in the sentence, the verb needs to agree in number with the object we're talking about. So, if we wanted to talk about *hamburguesas*, for example, we would say *En este restaurante **se comen unas hamburguesas** increíbles*. As you can see, the object (the *paella* or the *hamburguesas*) here is working as the subject, which is why the verb needs to agree in number with it. However, these objects don't do the action. Of course, the clients of the restaurant are the ones who eat, but they never appear in the sentence. Instead, we've purposely "hidden" the people who do the action to focus the attention on the objects.

In fact, in these cases, we can't add the subject in the impersonal sentence with *se* without there being a change of meaning. If we said *En este restaurante los clientes se comen unas hamburguesas increíbles*, the sentence would stop being impersonal and it would, instead, have a reflexive or emphatic value that emphasizes the subject.

Passive voice

Both in Spanish and in English, the passive voice is a quintessential construction to make impersonal sentences and focus the attention on the object instead of the subject. In these constructions, we do so by presenting the object as a subject, even though it isn't responsible for the action.

In Spanish, the passive voice is formed with the conjugation of the verb *ser* and the participle form of the main verb, following this prototype formula:

- Patient (direct object of the active voice) + *ser* + participle

An example of this could be the active voice sentence *Unos ladrones robaron la pintura* ("Some thieves stole the painting"), which in the passive voice would turn into *La pintura **fue robada*** ("the painting was stolen").

In this sentence, it is understood that the painting was stolen by thieves, so it is not necessary for us to specify who it was stolen by. However, in Spanish, just like in English, we can add the information about the agent of the action (that is, the "real" subject who does the action) by adding the preposition *por* followed by the subject. So, following the previous example, we could add who the agent is in the following way: *La pintura fue robada **por unos ladrones*** ("the painting was stolen by the thieves").

If we add the agent to our previous formula, it would change into:

- Patient (direct object of the active voice) + *ser* + participle (+ agent (subject of the active voice))

We've seen the roles that the subject and the direct object take in passive sentences, but what about the indirect object (that is, the person or thing we do the action for)? Well, we simply cannot use the passive voice when we have an indirect object.

However, we should keep in mind that we cannot turn sentences with verbs of emotion or perception as their main verbs into passive voice. For example, we could never say *Juan es querido por mí* ("Juan is loved by me") or *Juan es visto por mí* ("Juan is seen by me"). Moreover, we can't use the passive voice with the progressive tense, so we can't say *El té está siendo preparado por Juan* ("The tea is being prepared by Juan").

Lastly, it should be noted that we don't use passive voice in Spanish as much as in English. Instead, we prefer the construction with *se* + third-person singular/plural, which we sometimes call "passive voice with *se*".

Key Takeaways

In this chapter, we've dealt with the different resources to make impersonal sentences when the subject is obvious, unknown, irrelevant, or we don't want to disclose it and to make generalized statements.

These resources are:

- Using verbs in the third-person plural.
- Using verbs in the third-person singular or plural, usually with the following phrases:
  - *Está* + weather
  - *Está* + *prohibido/permitido*
    - *Está prohibido/a / permitido/a + singular noun*
    - *Está prohibido/permitido + infinitive verb*
    - *Están prohibidos/as / permitidos/as + plural noun*
  - *Es* + adjective + infinitive
  - *Hay que* + infinitive
  - *Resulta/parece que*
- Using verbs in the second-person singular.
- Using the pronouns *se:*
  - *Se* + verb in the third-person singular

○ *Se* + verb in the third-person singular/plural + object

- Using the passive voice, following this formula:

  ○ Patient (direct object of the active voice) + *ser* + participle (+ agent (subject of the active voice))

In the next chapter, we're going to be dealing with the only Spanish mood we haven't talked about yet: the imperative.

Exercises

1. Can you make these sentences impersonal by changing the verbs into the third-person plural?

   a. Juana me contó que te irás de viaje.

   b. Pedro Sánchez dijo los resultados de la votación en la radio.

   c. Alguien llama al teléfono, ¿atiendes tú?

   d. ¿Vino alguien mientras yo no estaba?

2. Choose between the singular or plural third-person form of the verbs in parentheses in the following sentences:

   a. Está/Están lloviendo.

   b. Está/Están prohibido nadar en el río.

   c. Está/Están permitidas las llamadas telefónicas.

   d. Es/Son difícil cruzar la selva a pie.

   e. Es/Son importante mirar a ambos lados antes de cruzar la calle.

   f. Hay/Han que hacer ejercicio al menos dos veces por semana.

   g. Resulta/Resultan que no había dinero para ir de viaje.

3. Are these second-person singular sentences impersonal?

   a. Si no llevas paraguas cuando llueve, te mojarás.

   b. Gabriel, con esfuerzo, puedes hacer lo que te propongas.

   c. Hoy en día, Paloma no sabe estudiar.

   d. Con esta economía, no sabes en cuánto saldrán las cosas mañana.

   e. Hoy en día, puedes encontrar restaurantes abiertos las 24 horas.

   f. Tú no puedes seguir así.

   g. En la actualidad, si no estudias idiomas no tienes tantas oportunidades.

4. Choose the right verb to form impersonal sentences with *se*.

   a. En mi país .... mucho la honestidad.

      i. valóranse

      ii. se valora

      iii. se valoran

   b. En verano .... desde temprano.

      i.   amanece

      ii.   se acuestan

      iii. se toma mate

c. Cuando llueve .... tanto.

      i.   no se camina

      ii.   no se corren

      iii. no se moja

d. En Argentina, el 9 de julio .... el Día de la Independencia.

      i.   se festejan

      ii.   se reúne

      iii. se celebra

e. En este hotel .... muy bien, no hay nada de ruido.

      i.   se duerme

      ii.   se duermen

      iii. dormirse

5. Fill in the gaps with the correct form of the verbs in parentheses to form impersonal sentences with *se*.

a. Allí .... (jugar) al fútbol.

b. En verano .... (beber), sobre todo, tragos con ron y vodka.

c. ¿Este es el lugar en el que .... (servir) unas gambas exquisitas?

d. En esta tienda .... (pagar) lo que se rompe.

e. Hoy en día .... (comer) más hamburguesas que pastas.

6. Fill in the gaps with the correct form of the verbs in parentheses to make sentences in the passive voice.

a. Esta casa .... (construir) por mi padre.

b. La obra más destacada .... (pintar) por Santiago.

c. Esta estatua .... (modificar) todos los días por el viento y la lluvia.

d. Me dijeron que la revista .... (diseñar) en 2020.

e. No os preocupéis, el asunto .... (investigar) y todo indica que fue un malentendido.

f. ¿Es cierto que el periodista .... (asaltar) ayer?

g. Este libro .... (leer) por cientos de personas cada año.

7. Turn the following active sentences into the passive.

a. Ayer Juana cantó el himno nacional.

b. Plantaron tres árboles en la plaza.

c. Adoptaron a todos los gatitos de Milagros.

d. Algunas personas vieron el partido de tenis en el bar.

e. Solucionaron el problema.

f. Un detective resolvió el misterio.

g. Ayer derrotaron a mi equipo de fútbol.

8. How do we form sentences with the indirect object into the passive?

   a. We put the indirect object before the verb.

   b. We put the indirect object in the place of the subject.

   c. We can't form passive sentences with indirect objects.

9. Are the following sentences personal (P) or impersonal (I)?

   a. Está prohibido fumar en espacios cerrados.

   b. Las mozas prohíben fumar en el restaurante.

   c. Sebastián, el de la radio, dijo que hoy hará mucho calor.

   d. En la radio dijeron que hoy hará mucho calor.

   e. Aquí los clientes comen una rica paella.

   f. Aquí se come una rica paella.

   g. Los dueños se comieron toda la comida.

   h. Toda la comida fue comida.

   i. Hay que esforzarse mucho para mejorar.

   j. Tienes que esforzarte mucho para mejorar.

10. Complete the following sentences with the correct form of the verbs in parentheses to make impersonal sentences.

    a. En mi país .... (jugar) mucho al polo.

    b. La comida .... (preparar) por Susana.

    c. .... (decir) que esa actriz está aquí en la ciudad.

    d. En esta institución .... (prohibir) gritar.

    e. No .... (haber/saber) mucho para aprobar este examen.

    f. En México .... (comer) unos tacos increíbles.

    g. ¡Mira el estado de estas calles! Así .... (poder) hacer daño en cualquier momento.

Answer Key

1.

    a. Me contaron que te irás de viaje.

    b. En la radio dijeron los resultados de la votación.

    c. Llaman al teléfono, ¿atiendes tú?

    d. ¿Vinieron mientras yo no estaba?

2.

    a. Está lloviendo.

    b. Está prohibido nadar en el río.

    c. Están permitidas las llamadas telefónicas.

    d. Es difícil cruzar la selva a pie.

    e. Es importante mirar a ambos lados antes de cruzar la calle.

    f. Resulta que no había dinero para ir de viaje.

3.

    a. Yes

    b. No

    c. No

    d. Yes

    e. Yes

    f. No

    g. Yes

4.

    a. ii. se valora

    b. iii. se toma mate

    c. i. no se camina

    d. iii. se celebra

    e. i. se duerme

5.

    a. se juega

    b. se bebe

    c. se sirven

    d. se paga

    e. se comen

6.

a. fue construida

b. fue pintada

c. es modificada

d. fue diseñada

e. fue investigado

f. fue asaltado

g. es leído

7.

a. Ayer el himno nacional fue cantado por Juana.

b. Tres árboles fueron plantados en la plaza.

c. Todos los gatitos de Milagros fueron adoptados.

d. El partido de tenis fue visto (por algunas personas) en el bar.

e. El problema fue solucionado.

f. El misterio fue resuelto por un detective.

g. Mi equipo de fútbol fue derrotado ayer.

8. c. We can't form passive sentences with indirect objects.

9.

a. I

b. P

c. P

d. I

e. P

f. I

g. P

h. I

i. I

j. P

10.

a. En mi país se juega mucho al polo.

b. La comida fue preparada por Susana.

c. Dicen que esa actriz está aquí en la ciudad.

d. En esta institución está prohibido gritar.

e. No hay que saber mucho para aprobar este examen.

f. En México se comen unos tacos increíbles.

g. ¡Mira el estado de estas calles! Así te puedes hacer daño en cualquier momento.

Chapter 7: That's an order!

⁂

Las órdenes y las costumbres tienen una cosa en común: parece que vienen de fuera, que se te imponen sin pedirte permiso. En cambio, los caprichos te salen de dentro, brotan espontáneamente sin que nadie te los mande ni a nadie en principio creas imitarlos.

- Fernando Savater

The last one of the Spanish verbal moods is the imperative, which also exists in English. The imperative is used to give orders, advice, recommendations or to request something in a straightforward manner.

In Spanish, using the imperative isn't always a signal of power or an impolite way to ask for something. It is actually fairly commonly used in many set phrases and in everyday conversations.

Let's take a look at the forms of the imperative in Spanish!

Affirmative and negative imperative

Affirmative imperative

In Spanish, the imperative has only four possible conjugations, which correspond to the gender and number of *tú, usted, vosotros/vosotras,* and *ustedes.*

Let's look at the imperative conjugation of the three prototype verbs we've been using so far:

		Cantar	Comer	Vivir
Singular	tú	canta	come	vive
	usted	cante	coma	viva
Plural	vosotros / vosotras	cantad	comed	vivid
	ustedes	canten	coman	vivan

As with many other Spanish conjugations, the imperative conjugation of verbs ending in *-er* and *-ir* both end in the same way. Which is a relief, right?

The form with *tú* is formed by eliminating the final *-s* from the present indicative second person singular form. Which means that *cantas, comes,* and *vives* turn into *canta, come* and *vive.* But, we should also note that the conjugations for *tú* and *usted* seem to be swapped. Can you see it? With *tú,* verbs ending in *-ar* end in *a,* while verbs ending in *-er* and *-ir* end in *e.* But with *usted* it is the other way around: verbs ending in *-er* and *-ir* end in *a,* and verbs ending in *-ar* end in *e.*

The conjugation with *vosotros/vosotras* is formed by substituting the final *-r* from the infinitive with *-d*. It's that easy!

Let's see these verbs in use!

- *Lara, ¡**canta** una canción bonita!*
- *Usted **coma** y no haga tantas preguntas.*
- *¡**Vivid** como si fuera el último día en la Tierra!*

As you already know, we can also apply the endings of these verbs to other regular verbs to form the imperative. Let's see some examples.

- *¡**Dejen** de pelear y **hagan** la tarea!*
- *Para hacer una tortilla, primero **rompa** el huevo...*
- *¡**Salid** de mi vista!*

There are also some irregular verbs that do not follow the conjugation we've seen. Let's see some of them.

		Poner	Hacer	Tener	Ir	Decir
Singular	tú	pon	haz	ten	ve	di
	usted	ponga	haga	tenga	vaya	diga
Plural	vosotros/vosotras	poned	haced	tened	id	decid
	ustedes	pongan	hagan	tengan	vayan	digan

Now let's see these irregular verbs in use!

- *Camila, **pon** el pastel en el horno, por favor.*
- *__Haga__ un dibujo de su familia.*
- *__Tengan__ a mano sus pasaportes.*
- *__Abrid__ la boca y **decid** "Ahh".*
- *__Ve__ a la tienda y **pide** un kilo de pan.*

Negative imperative

If you paid attention to the titles, you might have already realized that there are two types of imperative: the affirmative, which is the one we've seen in the previous section, and the negative, which is the one we'll see now.

The negative is formed with the negative adverb *no* + the present subjunctive form of the verbs. Let's see how the regular verbs we've seen before are conjugated with the negative imperative:

	Cantar	Comer	Vivir

444

Singular	tú	no cant<u>es</u>	no com<u>as</u>	no viv<u>as</u>
	usted	no cant<u>e</u>	no com<u>a</u>	no viv<u>a</u>
Plural	vosotros / vosotras	no cant<u>éis</u>	no com<u>áis</u>	no viv<u>áis</u>
	ustedes	no cant<u>en</u>	no com<u>an</u>	no viv<u>an</u>

Notice that the negative imperative forms for *usted* and *ustedes* are the same as the affirmative imperative forms, only with the adverb *no*.

Let's see some examples!

- *¡Pedro, **no cantes** esa canción todo el día!*
- ***No vivan** en esta casa, está llena de fantasmas.*
- ***No coma** esa sopa, ¡tiene una mosca!*

Let's take a look at what happens in the negative imperative with the irregular verbs we've seen with the affirmative imperative.

		Poner	Hacer	Tener	Ir	Decir
Singular	tú	no pongas	no hagas	no tienes	no vayas	no digas
	usted	no ponga	no haga	no tenga	no vaya	no diga
Plural	vosotros / vosotras	no pongáis	no hagáis	no tengáis	no vayáis	no digáis
	ustedes	no pongan	no hagan	no tengan	no vayan	no digan

Let's see these irregular verbs in use now:

- *¡**No pongas** agua en el aceite!*
- ***No hagáis** un desastre en la cocina, por favor.*
- ***No tengan** tanto cuidado, es solo un trapo viejo.*
- ***No vayan** a la playa hoy, está muy nublado.*
- *Usted haga lo que quiera, pero **no diga** que no le avisé.*

Reflexive verbs

With reflexive verbs, the affirmative and negative imperative are formed very differently from what we've seen so far. On the one hand, we have the affirmative, which is formed with the reflexive pronoun joint to the verb. On the other hand, we have the negative imperative, for which we put the reflexive pronoun between the *no* and the verb. Let's see some examples with the verbs *levantarse* and *vestirse*.

445

	Levantarse		Vestirse	
	Affirmative	Negative	Affirmative	Negative
tú .	levánt**ate**	no **te** levant**es**	víst**ete**	no **te** vist**as**
usted	levánt**ese**	no **se** levant**e**	vist**ase**	no **se** vist**a**
vosotros / vosotras	levant**aos**	no **os** levant**éis**	vest**íos**	no **os** vist**áis**
ustedes	levánt**ense**	no **se** levant**en**	vist**anse**	no **se** vist**an**

The regular affirmative imperative conjugation of reflexive verbs like *levantarse* follow almost the same conjugation as regular imperative verbs, except in the second-person plural form, in which we get rid of the *d*, and, of course, we also add the corresponding reflexive pronoun afterwards.

As you may have noticed, *vestirse* is an irregular verb. For irregular affirmative reflexive verbs in the imperative, the irregularities are similar to that of other tenses, but they aren't exactly the same as any of them, so you should resort to your memory to remember how they should be conjugated.

And, in both cases, the negative conjugation of reflexive verbs depends on the subjunctive conjugation of the verbs.

To sum up, then, here's a simple formula to form the imperative of reflexive verbs:

- Affirmative: verb in the imperative + reflexive pronoun (added to the end of the verb)
- Negative: *no* + reflexive pronoun + verb in the present subjunctive

Now, let's see some examples using these and other reflexive verbs to see how they work in a sentence:

- ***Levántate***, *Jaime, que llegas tarde a la escuela.*
- ***No se despida*** *de mí aún, nos veremos en unos minutos.*
- *Chicos, apaguen las luces y* **duérmanse**, *que es tarde.*
- *¡Esperen!* **No se abrochen** *los cinturones que hay que bajar del auto.*

Imperative with Direct and Indirect Objects

The direct and indirect objects in imperative sentences work in a very similar way to any other normal sentence.

Let's start talking about the direct object (DO) with an example. We can say *Canta la canción* where *la canción* is the DO of the sentence. And, following the previous example, we could say *No cantes la canción* in the negative imperative form. Just like any other Spanish sentence, right?

Well, the thing about Spanish is that we also have DO pronouns that are used when the DO is understood by context. So, if we were already talking about a song, we could simply say *Cántala* where the pronoun *la* replaces *la canción*. In the negative imperative form, however, the pronoun isn't added to the end of the verb. Instead, it is added to the sentence between *no* and the verb. For example, we can say *No la cantes.*

Of course, pronouns in Spanish change depending on the person, gender and number, so here is a table with the different Spanish DO pronouns:

	Masculine	Feminine	Neuter
first-person singular	-	-	me
second-person singular	-	-	te
third-person singular	lo	la	-
first-person plural	-	-	nos
second-person plural	-	-	os
third-person plural	los	las	-

So, following the previous example, if we wanted to ask someone to sing a verse instead of a song, we would tell them *Cántalo*, because *verso* is a masculine word in Spanish. And, in the negative imperative form, we would say *No lo cantes*.

Let's see some other examples:

- *¿Has probado los espárragos? Pruéba**los**, están buenísimos.*
- *¿Te gusta esa playera? No **la** compres, es muy cara.*
- *¿Ves esas ventanas? Por favor, no **las** cierres, quiero que corra aire.*
- *¡Quiére**te** más! Eres increíble, no **lo** dudes.*

Okay, now, it's time to talk about the indirect object (IO). Let's start with an example similar to the one we've used for the DO. We can say: *Canta una canción a tu hermana*. In this sentence, *una canción* is the DO, while *a tu hermana* is the IO of the sentence. In the negative imperative form, this sentence would turn into *No cantes una canción a tu hermana*.

However, just like there are pronouns for the DO, in Spanish there are pronouns for the IO as well. These pronouns are used if we are already talking about the person the action is destined to. In the affirmative, the IO pronoun is added to the end of the verb. For example, we can say *Cántale una canción* if we were already talking about this person's sister. In the negative, however, the pronoun comes between *no* and the verb in this way, for example: *No le cantes una canción*.

Luckily, there are only six IO pronouns (instead of nine for the DO) which do not change depending on the gender, but only on person and number. Here they are:

first-person singular	me
second-person singular	te
third-person singular	le

first-person plural	nos
second-person plural	os
third-person plural	les

So, if we wanted to say "sing a song to your brother" we would still say *Cántale una canción*, but if we wanted to say "sing me a song", the pronoun would change and we would have to say *Cánta<u>me</u> una canción*.

Now, here's another thing about the Spanish IO and DO pronouns: you can have both in one sentence! In affirmative imperative sentences, both pronouns are added to the end of verb. The IO pronoun always comes first and the follows the DO pronouns. For example we can say: *¿Tienes unas tijeras? Préstamelas*. In this example, *me* is the IO pronoun that is replacing the IO *a mí*, and *las* is the DO pronoun that is replacing the DO *las tijeras*.

In the negative imperative form, the pronouns go separately between *no* and the verb, and the IO pronoun always precedes the DO pronoun. So the example sentence would become: *No <u>me</u> <u>las</u> prestes*.

However, we should note that when there is a third-person (singular or plural) DO pronoun with another third-person (singular or plural) IO pronoun, the IO pronoun turns into *se*, so as not to have something like **Préstalelos* or **Préstalesla*. In this way, if we wanted to ask someone to lend the scissors to their sister or brother, for example, we would say: *¿Tienes unas tijeras? Présta<u>se</u>las*. And, in the negative imperative form, we could say *No <u>se</u> <u>las</u> prestes*.

In the same way, with the IO and DO pronouns, the example *Canta una canción a tu hermana* would turn into *Cánta<u>se</u>la* or, in the negative, *No <u>se</u> <u>la</u> cantes*.

Now, let's see some other examples using the IO and DO pronouns:

- *Regála**le** unas flores y unos chocolates, nunca falla.*
- *No **te** compres esos vasos, **te los** regalo.*
- *Cocína**selo**, le va a encantar la sorpresa.*
- *¿Qué les pedirás a los abuelos de París? ¿Unos llaveros? Pidámo**selos**.*

We should also bear in mind that, fairly often, the DO and IO be duplicated in sentences. But what does this imply? This implies that the DO and the IO can appear both in full and through their pronouns in a single sentence. This is done to reinforce the DO or IO, but, in some Spanish-speaking countries, the standard is to duplicate (especially the IO), and they do it all the time.

Let's see some examples: in *Cánta<u>le</u> una canción <u>a tu hermana</u>*, both the pronoun *le* and *a tu hermana* refer to the same indirect object of the sentence. In *Ve<u>lo</u> <u>a Juan</u>*, the pronoun *lo* and *a Juan* both refer to the same direct object of the sentence.

Uses of the imperative

In Spanish, the imperative can be used to give orders, instructions, advice, and to make requests, proposals, and suggestions. Let's look at some examples of these different uses of the imperative.

Giving instructions and orders

448

- *Primero, **sala** la carne, luego **ponla** en el horno y **déjala** por media hora. Por último, **sírvela** con el puré, pero **no la sirvas** con la salsa.*

- ***Lea** las instrucciones que se encuentran dentro de la caja antes de utilizar el producto. **No deje** el producto al alcance de los niños.*

- *¡Ana, **ven** y **pon** la mesa que la comida ya está lista!*

- *¡**Detenga** el vehículo y **baje** la ventanilla!*

Giving recommendations and advice

- ***Vayan** en taxi a la reunión, yo las paso a buscar cuando terminen.*

- ***Prueba** esta nueva crema, ¡te hará bien a la piel!*

- *Si quieres llegar temprano, **sal** ahora mismo.*

- *¿Te duele la cabeza? **Toma** esta pastilla, a mí me ayudó muchísimo.*

Make requests and proposals

- *Necesito pedirte un favor. **Baja** las escaleras y **apaga** mi computadora, por favor.*

- *¡**Corre** al mercado y trae un kilo de pan, por favor, que ya está por cerrar!*

- *¡**Cántenle** esa canción que le gusta! Se pondrá contenta.*

- ***Pídeme** ayuda cuando lo necesites.*

Make suggestions

- ***Tomad** el tren y podréis llegar más rápido.*

- *Si te gusta el rock, **escucha** a Pink Floyd.*

- *¿Estás en Palermo? **Ve** a comer a Don Sancho, todo allí es riquísimo.*

Key Takeaways

We've talked about the imperative mood in this chapter, which is the last one of the three Spanish verbal moods, alongside the indicative and the subjunctive.

- The imperative is conjugated with only *tú, usted, vosotros/vosotras*, and *ustedes*.

- The negative imperative is formed with *no* + the present subjunctive.

- The imperative form of reflexive verbs follow these formulas:

  - Affirmative: verb in the imperative+reflexive pronoun (added to the end of the verb)

  - Negative: no + reflexive pronoun + verb in the present subjunctive

- With direct objects, we can use the DO pronouns *me, te, lo, la, nos, os, los*, and *las* with the following formulas:

  - Affirmative: verb in the imperative+DO pronoun (added to the end of the verb)

  - Negative: no + DO pronoun + verb in the present subjunctive

- With indirect objects, we can use the IO pronouns *me, te, le, nos, os*, and *les* with the following formulas:

  - Affirmative: verb in the imperative+IO pronoun (added to the end of the verb) + DO

○ Negative: no + IO pronoun + verb in the present subjunctive + DO

• When we have both direct and indirect objects, we can use both DO and IO pronouns with the following formula:

○ Affirmative: verb in the imperative+IO pronoun+DO pronoun (both added to the end of the verb)

○ Negative: no + IO pronoun + DO pronoun + verb in the present subjunctive

○ Exception: When we have a third-person DO pronoun (singular or plural) and a third-person IO pronoun (singular or plural), the IO pronoun changes from *le* or *les* to *se*.

• The imperative is used to:

○ give instructions

○ give orders

○ give recommendations

○ give advice

○ make requests,

○ make proposals

○ make suggestions

The next chapter is also the last one of this whole intermediate book. There, we will be dealing with the future so that you can start projecting what you will do with all of this Spanish knowledge. See you there!

Exercises

1. How many conjugations of the imperative are there?

   a. six

   b. three

   c. five

   d. four

2. Complete the following sentences with the affirmative imperative form of the verbs in parentheses.

   a. .... (vosotras/bailar) mucho esta noche y, sobre todo, ¡........................ (vosotras/disfrutar)!

   b. Pablo, ... (tú/ir) al cine con tus amigos, pero .... (volver) temprano.

   c. .... (tú/salir) temprano hoy. Te prepararé una rica cena.

   d. .... (ustedes/visitar) a su abuela hoy y .... (llevar) estas revistas al puerto, por favor.

   e. Señor, por favor .... (usted/guardar) su celular.

3. Complete the following sentences with the negative imperative form of the verbs in parentheses.

a. ¡Clara! ¡....................... (tú/comer) con las manos sucias!

b. Por favor, ... (usted/pisar) el césped.

c. Disculpen, ... (ustedes/poder) sacar fotos en el museo.

d. Joaquín, ... (tú/escuchar) la música tan fuerte, por favor.

e. ¡....................... (vosotros/almorzar) antes de venir, así tienen hambre!

4. Complete the following sentences with the imperative form of the reflexive verbs in parentheses.

a. .... (tú/ponerse) lindo esta noche que saldremos a comer.

b. .... (ustedes/levantarse) temprano, que mañana tienen muchas cosas que hacer.

c. Para no separarse, ... (vosotras/encontrarse) en esta plaza cuando termine el show.

d. ¡....................... (ustedes/no/sentarse) ahí! Está recién pintado.

e. Por favor, ... (usted/no/retirarse) del establecimiento.

5. Complete the table with the missing DO and IO pronouns

	DO pronouns	IO pronouns
first-person singular	me	....
second-person singular	....	....
third-person singular	lo /	....
first-person plural	nos	nos
second-person plural	....	os
third-person plural	.... / las	les

6. Rewrite these sentences with the corresponding DO pronouns.

a. Compra un zapallo, por favor.

b. Ayúdame a sacar la carne del congelador.

c. Limpia tus zapatos, están muy sucios.

d. Mira las estrellas, están muy bonitas.

e. ¿Vendrás al acuario a ver a los peces?

7. Rewrite these sentences with the corresponding IO pronouns

a. Pide la cuenta al mozo cuando lo veas.

b. Compra unas manzanas a Nora.

    c. Ayuda a Pedro con esas bolsas.

    d. Limpia el piso a Laura antes de irte.

    e. Saca unas entradas de cine para Cleo.

8. Put the words in the correct order to form negative imperative sentences.

    a. busques / anillo / el / ya / no / encontré / lo

    b. vengas / teatro / no / al / ven / a

    c. me / Pedro, / verdad! / la / sé / ¡No / ya / mientas,

    d. no / arregladas / nos / miren / ¡No / estamos!

    e. escondáis, / ayudarlos! / venimos / os / ¡No / a

9. Complete the following text with the right IO and/or DO pronouns. Escuché que Juan había hecho trampa en el examen, así que le dije "¡Cuenta..... a mamá ahora mismo!", pero me dijo "No ..... cuentes a mamá, por favor". Así que le señalé el examen y le dije "Muéstra....." y él me respondió "Bueno, míra....., ¡pero no ..... juzgues (a mí)!". Una vez que lo vi y él me explicó en qué había hecho trampa, le dije "No le contaré a mamá, pero (tú) prepára..... para hacer todo lo que te pida a cambio".

10. Rewrite these sentences so that they are in the imperative form.

    a. Primero, limpiar la cocina con el producto y una esponja.

    b. Deben detener el auto y abrir la capota.

    c. Si te gusta el teatro, tienes que ir a ver Romeo y Julieta.

    d. Para esas lastimaduras, deberíais poneros un ungüento.

    e. Este producto no se debe dejar al sol.

Answer Key

1. d. four

2.

    a. Bailad mucho esta noche y, sobre todo, ¡disfrutad!

    b. Pablo, ve al cine con tus amigos, pero vuelve temprano.

    c. Sal temprano hoy. Te prepararé una rica cena.

    d. Visiten a su abuela hoy y lleven estas revistas al puerto, por favor.

    e. Señor, por favor guarde su celular.

3.

    a. ¡Clara! ¡No comas con las manos sucias!

    b. Por favor, no pise el césped.

    c. Disculpen, no pueden sacar fotos en el museo.

    d. Joaquín, no escuches la música tan fuerte, por favor.

    e. ¡No almorcéis antes de venir, así tenéis hambre!

4.

    a. Ponte lindo esta noche que saldremos a comer.

    b. Levántense temprano, que mañana tienen muchas cosas que hacer.

    c. Para no separarse, encontraos en esta plaza cuando termine el show.

    d. ¡No se sienten ahí! Está recién pintado.

    e. Por favor, no se retire del establecimiento.

5.

	DO pronouns	IO pronouns
first-person singular	me	<u>me</u>
second-person singular	<u>te</u>	<u>te</u>
third-person singular	lo / <u>la</u>	<u>le</u>
first-person plural	nos	nos
second-person plural	<u>os</u>	os
third-person plural	<u>los</u> / las	les

6.

    a. Cómpralo, por favor.

    b. Ayúdame a sacarla del congelador.

c. Limpialos, están muy sucios.

d. Míralas, están muy bonitas.

e. ¿Vendrás al acuario a verlos?

7.

a. Pídele la cuenta cuando lo veas.

b. Cómprale unas manzanas.

c. Ayúdalo con las bolsas.

d. Límpiale el piso antes de irte.

e. Sácale unas entradas de cine.

8.

a. No busques el anillo, ya lo encontré.

b. ¡No vengas a verme al teatro!

c. ¡No me mientas, Pedro, ya sé la verdad!

d. ¡No nos miren, no estamos arregladas!

e. ¡No os escondáis, venimos a ayudarlos!

9.

Escuché que Juan había hecho trampa en el examen, así que le dije "¡Cuéntale a mamá ahora mismo!", pero me dijo "No se lo cuentes a mamá, por favor". Así que le señalé el examen y le dije "Muéstramelo" y él me respondió "Bueno, míralo, ¡pero no me juzgues!". Una vez que lo vi y él me explicó en qué había hecho trampa, le dije "No le contaré a mamá, pero prepárate para hacer todo lo que te pida a cambio".

10.

a. Primero, limpia la cocina con el producto y una esponja.

b. Detengan el auto y abran la capota.

c. Si te gusta el teatro, ve a ver Romeo y Julieta.

d. Para esas lastimaduras, ponéos un ungüento.

e. No deje este producto al sol.

Chapter 8: Step into the Future

❧

El futuro no es lo que va a pasar sino lo que vamos a hacer.

- Jorge Luis Borges

We'll talk some more about the future in the last chapter of this book. We started with this tense in Chapter 5, the one dedicated to hypotheses, but that was just the beginning. There's a lot more to be said about the Spanish future.

Something curious about Spanish is that we can use the present of the indicative to talk about the future. See for example the following sentence:

- *No te preocupes. Mañana se lo **digo***.

But that's not all. As we saw in Chapter 5, we can also use the simple future to make hypotheses about the present, as in this examples:

- *María **estará** cenando, por eso no atiende el teléfono.*

This can be a little confusing, but don't worry! We'll go step by step so that you can fully understand it.

Forms of the future

Presente del indicativo

When we present the result of a firm decision or when we want to guarantee the fulfillment of an action, we can use the present of the indicative to talk about the future.

- *La semana que viene **voy** al banco y **retiro** el dinero.*
- ***Salimos** el martes a las ocho de la mañana.*
- ***Trabajan** mucho el mes que viene y después **se toman** vacaciones.*

As you can see in this last example, the verb *trabajar* is conjugated in the present indicative. But, can you see the difference in meaning between that sentence and this one?

- ***Trabajan** mucho todos los días y no les pagan lo suficiente.*

Even though the verb is conjugated in the same tense, we have time markers that help us decide if the speaker is talking about the present (*todos los días*) or the future (*el mes que viene*). We'll go into them later in this chapter.

Ir + a + infinitivo (o futuro perifrástico)

We use this tense to talk about decisions, plans or future actions with a strong link to the present moment. They tend to be actions which had prior planning or intent.

- *-¿Qué **vais a hacer** este fin de semana? -**Vamos a ir** a la playa.*

- *Durante las vacaciones, **voy a leer** muchos libros.*
- *Cuando termine el colegio, **voy a estudiar** medicina.*

As you can see in the examples, the verb *ir* is conjugated in the present indicative. Here's a chart with the conjugation of this verb:

yo	voy		
tú	vas		
él / ella / usted	va	+ a	+ infinitive
nosotros / nosotras	vamos		
vosotros / vosotras	vais		
ellos / ellas / ustedes	van		

The verb *ir* together with the preposition *a* add the sense of future. However, it's the second verb, the one that stays in the infinitive, that carries the actual meaning of the action. This construction is very similar to the English "to be going to". Take a look at the translation of the previous examples:

- *-What **are** you **going to do** this weekend? -**I'm going to go** to the beach.*
- *During the holidays, **I'm going to read** lots of books.*
- *When I finish school, **I'm going to study** medicine.*

Futuro imperfecto (o futuro simple)

We use this tense to talk about what we will do in the future. However, as we saw in Chapter 5, we can also use it to talk about conjectures, possibilities, and probabilities in the present. Lastly, we can also use it to make predictions about the future and to give solemn commands. Let's take a look at some examples of all of these uses:

The future simple used to talk about the future:

- *Mañana **visitaré** a mi abuela.*
- ***Tendremos** un examen la semana que viene.*
- ***Llegarán** el sábado por la tarde.*

The future simple used to make hypothesis about the present:

- *Salió hace una hora, ya **estará** en su casa.*
- *Llamé a la heladería y no contestó nadie. **Estará** cerrada.*
- *Son las dos de la tarde, los niños **tendrán** hambre. Diles que vengan a almorzar.*

The future simple used to make predictions about the future:

- *Estoy segura de que te **gustará** este libro.*
- *Creo que **buscará** trabajo como voluntario cuando termine la universidad.*
- *Seguramente **aprenderás** un montón de cosas nuevas en ese curso.*

The future simple used to give solemn commands:

- *Me **esperarás** aquí hasta que vuelva.*
- ***Harás** caso al maestro.*
- *No **robarás**.*

We've already described how to form this tense, which, by the way, is easier than many other Spanish tenses. Go back to Chapter 5 if you need a refresher!

Futuro perfecto (o futuro compuesto)

This tense is used to talk about a future action that will have finished before another future action takes place. It may seem a little complicated, but don't worry, we'll see some examples for you to fully comprehend it:

- *Salieron en auto muy temprano a la mañana. Para el mediodía, **habrán llegado** a destino.*
- *No te preocupes, cuando regreses, **habré terminado** de cocinar.*
- *Mejor ve a comprar la comida ahora, porque por la noche se **habrá agotado**.*
- *Mañana a esta hora ya **habrás llegado** a Málaga.*

In these cases, the speakers are placing themselves in a concrete future moment (*para el mediodía, cuando regreses, por la noche, mañana a esta hora*), and they want to indicate that the actions they are talking about will have finished by then.

This tense can also be used to express the supposition that an action may have happened in the past. We use the perfect future in the same cases where we would use *pretérito perfecto*. However, we use *pretérito perfecto* to talk about actions that we know for a fact took place in the past, whereas we use the perfect future for things we assume took place in the past. Let's see some examples:

- *Mira, lleva un brazo enyesado. Se **habrá caído** de la bicicleta.*
  (We don't know what happened to their arm, we assume they fell off the bike.)

- *-¿Por qué está tan cansada Clara?*
  *-No sé, **habrá dormido** mal anoche.*
  (We are making a supposition.)
  *-Durante el desayuno me contó que **durmió** mal anoche.*
  (We know for a fact what happened.)

- *-¿Sabes por qué no ha venido Marcos?*
  *-Se **habrá quedado dormido**, como siempre.*
  (We don't know, we are guessing.)
  *-Se **quedó dormido**, como siempre.*
  (We know what happened.)

Now that we know when to use the *futuro perfecto*, let's see how to form it. It's pretty simple. As with all other "perfect" tenses, we use the auxiliary verb *haber* conjugated in the *futuro simple* followed by the participle of the main verb. Here's a chart with the conjugations:

yo	habré	
tú	habrás	
él / ella / usted	habrá	+ participle
nosotros / nosotras	habremos	

vosotros / vosotras	habréis	
ellos / ellas / ustedes	habrá	

Bear in mind that, for reflexive verbs, the reflexive pronoun (*me, te, se, nos, os, se*) is always placed before the auxiliary verb *haber*, like this:

- ***Me habrán dejado*** *las llaves en casa.*
- ***Se habrá quedado*** *dormido.*

Time markers for the future

The time markers for the future are the words and phrases that trigger this tense or that tell us that the action we are talking about is a future one. Let's take a look at some of these words and expressions.

- *Mañana* ("tomorrow"): **Mañana** *saldremos a cenar con mis compañeros del instituto.*
- *Esta mañana / tarde / noche / semana* ("this morning / afternoon / evening / week"): **Esta semana** *tendremos todo listo para partir.*
- *Este jueves / mes / año / siglo* ("this Thursday / month / year / century"): **Este mes** *será durísimo en el trabajo, tenemos muchas cosas que hacer.*
- *Pasado mañana* ("the day after tomorrow"): **Pasado mañana** *vamos a ir a visitar a mis padres a su casa de campo.*
- *Dentro de unos días / un par de meses / dos años* ("in a few days / a couple of months / two years"): **Dentro de un par de meses**, *ya habremos terminado la construcción de la casa y podremos mudarnos.*
- *El lunes / mes / trimestre / año que viene* ("Next Monday / month / term / year"): *No os preocupéis si no entendéis algo de esta unidad, la vamos a repasar **el trimestre que viene**.*
- *El lunes / mes / trimestre / año próximo* ("The coming Monday / month / term / year"): *Darán la última función **el sábado próximo**, y no me la quiero perder.*

Resources to make hypothesis about the future

These are some of the words and expressions we use to make assumptions about the future:

Word/Expression	Pronunciation	Translation
seguramente	seh-goo-rah-MEHN-teh	very likely
probablemente	proh-bah-bleh-MEHN-teh	probably
posiblemente	poh-see-bleh-MEHN-teh	possibly
seguro que	seh-GOO-roh keh	surely
supongo que	soo-POHNG-goh keh	suppose

458

Here are a few examples of these words and expressions in use:

- ***Seguramente*** *llegarán tarde. Son muy impuntuales*
- ***Probablemente*** *volverán muy cansados después de la excursión y querrán acostarse sin cenar.*
- *El Partido Socialista* ***posiblemente*** *ganará las elecciones.*
- *No te pongas triste por la despedida.* ***Seguro que*** *nos veremos pronto.*
- ***Supongo que*** *iremos de vacaciones a Mallorca, como siempre.*

Expressing conditions

To finish this chapter about the future, we'll do a quick review of the ways to express conditions in Spanish:

Si + presente, futuro:

- *Si estudias mucho, aprobarás el examen.*

Si + presente, presente:

- *Si mañana nieva, no voy al trabajo.*

Depende de + sustantivo:

- *-¿Vendrás a cenar el viernes por la noche?*
  -No sé... depende del estudio. Si termino de leer todo, voy.

Depende de si + presente de indicativo:

- *-¿Saldrás del trabajo temprano?*
  -Depende de si termino el informe a tiempo.

Key Takeaways

Here are the different ways we have to talk about the future:

- **Presente del indicativo**. We use this tense to talk about the future when we present the result of a firm decision or when we want to guarantee the fulfillment of an action.

- **Ir + a + infinitivo**. We use this tense to talk about decisions, plans or future actions with a strong link to the present moment and had prior planning or intent. We conjugate the verb *ir* in the present indicative and then we add the preposition *a* and the infinitive, which carries the actual meaning of the action.

- **Futuro imperfecto**. We use this tense to:
  - talk about what we will do in the future.
  - talk about conjectures, possibilities, and probabilities in the present.
  - make predictions about the future.
  - give solemn commands.

- **Futuro perfecto**: We use this tense to:

- talk about a future action that will have finished before another future action takes place. The speakers place themselves in a concrete future moment, and they want to indicate an actions that will have finished by then.

- express the supposition that an action may have happened in the past.

To form the future perfecto, we use the auxiliary verb *haber* conjugated in the *futuro simple* followed by the participle of the main verb.

The reflexive pronoun is always placed before the auxiliary verb *haber* when used with reflexive verbs.

- **Time markers for the future**. These are the words and phrases that trigger this tense: *mañana*; *esta mañana / tarde / noche / semana*; *este jueves / mes / año / siglo*; *pasado mañana*; *dentro de unos días / un par de meses / dos años*; *el lunes / mes / trimestre / año que viene*; *el lunes / mes / trimestre / año próximo*.

- **Resource to make hypotheses about the future**. These are some of the words and expressions we use to make assumptions about the future: *seguramente, probablemente, posiblemente, seguro que, supongo que*.

- **Expressing conditions**. These are the ways to express conditions in Spanish:
  - Si + presente, futuro
  - Si + presente, presente
  - Depende de + sustantivo
  - Depende de si + presente de indicativo

Congratulations! You've reached the end of the book! However, before saying goodbye, let's see how much you've learned from this last chapter.

Exercises

1. How many ways to talk about the future we mentioned in this chapter?
   - a. six
   - b. three
   - c. five
   - d. four

2. Complete with the correct tense (*presente del indicativo, futuro perifrástico, futuro imperfecto* or *futuro perfecto*):
   a. .... is used to make predictions about the future.
   b. .... is used to talk about decisions, plans or future actions with a strong link to the present moment.
   c. .... is used to talk about a future action that will have finished before another future action takes place.

3. Complete with the correct tense (*presente del indicativo, futuro perifrástico, futuro imperfecto* or *futuro perfecto*):
   a. .... is used to talk about the future when we present the result of a firm decision.
   b. .... is used to give solemn commands.
   c........................ is used to talk about conjectures, possibilities, and probabilities in the present.

4. Decide whether these sentences are referring to the past (p) or the future (f):
   a. Dentro de dos años, nos habremos mudado a Madrid.
   b. Hace mucho no veo a mi vecino. Se habrá mudado a otro barrio.
   c. Cuando nos volvamos a ver, habré terminado de escribir mi novela.
   d. Lucas está de muy mal humor. No sé qué le habrá pasado.

5. Decide whether these sentences are referring to the present (p) or the future (f):
   a. El avión sale muy temprano mañana.
   b. Salen del colegio a las 15 todos los días.
   c. La semana que viene trabajamos horas extra todos los días.
   d. En las próximas vacaciones, vamos a París.

6. Complete the following sentences with the correct conjugation of the verb *ir* to form the *futuro perifrástico*.
   La semana que viene comienzan mis vacaciones y tengo muchos planes. El primer día, ... a dormir hasta tarde. La alarma no .... a sonar, y .... a salir de la cama cuando se me dé la gana. También tengo planes con mis amigas. .... a ir a cenar a un restaurante que abrió hace poco. .... a pedir la especialidad de la casa: pizzas napolitanas. Pero no .... a ser todo placer, porque también tengo cosas que hacer. .... a ponerme al día con el estudio. Paula, mi compañera de la universidad, ... a venir a mi casa, y .... a estudiar juntas. Y creo que esos son todos mis planes para las vacaciones.

7. Complete the following sentences with you plans for the future:
   a. Pasado mañana ....
   b. Este sábado ....
   c. El martes que viene ....
   d. Dentro de dos meses ....

8. Complete the following sentences with the future form of the verbs in parentheses.
   a. Se calcula que en la India .... (haber) unos 1.600 millones de habitantes en el año 2075.
   b. Estoy cansado de trabajar tantas horas. Mañana creo que .... (hablar) con mi jefe.
   c. Mira, Juan, solamente .... (aprobar) el examen si estudias.
   d. Creo que Luis .... (terminar) los estudios dentro de dos años.

9. Which of the following words and expressions are used to make assumptions about the future?
   momentáneamente; *supongo que*; *seguramente*; *seguro que*; *me imagino que*; *actualmente*; *posiblemente*.

10. Use the words and expressions from the previous exercise to write 5 predictions about the future. What do you think the world will look like in 100 years?

Answer Key

1. d. four.

2. a. *futuro imperfecto* is used to make predictions about the future.
   b. *futuro perifrástico* is used to talk about decisions, plans or future actions with a strong link to the present moment.
   c. *futuro perfecto* is used to talk about a future action that will have finished before another future action takes place.

3. a. *presente del indicativo* is used to talk about the future when we present the result of a firm decision.
   b. *futuro imperfecto* is used to give solemn commands.
   c. *futuro imperfecto* is used to talk about conjectures, possibilities, and probabilities in the present.

4. a. future.
   b. past.
   c. future.
   d. past.

5. a. future.
   b. present.
   c. future.
   d. future.

6. voy; va; voy; Vamos; Vamos; va; Voy; va; vamos.

7.

8. a. habrá
   b. hablaré
   c. aprobarás
   d. terminará

9. *supongo que*; *seguramente*; *seguro que*; *me imagino que*; *posiblemente*.

10.

Conclusion

When you started this book, you had the wish to become an intermediate Spanish student, and now you've come out the other side a fully-grown intermediate Spanish student. How does it feel?

We've touched on many topics in this book. Some grammar topics were particularly difficult, but, if you're reading this, it means you've gone through it all: you've read, you've practiced, subjunctives have made you sweat and you've successfully completed this book. *¡Felicitaciones!*

Before we say goodbye for good, how about we go through everything we've covered? This way, you can make sure that you've studied all of the topics in this book. *¿Vamos?*

In the first chapter, we dealt with three past tenses: the *pretérito perfecto simple,* the *pretérito perfecto compuesto,* and the *pretérito imperfecto.* We learned that the *pretérito perfecto simple* is used to talk about specific events, while the *pretérito perfecto compuesto* is used to talk about events that are connected to the time of speaking, and the *pretérito imperfecto* is used to talk about things that used to happen. In this chapter, we also went over some useful time markers for each of these past tenses and saw some verbal phrases to express beginning, ending, duration and repetition. You probably already knew some of the things we saw in this chapter you, but we really did start with a bang, didn't we?

In chapter 2, we moved on to the topic of describing people, places and things. To do this, we learned about the relative pronouns (*que; definite article + que; lo que; cual, cuales; quien, quienes,* and *cuyo, cuya, cuyos,* and *cuyas*) which are used to link a main sentence with a defining or non-defining relative clause. Then, we talked about adjectives: demonstrative, possessive, limiting, essential quality adjectives, invariable adjectives, and adjectives that change meaning depending on their position. Besides talking about the characteristics of adjectives, we also saw a few lists of adjectives that will definitely come in handy.

Then, in chapter 3, we finally talked about the subjunctive mood with a practical perspective. We learned how to conjugate it and some words that trigger its use. We also dealt with the use of the subjunctive and saw that it can be used to express desire, necessity, interests, doubt, probability, and purpose, to state an opinion, and give advice and orders.

In chapter 4, we learned how to tell anecdotes by mixing the different past tenses with some connectors, and we also saw a new past tense: the *pretérito pluscuamperfecto* which is used to talk about an action that happened before another action in the past. Finally, we saw many phrases that we can use to react when someone else tells us an anecdote so that you can go way beyond simply nodding along.

In the fifth chapter, we learned how to hypothesize in Spanish like true philosophers. To make hypotheses, we went through the *futuro simple*: its conjugation, and its uses (to talk about something that will happen and to express a hypothesis). We also talked about the uses and conjugations of the *condicional simple*, which is another Spanish tense used to talk about hypothetical situations that might be true in the present or future.

The last tense we dealt with in this chapter was the *condicional compuesto*, which is used to talk about things that were supposed to happen or could have happened in the past. Then, we saw four different ways to form conditional sentences using these and other tenses you already know. Finally, we saw some phrases used to express doubt or uncertainty with the subjunctive. To be honest, this chapter was rather intense and packed with knowledge, but I'm sure you got everything! If you didn't, you can always go back and review!

Then, in chapter 6, we talked about impersonal constructions. We learned how to use third-person verbs, second-person singular verbs, the pronouns *se* and the passive voice to make impersonal sentences. Impersonal sentences are used when we don't know who does the action, don't want to disclose it, it is irrelevant, unknown or obvious, or we are talking about generalized topics.

Chapter 7 dealt with the last one of the three Spanish verbal moods: the imperative. This mood is used to give instructions, orders, recommendations, advice, and requests and to make requests, proposals, and suggestions. We learned how to conjugate the imperative in the affirmative and the negative form, and how to form it with reflexive verbs. We also learned about the direct object and indirect object pronouns, which are used to replace or complement the direct and indirect objects. We also learned how to use them with the imperative.

Finally, in chapter 8, we talked about different ways to talk about the future. We learned that we can talk about the future with the present indicative, which is used when we are talking about the result of a decision or we want to guarantee the fulfillment of an action. We also talked about the *futuro perifrástico,* which is formed with *ir + a +* infinitive and is used to talk about decisions, plans or future actions with a strong link to the present.

Then, we dealt with the *futuro imperfecto* and the *futuro perfecto.* The first tense is used to talk about what we will do in the future, conjectures, possibilities, predictions and to give solemn commands. The latter, however, is used to talk about a future action that will have finished before another future action takes place, and to suppose that an action may have happened in the past. We finally finished with time markers for the future, resources to make hypotheses about the future and the different ways to express conditions in Spanish.

Our ride through the intermediate level of Spanish was concise but definitely intense and filled with important content that is necessary to learn Spanish. Did you even know that there were that many tenses?

And what can you do now? Well, after everything you've learned here, we encourage you to go out and put all your new knowledge into practice. And that doesn't only mean that you should find more exercises to practice–it also means that you should go out and start speaking the language. I don't think it will be hard to find a Spanish speaker to practice with, but you can always find someone online, find conversation courses and even clubs for practicing languages. It doesn't matter who you practice with, as long as you practice all of the grammar and vocabulary you've learned and practice your pronunciation. You'll also find out how everything you've learned is used in real scenarios!

Above all, what you should definitely do is keep on learning the language! You're close to becoming an expert Spanish speaker, so keep it up!

It's time to say goodbye. We hope you continue your Spanish-speaking journey. *¡Adiós y buena suerte!*

BOOK 5

Learn Intermediate Spanish with Short Stories for Adults

Shortcut Your Spanish Fluency! (Fun & Easy Reads)

Explore to Win

Book 5 description

Do you have some knowledge of Spanish basics? Do you want to get to Spanish fluency but can't quite get there? We have just the right thing for you: ***Learning Intermediate Spanish with Short Stories for Adults***.

Our high-quality short stories are just what you need to take your Spanish skills to the next level. They are specifically designed for those who know the basics and want to get to intermediate at their own pace. Every story in this book is engaging and easy to follow, we will challenge you with quizzes that, just like our stories, will get progressively harder as you go on. You'll learn rich vocabulary and earn the confidence you need to put your Spanish to the test out there, with real Spanish speakers.

Getting to an intermediate level doesn't have to be an uphill struggle. Let's make it fun and simple!

In *Learning Intermediate Spanish with Short Stories for Adults* you will discover:

- Engaging stories
- Rich vocabulary and useful everyday phrases
- Stories tailored around a particular structure to challenge your Spanish every time
- Specific verb conjugations within the stories
- The indefinite and imperfect preterite tenses simplified
- The pluperfect tense
- The present perfect tense and other similar structures
- The future simple
- The passive "se"
- Tons of idiomatic expressions
- Tips and tricks on how to get the best from our stories
- Helpful glossaries
- A summary of every story
- Exercises to put your reading skills to the test
- Answer keys for every exercise set
- Some key takeaways at the end of every chapter

This incredible book was written by Spanish linguists, which means they have a deep understanding of the Spanish language, while also being able to teach you the language and phrases spoken in real life.

If you're ready to take your Spanish to the next level, then scroll up and click "add to cart" NOW!

Introduction

So you've just put down our book *Learn Spanish with Short stories for Adult Beginners* and feel like you need more? Are you looking for more high-quality short stories in Spanish? Don't worry, we've got you covered!

With this edition of *Learn Intermediate Spanish with Short stories for Adults* you will learn essential every-day vocabulary while dwelling into more complex structures such as the future, the indefinite and the imperfect preterite, and the dreaded subjunctive. But don't start panicking! Remember our short stories are carefully designed for you, our intermediate learner, meaning they will challenge you but in a way you won't feel frustrated. Quite the opposite, actually. You will feel motivated every step of the way as you notice your Spanish skills improving more and more.

Each of our chapters is meant to teach you a key element of the Spanish language while keeping you hooked with the compelling story. We won't be putting you to sleep with boring stories or tales for kids. We promise! And our exercises at the end of the chapter will test your Spanish skills every time.

If you're coming to us after finishing *Learn Spanish with Short stories for Adult Beginners*, it's good to have you back. And if you just stumbled upon our book looking for new material to read, then welcome aboard! Great stories await with *Learn Intermediate Spanish with Short stories for Adults*.

How to use this book

You will notice that each story in our book follows the same structure:

Short story in Spanish

A summary in Spanish

A summary in English

A glossary with Spanish words and phrases and their English translation

Quizzes to test your understanding of the story

Answers to verify if you were correct

Key takeaways from the chapter

We suggest you follow these tips to get the most out of our stories:

1. **Read the story all the way through**. Don't worry about trying to understand every single word right away. Follow the plot of the story as much as you can, and use the context to fill in those mental gaps you may have.

2. **Take a moment to reflect on the plot of the story**. Think about how much you understood on your own, and if it helps, write down in English what you think the story was about.

3. **Read the Spanish summary**. See if the idea of the story is the same as what you had in your head. If the Spanish summary seems too complicated at first, try reading the English one. And don't worry, even if it feels hard at first, it will get easier as you train your mind.

4. **Read the story once again**. This time focus more on the details you may have missed on your first read.

5. **Review the glossary**. Make sure you understand the words in the list, and if you're unsure of the meaning of any of the words, go to the story to put them in context. This will help you fully grasp the meaning of the more complicated phrases or expressions.

6. **Test yourself**. Do the quizzes to make sure you understood the story from beginning to end.

7. **Check the answers**. Make sure the answers are similar or the same as the ones you wrote. But don't worry if you didn't get all the answers right. Making mistakes isn't failing. If you made a mistake, review that part of the story. You'll have a better understanding of both the story as a whole and the concept, phrase or structure that you didn't get the first time around.

8. **Congratulate yourself**. Think about how much you understood on your own, even if it wasn't much at first. Remember that the key here is practice and consistency. The more you read and train your brain, the better you will get at this.

9. **Go to the next story**. Once you've gotten everything you could out of the story, go to the next one. Remember that each story has its own set of structures and vocabulary that gets progressively more challenging. The more you read, the closer you will be to your goal of mastering the Spanish language.

Chapter 1: La fiebre – The fever

❧

Si traes hijos al mundo, ámalos con el corazón y el alma.

\- Alice Walker

Hoy Carlos se quedó en casa porque **le dolía la cabeza** y **se sentía mal**. Su madre, Marisol, va al trabajo pensando que es solo **un resfriado**. Cuando llega a casa, Marisol se da cuenta que su hijo **tiene fiebre**. **Ella manda a su hija a comprar medicina** para Carlos, y **mientras tanto** prepara una **sopa de pollo** con muchos vegetales **para que el niño recupere sus fuerzas. Pica cebolla**, **papas**, zanahorias, **cilantro** y también **perejil** y **lo echa todo** a la sopa. El niño **tiene casi 39 grados de temperatura**, claramente tiene fiebre. Marisol le pregunta si **tiene dolor de estómago** y él le dice que no, así que **le da la sopa** a Carlos mientras él ve la televisión. A Carlos **no le apetece comer sopa**, pero lo hace porque Marisol le dice que **es por su bien**. Cuando Carlos se termina la sopa, **se toma una pastilla** para la fiebre y descansa un rato en la cama de Marisol porque **ella necesita estar atenta de su temperatura**. Marisol **le pone un pañuelo frío en la frente para bajarle la fiebre. Si la temperatura no baja**, Marisol **tendrá que darle una ducha con agua fría**.

Marisol piensa qué puede hacer. Ella no tiene carro para llevar a su hijo al hospital y **a estas horas de la noche el transporte público no está disponible**. Tal vez **podría pedirle a algún vecino con carro que loslleve al hospital**, aunque **no sabe a quién pedirle el favor** y ya son las 11 de la noche. Marisol **le toma la temperatura** a Carlos cada 20 minutos **esperando algún cambio**, pero la fiebre **no cede**, así que ella lleva a su hijo al baño para que se duche con agua fría.

Marisol espera 20 minutos luego de la ducha para tomarle la temperatura a Carlos de nuevo. Carlos continúa con 39 grados de temperatura. Marisol empieza a preocuparse y llama a su hermana.

–**Perdón que te llame a esta hora**, Carlos tiene mucha fiebre.

–**¿Cuánto tiene de temperatura?** –pregunta la hermana de Marisol.

–**Tiene 39 grados de fiebre**.

–**Ay, sí, es altísima**.

–**¿Tú conoces a alguien que pueda llevarme al hospital** a esta hora?

–Mi vecino Ramón tiene carro. **Le voy a preguntar y te llamo de vuelta**.

–**Dale**.

Carlos **sigue viendo caricaturas** en la televisión, pero **está temblando** un poco, parece que **tiene escalofríos**.

La hermana de Marisol la llama de vuelta.

–El carro de Ramón tiene **una llanta pinchada**.

–Ay, no sé qué hacer, hermana. Estoy muy **angustiada** porque **no se le baja la fiebre** con nada.

–**Cálmate**, no pasa nada. También llamé a una vecina que es **enfermera** y **le puede poner una inyección** para bajarle la fiebre.

–¿En serio? Ay, gracias, hermanita.

–**En 10 minutos estamos allá**.

Marisol espera a su hermana en la puerta, con mucha impaciencia. Cuando ella llega con su vecina, Marisol les da las gracias por venir a esta hora. La enfermera pasa al cuarto de Marisol y habla con Carlos, **con un tono muy dulce** y calmado le dice que **necesita que sea un niño valiente** porque **le tiene que poner una inyección**. Carlos **está asustado** y **le aprieta la mano a su mamá** mientras la enfermera le pone una inyección **en su nalga izquierda**. Carlos **se queja cuando siente la aguja y** luego llora. Marisol **lo consuela** y le da un chocolate **como premio** por **portarse bien**.

La enfermera le dice a Marisol que **ya puede estar tranquila**, que con la inyección **la fiebre bajará** en un par de horas. También le da su número de teléfono y **le dice que la llame si la necesita**. Marisol **ofrece pagarle** a la enfermera pero ella **no lo acepta**, le dice que es un favor y **espera que Carlos se mejore**.

Con el pasar de las horas, a Carlos se le baja un poco la fiebre. Marisol duerme con él **por si acaso**. En la mañana, cuando Marisol le toma la temperatura, Carlos ya no tiene fiebre, aun así, Marisol le dice a Carlos que es mejor que se quede en casa, y ella **falta al trabajo para cuidar de él**.

Resumen

Carlos, el hijo de Marisol, se siente mal y no va a clases. Con el progresar del día, a Carlos le da fiebre y Marisol hace de todo para bajarle la temperatura. Le da sopa, le da medicina, le da un baño de agua fría, pero nada funciona. Es de noche y Marisol está angustiada porque no sabe qué hacer, así que llama a su hermana. Su hermana llega a la casa con una vecina que es enfermera y le pone una inyección a Carlos para la fiebre. Con el pasar de las horas, el niño mejora.

Summary

Carlos, Marisol's son, feels unwell so he misses class. During the day Carlos gets a fever and Marisol does everything she can to lower his temperature. She feeds him soup, gives him medicine, she gives him a bath, but nothing works. It's late at night and Marisol is worried because she doesn't know what to do, so she calls her sister. Her sister comes to her house with a neighbor who is a nurse, and she gives Carlos a shot for the fever. With the passing of the hours, the boy gets better.

Glosario – Glossary

Le dolía la cabeza: he had a headache

Se sentía mal: he felts unwell

Un resfriado: a cold

Tiene fiebre: he has a fever

Ella manda a su hija a comprar medicina: she asks her daughter to buy some medicine

Mientras tanto: meanwhile

Sopa de pollo: chicken soup

Para que el niño recupere sus fuerzas: so that the boy regain strength

Pica, cebolla, papas, cilantro y perejil: she chops onion, potatoes, cilantro and parsley

Lo echa todo: she adds everything

Tiene casi 39 grados de temperatura: his temperature is almost 39 degrees

Tiene dolor de estómago: he has a stomachache

Le da la sopa: she feeds him some soup

No le apetece comer sopa: he doesn't feel like eating soup

Es por su bien: it's for his own good

Se toma una pastilla: he takes a pill

Ella necesita estar atenta de su temperatura: she needs to monitor his temperature

Le pone un pañuelo frío en la frente: she puts a cold washcloth on his forehead

Para bajarle la fiebre: to lower his fever

Si la temperatura no baja: if the temperature doesn't lower

Tendrá que darle una ducha con agua fría: she will have to give him a cold shower

A estas horas de la noche: this late at night

El transporte público no está disponible: public transportation is not available

Podría pedirle a algún vecino con carro que los lleve al hospital: she could ask a neighbor with a car to take them to the hospital

No sabe a quién pedirle el favor: she doesn't know who to ask for a favor

Le toma la temperatura: she takes his temperature

Esperando algún cambio: waiting for a change

No cede: it doesn't go down

Perdón que te llame a esta hora: sorry for calling you this late

¿Cuánto es su temperatura?: what's his temperature?

Tiene 39 grados de fiebre: he has a fever of 39 degrees

Está altísima: it's really high

¿Tú conoces a alguien que me pueda llevar al hospital?: do you know anyone that can take me to the hospital?

Le voy a preguntar y te llamo de vuelta: I will ask him and then I'll call you back

Dale: okay

Sigue viendo caricaturas: he keeps watching cartoons

Está temblando: he's shaking

Tiene escalofríos: he has chills

Tiene una llanta pinchada: it has a flat tire

Angustiada: worried

No se le baja la fiebre: his fever won't go down

Cálmate: calm down

Enfermera: nurse

Le puede poner una inyección: she can give him a shot

En 10 minutos estamos allá: we will be there in 10 minutes

Con un tono muy dulce: with a very sweet tone of voice

Necesita que sea un niño valiente: she needs him to be a brave boy

Le tiene que poner una inyección: she has to give him a shot

Está asustado: he's scared

Le aprieta la mano a su mamá: she squeezes her mom's hand

En su nalga izquierda: on his left butt cheek

Se queja cuando siente la aguja: he groans when he feels the needle

Lo consuela: she comforts him

Como premio: as a reward

Portarse bien: behaving well

Ya puede estar tranquila: she can relax now

La fiebre bajará: the fever will go down

Le dice que la llame si la necesita: she tells her to call her if she needs her

Ofrece pagarle: she offers to pay her

No lo acepta: she doesn't accept it

Espera que Carlos se mejore: she hopes that Carlos gets better

Con el pasar de las horas: with the passing of the hours

Por si acaso: just in case

Falta al trabajo para cuidar de él: she misses work to take care of him

Ejercicio 1

Contesta las siguientes preguntas – answer the following questions

1- **¿Qué manda Marisol a su hija a comprar?** – what does Marisol ask her daughter to buy?

_____

2- **¿Qué le prepara Marisol a Carlos?** – what does Marisol prepare for Carlos?

_____

3- **¿Dónde duerme Carlos?** – where does Carlos sleep?

_____

4- **¿Por qué ella no lleva a su hijo al hospital?** – why doesn't she take her son to the hospital?

5- ¿Cada cuánto tiempo Marisol le toma la temperatura a Carlos? – how often does Marisol take Carlos' temperature?

6- ¿A qué hora Marisol llama a su hermana? – what time does Marisol call her sister?

7- ¿Qué le pasa al carro de Ramón? – what's wrong with Ramón's car?

8- ¿Dónde inyecta la enfermera a Carlos? – where does the nurse give Carlos the shot?

9- ¿Por qué la enfermera no acepta el dinero? – why doesn't the nurse accept the money?

10- ¿Qué hace Marisol al día siguiente? – what does Marisol do the next day?

Ejercicio 2

Elige entre "verdadero" o "falso" – choose "true" or "false"

1- **La sopa tiene tomate.** – The soup has tomato in it.

2- **A Carlos no le gusta mucho la sopa.** – Carlos doesn't like soup very much.

3- **Marisol deja que Carlos duerma un rato.** – Marisol lets Carlos sleep for a while.

4- **Carlos toma una ducha con agua caliente.** – Carlos takes a shower with hot water.

5- La temperatura de Carlos es de 40 grados. – Carlos temperature is 40 degrees.

6- **La enfermera da miedo.** – The nurse is scary.

7- **Carlos llora por la inyección.** – Carlos cries because of the shot.

8- **Marisol le da un chocolate a Carlos.** – Marisol gives Carlos a chocolate.

9- **La enfermera le pone dos inyecciones a Carlos.** – The nurse gives Carlos two shots.

10- **Carlos se mejora con rapidez.** – Carlos gets better pretty fast.

Respuestas – Answers

Ejercicio 1

1- Marisol manda a su hija a comprar medicina para Carlos.

2- Marisol le prepara una sopa de pollo a Carlos.

3- Carlos duerme en la cama de Marisol.

4- Marisol no lleva a su hijo al hospital porque no tiene carro y el transporte público no está disponible en la noche.

5- Marisol le toma la temperatura a Carlos cada 20 minutos.

6- Marisol llama a su hermana a las 11 de la noche.

7- El carro de Ramón tiene una llanta pinchada.

8- La enfermera inyecta a Carlos en la nalga izquierda.

9- La enfermera no acepta el dinero porque es un favor.

10- Al día siguiente, Marisol le dice a Carlos que se quede en casa y ella falta al trabajo para cuidar de él.

Ejercicio 2

1- Falso

2- Verdadero

3- Verdadero

4- Falso

5- Falso

6- Falso

7- Verdadero

8- Verdadero

9- Falso

10- Verdadero

Puntos clave — Key takeaways

- *Apetecer, doler,* and *dar miedo* are verbs/constructions similar to *gustar* in the way they are conjugated.

- The indirect objective pronouns *me, te, le, nos,* and *les* are used with these verbs.

- *Me duele la cabeza* and *tengo dolor de cabeza* are different ways to say "I have a headache", and the same structure can be applied to other aches.

- *Mandar* can be used as "to ask" when talking about commands.

- Remember that direct and indirect objective pronouns go before the verb in Spanish, as in, *Yo lo ayudo* (I help him), or *Yo le doy un libro* (I give him a book).

In the next chapter, you will read Cristina's touching story, where she talks about her grandmother who passed away the year before. Here, we will introduce the indefinite preterite tense.

Chapter 2: La abuela – Grandma

Los abuelos, al igual que los héroes, son tan necesarios para el crecimiento de los niños como las vitaminas.

- Joyce Allston

Hoy es **el aniversario de la muerte de** la abuela de Cristina. Es un día muy triste para la familia, pero como **ellos se apoyan los unos a los otros**, es un poco **más llevadero**. Cristina va al cuarto que **antes pertenecía a** su abuela. **Ya nadie duerme en ese cuarto**, aunque la cama de su abuela **todavía está ahí**. Cristina se sienta en la cama y comienza a pensar mucho en su abuela, **casi puede sentirla** en el aire. La madre de Cristina era muy joven **cuando la tuvo** así que en el año 1990, cuando Cristina tenía cuatro años, **pasó al cuidado de su abuela** Lucía. Cristina **durmió** muchas noches en esa misma cama con su abuela, como **cuando se enfermaba**. La abuela Lucía era **una mujer muy amorosa**, especialmente con sus nietos, a todos **les daba el mismo cariño**. Varios de sus nietos **vivieron** en su casa **en algún punto de** sus vidas. Cristina **creció** en esa casa, **estudió** en el colegio a cinco cuadras de allí y **trabajó en la tienda de zapatos** de enfrente. Cristina recuerda **muy vívidamente** un diciembre en que su madre **vino** a la casa a visitarla. La abuela Lucía **había preparado** mucha comida con la ayuda de todos sus nietos, Cristina **preparó la ensalada de pollo con papas y zanahoria**. Esa noche la madre de Cristina **le trajo unos regalos**, un vestido hermoso y **un oso de peluche**. **Les contó a todos** que **tenía** un nuevo esposo, un abogado exitoso que **complacía todos sus caprichos**, y que ahora vivía en una linda casa al este de la ciudad. Cuando todos **terminaron de comer**, en la privacidad del cuarto de su abuela, **le preguntó a Cristina si quería vivir con ella. Le prometió** que ahora **todo sería distinto**, que **ella sería** una mejor madre y **le daría todo lo que ella merecía**, que **le compraría mucha ropa** y **estudiaría en un colegio privado. Cristina tenía diez años en aquel entonces**, una niña **muy madura para su edad**. Esta era **la primera vez que veía** a su madre así. **Se sentía** muy contenta de estar con su madre y de todo lo que ella le prometía, pero luego de pensarlo un momento, **rechazó la oferta**. Le dijo que en la casa de su abuela quizás **no tenía muchos lujos**, que quizás no tenía **su propia habitación**, o sus propios juguetes, pero que ella era una niña muy feliz, y que al final **eso era todo lo que importaba**. Su madre **estaba muy herida y decepcionada**, pero con los años **entendió la decisión que tomó Cristina**.

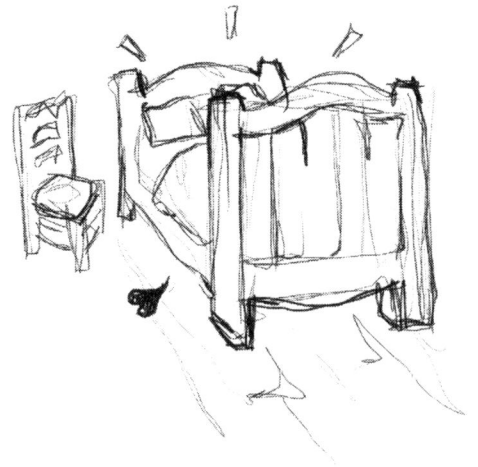

Cristina **nunca se arrepintió**.

—¿Qué haces? —preguntó Iván, el primo de Cristina, entrando a la habitación.

—Nada. Recordando.

—La abuela **te quería** mucho. Lo sabes, ¿no?

—Claro que lo sé. Nos quería a todos, y nos **lo demostraba**.

−¿**Ya preparaste lo que vas a decir** en la ceremonia?

Cristina sostiene un papel en sus manos. −Sí, aquí lo tengo.

Iván y Cristina salen de la casa, se montan en el carro y conducen hasta la iglesia El Corazón de Jesús. Ahí **se encuentran** con algunos primos, sus tíos, amigos. **Ha pasado un año desde** la muerte de la abuela Lucía y todos demuestran su cariño con su presencia. **El sacerdote** de la iglesia dice unas palabras y llama a Cristina para que diga unas palabras sobre su abuela. Hay una foto de su abuela y Cristina **la observa** por un momento. **Las palabras se le atascan en la garganta** y **se le salen las lágrimas** mientras lee **lo que escribió**. Cuando termina, **todos se levantan de sus asientos** y le **aplauden**.

−Mi niña, **no sabes cuánto te quería tu** abuela.

Cristina responde: Sí, sí lo sé.

Resumen

Es el aniversario de la muerte de la abuela de Cristina y ella está en el cuarto de su abuela, pensando mucho en ella. Reflexiona sobre su infancia viviendo con su abuela, y sobre una noche en la que su madre le pidió que se mudara con ella. Luego, junto con su primo Iván, Cristina va a la iglesia El Corazón de Jesús y lee unas hermosas palabras en honor a su abuela. Todos le aplauden y le recuerdan cuánto la quería su abuela.

Summary

It is the anniversary of Cristina's grandma's death, and she's in her grandma's room, thinking a lot about her. She reflects on her childhood living with her grandma, and about a night when her mother asked her to move in with her. Then, along with her cousin Iván, Cristina goes to the church *El Corazón de Jesús* and she reads some beautiful words in her grandma's honor. Everyone gives her a round of applause and reminds her how much her grandma loved her.

Glosario − Glossary

El aniversario de la muerte de: the anniversary of the death of

Ellos **se apoyan los unos a los otros**: they support each other

Más llevadero: more bearable

Antes pertenecía a: it used to belong to

Ya nadie duerme en ese cuarto: no one sleeps in that room anymore

Todavía está ahí: it's still there

Casi puede sentirla: she can almost feel her

Cuando la tuvo: when she had her

Pasó al cuidado de su abuela: she was placed in the care of her grandma

Durmió: she slept

Cuando se enfermaba: when she would get sick

Una mujer muy amorosa: a very loving woman

Le daba el mismo cariño: she gave them the same affection

Vivieron: they lived

En algún punto: at one point

Creció: she grew up

Estudió: she studied

Trabajó en la tienda de zapatos: she worked at the shoe store

Muy vívidamente: very vividly

Vino: she came

Había preparado: she had prepared

Preparó la ensalada de pollo con papas y zanahoria: she prepared the chicken salad with potatoes and carrot

Le trajo unos regalos: she brought her some presents

Un oso de peluche: a teddy bear

Les dijo a todos: she told everyone

Tenía: she had

Complacía todos sus caprichos: he would indulge all of her whims

Terminaron de comer: they were done eating

Le preguntó a Cristina si quería vivir con ella: she asked Cristina if she wanted to live with her

Le prometió: she promised her

Todo sería distinto: everything would be different

Ella sería: she would be

Le daría todo lo que ella merecía: she would give her everything she deserved

Le compraría mucha ropa: she would buy her a lot of clothes

Estudiaría en un colegio privado: she would study in a private school

Cristina tenía diez años: Cristina was ten years old

En aquel entonces: back then

Muy madura para su edad: very mature for her age

La primera vez que veía: the first time she saw

Se sentía: she felt

Rechazó la oferta: she declined the offer

No tenía muchos lujos: she didn't have a lot of luxuries

Su propia habitación: her own room

Eso era todo lo que importaba: that was all that mattered

Estaba muy herida y decepcionada: she was pretty hurt and disappointed

Entendió la decisión que tomó Cristina: she understood the decision Cristina made

Nunca se arrepintió: she never regretted it

Te quería: she loved you

Lo demostraba: she showed it

¿Ya preparaste lo que vas a decir?: did you already prepare what you're going to say?

Se encuentran: they meet

Ha pasado un año desde: it's been a year since

El sacerdote: the priest

La observa: she looks at it

Las palabras se le atascan en la garganta: the words get stuck in her throat

Se le salen las lágrimas: she sheds some tears

Lo que escribió: what she wrote

Todos se levantan de sus asientos: they all rise from their seat

Le **aplauden**: they give her a round of applause

No sabes cuánto te quería: you don't know how much she loved you

Ejercicio 1

Contesta las siguientes preguntas – answer the following questions

1- **¿Qué edad tenía Cristina cuando comenzó a vivir con su abuela?** – how old was Cristina when she started living with her grandma?

_____

2- **¿Cuándo solía Cristina dormir con su abuela?** – when did Cristina use to sleep with her grandma?

_____

3- **¿En qué tipo de tienda trabajó Cristina?** – what type of store did Cristina work at?

_____

4- **¿Cuándo apareció la mamá de Cristina?** – when did Cristina's mom show up?

_____

5- **¿Qué regalos trajo la mamá de Cristina?** – what presents did Cristina's mom bring?

_____

6- **¿Dónde vivía la mamá de Cristina?** – where did Cristina's mom live?

_____

7- **¿Qué le preguntó la mamá a Cristina?** – what did Cristina's mom ask her?

_____

8- **¿Por qué Cristina rechazó la oferta?** – why did Cristina decline the offer?

_____

9- ¿A quién ve Cristina en la iglesia? – who does Cristina see in the church?

_____

10- ¿Qué le dicen todos a Cristina? – what does everyone keep telling Cristina?

_____

Ejercicio 2

Elige entre "verdadero" o "falso" – choose "true" or "false"

1- **Cristina se mudó con su abuela en 1990.** – Cristina moved with her grandma in 1990.

_____

2- **Cristina siempre dormía con su abuela.** – Cristina always slept with her grandma.

_____

3- **Cristina vivía con algunos primos.** – Cristina lived with some cousins.

_____

4- **La ensalada tenía tomates.** – The salad had tomatoes in it.

_____

5- **La mamá de Cristina tenía un nuevo esposo.** – Cristina's mom had a new husband.

_____

6- **Cristina no tenía su propia habitación.** – Cristina didn't have her own room.

_____

7- **La mamá de Cristina se la llevó a la fuerza.** – Cristina's mom took her by force.

_____

8- **La iglesia se llamaba El Corazón de Cristo.** – The church was called _El Corazón de Cristo_.

_____

9- **Lucía murió hace 10 años.** – Lucía died 10 years ago.

_____

10- **Cristina lee el discurso sin problemas.** – Cristina reads her speech effortlessly.

_____

Respuestas – Answers

Ejercicio 1

1- Cristina comenzó a vivir con su abuela a los cuatro años.

2- Cristina solía dormir con su abuela cuando se enfermaba.

3- Cristina trabajó en una tienda de zapatos.

4- La mamá de Cristina apareció una noche de diciembre.

5- La mamá de Cristina trajo un vestido y un oso de peluche para ella.

6- La mamá de Cristina vivía en una linda casa en el este de la ciudad.

7- La mamá de Cristina le preguntó si quería ir a vivir con ella.

8- Cristina rechazó la oferta porque ella era feliz con su abuela.

9- Cristina ve a sus primos, tíos y amigos en la iglesia.

10- Todos le dicen a Cristina que su abuela la quería mucho.

Ejercicio 2

1- Verdadero

2- Falso

3- Verdadero

4- Falso

5- Verdadero

6- Verdadero

7- Falso

8- Falso

9- Falso

10- Falso

Puntos clave — Key takeaways

- The indefinite preterite is one of the tenses in Spanish that we use to talk about the past.
- Vivió and estudió are examples of regular-verb conjugations in Spanish.
- *Dijo* and *durmió* are examples of irregular-verb conjugations in Spanish.
- Irregular verbs fall into certain conjugation categories. We can choose to study these categories, or memorize each verb with an irregular conjugation.
- A few verbs, such as *ser*, change so drastically when conjugated in indefinite preterite that the only thing we can do is memorize them.

In the next chapter, you will read Tomas' crazy story about what he and his friends did on the night of his birthday. Keep your eyes open! We will be making emphasis in the indefinite preterite as well as the imperfect preterite.

Chapter 3: El cumpleaños de Tomás – Tomás' birthday

No envejecemos con los años, sino que somos más nuevos cada día.

\- Emily Dikinson

Tomás despierta con un fuerte dolor de cabeza, toda **la habitación da vueltas**. El reloj marca las 2 de la tarde y él no recuerda mucho sobre **lo que pasó** la noche anterior. Tomás todavía tiene puesta la ropa de anoche, dos de sus amigos duermen en unos **colchones** en el piso de su habitación. Luis despierta igual de **desorientado** que él, y le pregunta qué hora es.

—¿**Te acuerdas** algo de anoche? —pregunta Tomás.

—Claro, ¿Por qué? ¿Tú no?

—No mucho, **la verdad**.

Luis **comienza a decirle lo que sucedió** la noche anterior. Sus amigos vinieron a su casa alrededor de las 10 de la noche y **tomaron un poco**. Luis **trajo una botella de ron**, otro amigo trajo vodka. **Ninguno sabía preparar tragos complicados**, así que tomaron vodka con jugo de naranja, y ron con **gaseosa**. **Estuvieron bebiendo** y hablando **como por tres horas** y luego tomaron dos taxis hasta la **discoteca** Blue, a unos treinta minutos de camino. La entrada a la discoteca **costaba** 200 pesos, pero Tomás **entró gratis** porque era su cumpleaños. También **le dieron un cóctel como obsequio. El DJ ponía mayormente** las canciones pop más populares del momento, y todos en **la multitud cantaban mientras bailaban**. Las **luces giratorias alumbraban** el lugar **al ritmo de la música**. Había chicas muy lindas, y en poco tiempo los chicos **habían conseguido con quien bailar**. Tomás **conoció** a **una chica llamada** Valentina, tenía el cabello rubio y corto y una sonrisa muy bonita. Ella **lo felicitó por su cumpleaños** y **le invitó un trago**. Después de bailar un rato, Tomás **se sentó** con Valentina y **charlaron** sobre varias cosas. Ambos **estaban tan concentrados en la conversación** que casi no **notaron** la conmoción en **la pista de baile**, y cuando Tomás **se dio cuenta**, Luis **estaba discutiendo con** uno de los **guardias de seguridad**. Tomás **fue a preguntar qué sucedía**, y **para su sorpresa** los guardias de seguridad **los echaron** a él y a sus amigos del lugar. Tomás estaba **enfurecido**, no solo porque estaba un poco borracho sino porque **no entendía** nada de lo que estaba pasando. Luis estaba igual de furioso y **le explicó** que **alguien le había sacado el celular de su bolsillo** y que **pensaba que había sido** uno de los guardias que estaba en la pista de baile, y que cuando **lo confrontó**, el hombre **negó** todo y les dijo a los otros guardias que los sacaran porque **estaban haciendo una escena**. Tomás le preguntó si estaba totalmente seguro de **si el guardia le había robado el celular** y él le dijo que no, que estaba muy oscuro. A pesar de **lo que había pasado**, y de que Tomás estaba frustrado porque **no tuvo tiempo de pedirle a Valentina su número**, los chicos **no querían regresar a casa todavía**, así que **fueron** a otra discoteca llamada Caribe, donde la música era salsa, merengue y reggaetón. **Había barra libre** hasta las 4 de la mañana, así que **aprovecharon** para tomar **tanto como podían**.

Tomás tomó demasiado y **tuvo que ir** al baño porque **pensaba que iba a vomitar**, aunque por suerte solo **fue una falsa alarma**. A las 2 de la mañana **hubo** un show de *drag queens*, y finalmente los chicos se dieron cuenta de que estaban en una discoteca gay. **Se sentían tontos por ser tan despistados**, pero igual encontraron a chicas que pensaban que ellos eran **de mente abierta** por estar en un lugar como ese y **los invitaron a bailar**. La pasaron genial el resto de la noche, hasta que la discoteca **cerró**. Luego de ahí, todos **regresaron** en taxi a la casa de Tomás.

—¿**Ahora sí te acuerdas?** –pregunta Luis.

—Más o menos.

El celular de Tomás **vibra**, es un mensaje de **un número desconocido**. –Hola, es Rebeca, la chica de la discoteca de anoche, este es mi número.

Resumen

Tomás se despierta con un fuerte dolor de cabeza sin recordar mucho lo que pasó la noche anterior. Luis le cuenta que celebraron su cumpleaños tomando un poco en su casa y luego yendo a una discoteca donde Tomás conoció a una chica llamada Valentina. Hubo un problema con uno de los guardias de seguridad del lugar y a Tomás y sus amigos los echaron de la discoteca, pero como no querían ir a casa aún, fueron a Caribe, donde tomaron mucho y bailaron con unas chicas. Fue una noche loca que sin duda recordarán por muchos años.

Summary

Tomás wakes up with a throbbing headache without remembering much of what happened the previous night. Luis tells him that they celebrated Tomás' birthday drinking a bit at his house and then going to a club where Tomás met a girl called Valentina. There was a problem with one of the security guards of the place and Tomás and his friends got kicked out of the club, but since they didn't want to go home yet, they went to Caribe, where they drank a lot and danced with some girls. It was a crazy night that they will definitely remember for many years.

Glosario – Glossary

La habitación da vueltas: the room spins

Lo qué pasó: what happened

Colchones: mattresses

Desorientado: disoriented

¿Te acuerdas?: do you remember?

La verdad: honestly

Comienza a decirle: he starts telling him

Lo que sucedió: what happened

Tomaron un poco: they drank a bit

Trajo: he brought

Una botella de ron: a bottle of rum

Ninguno sabía preparar tragos complicados: none of them knew how to make complicated cocktails

Gaseosa: soda

Estuvieron bebiendo: they were drinking

Como por tres horas: for about three hours

Discoteca: night club

Costaba: it cost

Entró gratis: he entered for free

Le dieron un cóctel como obsequio: they gave him a cocktail as a gift

El DJ ponía: the DJ played

Mayormente: mostly

La multitud: the crowd

Cantaban mientras bailaban: they were singing while dancing

Las luces giratorias alumbraban: the rotating lights lit up

Al ritmo de la música: to the rhythm of the music

Habían conseguido: they had found

Con quien bailar: who to dance with

Conoció: he met

Una chica llamada: a girl called

Lo felicitó por su cumpleaños: she said happy birthday to him

Le invitó un trago: she bought him a drink

Se sentó: he sat

Charlaron: they talked

Estaban tan concentrados en la conversación: they were so focused on the conversation

Notaron: they noticed

La pista de baile: the dance floor

Se dio cuenta: he noticed

Estaba discutiendo con: he was arguing with

Guardias de seguridad: security guards

Fue a preguntar qué sucedía: he went to ask what was happening

Para su sorpresa: to his surprise

Los echaron: they kicked them out

Enfurecido: enraged

No entendía: he didn't understand

Le explicó: He explained

Alguien le había sacado el celular de su bolsillo: someone had grabbed his phone from his pocket

Pensaba que había sido: he thought that it had been

Lo confrontó: he confronted him

Negó: he denied it

Estaban haciendo una escena: they were making a scene

Si el guardia le había robado el celular: if the guard had stolen his phone

Lo que había pasado: what had happened

No tuvo tiempo de pedirle a Valentina su número: he didn't have time to ask Valentina for her number

No querían regresar a casa todavía: they didn't want to go back home yet

Fueron: they went

Había barra libre: there was an open bar

Aprovecharon para tomar tanto como podían: they took advantage of the situation to drink as much as they could

Tuvo que ir: he had to go

Pensaba que iba a vomitar: he thought he was going to throw up

Fue una falsa alarma: it was a false alarm

Se sentían tontos: they felt stupid

Por ser tan despistados: for being so absent-minded

De mente abierta: open-minded

Los invitaron a bailar: they asked them to dance

Cerró: it closed

Regresaron: they went back

¿Ahora sí te acuerdas?: do you remember now?

Vibra: it vibrates

Un número desconocido: an unknown number

Ejercicio 1

Contesta las siguientes preguntas – answer the following questions

1- **¿A qué hora despierta Tomás?** – what time does Tomás wake up?

_____

2- **¿Qué tomaron en casa de Tomás?** – what did they drink in Tomas' house?

_____

3- **¿Cuánto pagó Tomás para entrar a la discoteca?** – how much did Tomás pay to enter the club?

4- **¿Cómo era Valentina?** – what did Valentina look like?

5- **¿Con quién discutía Luis?** – who was Luis arguing with?

6- **¿Qué le pasó a Luis?** – what happened to Luis?

7- **¿Qué tipo de música ponían en Caribe?** – what type of music did they play in Caribe?

8- **¿Cuántas veces vomitó Tomás en la discoteca?** – how many times did Tomás throw up in the club?

9- **¿Por qué las chicas los invitaron a bailar?** – why did the girls ask them to dance with them?

10- **¿Quién le manda un mensaje a Tomás en la mañana?** – who texts Tomás in the morning?

Ejercicio 2

Elige entre "verdadero" o "falso" – choose "true" or "false"

1- **Tomás despierta en casa de Luis.** – Tomás wakes up at Luis' house.

2- **Luis trajo una botella de ron.** – Luis brought a bottle of rum.

3- **La entrada a la discoteca costaba 300 pesos.** – The entry to the club was 300 pesos.

4- **Valentina tenía el cabello negro.** – Valentina had black hair.

5- **Luis se peleó con alguien.** – Luis had a fight with someone.

6- **Tomás le pidió el número a Valentina.** – Tomás asked Valentina her phone number.

7- **En Caribe había barra libre hasta las 4 a.m.** – At Caribe there was an open bat until 4 a.m.

8- **Hubo un concurso a las 2 a.m.** – There was a contest at 2 a.m.

9- **Tomás bailó con Rebeca.** – Tomás danced with Rebeca.

10- **Tomás condujo hasta su casa.** – Tomás drove home.

Respuestas – Answers

Ejercicio 1

1- Tomás despierta a las 2 de la tarde.

2- En casa de Tomás tomaron vodka con jugo de naranja y ron con gaseosa.

3- Tomás no pagó para entrar, la entrada fue gratis porque él estaba cumpliendo años.

4- Valentina tenía el cabello rubio y corto y una linda sonrisa.

5- Luis discutía con uno de los guardias de seguridad de la discoteca.

6- Alguien le sacó el teléfono del bolsillo a Luis.

7- En Caribe ponían salsa, merengue y reggaetón.

8- Tomás no vomitó, solo fue una falsa alarma.

9- Las chicas los invitaron a bailar porque pensaban que ellos eran de mente abierta por estar en un lugar así.

10- Rebeca, la chica con la que Tomás bailó la noche anterior, le mandó un mensaje.

Ejercicio 2

1- Falso

2- Verdadero

3- Falso

4- Falso

5- Falso

6- Falso

7- Verdadero

8- Falso

9- Verdadero

10- Falso

Puntos clave — Key takeaways

- The imperfect preterite is the other of the tenses in Spanish that we use to talk about the past.
- *Cantaban* and *bailaban* are examples of regular-verb conjugations in Spanish.
- *Podían* and *querían* are examples of irregular-verb conjugations in Spanish.
- Just like verbs in the indefinite preterite, irregular verbs in the imperfect preterite fall into certain conjugation categories. We can choose to study these categories, or memorize each verb with an irregular conjugation.

In the next chapter, you will go deep into Tomás' childhood and how he used to spend the summers with his family. We will also delve into the imperfect preterite tense, learning how to use verbs such as *soler* in the past tense.

Chapter 4: Mi niñez – My childhood

El niño que no juega no es niño, pero el hombre que no juega perdió para siempre al niño que vivía en él, y que le hará mucha falta.

- Pablo Neruda

Cuando Tomás era pequeño, **solía** pasar las vacaciones de verano en la casa de sus abuelos **en el campo**. **No podía esperar a que llegaran las vacaciones**. Siempre **se portaba bien** el mes anterior a las vacaciones **para que sus padres lo dejaran ir** al campo. La casa de los abuelos de Tomás era enorme, tenían un **terreno extenso** donde **había** muchas plantas y **sembraban** tomates y papas, e incluso **cocos** y bananas. También tenían más de diez perros, el perro favorito de Tomás era Girasol, una golden retriever muy **traviesa que se ponía muy contenta cada vez que veía a Tomás**. También tenían otros animales como **caballos, patos y gallinas**. **Nunca había silencio** en la casa.

Esos días de vacaciones Tomás **se levantaba** a las 8 de la mañana y **ayudaba** a su abuela a preparar los huevos para el desayuno, luego **veía caricaturas** mientras comía. Al rato **salía a jugar** con los perros o a ver a sus primos más grandes **montar a caballo**. A él **no lo dejaban** montar a caballo porque era muy pequeño, pero a veces su primo Juan lo dejaba subirse al caballo con él, y **no le decían** a la abuela **para que no se enfadara**. A Tomás también **le gustaba meterse en la piscina** todos los días, **incluso cuando llovía**. A veces Girasol **entraba** a la piscina con él y **jugaban un rato en el agua**. Las noches en el campo eran un poco frías, así que la abuela **no dejaba que Tomás estuviera en la piscina para que no se resfriara**. Una noche, Tomás **no le hizo caso a su abuela** y se resfrió tanto **que hasta tuvo fiebre**, esa vez **aprendió su lección**. En la noche Tomás normalmente jugaba **juegos de mesa** con sus primos, dibujaba en su cuarto, o veía **las noticias** con el abuelo.

Tomás **era un nieto muy consentido**. Sus primos normalmente **tenían que compartir habitación**, pero él **tenía un cuarto para él solo**, quizás era porque era el más joven, pero él cree que fue así porque **era el único nieto que pasaba todos los veranos** en casa de sus abuelos. Sus primos a veces **viajaban** a otros lugares, pero Tomás **le pedía a sus padres que lo llevaran** a casa de sus abuelos todos los años porque le encantaba.

Lo único que a Tomás no le gustaba era cuando su tío Manuel **los llevaba a todos de cacería**. Le gustaba pasar tiempo con sus primos en el campo, pero cada vez que **veía morir a los animales** Tomás **se ponía a llorar**. Una vez incluso su tío se molestó con él porque Tomás **se rehusó a comer el conejo que ellos habían cazado**, pensaban que Tomás **estaba siendo malcriado** y hasta **lo castigaron**. Le dijeron que esa noche no comería nada, que **se acostaría con el estómago vacío**, pero su abuela, **a escondidas, le dio un buen pedazo de tarta de manzana. Hasta el día de hoy nadie sabe que eso pasó**. Desde esa noche, Tomás decidió que **ya no comería carne**, y aunque **nadie lo entendía al principio, con el tiempo**, lo entendieron y **lo respetaron**.

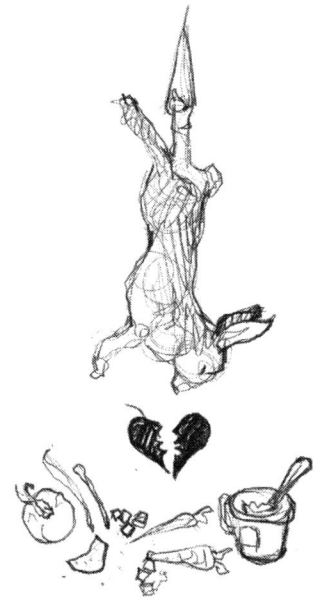

Desde entonces, cada vez que Tomás **iba** a casa de sus abuelos, la abuela **le preparaba** algo especial a él con vegetales. Junto con Tomás, la abuela **sembró pepinos, pimentones y aguacates**, luego una de las actividades favoritas de Tomás era **cuidar de las plantas** y **recoger los frutos** que dejaban. A pesar de algunos momentos **no tan buenos**, Tomás recuerda **su infancia** con mucha alegría y a menudo **desearía volver a vivir** esos momentos.

Resumen

Cuando Tomás era pequeño, solía pasar cada verano en casa de sus abuelos en el campo. Le gustaba jugar con los animales y pasar tiempo con sus primos, además de nadar en la piscina. Un día en particular tuvo un problema con su tío Manuel y lo castigaron por rehusarse a comer la carne de un animal que habían cazado, entonces Tomás decidió que nunca más volvería a comer carne. A pesar de algunos momentos no tan buenos, Tomás era muy feliz en el campo con sus abuelos y recuerda esos días con mucho cariño.

Summary

When Tomás was little, he used to spend every summer in his grandparents' house in the countryside. He liked playing with the animals and spending time with his cousins, as well as swimming in the pool. One day in particular he had a problem with his uncle Manuel and they grounded him for refusing to eat the meat of an animal they had hunted, then Tomás decided he would never eat meat again. Despite some not so great moments, Tomás was really happy in the country with his grandparents and he remembers those days fondly.

Glosario – Glossary

Solía: he used to

En el campo: in the countryside

No podía esperar a que llegaran las vacaciones: he couldn't wait for vacations to arrive

Se portaba bien: he would behave well

Para que sus padres lo dejaran ir: so that his parents would let him go

Terreno extenso: extensive land

Había: there was/there were

Sembraban: they would plant

Cocos: coconut

Traviesa: mischievous

Que se ponía contenta: who would get happy

Cada vez que veía a Tomás: every time she saw Tomás

Caballos, patos y gallinas: horses, ducks and hens

Nunca había silencio: there was never silence

Se levantaba: He would get up

Ayudaba: He would help

Veía caricaturas: he would watch cartoons

Salía a jugar: he would go out to play

Montar a caballo: to ride a horse

No lo dejaban: they wouldn't let him

No le decían: they wouldn't tell

Para que no se enfadara: so that she wouldn't get mad

Le gustaba meterse en la piscina: he used to like getting in the pool

Incluso cuando llovía: even when it was raining

Entraba: she would get in

Jugaban un rato en el agua: they would play for a while in the water

No lo dejaba estar en la piscina: she wouldn't let him be in the pool

Para que no se resfriara: so that he wouldn't catch a cold

No le hizo caso a su abuela: he didn't listen to his grandmother

Se resfrió: he caught a cold

Tanto **que hasta tuvo fiebre**: it was so strong that he even had fever

Aprendió su lección: he learned his lesson

Juegos de mesa: board games

Las noticias: the news

Era un nieto muy consentido: he was a very spoiled grandson

Tenían que compartir habitación: they had to share a room

Tenía un cuarto para él solo: he had a room just for him

Era el único nieto que pasaba todos los veranos: he was the only grandson that would spend every summer

Viajaban: they would travel

Le pedía a sus padres que lo llevaran: he would ask his parents to take him

Los llevaba a todos de cacería: he would take them all hunting

Veía a los animales morir: he would watch the animals die

Se ponía a llorar: he would start crying

Se rehusó a comer: he refused to eat

El conejo que ellos habían casado: the rabbit they had hunted

Estaba siendo malcriado: he was being a brat

Lo castigaron: they grounded him

Se acostaría con el estómago vacío: he would go to bed with an empty stomach

A escondidas: behind their backs

Le dio un buen pedazo de tarta de manzana: she gave him a generous piece of apple pie

Hasta el día de hoy: to this day

Nadie sabe que eso pasó: no one knows that that happened

Ya no comería carne: he wouldn't eat meat anymore

Nadie lo entendía al principio: no one understood it at first

Con el tiempo: with time

Lo respetaron: they respected it

Desde entonces: since then

Iba: he would go

Sembró pepinos, pimentones y aguacates: she planted cucumber, pepper and avocado

Cuidar de las plantas: to take care of the plants

Recoger los frutos: to reap the fruits

No tan buenos: not so good

Su infancia: his childhood

Desearía volver a vivir: he wishes he could relive

Ejercicio 1

Contesta las siguientes preguntas – answer the following questions

1- **¿Por qué Tomás solía portarse bien?** – why did Tomás use to behave well?

_____

2- **¿Cómo era Girasol?** – how was Girasol like?

_____

3- **¿Qué otros animales había?** – what other animals where there?

_____

4- **¿Por qué no lo dejaban montar a caballo?** – why wouldn't they let him ride a horse?

_____

5- **¿Qué hacía su primo Juan?** – what would his cousin Juan do?

_____

6- **¿Qué le pasó a Tomás cuando no escuchó a su abuela?** – what happened to Tomás when he didn't listen to his grandma?

_____

7- **¿Por qué piensa Tomás que sus abuelos lo consentían?** – what does Tomás think is the reason his grandparents spoiled him?

_____

8- **¿Qué pasaba cuando Tomás iba de cacería?** – what would happen when Tomás went hunting?

_____

496

9- **¿Por qué castigaron a Tomás?** – why did they ground Tomás?

_____

10- **¿Cuál era la actividad favorita de Tomás?** – what was Tomás' favorite activity?

_____

Ejercicio 2

Elige entre "verdadero" o "falso" – choose "true" or "false"

1- **Los abuelos de Tomás sembraban frutas.** – Tomás' grandparents would plant fruits.

_____

2- **Ellos también tenían gatos.** – They also had cats.

_____

3- **Tomás preparaba el café para los demás en las mañanas.** – Tomás would make coffee for everybody in the morning.

_____

4- **A Tomás no lo dejaban alimentar a los caballos.** – They wouldn't let Tomás feed the horses.

_____

5- **Las noches eran frías.** – The nights were cold.

_____

6- **Tomás compartía cuarto con Juan.** – Tomás shared a room with Juan.

_____

7- **A Tomás no le gustaba ir de cacería.** – Tomás didn't like to go hunting.

_____

8- **A Tomás lo castigaron por pelearse con un primo.** – Tomás was grounded because he was fighting with a cousin.

_____

9- **Tomás decidió ya no comer carne.** – Tomás decided not to eat meat anymore.

_____

10- **Tomás recuerda su infancia con cariño.** – Tomás remembers his childhood fondly.

_____

Respuestas – Answers

Ejercicio 1

1- Tomás se portaba bien para que sus padres lo dejaran ir a casa de sus abuelos en el campo.

2- Girasol era una golden retriever muy traviesa.

3- En el campo también había caballos, patos y gallinas.

4- A Tomás no lo dejaban montar a caballo porque era muy pequeño.

5- Su primo Juan lo dejaba montar a caballo con él.

6- Cuando Tomás no escuchó a su abuela, se resfrió tanto que hasta tuvo fiebre.

7- Tomás cree que sus abuelos lo consentían mucho porque él era el único nieto que los visitaba todos los veranos.

8- Cuando Tomás iba de cacería y veía a los animales morir, se ponía a llorar.

9- Castigaron a Tomás porque se rehusó a comer el conejo que ellos habían cazado.

10- La actividad favorita de Tomás era cuidar de las plantas y recoger los frutos que ellas dejaban.

Ejercicio 2

1- Verdadero

2- Falso

3- Falso

4- Falso

5- Verdadero

6- Falso

7- Verdadero

8- Falso

9- Verdadero

10- Verdadero

Puntos clave — Key takeaways

- We usually use the imperfect preterite to talk about past habits or repeated situations in the past.
- Used to or would are the structures we can use as equivalent to the imperfect preterite.
- The verb *soler* can be translated as used to, that way, *Yo solía viajar*, would be (I used to travel).
- When reading a story narrated in the past tense in Spanish, you will find both the indefinite preterite and the imperfect preterite.

In the next chapter, you will read about Marisol and her struggles with her hyperactive son. Stay focused! We will be introducing the pluperfect tense.

Chapter 5: El pequeño karateca – The little karate fighter

❦

La recreación y la diversión son tan necesarias para nuestro bienestar como las actividades más serias de la vida.

- Brigham Young

Carlos, el hijo de Marisol, **siempre ha sido** un niño muy **inquieto** y con mucha energía, es por eso que **ha probado todo tipo de pasatiempos** o simples actividades para usar toda esa energía. Probó con los instrumentos, Marisol **le consiguió una profesora privada que le enseñara a tocar el piano**, pero Carlos no tenía la **paciencia suficiente para memorizar las notas. La guitarra** fue **el mismo cuento**, y **ni hablar del violín. Un tío lejano de Carlos** le compró un violín **carísimo** en Alemania porque Carlos **prometió que practicaría hasta dominar el instrumento**, pero luego de solo un mes el niño **perdió todo el interés**. Ahora **el violín importado lleva dos años acumulando polvo en el closet de Carlos**.

Con eso Marisol aprendió que **lo mejor sería que el niño se enfocara en los deportes**. Comenzó con **la natación**, y por un tiempo parecía **que le gustaba**. Iba a una gran piscina en La Universidad Nacional a practicar todas las semanas, pero luego de un par de meses **se aburrió. El fútbol también se le daba muy bien**. Le encantaba ver los partidos en televisión así que **Marisol supuso que le gustaría**. Carlos jugó fútbol por casi un año, incluso **estuvo muy cerca de entrar en el equipo de fútbol de su escuela**. Pero como sucedió en todos los casos anteriores, el niño simplemente se aburrió. **A dos semanas de hacer la prueba para entrar en el equipo**, Carlos **dijo que ya no le interesaba**.

Por suerte, **luego de un mes de obsesión** con películas sobre **artes marciales**, Carlos comenzó a practicar karate. Al principio **hubo un problema** porque Carlos originalmente quería practicar taekwondo, que es un arte marcial muy distinto, y en la escuela de artes marciales **le habían dicho a Marisol que también enseñaban taekwondo, pero no era así**. Carlos fue a la primera clase muy **entusiasmado por aprender**, escuchó al profesor **en todo momento** e **hizo todo lo que él les enseñaba**. En un punto de la clase, Carlos se dio cuenta de que les estaban enseñando karate y no taekwondo, y se levantó y **se retiró del salón sin decir una palabra**. Marisol se sentía muy apenada por la reacción de su hijo y **le pidió disculpas al profesor por lo que él hizo**. En el pasillo de la escuela, Marisol habló con su hijo. Carlos decía que **ella lo había engañado**, que la clase era de karate y no de lo que él quería, así que no iba a continuar, pero Marisol habló con él y le explicó la situación, **le dijo que lo intentara al menos un mes** porque **ella ya había pagado por un mes de clases** para él, y también **le había comprado un uniforme de karate**. Aunque **le costó un**

poco convencerlo, al final Carlos **le hizo caso a su madre**, y luego de dos semanas **le empezó a gustar** mucho el karate, **hasta el punto de que no hablaba de otra cosa**.

Marisol se puso muy contenta porque pensó que **al fin había encontrado el hobby perfecto** para su hijo, **y así fue. Ya Carlos lleva dos años practicando karate** y **no solo le gusta mucho sino que es muy bueno**. El mes pasado fue **la ceremonia para avanzar de nivel** y Carlos **pasó a ser cinturón azul**. Marisol está orgullosa de él y **le gusta lo motivado que está** su hijo **ya que nunca lo había visto poner tanto empeño** en algo. Marisol **espera que Carlos siga practicando** karate por muchos años ya que **le enseña disciplina**, y **quizás lo ayude para defenderse** en el futuro.

Resumen

Carlos es un niño con mucha energía y por eso ha tenido todo tipo de pasatiempos. Ha probado algunos instrumentos, como el violín, la guitarra y el piano, pero todos los dejó al poco tiempo. Lo mismo pasó con ciertos deportes. La natación la abandonó luego de un par de meses y también se aburrió del fútbol. Marisol inscribió a Carlos en una escuela de artes marciales donde le dijeron que enseñaban taekwondo, pero al final no era cierto, y Carlos terminó en una clase de karate, que al principio no le gustaba pero con el tiempo eso cambió. Ahora Carlos es cinturón azul y le sigue gustando mucho el karate.

Summary

Carlos is a really energetic kid and that's why he's had all kinds of hobbies. He's tried some instruments, such as the violin, the guitar and the piano, but he quit before long. The same thing happened with certain sports. He quit swimming after a couple of months and also got bored of soccer. Marisol enrolled Carlos in a martial arts school where they told her they taught taekwondo, but in the end that was not true. Carlos ended up in a karate class, which at the beginning he didn't like but with the time that changed. Now, Carlos is a blue belt and he still likes karate a lot.

Glosario – Glossary

Siempre ha sido: he has always been

Inquieto: restless

Ha probado todo tipo de pasatiempos: he has tried all kinds of hobbies

Le consiguió: she got him

Una profesora privada que le enseñara a tocar el piano: a private teacher who would teach him to play the piano

Paciencia suficiente para memorizar las notas: enough patience to memorize the notes

La guitarra: the guitar

El mismo cuento: the same story

Ni hablar del violín: not to mention the violin

Un tío lejano de Carlos: a distant uncle of Carlos'

Carísimo: super expensive

Prometió que practicaría hasta dominar el instrumento: he promised he would practice until he had mastered the instrument

Perdió todo el interés: he lost all interest

El violín importado lleva dos años acumulando polvo en el closet de Carlos: the imported violin has been collecting dust for two years in Carlos' closet

Lo mejor sería que el niño se enfocara en los deportes: the best thing to do would be for him to focus on sports

La natación: swimming

Parecía **que le gustaba**: he seemed to like it

Se aburrió: he got bored

El fútbol también se le daba bien: he was good at soccer too

Marisol supuso que le gustaría: Marisol assumed he would like it

Estuvo cerca de entrar en el equipo de fútbol de su escuela: he was close to getting into his school's soccer team

A dos semanas de hacer la prueba para entrar en el equipo: two weeks away from the team tryouts

Dijo que ya no le interesaba: he said he was no longer interested

Luego de un mes de obsesión: after a month of obsession

Artes marciales: martial arts

Hubo un problema: there was a problem

Le habían dicho a Marisol que también enseñaban taekwondo: they had told her that they also taught taekwondo

No era así: but that wasn't the case

Entusiasmado por aprender: excited to learn

En todo momento: at all moments

Hizo todo lo que él les enseñaba: he did everything he would teach them

Se retiró del salón: he left the room

Sin decir una palabra: without saying a word

Le pidió disculpas al profesor: she apologized to the teacher

Por lo que él hizo: for what he had done

Ella lo había engañado: she had deceived him

Le dijo que lo intentara al menos por un mes: she told him to try it at least for a month

Ella ya había pagado por un mes de clases: she had already paid for a month of lessons

Le había comprador un uniforme de karate: she had bought him a karate uniform

Le costó un poco convencerlo: it was a bit hard to convince him

Le hizo caso a su madre: he listened to his mother

Le empezó a gustar: he started liking it

Hasta el punto de que no hablaba de otra cosa: to the point he wouldn't talk about anything else

Al fin había encontrado el hobby perfecto para su hijo: she had finally found the perfect hobby for her son

Y así fue: and that was the case indeed

Ya Carlos lleva dos años practicando karate: Carlos has been practicing karate for two years now

No solo le gusta sino que es bueno: not only does he like it but he's also good

La ceremonia para avanzar de nivel: the ceremony to get to the next level

Pasó a ser cinturón azul: he became a blue belt

Le gusta lo motivado que está: she likes how motivated he is

Ya que nunca lo había visto poner tanto empeño en algo: because she had never seen him putting so much effort into something

Espera que Carlos siga practicando: she hopes he keeps practicing

Le enseña disciplina: it teaches him discipline

Quizás lo ayude a defenderse: maybe it will help him defend himself

Ejercicio 1

Contesta las siguientes preguntas – answer the following questions

1- **¿Qué instrumentos probó Carlos?** – what instruments did Carlos try?

_____

2- **¿Por qué él no continuó practicando el piano?** – why didn't he continue practicing the piano?

_____

3- **¿Qué sucedió con el violín de Carlos?** – what happened to Carlos' violin?

_____

4- **¿En dónde él practicaba natación?** – where did he use to practice swimming?

_____

5- **¿Por qué Marisol pensó que a Carlos le gustaría jugar fútbol?** – why did Marisol think Carlos would like to play soccer?

_____

6- **¿Cuándo Carlos perdió el interés por el fútbol?** – when did Carlos lose interest in soccer?

_____

7- **¿Cuál fue el problema con las clases de taekwondo?** – what was the problem with the taekwondo lessons?

_____

8- **¿Qué hizo Marisol luego de la reacción de su hijo durante la clase de karate?** – what did Marisol do after her son's reaction during the karate lesson?

_____

9- ¿Por qué Marisol insistió en que su hijo continuara con las clases? – why did Marisol insist her son continue with the lessons?

_____

10- ¿Cómo le va a Carlos en karate ahora? – how is Carlos' karate going now?

_____

Ejercicio 2

Elige entre "verdadero" o "falso" – choose "true" or "false"

1- Carlos aprendió a tocar la batería. – Carlos learned to play the drums.

_____

2- Su tío le compró el violín en Argentina. – His uncle bought him the violin in Argentina.

_____

3- Carlos practicó el violín por solo un mes. – Carlos practiced the violin for just a month.

_____

4- Carlos jugó fútbol por un año. – Carlos played soccer for a year.

_____

5- El taekwondo y el karate son muy similares. – Taekwondo and karate are pretty similar.

_____

6- Carlos perdió su primera clase de karate. – Carlos missed his first karate lesson.

_____

7- Carlos le gritó a su profesor de karate. – Carlos yelled at his karate teacher.

_____

8- Marisol pagó por dos meses de clases de karate. – Marisol paid for two months of karate lessons.

_____

9- Carlos es cinturón azul en karate ahora. – Carlos is a blue belt in karate now.

_____

10- A Marisol le gusta que su hijo practique karate. – Marisol likes that her son practices karate.

_____

Respuestas – Answers

Ejercicio 1

1- Carlos probó el piano, la guitarra y el violín.

2- Carlos no continuó practicando el piano porque no tenía la concentración suficiente para memorizar las notas.

3- El violín de Carlos lleva dos años acumulando polvo en su closet.

4- Carlos practicaba natación en la piscina de la Universidad Nacional.

5- Marisol pensó que a Carlos le gustaría el fútbol porque le encantaba ver partidos de fútbol en la televisión.

6- Carlos perdió el interés por el fútbol a dos semanas de hacer la prueba para entrar en el equipo de fútbol de su escuela.

7- Carlos quería aprender taekwondo y a Marisol le habían dicho que en esa escuela enseñaban taekwondo, pero no era cierto.

8- Marisol se sentía muy apenada y le pidió disculpas al profesor por la reacción de su hijo.

9- Marisol insistió en que su hijo continuara con las clases de karate porque ya había pagado por un mes y también le había comprado un uniforme de karate nuevo.

10- A Carlos le sigue gustando el karate y es muy bueno en ello, ahora es cinturón azul.

Ejercicio 2

1- Falso

2- Falso

3- Verdadero

4- Verdadero

5- Falso

6- Verdadero

7- Falso

8- Falso

9- Verdadero

10- Verdadero

Puntos clave — Key takeaways

- When we're narrating something that happened in the past, we can use the pluperfect to talk about an action that happened prior to the event we're describing.
- The pluperfect is formed with the imperfect preterite conjugation of *haber* and a verb in its past participle form, *Yo había hecho eso*, as in (I had done that).
- Using the pluperfect tense is the furthest back in time we can go in Spanish.

- The pluperfect tense is mostly a supporting tense, meaning it's usually accompanied by another sentence in the indefinite or imperfect preterite. It rarely acts on its own.

In the next chapter, you will live vicariously through Cristina as you learn the present perfect tense and how to use it.

Chapter 6: El viaje de Cristina – Cristina's trip

∾

Hay una especie de magia cuando nos vamos lejos y, al volver, hemos cambiado.

- Kate Douglas Wiggin

Este año a Cristina **le ha ido muy bien en el trabajo.** Trabaja **más horas que nunca**, pero **gracias a eso ha podido ahorrar mucho dinero.** Su novio **le preguntó qué planeaba hacer** con todo ese dinero, **a lo que ella no tenía respuesta** en ese momento, luego, después de pensarlo mucho, recordó que **uno de sus sueños siempre había sido viajar por el mundo.** Pensó en Francia, Italia y Portugal, países con mucha historia **que a ella le parecían muy fascinantes.**

Y así Cristina pasó las últimas tres semanas de viaje, **mañana será su último día en Portugal** y **se lleva recuerdos inolvidables.** Al fin **ha podido ver esos castillos antiguos donde la realeza vivía hace siglos,** con una arquitectura **fuera de este mundo.** En las fotos que tomó, **es casi imposible distinguir a la gente**, todos parecen pequeños insectos **al lado de los majestuosos castillos.** Por un momento vivió **aquella fantasía que tenía de pequeña**, se sintió como **una princesa de cuentos de hadas** con **esos collares y anillos de oro extravagantes.** En su viaje a Lisboa, Cristina también **ha podido probar platos deliciosos de comida marina.** Cristina **no acostumbra comer cosas tan exóticas,** pero decidió hacerlo **porque sabía que se arrepentiría si no lo hacía.** Ha probado los **camarones, pulpos y almejas** en varios restaurantes del área. **Si tuviese que elegir** su favorito, **ella escogería** el restaurante que queda **a dos cuadras del lugar donde se está quedando,** un lugar muy **acogedor que lo atiende una señora mayor muy dulce que a Cristina le recuerda a su abuela.**

Aunque al principio **el plan era que el novio de Cristina la acompañara,** al final **no pudo** porque **tenía que trabajar,** así que **Cristina emprendió este viaje sola.** A pesar de eso, ella no se arrepiente. **Ella ha tenido la oportunidad de conocer** a personas muy interesantes, como unas **chicas de Alemania que hablaban un poco de español.** Una de ellas era una chica muy alta **que había venido a Lisboa a buscar inspiración para una novela que estaba escribiendo.** Cristina pasó tres días con ellas, y la escritora **le hacía todo tipo de preguntas, parecía fascinada con todo lo que Cristina tenía para decir.** También conoció a **una pareja de recién casados** que estaban en Portugal por su **luna de miel. Las circunstancias de cómo se conocieron** fueron bastante inusuales, el chico le habló a Cristina porque pensaba que era su hermana, **lo que a Cristina le pareció extraño** y por un momento pensó que era **alguna estrategia para robarla** o algo por el estilo, pero el chico **le enseñó unas fotos** a Cristina, y efectivamente **la hermana del chico se parecía mucho a ella.** Después del suceso tan extraño, Cristina **almorzó con ellos**, pero era difícil comunicarse porque los chicos no hablaban español, solo un poco de inglés.

Por desgracia **no todo ha sido color de rosa** en este viaje. Cristina **se ha quedado** en siete lugares distintos **a lo largo de su viaje** en Portugal, y en el único sitio donde tuvo problemas fue en un hotel, que la verdad fue un poco costoso. En su segundo día de estadía en el hotel, Cristina perdió su **secador de pelo** y algunos euros que tenía en la **maleta**, **lo cual reportó a los encargados del hotel** y ellos no hicieron nada, solo le dijeron que **ellos no se harían responsables de sus pérdidas**. Cristina **supone que la responsable fue la mucama** que entró a limpiar su cuarto **cuando ella no se encontraba en el hotel**. Pero **dejando eso de lado**, la experiencia ha sido muy **enriquecedora** para Cristina y piensa continuar viajando tanto como pueda.

Resumen

El sueño de Cristina siempre ha sido viajar por el mundo y ahora que trabaja en una empresa donde tiene un buen salario, puede darse la oportunidad de hacerlo. Ella escoge Portugal como su primer destino y la ha pasado muy bien allí, especialmente en Lisboa, donde visita algunos castillos majestuosos y conoce a varias personas interesantes. No todo fue perfecto en esta aventura, pero fue una experiencia muy enriquecedora.

Summary

Cristina's dream has always been traveling around the world and now that she works at a company where she has a good salary, she can have a chance to do that. She chooses Portugal as her first destination and has had a great time there, especially in Lisbon, where she visits some majestic castles and meets several interesting people. Not everything was perfect in this adventure, but it was a very rewarding experience.

Glosario – Glossary

Le ha ido muy bien en el trabajo: things have been going great for her at work

Más horas que nunca: more hours than ever

Gracias a eso: thanks to that

Ha podido ahorrar mucho dinero: she has been able to save a lot of money

Le preguntó qué planeaba hacer: he asked her what she was planning to do

A lo que ella no tenía respuesta: to which she had no answer

Uno de sus sueños siempre había sido viajar por el mundo: one of her dreams had always been to travel around the world

Que a ella le parecían muy fascinantes: which she found so fascinating

Mañana será su último día en Portugal: tomorrow will be her last day in Portugal

Se lleva recuerdos inolvidables: she's taking unforgettable memories with her

Ha podido ver esos castillos antiguos: she has been able to see those old castles

Donde la realeza vivía hace siglos: where the royalty lived centuries ago

Fuera de este mundo: out of this world

Es casi imposible distinguir a la gente: it's almost impossible to distinguish the people

Aquella fantasía que tenía de pequeña: that fantasy she had as a little girl

Una princesa de cuentos de hadas: a princess from fairy tales

Esos collares y anillos de oro extravagantes: those extravagant gold necklaces and rings

Ha podido probar todo tipo de platos de comida marina: she has been able to try all kinds of seafood dishes

No acostumbra a comer cosas tan exóticas: she's not used to eating exotic things

Porque sabía que se arrepentiría si no lo hacía: because she knew she would regret it if she didn't

Camarones, pulpos y almejas: shrimp, octopus and clam

Si tuviese que elegir: if she had to choose

Escogería: she would pick

A dos cuadras del lugar donde se está quedando: two blocks away from the place she's staying

Acogedor: cozy

Que lo atiende una señora mayor muy dulce: which is run by a sweet old lady

Que a Cristina le recuerda a su abuela: who reminds Cristina of her grandmother

El plan era que el novio de Cristina la acompañara: the plan was for Cristina's boyfriend to go with her

No pudo: he couldn't

Tenía que trabajar: he had to work

Cristina emprendió en este viaje ella sola: Cristina embarked on this trip alone

Ella ha tenido la oportunidad de conocer: she has had the opportunity to meet

Chicas de Alemania que hablaban un poco de español: girls from Germany who spoke a little Spanish

Que había venido a Lisboa: who had come to Lisbon

A buscar inspiración para una novela que estaba escribiendo: to search for inspiration for the novel she was writing

Le hacía todo tipo de preguntas: she made her all kinds of questions

Fascinada con todo lo que Cristina tenía para decir: fascinated with everything Cristina had to say

Una pareja de recién casados: a couple of newlyweds

Luna de miel: Honeymoon

Las circunstancias de cómo se conocieron: the circumstances of how they met

A Cristina le pareció extraño: Cristina found strange

Alguna estrategia para robarla: some strategy to rob her

Algo por el estilo: something like that

Le enseñó unas fotos: he showed her some pictures

La hermana del chico se parecía a ella: the guy's sister looked like her

Almorzó con ellos: she had lunch with them

No todo ha sido color de rosas: it hasn't all been peaches and cream

Se ha quedado: she has stayed

A lo largo de su viaje: throughout her journey

Secador de pelo: hairdryer

Maleta: suitcase

Lo cual reportó a los encargados del hotel: which she reported to the hotel managers

No se harían responsable de sus pérdidas: they wouldn't take responsibility for her lost item

Supone que la responsable fue la mucama: she assumes the responsable was the housekeeper

Cuando ella no se encontraba en el hotel: when she wasn't in the hotel

Dejando eso de lado: leaving that aside

La experiencia ha sido enriquecedora: the experience has been rewarding

Ejercicio 1

Contesta las siguientes preguntas – answer the following questions

1- **¿Qué ha podido hacer ella gracias a su trabajo?** – what has she been able to do thanks to her job?

_____

2- **¿Cuánto tiempo ha estado de viaje?** – how long has she been on her trip?

_____

3- **¿A qué parte de Portugal fue ella?** – what part of Portugal did she go to?

_____

4- **¿Qué comida ha probado en Portugal?** – why food has she tried in Portugal?

_____

5- **¿Cómo era la persona que atendía el restaurante?** – what was the person who ran the restaurant like?

_____

6- **¿A qué vino la chica alemana a Portugal?** – what did the German girl come to Portugal to do?

_____

7- **¿Cómo ella conoció a la pareja de recién casados?** – how did she meet the newlyweds?

_____

8- **¿Por qué era difícil hablar con ellos?** – why was it difficult to talk to them?

_____

9- **¿Qué sucedió en el hotel?** – what happened in the hotel?

_____

10- **¿Qué hicieron los encargados del hotel?** – what did the hotel managers do?

Ejercicio 2

Elige entre "verdadero" o "falso" – choose "true" or "false"

1- **Ella piensa que Portugal es fascinante.** – She thinks Portugal is fascinating.

2- **Ella siempre come cosas exóticas.** – She always eats exotic food.

3- **El restaurante queda a 1 kilómetro.** – The restaurant is 1 kilometer away.

4- **Cristina viajó sola.** – Cristina traveled by herself.

5- **Ella conoció a dos chicas rusas.** – She met two Russian girls.

6- **La chica era profesora.** – The girl was a teacher.

7- **Cristina se parece a la hermana del chico.** – Cristina looks like the guy's sister.

8- **Cristina cena con ellos.** – Cristina has dinner with them.

9- **Cristina se ha quedado en cinco lugares diferentes.** – Cristina has stayed in five different places.

10- **Los encargados del hotel no hicieron nada por ella.** – The hotel managers didn't do anything for her.

Respuestas – Answers

Ejercicio 1

1- Cristina ha podido ahorrar mucho dinero con su nuevo trabajo y gracias a eso puede viajar.

2- Cristina ha estado de viaje por tres semanas.

3- Cristina fue a Lisboa.

4- Cristina ha probado comida marina como camarones, pulpo y almejas.

5- La persona que atendía el restaurante era una señora mayor muy dulce que a Cristina le recordaba a su abuela.

6- La chica alemana vino a Portugal a buscar inspiración para la novela que está escribiendo.

7- Ella conoció a la pareja de recién casados ya que el chico le habló a Cristina porque pensaba que era su hermana que se parece mucho a ella.

8- Era difícil hablar con ellos porque no hablaban español, solo un poco de inglés.

9- En el hotel Cristina perdió su secador de pelo y algo de dinero que tenía en la maleta, ella cree que fue robado.

10- Los encargados del hotel no hicieron nada, solo le dijeron que ellos no se harían responsables de sus pérdidas.

Ejercicio 2

1- Verdadero

2- Falso

3- Falso

4- Verdadero

5- Falso

6- Falso

7- Verdadero

8- Falso

9- Falso

10- Verdadero

Puntos clave — Key takeaways

- When we're talking about something that started happening in the past and continues in the present, we can use the present perfect tense.

- The present perfect is formed with the present conjugation of *haber* and a verb in its past participle form, *Yo he viajado*, as in (I have traveled).

- The use of this tense is usually regional, meaning some Spanish speaking countries don't use it as often since there are other constructions and structures in Spanish with the same end.

In the next chapter, you will read about Tomás and how hard it is for him to say goodbye to one of his closest friends. We will be covering structures similar to the present perfect tense.

Chapter 7: La despedida – The farewell

❧

El dolor de la separación no es nada comparado con la alegría de reunirse de nuevo.

- Charles Dickens

Gerardo es uno de los mejores amigos de Tomás, los dos han **sido amigos por más de diez años**. Gerardo no habla mucho de Venezuela, el país de donde viene, Tomás no sabe por qué pero piensa que **quizás sea porque le da tristeza pensar en su país** y en **su familia que dejó allá**. Tomás ha conocido a los padres de Gerardo, también a algunos de sus primos y a su abuelo. Cada vez que Tomás va a casa de Gerardo lo reciben con mucho cariño y siempre le ofrecen comida, mucha comida, la mamá de Gerardo cocina delicioso. Hace un par de años, en el cumpleaños de Gerardo, su mamá preparó una lasaña deliciosa, **tan exquisita** que Tomás **no la ha olvidado hasta el día de hoy**.

Gerardo **ha podido estudiar** y prepararse en la ciudad de Bogotá, pero encontrar trabajo **no ha sido nada fácil**. Ha **tenido muchos problemas** ya que a veces **quieren aprovecharse de él por ser inmigrante, le quieren pagar menos** o **no le quieren dar ciertos beneficios** que otros trabajadores de la empresa sí tienen. Una vez, cuando trabajaba en Computers Inc, a todos en la empresa les dieron un **bono navideño** y él fue el único que no recibió nada, y cuando **confrontó** a su jefe, el hombre le dijo que **podía renunciar si quería**, que **había muchos candidatos disponibles** y listos **para tomar su puesto de trabajo**. Gerardo **renunció apenas encontró un mejor trabajo**. Por suerte con los años encontró un buen trabajo en una empresa **donde lo tratan bien** y tiene los mismos beneficios que el resto, **hace dos años trabaja como programador** en Future Technologies.

El año pasado Gerardo conoció a una chica llamada Valeria en una fiesta de la compañía, ella es programadora como él, pero trabajaba en un piso diferente y **por eso nunca la veía. Desde ese día se volvieron** buenos amigos y ahora **tienen seis meses de novios. Se nota que están muy enamorados**, por eso **decidieron mudarse juntos** a España.

La semana pasada Gerardo le contó a Tomás y a **sus amigos más cercanos** que se iba con Valeria a España porque **a ella le habían ofrecido un trabajo** y **él no quería que la relación terminara**. Tomás **sabía que algo le preocupaba a Gerardo, llevaba varios días actuando extraño**, pero Tomás **no se imaginaba que la noticia era que él se iría**. Tomás se siente muy feliz por su amigo, **de que pueda vivir** en un país hermoso y **que lo haga** con la persona que ama. Pero también se siente un poco triste porque **va a perder a un gran amigo**, es un sentimiento **egoísta**, pero **es lo que él siente**.

Esta noche Tomás va a ir a **la fiesta de despedida** de Gerardo. Se siente algo nervioso o quizás triste, **lleva una hora escogiendo qué ropa se va a poner** y no puede decidirse. Los amigos más cercanos de Gerardo y su familia se reúnen en su casa, hay bebidas, mucha comida y la música está a todo volumen. Todos celebran, toman fotos y cuentan historias sobre Gerardo. Gerardo les cuenta que Valeria ya está en España y que él se reunirá con ella mañana, también les muestra **un video que Valeria grabó mostrando el departamento donde vivirán** los dos. **Se hace muy tarde** y las personas comienzan a irse, se despiden de Gerardo porque **ya no lo verán más**, **el vuelo** de Gerardo sale a las 3 de la mañana. Gerardo se va a despedir de Tomás pero él le dice que **quiere acompañarlo al aeropuerto**, así que se queda con él un rato más y luego van en la camioneta del papá de Gerardo a llevarlo al aeropuerto. Tomás se despide de Gerardo con un abrazo, los dos lloran. Tomás se queda un rato más **hasta que ve despegar el avión donde va Gerardo**.

Resumen

Gerardo y Tomás han sido amigos por más de 10 años. Tomás ha conocido a muchos miembros de su familia, ha ido mucho a su casa y conoce muy bien la situación de Gerardo. Sabe que las cosas no siempre han sido fáciles para Gerardo por ser inmigrante, especialmente cuando se trata de trabajo. La noticia de la partida de Gerardo toma por sorpresa a Tomás. Pasa un rato con él en su fiesta de despedida y luego lo acompaña al aeropuerto, donde se despide de él quizás para siempre.

Summary

Gerardo and Tomás have been friends for over 10 years. Tomás has met many of his relatives, he has also gone to his house a lot and knows Gerardo's situation pretty well. He knows things haven't been so easy for Gerardo because he's an immigrant, especially when it comes to work. The news of Gerardo's departure comes as a surprise to Tomás. He spends some time with him at his farewell party, then he goes with him to the airport, where he says goodbye to him perhaps forever.

Glosario – Glossary

Han sido amigos por más de diez años: they have been friends for more than ten years

Quizás sea porque le da tristeza pensar en su país: maybe it's because it saddens him to think about his country

Su familia que dejó allá: his family that he left there

Lasaña: lasagna

Tan exquisita: so delicious

No la ha olvidado hasta el día de hoy: he hasn't forgotten about it to this day

Ha podido estudiar: he has been able to study

No ha sido nada fácil: it hasn't been easy at all

Ha tenido muchos problemas: he has had many problems

Quieren aprovecharse de él por ser inmigrante: they want to take advantage of him for being an immigrant

Le quieren pagar menos: they want to pay him less

No le quieren dar ciertos beneficios: they don't want to give him certain benefits

Bono navideño: Christmas bonus

Confrontó: confronted

Podía renunciar si quería: he could quit if he wanted to

Había muchos candidatos disponibles: there were lots of available candidates

Para tomar su puesto de trabajo: to take his job

Renunció apenas encontró un mejor trabajo: he quit as soon as he found a better job

Lo tratan bien: they treat him well

Hace dos años que trabaja como programador: he has been working as a programmer for two years

Por eso nunca la veía: that's why he never saw her

Desde ese día se volvieron: from that day on they became

Tienen seis meses de novios: they have been dating for six months

Se nota que están enamorados: you can tell they're very in love

Decidieron mudarse juntos: they decided to move in together

Sus amigos más cercanos: his closest friends

A ella le habían ofrecido un trabajo: she had been offered a job

Él no quería que la relación terminara: he didn't want the relationship to end

Sabía que algo le preocupaba a Gerardo: he knew Gerardo was worried about something

Llevaba varios días actuando raro: he had been acting strange for several days

No se imaginaba que la noticia era que él se iba: he didn't imagine that the news was that he was leaving

De que pueda vivir: that he can live

Que lo haga: that he can do it

Va a perder a un gran amigo: he's going to lose a great friend

Egoísta: selfish

Es lo que él siente: it's how he feels

La fiesta de despedida: the farewell party

Lleva una hora escogiendo qué ropa se va a poner: he has been picking an outfit for about an hour

Un video que Valeria grabó mostrando el departamento donde vivirán: a video that Valeria recorded showing the apartment they will live in

Se hace muy tarde: it gets pretty late

Ya no lo verán más: they won't see him anymore

El vuelo: the flight

Quiere acompañarlo al aeropuerto: he wants to go with him to the airport

Hasta que ve despegar el avión donde va Gerardo: until he sees the plane Gerardo is in take off

Ejercicio 1

Contesta las siguientes preguntas – answer the following questions

1- ¿Cuánto tiempo llevan Tomás y Gerardo siendo amigos? – how long have Tomás and Gerardo been friends?

_____

2- ¿Por qué quizás Gerardo no habla de su país de origen? – what's perhaps the reason Gerardo doesn't talk about his country of origin?

_____

3- ¿Qué cocinaron en el cumpleaños de Gerardo? – what did they cook on Gerardo's birthday?

_____

4- ¿Qué problemas ha tenido Gerardo? – what problems have Gerardo faced?

_____

5- ¿Qué le pasó en Computers Inc? – what happened to him in Computers Inc?

_____

6- ¿Cuánto tiempo lleva en su último trabajo? – how long has he been in his last job?

_____

7- ¿Cuánto tiempo ha estado saliendo con Valeria? – how long has he been dating Valeria?

_____

8- ¿Por qué él se va a ir España? – why is he going to Spain?

_____

9- ¿Cómo se siente Tomás? – how does Tomás feel?

_____

10- ¿A qué hora es el vuelo de Gerardo? – what time is Gerardo's flight?

_____

Ejercicio 2

Elige entre "verdadero" o "falso" – choose "true" or "false"

1- Tomás ha conocido a toda la familia de Gerardo. – Tomás has met all of Gerardo's relatives.

_____

2- Gerardo estudió en Bogotá. – Gerardo studied in Bogotá.

_____

3- Algunos han querido aprovecharse de Gerardo por ser inmigrante. – Some have wanted to take advantage of Gerardo because he's an immigrant.

_____

4- Gerardo fue despedido de Computers Inc. – Gerardo got fired from Computers Inc.

_____

5- Él conoció a Valeria en una fiesta del trabajo. – He met Valeria at a work party.

516

6- **Él está muy enamorado de Valeria.** – He's deeply in love with Valeria.

7- **A Tomás no le sorprendió la noticia.** – Tomás wasn't surprised by the news.

8- **La fiesta de Gerardo es en su casa.** – Gerardo's party is at his house.

9- **Gerardo y Valeria alquilaron una casa en España.** – Gerardo and Valeria rented a house in Spain.

10- **Tomás acompaña a Gerardo al aeropuerto.** – Tomás goes with Gerardo to the airport.

Respuestas – Answers

Ejercicio 1

1- Tomás y Gerardo han sido amigos por 10 años.

2- Quizás Gerardo no habla de su país de origen porque se siente triste al pensar en su país y la familia que dejó allá.

3- La mamá de Gerardo cocinó una lasaña deliciosa.

4- A veces quieren aprovecharse de él por ser inmigrante, le quieren pagar menos o no le quieren dar ciertos beneficios que otros trabajadores de la empresa sí tienen.

5- A todos en la empresa les dieron un bono navideño y él fue el único que no recibió nada.

6- Hace dos años que trabaja como programador en Future Technologies.

7- Gerardo tiene seis meses saliendo con Valeria.

8- Gerardo se va a ir a España porque a Valeria le ofrecieron un trabajo y él no quiere que la relación termine.

9- Tomás se siente feliz por Gerardo pero a la vez triste porque siente que va a perder a un gran amigo.

10- El vuelo de Gerardo sale a las 3 de la mañana.

Ejercicio 2

1- Falso

2- Verdadero

3- Verdadero

4- Falso

5- Verdadero

6- Verdadero

7- Falso

8- Verdadero

9- Falso

10- Verdadero

Puntos clave — Key takeaways

- We can use these constructions with *llevar, tener* and *hacer + que* the same way we would use the present perfect tense.

- These constructions have no direct translation in English, which is why we would use the present perfect tense in English as an equivalent.

- These constructions are often a bit difficult for Spanish learners to grasp because of how different they would be from their English equivalent, since the structure of the sentence is basically turned upside down. *Hace dos años que somos amigos*, is an equivalent of (We have been friends for two years).

- All of these structures place the time reference first, *Tengo días escribiendo; llevo días escribiendo; Hace días que escribo*, these would be an equivalent of (I have been writing for days)

In the next chapter, you will accompany Daniela as she struggles to find a new apartment. Keep your eyes open! We will be introducing the future simple tense.

Chapter 8: La mudanza – The move

❦

Mudan los tiempos y las voluntades; se muda el ser, se muda la confianza; el mundo se compone de mudanza tomando siempre nuevas calidades.

- Luís de Camões

Daniela **vive con sus dos compañeras de piso desde hace más de tres años** porque **los alquileres** en la ciudad son muy costosos. Para ella, tener compañeros de piso, **en parte** tiene sus **ventajas**, no solo porque **gasta menos dinero** en el alquiler y los servicios como el agua o el internet, **sino** que también tiene compañía. Aunque a veces a Daniela **le gustaría tener más privacidad**, ella **no está segura de cómo sería su vida si viviera sola, quizás sería mucho mejor**, pero **puede que no, puede que con el tiempo extrañe** a sus compañeras.

El mes que viene a Daniela y a sus compañeras **se les terminará el contrato** del departamento donde viven en el barrio Belgrano. Raquel y ella **tenían intenciones de renovar el contrato** por tres años más, pero su otra compañera, Martina, les dijo que ella **no quería seguir viviendo en esa parte de la ciudad** y que **se iba a mudar con su novio**. Eso tomó por sorpresa a Raquel y Daniela, por unos días **pensaron en buscar** a una nueva compañera **para compartir los gastos**, pero **al final** tomaron una decisión distinta.

—**Yo quiero seguir viviendo contigo** —le dijo Raquel cuando tomaban la decisión.

—Yo también —respondió Daniela.

Así comenzó la búsqueda de un nuevo departamento **para solo ellas dos**. Buscaron en varias páginas web y encontraron tres departamentos **que les gustaron**. El primero quedaba en el sur, afuera de la ciudad, pero bastante cerca de la estación de metro. Era un lindo departamento, muy amplio y con bastante iluminación, a un precio accesible, pero **lo descartaron** por la distancia, ya que ambas trabajan en la ciudad y sabían que con el tiempo **se volvería un problema** llegar a casa. El segundo departamento quedaba en Palermo, a un poco más de 20 cuadras de su actual departamento. Tenía tres habitaciones y **venía con muebles** y una televisión. A las chicas **les pareció un poco raro el precio**, el alquiler **estaba demasiado barato para la zona donde se encontraba** el departamento, su tamaño y las cosas con las que venía, después el dueño les explicó que **hace rato que él quería alquilar el departamento pero nadie concretaba el contrato con él**. A las chicas les encantó tanto el departamento que decidieron alquilarlo, pero por desgracia, **el día que iban a firmar** el contrato con el dueño, él las contactó y les dijo que ya había firmado contrato con otras personas.

Raquel y Daniela **estaban desilusionadas, ya se habían hecho a la idea de que vivirían ahí**, hasta tenían el dinero en mano. El tercer departamento al que fueron era más pequeño que los otros dos, estaba todo pintado de blanco y solo venía con un mueble verde que estaba **en buen estado** y una nevera totalmente funcional, **había una habitación para cada una** y el baño era amplio. **La**

dueña del departamento era una **señora mayor** muy amable, y **les dijo que lo pensaran unos días y tomarán una decisión.**

Las chicas lo pensaron seriamente toda la noche, el departamento quedaba enr el centro de la ciudad, muy cerca del trabajo de Daniela, el alquiler no era tan barato como el de los otros dos departamentos, pero casi todos **los otros que ellas habían visto** tenían los mismos precios. Al día siguiente firmaron contrato con la dueña y comenzaron a planear **lo que pasará el día que se muden.** Daniela **irá** al otro departamento para limpiar un poco, mientras Raquel va en el **camión de la mudanza** con las cosas. Ese día **las dos comerán** en un restaurante de comida italiana para celebrar, y brindarán **con una botella de vino.** Ese es su plan, no están seguras de **si las cosas pasarán como ellas quieren,** pero **aceptarán lo que venga** con optimismo.

Resumen

Cuando la compañera de piso de Daniela y Raquel les dice que se irá a vivir con su novio a otro lado, ellas se encuentran con la necesidad de buscar un nuevo lugar donde vivir. Buscan un departamento que a ambas les guste y terminan con tres opciones. Descartan el primer departamento, el segundo se lo alquilan a otra persona, así que el tercero parece ser la mejor opción. Las chicas planean todo lo que harán el día de la mudanza con la esperanza de que todo salga bien ese día.

Summary

When Daniela and Raquel's roommate tells them she will go live with her boyfriend someplace else, they find themselves having to find a new place to live. They look for an apartment they both like and end up with three options. They rule out the first apartment, the second one gets rented to someone else, so the third one seems like the best option. The girls plan everything they will do the day of the moving with hopes that everything goes great that day.

Glosario – Glossary

Vive con sus compañeras de piso desde hace más de tres años: she has been living with her roommates for more than three years

Los alquileres: the rent

En parte: partly

Ventajas: advantages

Gasta menos dinero: she spends less money

Sino: but

Le gustaría tener más privacidad: she would like to have more privacy

No está segura de cómo sería su vida si viviera sola: she's not sure what her life would be like if she lived alone

Quizás sería mucho mejor: maybe it would be much better

Puede que no: it might not

Puede que con el tiempo extrañe: with time she might miss

El mes que viene: next month

Se les terminará el contrato: their contract will end

Tenían la intención de renovar el contrato: they had the intention of renewing the contract

No quería seguir viviendo en esa parte de la ciudad: she didn't want to keep living in that part of the city

Se iba a mudar con su novio: she was going to move with her boyfriend

Pensaron en buscar: they thought about looking for

Para compartir los gastos: to share the expenses

Al final: in the end

Yo quiero seguir viviendo contigo: I want to keep living with you

Así comenzó la búsqueda: that's how the search started

Para solo ellas dos: for just the two of them

Que les gustaron: that they liked

Lo descartaron: they ruled it out

Se volvería un problema: it would become a problem

Actual: current

Venía con muebles: it came with furniture

Les pareció un poco raro el precio: the price seemed a bit odd to them

Estaba demasiado barato para la zona donde se encontraba: it was too cheap for the area where it was located

Hace rato que él quería alquilar el departamento pero nadie concretaba el contrato con él: he had been wanted to rent the apartment for a while but no one wanted to close the contract with him

El día que iban a firmar: the day they were going to sign

Estaban desilusionadas: they were disappointed

Ya se habían hecho a la idea de que vivirían ahí: they had already gotten used to the idea that they would live there

En buen estado: in good condition

Había una habitación para cada una: there was a room for each of them

La dueña del departamento: the owner of the apartment

Señora mayor: an old lady

Les dijo que lo pensaran unos días y tomarán una decisión: she told them to think about it for a few days and make a decision

Los otros que ellas habían visto: the other ones they had seen

Lo que pasará el día que se muden: what will happen the day they move

Irá: she will go

Camión de la mudanza: moving truck

Las dos comerán: they will both eat

Brindarán con una botella de vino: they will cheer with a bottle of wine

Si las cosas pasarán como ellas quieren: if things will happen the way they want

Aceptarán lo que venga: they will accept whatever comes

Ejercicio 1

Contesta las siguientes preguntas – answer the following questions

1- **¿Desde hace cuánto que Raquel y Martina son sus compañeras de piso?** – how long have Raquel and Martina been her roommates?

_____

2- **¿Qué es lo bueno de tener compañeras de piso?** – what's good about having roommates?

_____

3- **¿Cuándo terminará su contrato?** – when's their contract coming to an end?

_____

4- **¿Por qué se muda Martina?** – why is Martina moving?

_____

5- **¿Por qué descartaron el primer departamento?** – why did they rule out the first apartment?

_____

6- **¿Por qué era raro lo barato que era el segundo departamento?** – why was it weird how cheap the second apartment was?

_____

7- **¿Qué sucedió cuando iban a firmar el contrato?** – what happened when they were going to sign the contract?

_____

8- **¿Cómo era el tercer departamento?** – what was the third apartment like?

_____

9- **¿Cuál era el departamento con el alquiler más costoso de los tres?** – what was the apartment with the most expensive rent of the three?

_____

10- **¿Cómo celebrarán el día que se muden?** – how will they celebrate the day they move?

_____

Ejercicio 2

Elige entre "verdadero" o "falso" – choose "true" or "false"

1- **Los alquileres en la ciudad son costosos.** – The renting prices in the city are high.

_____

2- **A ella le gustaría tener privacidad.** – She would like to have some privacy.

3- **Ella no quería vivir más en ese departamento.** – She didn't want to live in that apartment anymore.

4- **El primer departamento queda al este.** – The first apartment is to the east.

5- **El segundo departamento queda en Belgrano.** – The second apartment is in Belgrano.

6- **Hace rato que el dueño quería alquilar el departamento.** – The owner had wanted to rent the apartment for a while.

7- **El tercer departamento es el más grande.** – The third apartment is the largest.

8- **La dueña les rebajó el precio del alquiler.** – The owner lowered the rent.

9- **El departamento no tiene muebles.** The apartment has no furniture.

10- **Ellas firmaron el contrato al día siguiente.** – They signed the contract the next day.

Respuestas – Answers

Ejercicio 1

1- Raquel y Martina han sido sus compañeras de piso por tres años.

2- Las ventajas de tener compañeras de piso es que gastas menos en el alquiler y otros servicios, y además tienes compañía.

3- El contrato se les vence el mes que viene.

4- Martina se muda porque no quiere vivir más en esa parte de la ciudad y se va a mudar con su novio.

5- Descartaron el primer departamento porque queda lejos de la ciudad.

6- Era raro lo barato que era el segundo departamento por la zona en dondc quedaba y las cosas con las que venía.

7- Cuando iban a firmar el contrato, el dueño las contactó para avisarles que ya había firmado contrato con alguien más.

8- El tercer departamento era más pequeño que los otros dos, estaba pintado de blanco y venía con un mueble verde y una nevera, habían dos habitaciones y el baño era amplio.

9- El tercer departamento era el más costoso de los tres.

10- Las chicas celebrarán el día que se muden comiendo en un restaurante de comida italiana y brindando con una botella de vino.

Ejercicio 2

1- Verdadero

2- Verdadero

3- Falso

4- Falso

5- Falso

6- Verdadero

7- Falso

8- Falso

9- Falso

10- Verdadero

Puntos clave — Key takeaways

- *Vivirán* and *comerán* are examples of the future simple tense in Spanish.

- Though the future simple is a fairly used tense, it often sounds more natural to use the simple present tense with a future meaning in Spanish, as in *Esta noche nos vemos*, instead of *Esta noche nos veremos*.

- The future simple tense often feels too formal or a bit over the top for native speakers, so try to use it in a context where you think it fits.

In the next chapter, you will accompany Marisol as she makes one of the hardest decisions in her career. We will be learning more about the simple future.

Chapter 9: Mis metas – My goals

Siempre estoy haciendo cosas que no puedo hacer. Así es como consigo hacerlas.

- Pablo Picasso

Marisol trabaja como escritora en una revista llamada La Mirada **desde** el año 2007. A ella le gusta trabajar ahí, **se lleva muy bien con todos** y **ha aprendido** mucho en **ese puesto todos estos años**, pero últimamente **se ha estado sintiendo insatisfecha**, y se siente **algo tonta** por eso. Tiene un trabajo **estable con el que puede mantenerse a sí misma** y, lo que es más importante aún, a sus hijos, es mucho más de lo que tienen otras personas.

Pero después de 15 años en la misma compañía, **haciendo el mismo trabajo** todos los días, Marisol siente que **no tiene nada más que aprender** en La Mirada. Su sueño en la universidad era convertirse en editora **algún día**, pero ella sabe que en esta revista eso es imposible porque **ese puesto lo tiene su jefa** Jasmine, que es la hija del **dueño de la empresa. Tampoco ganará más dinero** en su puesto actual, **a este paso, las cosas seguirán iguales** por **el resto de su vida, todos los días serán iguales** y Marisol **se sentirá cada vez peor**.

El martes Marisol va a una cita con su dentista y en la tarde **se reúne con** su hermana a tomar un café y le explica su situación.

–**¿Te sientes aburrida o qué?** –pregunta su hermana.

–Es más que eso, siento que ahí **no tengo oportunidad de crecer**.

–Pero **te costó mucho tener** un trabajo estable como escritora, ¿no?

–Sí, pero **ya no me llena**, quiero **un reto** más grande.

–**¿Hablaste con tu jefa?**

–Sí, y me dijo que **estaba contenta con mi trabajo**, pero que básicamente era lo único que podía hacer en la empresa. Y sé que es un trabajo estable y me gusta.

–Pero quieres ser una editora, ¿no? **¿Has pensado en trabajar** en otro lugar?

–Sí.

El 10 de agosto, Marisol **tendrá una entrevista de trabajo** en una de las revistas más importantes del país. **Hace muchos años que ella no va a una entrevista de trabajo,** así que está muy nerviosa, pero **ella confía** en sus habilidades y experiencia, así que **sabe que todo saldrá bien**. De igual manera, Marisol **se preparará** para la entrevista, **investigará el mercado laboral** del momento y **cuánto podría exigir como sueldo**.

Si las cosas salen como Marisol quiere, todo cambiará en su casa, ya que ella **tendrá que trabajar** más horas y **no podrá estar en casa** con sus hijos todo el tiempo. Marisol **tendrá que**

contratar a una niñera para que se quede con sus hijos hasta que ella llegue a casa, aunque mientras tanto ella sabe que cuenta con su hermana para que se haga cargo de sus hijos. Marisol tendrá que hacer **algunos sacrificios**, pero ella **está dispuesta a hacerlo, no solo por ella sino por sus hijos**. **Si Marisol consigue el trabajo** de editora **ganará** mucho más dinero, **lo cual significa que podrá invertir** más dinero en **la educación de sus hijos, podrá inscribirlos en una escuela privada** con mejores profesores. También **podrá llevarlos de viaje** más seguido. Ella **está segura** que a sus hijos les encanta viajar pero **no le dicen nada a ella** porque saben que en este momento no tiene el dinero para esos **lujos**. Esta noche Marisol **le prenderá una vela a la Virgen** y **rezará para que la ilumine** y **todo salga bien** mientras entra en **esta nueva etapa de su vida**.

Resumen

Marisol se siente insatisfecha en este punto de su vida, piensa en todos los años que lleva trabajando como escritora en la revista La Mirada, y en el hecho de que no tiene oportunidad de crecer más en la compañía. Su sueño siempre fue ser editora, pero eso no es posible en la empresa en la que trabaja actualmente. Luego de hablar con su hermana y poner las cosas en perspectiva, Marisol decide buscar empleo en otro lugar donde pueda explorar todo su potencial.

Summary

Marisol feels dissatisfied at this point in her life. She thinks about all the years she has been working as a writer in the magazine *La Mirada*, and the fact that she has no opportunity to grow more in the company. Her dream has always been to be an editor, but that's not possible in the company she currently works at. After talking to her sister and putting things into perspective, Marisol decides to look for a job in a place where she can explore her full potential.

Glosario – Glossary

Desde: since

Se lleva muy bien con todos: she gets along well with everybody

Ha aprendido: she has learned

Ese puesto: that position

Todos estos años: all these years

Se ha estado sintiendo insatisfecha: she has been feeling dissatisfied

Algo tonta: somewhat silly

Estable: stable

Con el que puede mantenerse a sí misma: with which she can support herself

Haciendo el mismo trabajo: doing the same work

No tiene nada que aprender: she has nothing else to learn

Algún día: some day

Ese puesto lo tiene su jefa: that position belongs to her boss

El dueño de la empresa: the owner of the company

Tampoco ganará más dinero: she's not going to earn more money either

A este paso: at this rate

Las cosas seguirán iguales: things will stay the same

El resto de su vida: the rest of her life

Todos los días serán iguales: every day will be the same

Se sentirá cada vez peor: she will feel worse as time goes on

Se reúne con: she meets with

¿Te sientes aburrida o qué?: do you feel bored or what?

No tengo oportunidad de crecer: I don't have the opportunity to grow

Te costó mucho tener: it was hard for you to have

Ya no me llena: it's not fulfilling for me anymore

Un reto: a challenge

Estaba contenta con mi trabajo: she was happy with my work

¿Has pensado en trabajar...?: have you thought about working...?

El 10 de agosto: on August 10th

Tendrá una entrevista de trabajo: she's going to have a job interview

Hace muchos años que ella no tiene una entrevista de trabajo: it has been many years since she last had a job interview

Ella confía: she trusts

Sabe que todo saldrá bien: she knows everything will go well

Se preparará: she will prepare herself

Investigará el mercado laboral: she will do research about the labor market

Cuánto podría exigir como sueldo: how much she could ask as salary

Si las cosas salen como Marisol quiere: if things go the way Marisol wants

Todo cambiará: everything will change

Tendrá que trabajar: she will have to work

Mientras tanto: in the meantime

Ella sabe que cuenta con su hermana para que se haga cargo de sus hijos: she knows she can count on her sister to take care of her kids

Tendrá que contratar una niñera para que se quede con sus hijos hasta que ella llegue a casa: she will have to hire a nanny to stay with her kids until she gets home

Algunos sacrificios: some sacrifices

Está dispuesta a hacerlo: she is willing to do it

No solo por ella sino por sus hijos: not only for her but for her kids

Si Marisol consigue el trabajo: if Marisol gets the job

Ganará: she will earn

Lo cual significa que podrá invertir: which means she will be able to invest

La educación de sus hijos: her kids' education

Podrá inscribirlos en una escuela privada: she will be able to enroll them in a private school

Podrá llevarlos de viaje: she will be able to take them on trips

Está segura: she is sure

No le dicen nada: they don't say anything to her

Lujos: luxuries

Le prenderá una vela a la Virgen: she will light a candle in the Virgen's name

Rezará para que la ilumine: she will pray for her to shine her light upon her

Todo salga bien: everything goes well

Esta nueva etapa de su vida: this new stage of her life

Ejercicio 1

Contesta las siguientes preguntas – answer the following questions

1- **¿Desde qué año Marisol trabaja en La Mirada?** – since what year has Marisol been working at La Mirada?

_____

2- **¿Cómo se ha estado sintiendo últimamente?** – how has she been feeling lately?

_____

3- **¿Cuál era su sueño en la universidad?** – what was her dream at college?

_____

4- **¿Quién es Jasmine?** – who is Jasmine?

_____

5- **¿Qué hace Marisol el martes?** – what does Marisol do on Tuesday?

_____

6- **¿Cuándo es su entrevista de trabajo?** – when's her job interview?

_____

7- **¿Cómo se prepara Marisol para la entrevista?** – how does Marisol prepare for the interview?

_____

8- **¿Cómo cambiarán las cosas en casa para ella?** – how will things change at home for her?

_____

9- **¿Con quién cuenta para cuidar de sus hijos mientras tanto?** – who can she count on to take care of her kids in the meantime?

_____

10- **¿Qué hará Marisol esta noche?** – what's Marisol going to do tonight?

Ejercicio 2

Elige entre "verdadero" o "falso" – choose "true" or "false"

1- **Ella se lleva bien con sus compañeros.** – She gets along well with her coworkers.

2- **Su trabajo actual es inestable.** – Her current job is unstable.

3- **Ella teme que todos sus días sean iguales por el resto de su vida.** – She fears that all her days will be the same for the rest of her life.

4- **Su hermana le dijo que no renunciara.** – Her sister told her not to quit.

5- **Ella tiene una entrevista en un periódico importante.** – She has an interview with an important newspaper.

6- **Ella siente que todo saldrá mal.** – She feels like everything will go wrong.

7- **Marisol trabajará más horas.** – Marisol will work more hours.

8- **Su esposo se quedará con los niños.** – Her husband will stay with the kids.

9- **Ella invertirá en la educación de sus hijos.** – She will invest in her kids education.

10- **Ella le prenderá una vela a Jesús.** – She will light a candle in Jesús' name.

Respuestas — Answers

Ejercicio 1

1- Marisol trabaja en La Mirada desde el año 2007.

2- Marisol se ha estado sintiendo insatisfecha últimamente.

3- Su sueño en la universidad era ser editora algún día.

4- Jasmine es su jefa, la editora de la revista y la hija del dueño de la compañía.

5- El martes Marisol va a su cita con el dentista y en la tarde se reúne con su hermana a tomar café.

6- La entrevista de Marisol es el 10 de agosto.

7- Marisol se prepara para su entrevista investigando el mercado laboral y cuánto podría exigir como salario.

8- Si Marisol obtiene el puesto, ya no podrá pasar tanto tiempo en casa con sus hijos.

9- Marisol cuenta con su hermana para que cuide de sus hijos cuando ella no puede.

10- Esta noche Marisol le prenderá una vela a la Virgen y pedirá que la ilumine.

Ejercicio 2

1- Verdadero

2- Falso

3- Verdadero

4- Falso

5- Falso

6- Falso

7- Verdadero

8- Falso

9- Verdadero

10- Falso

Puntos clave — Key takeaways

- *Seré, tendrá* and *podrá* are examples of irregular-verb conjugations in the future simple tense.

- Keep in mind that the fact a verb might be irregular in a tense such as the indefinite preterite, it doesn't necessarily mean it is the same case in every other tense.

- A common use of the future simple tense in Spanish is when you are trying to guess something, often phrased as a question, *¿Dónde estará mi celular?, ¿Cuántos gatos tendrá María?*, as in, (Where in the world is my phone?), (I wonder how many cats María has.)

In the next chapter, you will go alongside Tomás to one of the strangest stores he's ever been to. Stay focused! We will be introducing the passive "se".

Chapter 10: La extraña tienda – The odd store

La falta de dinero es la raíz de todo mal.

- Mark Twain

Tomás **lleva estudiando cine por un poco más de dos años**, su universidad es una de las mejores del país y **por ende** es una de las más caras. **Desde el principio** sus padres **se comprometieron a cubrir todos sus gastos**, pero en los últimos meses los padres de Tomás **han tenido gastos considerables. Las tuberías del baño** se dañaron y **tuvieron que gastar bastante dinero para repararlas.** El abuelo de Tomás también estuvo muy enfermo y las **citas del cardiólogo**, más los análisis y los medicamentos fueron **sumamente costosos.** Es por eso que los padres de Tomás le dijeron que **es muy probable que no tengan el dinero para pagarle el siguiente semestre** en la universidad. Tomás sintió mucha **rabia hacia sus padres** al principio, pero **luego de reflexionar** se dio cuenta de que esta situación **no era culpa de sus padres**, ellos **querían apoyarlo** como siempre, solo que **no estaban pasando por un buen momento económicamente.**

Si Tomás no quiere perder un semestre de clases, **tendrá que conseguir el dinero por su cuenta.**

Tomás **nunca ha tenido la necesidad de trabajar**, es muy afortunado en ese aspecto porque **así puede dedicar su tiempo a sus estudios.** Pensó que quizás podría buscar trabajo **como cajero en algún supermercado**, o tal vez como mesonero en un restaurante, lo malo es que esos trabajos son muy **demandantes** y **tendría que pasar muchas horas ahí. Es una lástima** que todavía sea muy **principiante** en su carrera y **no pueda usar lo que ha aprendido para ganar dinero** en el área. Luego de pensarlo un poco, **llegó a la conclusión** de que **lo mejor era que vendiera algunas de sus pertenencias.** Fue a casa de sus padres y buscó en su antigua habitación **qué podía vender.** Encontró una laptop algo vieja que funcionaba a la perfección, **solo que ya no la utilizaba**; también algo de **ropa de la que podría deshacerse**; unas **cadenas de oro que no se ponía desde** que era adolescente.

Puso un anuncio en **una página de venta de computadoras usadas** para ver si alguien estaba interesado en su laptop, después buscó algún lugar donde pudiera vender las cadenas de oro. A unas cuadras encontró una tienda llamada El Paraíso donde **parecía que vendían curiosidades**, así que fue a visitarla. Afuera de la tienda **había un cartel que decía "Se compra oro"** en letras grandes, entró caminando lentamente, observando todo tipo de cosas inusuales. Había un teléfono muy antiguo que parecía de oro y **tenía la forma de un hueso humano**, no sabía si era hermoso o un poco **escalofriante.** También había una lámpara con unas **estatuillas** de ángeles en la base. Había varias curiosidades como esas que **se veían costosas**, y otras de materiales como plástico, como un reloj con forma de gato con la cola como **péndulo**.

–**¿En qué te puedo ayudar?** –dijo un hombre con el cabello totalmente blanco.

Tomás actuó **como si el hombre no lo hubiese asustado**: Sí, compran oro, ¿no?

–Así es.

Tomás le mostró las cadenas al hombre y él las observó con **una lupa**.

–**Son de 14 quilates, las tengo desde que era pequeño.**

–**¿Por qué las vendes?**

–Necesito el dinero para pagar mi universidad.

–Una razón válida.

A la izquierda había un pasillo largo y había un cartel que decía **"Se reparan celulares"**.

–¿También reparan celulares aquí? –preguntó Tomás.

–Sí. ¿Por qué, te parece inusual?

–Un poco, sí.

En el mismo pasillo vio otro cartel que decía **"Se alquilan trajes"**.

–**¿Hasta alquilan trajes?**

–No, ya no. Antes sí.

–Es una persona con muchos talentos.

–O de muchos intereses –respondió el hombre.

Tomás sonrió pensando en lo inusual que era encontrar una tienda en **donde hicieran tantas cosas**. El hombre escribió en un papel **cuánto le pagaría por** las cadenas de oro y Tomás **intentó disimular su sorpresa, no se imaginaba** que esas cadenas **podían costar** tanto dinero. **Tendría lo suficiente como para pagar el semestre** de la universidad y parte del siguiente. **Antes de acceder a vender** las cadenas, Tomás investigó un poco el valor del oro **para asegurarse de que no lo estaban estafando**, aunque **era algo que debería haber hecho antes**. El precio parecía el adecuado así que aceptó y el hombre le entregó el dinero en efectivo.

Antes de irse, le preguntó cuánto costaba el reloj con forma de gato y lo compró porque le parecía un buen regalo de cumpleaños para **una amiga que cumpliría años** la próxima semana.

Resumen

Cuando los padres de Tomás le dicen que no tienen el dinero para pagar su universidad el siguiente semestre, él se ve en la necesidad de conseguir el dinero por su cuenta y rápido. Piensa en buscar un trabajo, pero luego de revisar su antigua habitación en la casa de sus padres, encuentra algunas cosas que ya no utiliza y que podría vender. Es así como Tomás termina en un tienda un poco inusual en donde al final consigue el dinero suficiente para poder continuar con sus estudios.

Summary

When Tomas' parents tell him that they don't have the money to pay for his university next semester, he finds himself having to get the money on his own, and fast. He thinks about looking for a job, but after checking his old room at his parents' house, he finds some items he doesn't use anymore and that he could sell. That's how he ends up in an odd store where he finally gets enough money to be able to continue with his studies.

Glosario – Glossary

Lleva estudiando cine por más de dos años: he has been studying film for over two years

Por ende: thus

Desde el principio: from the beginning

Se comprometieron a cubrir sus gastos: they promised they would cover all his expenses

Han tenido gastos considerables: they have had considerable expenses

Las tuberías del baño: the bathroom pipes

Tuvieron que gastar bastante dinero para repararlas: they had to spend a lot of money to repair them

Citas del cardiólogo: the cardiologist appointments

Sumamente costosa: extremely expensive

Es probable que no tengan dinero para pagarle el siguiente semestre: they probably don't have the money to pay for his next semester

Rabia hacia sus padres: anger towards his parents

Luego de reflexionar: after some reflection

No era culpa de sus padres: it wasn't his parents' fault

Querían apoyarlo: they wanted to support him

No estaban pasando por un buen momento económicamente: they weren't going through a good situation financially

Tendrá que conseguir el dinero por su cuenta: he will have to get the money on his own

Nunca ha tenido la necesidad de trabajar: he has never had the need to work

Así puede dedicar su tiempo a sus estudios: that way he can dedicate his time to his studies

Como cajero en algún supermercado: as a cashier in a supermarket

Demandantes: demanding

Tendría que pasar muchas horas ahí: he would have to spend many hours there

Es una lástima: it's a shame

Principiante: beginner

No pueda usar lo que ha aprendido para ganar dinero: he can't use what he has learned to make money

Llegó a la conclusión: he came to the conclusion

Lo mejor era que vendiera algunas de sus pertenencias: the best thing to do was to sell some of his belongings

Qué podía vender: what he could sell

Solo que ya no la utilizaba: he just didn't use it anymore

Ropa de la que podría deshacerse: clothes he could get rid of

Cadenas de oro que no se ponía desde: gold chains he had not worn since

Puso un anuncio: he put up an ad

Una página de venta de computadoras usadas: a website where they sold used computers

Parecía que vendían curiosidades: it seemed like they sold curiosities

Había un cartel que decía: there was a sign that said

Se compra oro: we buy gold

Tenía la forma de un hueso humano: it had the shape of a human bone

Escalofriante: creepy

Estatuilla: little statues

Se veían costosas: they looked expensive

Péndulo: pendulum

¿En qué te puedo ayudar?: what can I help you with?

Como si el hombre no lo hubiese asustado: as if the man had not scared him

Una lupa: a magnifying glass

Son de 14 quilates: they are 14 carats

Las tengo desde que era pequeño: I have had them since I was little

¿Por qué las vendes?: why are you selling them?

Se reparan celulares: we repair phones/phone repair

Se alquilan trajes: we rent suits

¿Hasta alquilan trajes?: you even rent suits?

Donde hicieran tantas cosas: where they did so many things

Cuánto le pagaría por: how much he would pay him for

Intentó disimular su sorpresa: he tried to hide his surprise

No se imaginaba: he did not imagine

Podían costar: they could cost

Tendría lo suficiente como para pagar el semestre: he would have enough to pay for his semester

Antes de acceder a vender: before agreeing to sell

Para asegurarse de que no lo estaban estafando: to make sure he wasn't being scammed

Antes de irse: before he left

Era algo que debería haber hecho antes: it was something he should have done before

Una amiga que cumpliría años: a friend that would have her birthday

Ejercicio 1

Contesta las siguientes preguntas – answer the following questions

1- **¿Por qué su universidad es tan cara?** – why is his university so expensive?

_____

2- **¿Por qué sus padres no pueden pagarle el semestre?** – why can't his parents pay for his semester?

_____

3- **¿Cómo se sintió Tomás?** – how did Tomás feel?

_____

4- **¿Dónde ha trabajado antes Tomás?** – where has Tomás worked at before?

_____

5- **¿Por qué es Tomás afortunado?** – why is Tomás lucky?

_____

6- **¿Qué encontró él en su antigua habitación?** – what did he find in his old room?

_____

7- **¿Qué había afuera de la tienda?** – what was there outside the store?

_____

8- **¿Cómo era el teléfono?** – what was the telephone like?

_____

9- **¿Cómo son las cadenas de Tomás?** – what are Tomás' chains like?

_____

10- **¿Qué compró Tomás de la tienda?** – what did Tomás buy from the store?

_____

Ejercicio 2

Elige entre "verdadero" o "falso" – choose "true" or "false"

1- **Sus padres gastaron dinero en las tuberías del baño.** – His parents spent some money on the bathroom pipes.

_____

2- **Su abuelo fue al dermatólogo.** – His grandpa went to the dermatologist.

_____

3- **Tomás culpa a sus padres de todo.** – Tomás blames his parents for everything.

4- **Él decidió vender sus cosas en vez de trabajar.** – He decided to sell his things instead of working.

5- **Tomás no se pone sus cadenas desde que era un niño.** – Tomás hasn't worn his chains since he was a kid.

6- **Puso un anuncio en una página web.** – He put up an ad on a website.

7- **La lámpara tenía estatuillas de perros.** – The lamp has little statues of dogs.

8- **El reloj de gato era de plástico.** – The cat clock was made of plastic.

9- **En la tienda también alquilan trajes.** – They also rent suits at the store.

10- **Él aún necesita dinero para pagar el semestre.** – He still needs some money to pay for the semester.

Respuestas – Answers

Ejercicio 1

1- La universidad de Tomás es así de cara porque es una de las mejores universidades de cine del país.

2- Sus padres no pueden pagarle la universidad este semestre porque han tenido gastos muy considerables últimamente.

3- Tomás sintió mucha rabia hacia sus padres al principio, pero luego entendió que no era su culpa.

4- Tomás no ha trabajado antes.

5- Tomás es muy afortunado porque no ha tenido la necesidad de trabajar y puede dedicar su tiempo a sus estudios.

6- Tomás encontró una laptop algo vieja, algo de ropa de la que se podía deshacer y unas cadenas de oro que no se ponía desde hace mucho.

7- Afuera de la tienda había un cartel que decía "Se compra oro" en letras grandes.

8- El teléfono parecía de oro y tenía la forma de un hueso humano.

9- Las cadenas de Tomás son de oro de 14 quilates.

10- Tomás compró un reloj con forma de gato como regalo de cumpleaños para una amiga.

Ejercicio 2

1- Verdadero

2- Falso

3- Falso

4- Verdadero

5- Falso

6- Verdadero

7- Falso

8- Verdadero

9- Falso

10- Falso

Puntos clave — Key takeaways

- The passive "se" is a passive structure and as such the subject is not mentioned because it's either unknown or irrelevant.

- We see tons of examples of the passive "se" in signs of advertising services, as in, *Se reparan celulares*, (We repair phones/phone repair).

- The passive "se" is also common in want ads or other types of announcements: *Se busca mesera con experiencia*; *Se venden carros*, as in (Wanted: waitress with experience); (Cars for sale).

In the next chapter, you will read about Daniela's time at a party where she loses her purse and has to do the impossible to get it back. Don't miss your chance to learn about indefinite pronouns because we'll be covering those.

Chapter 11: La cartera perdida – The lost purse

❧

La pérdida no es nada más que el cambio, y el cambio es el deleite de la naturaleza.

- Marco Aurelio

Daniela estaba muy emocionada por la fiesta de Ricardo, un compañero del trabajo que **tiene fama de celebrar sus cumpleaños por todo lo alto**. Ella necesitaba distraerse, últimamente **su vida solo se trataba de** su trabajo o de reparar cosas en su nuevo departamento, así que **le hacía mucha ilusión una noche para bailar y tomar** y **no pensar en nada más**. La fiesta era en la casa enorme de una **tía ricachona** de Ricardo, quedaba fuera de la ciudad, en una calle **rodeada** de otras casas iguales de hermosas, con una piscina y una **vista al lago**. Daniela pensó en **lo bien que se la debe de pasar en esta casa** en el verano, de momento **hacía un poco de frío como para meterse al agua**. Daniela se sentó en una mesa junto a Paula, **una compañera de trabajo que le caía bien**, y dos **chicos que no conocía**.

–¿Te puedo recomendar un cuba libre o un daiquiri? –dijo el chico que preparaba **los tragos**.

–**Dame cualquiera** –dijo Daniela.

Daniela se tomaba su cóctel mientras Ricardo hablaba por el micrófono, **agradeciéndoles a todos por venir**, luego **pusieron música** y todos se fueron a bailar. Daniela y Paula **se turnaban bailando**, así **una bailaba y la otra cuidaba las carteras**, lo hicieron así varias veces **hasta pasadas las 2 de la mañana** cuando Daniela vio que Paula bailaba cuando **era su turno** de quedarse en la mesa con las carteras. Daniela le preguntó dónde estaban sus cosas y **ella le dijo que no se preocupara**, que **se las había dejado a** uno de los chicos en la mesa, pero cuando las dos volvieron a la mesa **no había nadie**.

Paula **estaba tan apenada que se le quitó lo ebria** al instante, **le pidió disculpas** a Daniela y **le dijo que la ayudaría a encontrar** su cartera. Intentaron recordar información sobre el chico que estaba en la mesa con ellas pero no sabían su nombre, ni si su cabello era castaño oscuro o negro, no estaban muy seguras. Daniela **se puso a llorar** en el momento **de la angustia** y Paula no entendía por qué esa cartera era tan importante, así que **tuvo que confesarle** que en uno de los bolsillos de la cartera, había guardado unos aretes muy costosos **que su prima le había prestado** para la fiesta, eran muy pesados así que Daniela **prefirió guardarlos en su cartera para no perderlos** mientras bailaba.

Paula **se sentía aún más culpable** y fue a preguntarle a uno de los hombres de seguridad si tenía una lista de las personas en la fiesta, y buscó entre los nombres de los que estaban en su mesa **a ver si alguien le parecía familiar. Habían muchos, se tardó un par de minutos en leerlos todos**,

541

y **el único que le llamó la atención** fue Francisco, a Daniela también le parecía que **ese podía ser** el chico y **regresaron a buscarlo entre la gente**, **le preguntaron a varios si lo conocían**, pero **nadie sabía quién era**, excepto Ricardo. Él les dijo que **se había ido hace unos minutos** y les dio la dirección de su departamento.

Daniela **no se iba a rendir**. Tomaron un taxi hasta la casa de Francisco y **tocaron la puerta** hasta que un chico que no era Francisco **salió a ver quién era**, **se frotaba los ojos como si se acabara de despertar**. Les dijo que Francisco no estaba, que **se había ido** a la casa de su novia en un taxi. Las chicas **pensaban que él mentía** y **sin su permiso**, pasaron al departamento y llamaron el nombre de Francisco varias veces, pero el departamento estaba completamente vacío. Estaban apenadas así que le explicaron la situación al chico y luego de hablar unos minutos, él **accedió a darles la dirección** de la casa de la novia de Francisco.

Eran casi las 4 de la mañana y Daniela **se estaba quedando dormida** en el taxi, lo cual era raro porque también **le dolía la cabeza**, no sabía si era **por lo que había tomado** o **por todo el estrés de la situación en la que se había metido**. Tenía que encontrar a Francisco, tenía que encontrar esos aretes.

Tocaron el timbre por al menos cinco minutos **antes de que saliera Francisco**. Se les quedó viendo un momento **hasta que las reconoció** y **les preguntó a qué habían venido**. Francisco se sintió muy apenado y les dijo que **sí recordaba la cartera**, pero que **estaba tan ebrio que se la llevó con él** en el taxi, buscó unos minutos entre sus cosas en la sala, y luego fue a su cuarto. La novia de Francisco fue a la cocina a preparar algo de café y le dio una taza a cada una. Francisco **no encontró la cartera en ningún lado**, les dijo que **lo más probable era que la dejara en el taxi**, así que lo llamó **delante de ellas**. El hombre que manejaba el taxi le dijo que **sí había dejado** una cartera en el asiento y que en menos de una hora **podía pasar a dejarles la cartera**.

El cielo se aclaraba un poco y los cuatro tomaron café con unas tostadas que había preparado la novia de Francisco. A los minutos llegó el hombre con la cartera y luego de revisar los bolsillos y ver que los aretes estaban ahí, Daniela **sintió que al fin podía respirar**. En ese momento pensó que **había aprendido una nueva lección**, **nunca más pediría joyería cara prestada**.

Resumen

Daniela va a la fiesta de su amigo Ricardo esperando pasarla muy bien tomando y bailando toda la noche, se turna con su amiga Paula para cuidar sus cosas, pero en un descuido de Paula la cartera de Daniela desaparece. Preocupada por algo que se encuentra en la cartera, Daniela se pasa el resto de la fiesta intentando ver dónde está su cartera. Paula la acompaña a buscarla a la dirección de la persona que posiblemente la tiene, esperando que se la devuelvan.

Summary

Daniela goes to Ricardo's party hoping to have a great time drinking and dancing all night. She takes turns with her friend Paula to watch their things, but when Paula isn't paying attention Daniela's purse disappears. Worried about an item inside the purse, Daniela spends the rest of the party trying to find where her purse is. Paula goes with her to look for the purse at the address of the person who possibly has it, hoping they will give it back.

Glosario – Glossary

Tiene fama de celebrar su cumpleaños por todo lo alto: he was known for celebrating his birthday to the fullest

Su vida solo se trataba de: her life was only about

Le hacía mucha ilusión una noche para bailar y tomar: she was excited about a night dancing and drinking

No pensar en más nada: not think about anything else

Tía ricachona: wealthy aunt

Rodeada: surrounded

Vista al lago: view of the lake

Lo bien que se la debe de pasar en esta casa: how good it must be to be in this house

Hacía un poco de frío como para meterse al agua: it was a little cold to get in the water

Una compañera del trabajo que le caía bien: a coworker she liked

Chicos que no conocía: guys she didn't know

Los tragos: the drinks

Dame cualquiera: give me any

Agradeciéndoles a todos por venir: thanking everyone for coming

Pusieron música: they played the music

Se turnaban bailando: they took turns dancing

Una bailaba y la otra cuidaba las carteras: one of them would dance and the other would watch the purses

Hasta pasadas las 2 de la mañana: until after 2 in the morning

Era su turno: it was her turn

Ella le dijo que no se preocupara: she told her not to worry

Se las había dejado a: she had left them to

No había nadie: there was no one there

Estaba tan apenada que se le quitó lo ebria: she was so ashamed that she became sober

Le pidió disculpas: she apologized

Le dijo que la ayudaría a encontrar: she told her she would help her find

Se puso a llorar: she started crying

De la angustia: out of worry

Tuvo que confesarle: she had to confess

Su prima le había prestado: her cousin had lent her

Prefirió guardarlos en su cartera para no perderlos: she preferred to put them in her purse as not to lose them

Se sentía aún más culpable: she felt even more guilty

A ver si alguno le parecía familiar: to see if any of them seemed familiar

Habían muchos: there were many

Se tardó un par de minutos en leerlos todos: it took her a couple of minutes to read them all

El único que le llamó la atención: the only one that stood out to her

Ese podría ser: that could be

Regresaron a buscarlo entre la gente: they came back to look for him among the people

Le preguntaron a varios si lo conocían: they asked some if they knew him

Nadie sabía quién era: no one knew who he was

Se había ido hace unos minutos: he had left a few minutes ago

No se iba a rendir: she wasn't going to give up

Tocaron la puerta: they knocked on the door

Salió a ver quién era: he came out to see who it was

Se estrujaba los ojos: he was rubbing his eyes

Como si se acaba de despertar: as if he had just been woken up

Se había ido: he had left

Pensaban que él mentía: they thought he was lying

Sin su permiso: without his permission

Accedió a darles la dirección: he agreed to give them the address

Se estaba quedando dormida: she was falling asleep

Le dolía la cabeza: she had a headache

Por lo que había tomado: because of what she had drunk

Por todo el estrés de la situación en la que se había metido: because of all the stress of the situation she had gotten herself into

Tocaron el timbre: they rang the bell

Antes de que saliera Francisco: before Francisco came out

Hasta que las reconoció: until he recognized them

Les preguntó a qué habían venido: he asked them why they had come

Sí recordaba la cartera: he did remember the purse

Estaba tan ebrio que se la llevó con él: he was so drunk that he took it with him

No encontró la cartera en ningún lado:he could not find the purse anywhere

Lo más probable era que la dejó en el taxi: he most likely left it in the taxi

Delante de ellas: in front of them

Sí había dejado: he had indeed left

Podía pasar a dejarles la cartera: he could go give them the purse

El cielo se aclaraba un poco: the sky was getting brighter

Sintió que al fin podía respirar: she felt like she could finally breathe

Había aprendido una nueva lección: she had learned a new lesson

Nunca más pediría prestada joyería cara: she would never again borrow expensive jewelry

Ejercicio 1

Contesta las siguientes preguntas – answer the following questions

1- **¿Por qué necesitaba distraerse?** – why did she need some time to relax?

_____

2- **¿Cómo era la casa?** – what was the house like?

_____

3- **¿Con quién se sentó Daniela?** – who did Daniela sit with?

_____

4- **¿Por qué Daniela y Paula se turnaban bailando?** – why did Daniela and Paula take turns dancing?

_____

5- **¿Qué confesó Daniela?** – what did Daniela confess?

_____

6- **¿Qué hizo Ricardo?** – what did Ricardo do?

_____

7- **¿Quién estaba en casa de Francisco?** – who was at Francisco's place?

_____

8- **¿Por qué a Daniela le dolía la cabeza?** – why did Daniela have a headache?

_____

9- **¿Cómo reaccionó Francisco al verlas?** – how did Francisco react when he saw them?

_____

10- **¿Dónde estaba la cartera y cómo terminó ahí?** – where was the purse and how did it end up there?

_____

Ejercicio 2

Elige entre "verdadero" o "falso" – choose "true" or "false"

1- **Celebraron en la casa del tío de Ricardo.** – They celebrated at Ricardo's uncle's house.

_____

2- **Había otras casas hermosas alrededor.** – There were other beautiful houses around.

_____

3- **Paula no le caía muy bien.** – She didn't like Paula that much.

_____

4- **Paula dejó la cartera en el baño.** – Paula left the purse in the bathroom.

_____

5- **Daniela había dejado dinero en su cartera.** – Daniela had left money in her purse.

_____

6- **Casi nadie conocía a Francisco.** – Almost no one knew Francisco.

_____

7- **Francisco no estaba en su departamento.** – Francisco wasn't at his apartment.

_____

8- **Él estaba en casa de su novia.** – He was at his girlfriend's house.

_____

9- **La novia de Francisco llamó a la policía.** – Francisco's girlfriend called the police.

_____

10- **Daniela recuperó su cartera.** – Daniela got her purse back.

_____

Respuestas – Answers

Ejercicio 1

1- Daniela necesitaba distraerse porque su vida últimamente se había tratado solo sobre su trabajo y cosas que reparar en su nuevo departamento.

2- La casa es enorme, con piscina y vista al lago.

3- Daniela se sentó con Paula, una compañera de trabajo, y dos chicos que no conocía.

4- Porque así una bailaba y la otra se quedaba cuidando las carteras.

5- Daniela confesó que en uno de los bolsillos de la cartera, había guardado unos aretes muy costosos que su prima le había prestado para la fiesta.

6- Ricardo les dijo que Francisco se había ido hace unos minutos y les dio la dirección de su departamento.

7- En casa de Francisco se encontraba un chico, su compañero de piso.

8- Daniela no sabía si le dolía la cabeza por lo que había tomado o por todo el estrés de la situación en la que se había metido.

9- Francisco se les quedó viendo un momento hasta que las reconoció y les preguntó a qué habían venido.

10- Francisco estaba tan ebrio que cuando se fue se llevó la cartera de Daniela y sin querer la dejó en el taxi.

Ejercicio 2

1- Falso

2- Verdadero

3- Falso

4- Falso

5- Falso

6- Verdadero

7- Verdadero

8- Verdadero

9- Falso

10- Verdadero

Puntos clave — Key takeaways

- *Nadie*, *nada* and *muchos* are examples of indefinite pronouns.
- Indefinite pronouns may be the kinds of words that go under the radar; we use them to substitute a noun which is unknown, was previously mentioned or is implicit. An example would be: *Hay varios*, (There are several).

- Notice how in *Hay varios* we don't mention the noun, since the pronoun *varios* is substituting said noun, which in this short example is unknown. In normal conversations, there's usually a context of what these pronouns are substituting.

In the next chapter, you will hold Daniela's hand as she embarks on a romantic story with a foreign guy. Keep your eyes open for the common idiomatic phrases you'll encounter along the way.

Chapter 12: Un alma libre – A free soul

❧

Cada poema es único. En cada obra late, con mayor o menor grado, toda la poesía. Cada lector busca algo en el poema. Y no es insólito que lo encuentre. Ya lo llevaba adentro.

- Octavio Paz

Un par de meses atrás, Daniela **se inscribió en un curso de inglés con la finalidad de** aprender el idioma y **hacer nuevos amigos**. A ella le gusta conocer gente nueva, pero **no le gusta hacerlo de manera virtual**, prefiere conectar con las personas frente a frente, por eso le pareció que hacer un curso era la mejor opción para ella. Hasta ahora ha conocido a un grupo de personas que **le caen muy bien** y de vez en cuando después de clases van por un café o a dar una vuelta por el centro comercial que queda cerca. Esta vez quedaron en organizar **una salida a un bar**, algo nocturno, más aventurero. A Daniela le sorprendió un poco al principio que **sus compañeros hubieran elegido** ese plan, **pues** algunos de ellos tienen entre 50 y 60 años, y pensó que **no estarían interesados en ese tipo de cosas**. Estaba muy equivocada. Muchos de ellos tienen vidas más activas que ella. Ahí Daniela comenzó a **replantearse** todas esas pequeñas **creencias que fue construyendo con el pasar de los años**.

Estaban en un bar por la zona de San Telmo, con las **luces tenues** y un poco de música **de fondo**, pero aún así **los dejaba hablar cómodamente**. Conversaron un poco sobre su profesor actual del curso y **lo malhumorado que es, en eso todos estaban de acuerdo**, el hombre necesitaba encontrar una manera de alegrarse, no entendían cómo podía **estar de mal humor** todas las clases. **Pidieron una ronda de cervezas** y **unas papitas fritas con queso y tocino** que **estaban como para chuparse los dedos**.

Daniela se levantó para ir al baño **dando pasos lentos**, no porque el alcohol ya **estaba haciendo efecto**, sino porque tenía puesto unos tacones muy altos que **le estaban matando los pies**. En un momento **se resbaló** y **se agarró del brazo de un chico para no caerse**, le pidió disculpas al instante y **siguió su camino al baño**. Cuando salió del baño, **camino a su mesa**, el mismo chico de hace un momento le preguntó si estaba bien. Le dijo que sí y **comenzaron a charlar en la barra**. Su nombre era Théo, era francés y tenía un acento muy hermoso cuando hablaba español, a veces también hablaba en inglés porque **se le hacía más fácil, lo que a Daniela le encantaba** porque así ella también **podía practicar** y **poner a prueba lo que había aprendido en clases**. Hablaron unos veinte minutos y luego Daniela se despidió del chico para volver a la mesa con sus compañeros, pero antes de irse le dio su número a Théo, quizás fue algo impulsivo, pero **parte de ella creía que él no la iba a llamar**.

Daniela **la pasó genial** el resto de la noche, pero a eso de las 3 de la mañana ya **tenía sueño** así que pidió un taxi y al llegar a casa **fue directo a la cama**. La mañana siguiente, mientras desayunaba unas tostadas, recibió un mensaje de Théo. Él **le dio los buenos días** y le preguntó si le gustaba la poesía. **Hacía mucho tiempo que Daniela no leía un libro de poesía**, pero le dijo que sí.

A eso de las 6 de la tarde Daniela se encontró con Théo en una plaza en San Telmo, a solo unas cuadras del bar **donde se habían conocido**. Caminaron hasta una casa bastante antigua y **pintoresca**, con las paredes pintadas de colores vibrantes, había una pequeña cafetería donde solo vendían café y té. **Hicieron la cola** aunque solo tomó unos minutos. Los dos pidieron café y **luego del primer sorbo**, Daniela **no quería tomar más**, le parecía que **le hacía falta más azúcar**. Entraron a un salón inmenso donde se reunía la gente. Había algunas sillas y **un cartel que animaba a la gente a leer su poesía**, parecía que la idea era **estar de pie** y mirar al pequeño escenario en la esquina que tenía un micrófono. **Uno a uno fueron pasando las personas** a leer un poema, **en su mayoría eran en español**, pero algunos leyeron en inglés, francés, italiano y otros idiomas que Daniela no pudo reconocer. Le preguntaron a Daniela **si quería pasar a leer** pero ella dijo que no, no solo no escribía sino que **no tenía las agallas** para leer frente a todo el mundo. Théo sí accedió a pasar a leer uno de sus poemas, estaba en francés, y aunque Daniela no entendía lo que estaba diciendo, le parecía muy hermoso todo, su tono de voz, el ritmo, **la musicalidad** de sus palabras. **Le dio un fuerte aplauso** cuando terminó y a Théo **le dio pena** y **se sonrojó**.

Se fueron caminando, agarrados de la mano, sin un destino en especial en mente, solo hablando, **escuchándose el uno al otro**. Daniela sentía una conexión muy fuerte con Théo, **como si lo conociera de toda la vida** y no desde hace menos de 24 horas. Cuando **se besaron** se sintió de nuevo como una adolescente, incluso sabiendo que era **algo que no duraría**, que en cualquier momento **Théo regresaría a Francia** y **tendría que dejarlo ir**.

Resumen

Daniela se reúne con sus compañeros de clase en un bar de San Telmo una noche, y después de unos tragos, camino al baño se tropieza con un chico y comienzan a hablar. Al rato Daniela vuelve con sus amigos pero le deja su número de teléfono al chico, aunque cree que él no la va a llamar. Para su sorpresa, él le escribe al día siguiente y hacen planes para verse. Daniela la pasa muy bien con él y siente una conexión con él que jamás ha sentido con nadie, algo tan intenso y que probablemente pronto se acabe.

Summary

Daniela gets together with her classmates in a bar in San Telmo one night, and after a few drinks, on her way to the bathroom she stumbles onto some guy and they start talking. A while later Daniela gets back to her friends but she leaves him her number, even though she thinks he's not going to call her. To her surprise, he texts her the next day and they make plans to see each other. Daniela has a great time with him and she feels a connection with him that she had never felt with anyone, something so intense and that will probably be over soon.

Glosario – Glossary

Un par de meses atrás: a couple of months ago

Se inscribió en un curso de inglés: she enrolled in an English course

Con la finalidad de: with the purpose of

Hacer nuevos amigos: to make new friends

No le gusta hacerlo de manera virtual: she doesn't like to do it virtually

Le caen muy bien: she likes a lot

Una salida a un bar: an outing to a bar

Sus compañeros hubieran elegido: her classmates had chosen

Pues: because

No estarían interesados en ese tipo de cosas: they would not be interested in those kinds of things

Replantearse: reconsider

Creencias que fue construyendo con el pasar de los años: beliefs she started building throughout the years

Luces tenues: dim lights

De fondo: in the background

Los dejaba hablar cómodamente: it let them talk comfortably

Lo malhumorado que es: how grumpy he is

En eso todos estaban de acuerdo: they all agreed on that

Estar de mal humor: to be in a bad mood

Pidieron una ronda de cervezas: they ordered a round of beers

Unas papitas fritas con queso y tocino: French fries with cheese and bacon

Estaban como para chuparse los dedos: they were finger-liking good

Dando pasos lentos: taking slow steps

Estaba haciendo efecto: it was having an effect on her

Le estaban matando los pies: they were killing her feet

Se resbaló: she tripped

Se agarró del brazo de un chico para no caerse: she held onto a guy's arm to not fall

Siguió su camino al baño: she continued her way to the bathroom

Camino a su mesa: on the way to her table

Comenzaron a charlar en la barra: they started talking at the bar

Se le hacía más fácil: it was easier for him

Lo que a Daniela le encantaba: which Daniela liked

Podía practicar: she could practice

Poner a prueba lo que había aprendido en clase: to put to the test what she had learned in class

Parte de ella creía que él no la iba a llamar: part of her thought he wasn't going to call her

La pasó genial: she had a great time

Tenía sueño: she was sleepy

Fue directo a la cama: she went straight to bed

Le dio los buenos días: he said good morning

Hacía mucho que no leía un libro de poesía: it had been a while since she last read a poetry book

Donde se habían conocido: where they had met

Pintoresca: picturesque

Hicieron la cola: they waited in line

Luego del primer sorbo: after the first sip

No quería tomar más: she didn't want to drink any more

Le hacía falta más azúcar: it needed more sugar

Un cartel que animaba a la gente a leer su poesía: a sign that encouraged people to read their poetry

Estar de pie: to be on your feet

Uno a uno: one by one

Fueron pasando las personas: people were passing

En su mayoría eran en español: most of them were in Spanish

Si quería pasar a leer: if she wanted to take a turn reading

No tenía las agallas: she didn't have the courage

La musicalidad: the musicality

Le dio un fuerte aplauso: she gave him a big round of applause

Le dio pena: he was embarrassed

Se sonrojó: he blushed

Se fueron caminando: they strolled out

Agarrados de la mano: holding hands

Sin un destino en especial en mente: without a special destination in mind

Escuchándose el uno al otro: listening to each other

Como si lo conociera de toda la vida: as if she had known him all her life

Se besaron: they kissed

Algo que no duraría: something that would not last

Théo regresaría a Francia: Théo would return to France

Tendría que dejarlo ir: she would have to let him go

Ejercicio 1

Contesta las siguientes preguntas – answer the following questions

1- **¿Por qué se inscribió en el curso de inglés?** – why did she enrolled in the English course?

_____

2- **¿Qué hacen después de clase normalmente?** – what do they normally do after class?

3- **¿Qué sorprendió a Daniela?** – what surprised Daniela?

4- **¿Sobre quién estaban hablando?** – who were they talking about?

5- **¿Qué le pasó camino al baño?** – what happened to her on her way to the bathroom?

6- **¿Qué le gustaba de hablar con Théo?** – what did she like about talking to Théo?

7- **¿Qué pasó la mañana siguiente?** – what happened the next morning?

8- **¿Cómo era la casa?** – what was the house like?

9- **¿Qué pensó de la poesía de Théo?** – what did she think about Théo's poetry?

10- **¿Qué sentía ella por Théo?** – what did she feel about Théo?

Ejercicio 2
Elige entre "verdadero" o "falso" – choose "true" or "false"

1- **Le gusta hacer amigos por Internet.** – She likes making friends on the Internet.

2- **Algunos de sus amigos son mayores que ella.** – Some of her friends are older than her.

3- **La música estaba muy alta.** – The music was really loud.

4- **La comida estaba muy rica.** – The food was really tasty.

5- **Daniela casi se cae al suelo.** – Daniela almost fell on the floor.

6- **Daniela habla francés muy bien.** – Daniela speaks French really well.

7- **Théo la llamó la mañana siguiente.** – Théo called her the next morning.

8- **Daniela no se terminó el café.** – Daniela didn't finish her coffee.

9- **Théo leyó un poema en francés.** – Théo read a poem in French.

10- **Ella cree que pueden tener una relación estable.** – She thinks they can have a stable relationship.

Respuestas – Answers

Ejercicio 1

1- Daniela se inscribió en el curso de inglés para aprender el idioma y hacer nuevos amigos ya que le gusta conocer gente cara a cara.

2- Después de clases normalmente van por un café o a dar una vuelta por el centro comercial que está cerca.

3- A Daniela le sorprendió que sus compañeros hubieran elegido ir a un bar porque ellos son un poco mayor que ella.

4- Ellos estaban hablando sobre su profesor de inglés que es un malhumorado.

5- Camino al baño, Daniela se resbaló y se agarró del brazo de un chico para no caerse, le pidió disculpas y siguió su camino.

6- A Daniela le encantaba hablar con Théo porque ella podía practicar su inglés y poner a prueba lo que había aprendido en clases.

7- La mañana siguiente Daniela recibió un mensaje de Théo donde él le daba los buenos días y le preguntó si le gustaba la poesía.

8- La casa era bastante antigua y pintoresca, con las paredes pintadas de colores vibrantes.

9- Aunque Daniela no entendía lo que Théo estaba diciendo, su poesía le parecía muy hermosa, igual que su tono de voz, el ritmo, y la musicalidad de sus palabras.

10- Daniela sentía una conexión muy fuerte con Théo, como si lo conociera de toda la vida.

Ejercicio 2

1- Falso

2- Verdadero

3- Falso

4- Verdadero

5- Verdadero

6- Falso

7- Falso

8- Verdadero

9- Verdadero

10- Falso

Puntos clave — Key takeaways

- Idiomatic expressions don't have a literal meaning. This makes them tricky to guess what they mean, because though some of them are quite simple, there are a few out there that will leave you scratching your head and going for the dictionary.

- Unless the meaning of the idiomatic expression is obvious, the best thing you can do when you stumble into a new one is look it up to make sure you understand its meaning.

- *Estar, tener, hacer* and *dar* are the verbs with more idiomatic expressions in Spanish.

In the next chapter, you will accompany Tomás in his frustration with a problematic professor at college. Stay focused, there are more common idiomatic phrases to cover!

Chapter 13: El trabajo de historia – The history paper

La verdad no está de parte de quién más grite.

- Rabindranath Tagore

Este semestre Tomás empezó a ver clases de historia. Al principio él no entendía **por qué debían tomar esa clase** si estaban en la carrera de cine, **no le parecía que tuviera mucho sentido**. Además, el profesor era **detestable**, a nadie en el salón le caía bien. Casi siempre llegaba tarde a clases, parecía que **no preparaba bien sus clases** y era muy estricto. Una vez que Tomás llegó cinco minutos tarde a un examen, el profesor **no lo dejó entrar**, le dijo que era un irresponsable por no llegar a tiempo y que **debía haberse despertado más temprano** ese día. Tomás estaba furioso, **había estudiado muy duro** para el examen y también le parecía que el profesor era un **hipócrita** porque él llegaba tarde todo el tiempo.

Esa no fue la única vez que el profesor **trató a Tomás de manera injusta**. Luego de un tiempo, Tomás empezó a **darse cuenta** de que por alguna razón el profesor **parecía tener algo en su contra**. Eran pequeños gestos, como que a veces el profesor **ignoraba sus preguntas**, o que le hacía preguntas más difíciles que al resto, **como queriendo dejarlo en ridículo** frente a los otros alumnos. Y Tomás no fue el único que se dio cuenta de esto, otros de sus compañeros **comenzaron a notarlo** también, **los comentarios que le hacía** el profesor, **la forma como a veces lo miraba**. Tomás no entendía la razón, **se la pasaba pensando qué había hecho él para que el profesor le tuviera rencor**.

Pero el día que Tomás finalmente estuvo **seguro de que el profesor lo odiaba** fue cuando **tuvieron que hacer** el trabajo de historia. Muchos de sus compañeros **hicieron el trabajo en parejas**, pero él decidió hacerlo solo, siempre prefería hacerlo así porque podía tener el control de todo. A él y a varias personas **les tocó hacer el trabajo sobre** el rey Carlos IV, Tomás se esforzó mucho en el trabajo, inclusive ayudó a algunos a investigar y escribir partes de su trabajo, ya que a él siempre **se le daban bien las palabras**, así que cuando recibió su **calificación**, no lo podía creer. **Había reprobado el trabajo**, mientras que otros **habían obtenido notas más altas**, y cuando Tomás confrontó al profesor y **le pidió explicaciones de por qué le había puesto esa nota**, el profesor evadió la pregunta y **le dijo que aceptara la calificación que había obtenido**, y que **en el futuro se preparara mejor**. Fue un momento terrible, pero quizás lo peor fue que el profesor le dijo todo eso frente a los otros alumnos, **como si buscara humillarlo**.

A los días, Tomás habló con **el presidente del consejo estudiantil para preguntarle qué podía hacer él para solucionar la situación**, y él le dijo que **él no era el único que había tenido conflictos** con ese profesor, que ellos ya **estaban enterados de los comportamientos de él** porque ya varios estudiantes **se habían quejado**, pero como **la única persona que podía hacer** algo era **el decano de la facultad**, un hombre que **muchos encontraban intimidante, nadie se atrevía** a presentar una queja. Tomás se sentía muy frustrado y **le parecía insólito** que a los del consejo estudiantil **les daba lo mismo su situación**, pero **no se iba a rendir**. Escribió una carta esa misma tarde y al día siguiente se la llevó al decano de la facultad. Él **no lo pudo atender** porque estaba en una reunión, pero Tomás dejó la carta con su secretaria. Luego de dos semanas sin respuesta, Tomás se cuestionó **si la secretaria le había entregado la carta** al decano, o quizás que al decano no le importaba. No lo sabía, pero ya **estaba harto de la incertidumbre**.

Decidido a ponerle un fin a todo, una tarde, esperó al decano de la facultad en **donde él estacionaba su auto**. El hombre **se asustó** un poco cuando lo vio, le dijo que **estaba apurado** y no tenía tiempo para hablar pero Tomás **rápidamente** le explicó la situación, su frustración, que **el profesor le estaba haciendo la vida de cuadritos** y él ya no sabía qué hacer. El hombre **se quedó callado** por un momento.

Le preguntó: **¿Tú sabes cuántos años tiene él dando clases?**

Tomás no tenía idea, pero el hombre **parecía tener 50 y tantos,** así que puede que al menos unos 20 años.

–**¿Y eso qué tiene que ver?** –preguntó Tomás.

–Es **intocable**.

Tomás **no supo qué decir** después de eso, solo observó al hombre subirse a su auto y alejarse lentamente. Toda la ilusión que tenía de resolver el problema **se hizo pedazos**. Se sentó en un banco pensando en lo increíble que era que **nadie estuviera dispuesto a ayudarlo**, lo horrible que era estar en la posición donde **alguien podía hacer lo que quisiera** y los demás se **hacían los de la vista gorda** y no le decían nada y mucho menos **lo hacían afrontar las consecuencias de sus acciones**.

Resumen

Un día Tomás comienza a tener problemas con su profesor de historia, aunque al principio él cree que quizás lo está imaginando o que exagera, pero con el pasar del tiempo es cada vez más evidente que el profesor tiene algún tipo de rencor hacia él. Incluso comienza a afectar sus calificaciones y es ahí cuando Tomás se decide a buscar ayuda, alguien que se ponga de su lado y lo solucione todo.

Summary

One day Tomás starts having problems with his history professor, although at first he thinks maybe he's imagining it or exaggerating, but with the passing of time it is obvious that the professor has some sort of resentment towards him. It even starts affecting his grades and that's when Tomás makes up his mind and looks for help, someone to be on his side that fixes everything.

Glosario – Glossary

Por qué debían tomar esa clase: why they had to take that class

No le parecía que tuviera mucho sentido: it didn't seem to make much sense to him

Detestable: hateful

No preparaba bien sus clases: he didn't prepare his classes well

No lo dejó entrar: he didn't let him in

Debía haberse despertado más temprano: he should have woken up earlier

Había estudiado muy duro: he had studied really hard

Hipócrita: hypocrite

Trató a Tomás de manera injusta: he treated Tomás unfairly

Darse cuenta: to notice

Parecía tener algo en su contra: he seemed to have something against him

Ignoraba sus preguntas: he would ignore his questions

Como queriendo dejarlo en ridículo: as if he wanted to make a fool of him

Comenzaron a notarlo: they started to notice it

Los comentarios que le hacía: the comments he would make about him

La forma como a veces lo miraba: the way he would sometimes look at him

Se la pasaba pensando qué había hecho él para que el profesor le tuviera rencor: he would often think about what he had done for the professor to hold a grudge against him

Finalmente estuvo **seguro de que el profesor lo odiaba**: he was finally sure the professor hated him

Tuvieron que hacer: they had to do

Hicieron el trabajo en parejas: they wrote the papers with a partner

Les tocó hacer el trabajo sobre: they had to write the paper about

Se le daban bien las palabras: he had a way with words

Calificación: grades

Había reprobado el trabajo: he had failed the paper

Habían obtenido notas más altas: they had gotten highest grades

Le pidió explicaciones de por qué le había puesto esa nota: he asked him for an explanation why he had gotten that grade

Le dijo que aceptara la calificación que había obtenido: he told him to accept the grade he had gotten

En el futuro se preparara mejor: to prepare better in the future

Como si buscara humillarlo: as if he was looking to humiliate him

El presidente del consejo estudiantil: the president of the student council

Para preguntarle qué podía hacer él para solucionar la situación: to ask him what he could do to solve the situation

Él no era el único que había tenido conflictos: he wasn't the only one who had conflicts

Estaban enterados de los comportamientos de él: they were aware of his behavior

Se habían quejado: they had complained

La única persona que podía hacer algo: the only person who could do something

El decano de la facultad: the dean of the faculty

Muchos encontraban intimidante: many found intimidating

Nadie se atrevía: no one dared

Le parecía insólito: he thought it was unbelievable

Les daba lo mismo su situación: they didn't care about his situation

No se iba a rendir: he wasn't going to give up

No lo pudo atender: he couldn't see him

Se cuestionó si la secretaria le había entregado la carta: he questioned if the secretary had given him the letter

Estaba harto de la incertidumbre: he was sick of the uncertainty

Decidido a ponerle fin a todo: decided to put an end to everything

Donde él estacionaba su auto: where he parked his car

Se asustó: he was scared

Estaba apurado: he was in a hurry

Rápidamente: quickly

El profesor le estaba haciendo la vida de cuadritos: the professor was making his life miserable

Se quedó callado: he stayed quiet

¿Tú sabes cuántos años tiene él dando clases?: do you know how long he has been teaching?

Parecía tener 50 y tantos: he seemed to be 50 something

¿Y eso qué tiene que ver?: what does that have to do with it?

Intocable: untouchable

No supo qué decir: he didn't know what to say

Se hizo pedazos: it was shattered

Nadie estuviera dispuesto a ayudarlo: no one was willing to help him

Alguien podía hacer lo que quisiera: someone could do whatever they wanted

Hacían los de la vista gorda: they turned a blind eye

Lo hacían afrontar las consecuencias de sus acciones: they made him face the consequences of his actions

Ejercicio 1

Contesta las siguientes preguntas – answer the following questions

1- **¿Qué no entendía Tomás?** – what didn't Tomás understand?

_____

2- **¿Cómo era el profesor de historia?** – how was the history professor like?

_____

3- **¿Qué pasó el día del examen?** – what happened on the day of the exam?

_____

4- **¿Qué notó él que el profesor hacía?** – what did he notice the professor would do?

_____

5- **¿Por qué hizo el trabajo solo?** – why did he write the paper on his own?

_____

6- **¿Qué pasó con el trabajo de historia?** – what happened with the history paper?

_____

7- **¿Qué fue lo peor de ese momento?** – what was the worst thing about that moment?

_____

8- **¿Qué le dijo el presidente del consejo estudiantil?** – what did the president of the student council say?

_____

9- **¿Dónde habló con el decano?** – where did he talk to the dean?

_____

10- **¿Qué hizo el decano por él?** – what did the dean do for him?

_____

Ejercicio 2
Elige entre "verdadero" o "falso" – choose "true" or "false"
1- **Tomás llegó 15 minutos tarde al examen.** – Tomás arrived 15 minutes late to the exam.

_____

2- **El profesor era un hipócrita.** – The professor was a hypocrite.

_____

3- **Otros notaron cómo el profesor lo trataba.** – Others noticed how the professor treated him.

_____

4- **El trabajo era sobre el rey Carlos VI.** – The paper was about the king Carlos VI.

_____

5- **Tomás recibió ayuda para escribir el trabajo.** – Tomás got help writing the paper.

_____

6- **Tomás no entregó el trabajo a tiempo.** – Tomás didn't hand in the paper on time.

_____

7- **El presidente del consejo estudiantil lo ayudó con su problema.** – The president of the student council helped him with his problem.

_____

8- **Le escribió una carta al decano de la facultad.** – He wrote a letter to the faculty's dean.

9- **El decano no contestó a su carta.** – The dean didn't reply to his letter.

10- **Despidieron al profesor de historia.** – The history professor got fired.

Respuestas – Answers

Ejercicio 1

1- Tomás no entendía por qué debían tomar una clase de historia si estaban en la carrera de cine.

2- El profesor de historia era detestable, a nadie en el salón le caía bien. Casi siempre llegaba tarde a clases, parecía que no preparaba bien sus clases y era muy estricto.

3- Tomás llegó cinco minutos tarde al examen, así que el profesor no lo dejó entrar al salón de clases y le dijo que era un irresponsable por no llegar a tiempo.

4- Tomás notó que a veces el profesor ignoraba sus preguntas, o que le hacía preguntas más difíciles que al resto, como queriendo dejarlo en ridículo.

5- Tomás prefirió hacer el trabajo solo porque así podía tener el control de todo.

6- Tomás reprobó el trabajo de historia.

7- El profesor le dijo un montón de cosas horribles frente a los otros alumnos, como si buscara humillarlo.

8- El presidente del consejo estudiantil le dijo que Tomás no era el único que había tenido conflictos con ese profesor, que ya varios estudiantes se habían quejado.

9- Tomás habló con el decano en el lugar que él estacionaba su auto.

10- El decano no hizo absolutamente nada por él, solo dijo que el profesor era intocable.

Ejercicio 2

1- Falso

2- Verdadero

3- Verdadero

4- Falso

5- Falso

6- Falso

7- Falso

8- Verdadero

9- Verdadero

10- Falso

Puntos clave — Key takeaways

- Though you don't really need to learn idiomatic expressions to speak the language properly, they may come in handy since native speakers use them in everyday conversations. In essence, they will make your Spanish sound more natural.

- People often confuse idiomatic expressions and sayings. The difference between these two is that sayings usually carry some sort of lesson or truth behind them, while idiomatic expressions don't.

- Idiomatic expressions are very different from one language to another. Some expressions may have an equivalent in the other language, while others may not.

Conclusion

Wow, you sailed through the book. Good Job; we knew you had it in you! By reading all the stories and finishing all the exercises compiled in *Learn Intermediate Spanish with Short Stories for Adults*, you can confidently say you have the skills of a B2 Spanish learner. You have learned how to use both the indefinite and the imperfect preterite, as well as the pluperfect tense. Those are some tough ones, but that didn't stop you. You also mastered the present perfect tense and similar structures Spanish speakers use every day. You even learned how to talk about future plans, and how to use the tricky impersonal "se". You learned a ton of grammar there and you probably didn't notice. If you take that plus all the vocabulary you now know, you can go out into the world and have deeper and more meaningful conversations in Spanish. You left the basics behind.

And as always, the best part of this book is you can go back to the stories whenever you want. Any time you're feeling rusty or out of practice, you can review the stories, and find comfort while reinforcing what you already know.

We know that this isn't a goodbye, but a see you soon. When you feel ready, you can go ahead and pick up the next book in our series, *Learn Advanced Spanish with Short Stories for Adults*. Plenty of more exciting and challenging stories await, stories that will take you all the way to C1, to that level of confidence in Spanish you've always wanted. See you soon!

Ready To Start Speaking Spanish?

**Inside this Complete Spanish Phrasebook
+ digital Spanish flashcards combo you'll:**

✓ **Say what you want:** learn the most common words and phrases used in Spanish, so you can express yourself clearly, the first time!

✓ **Avoid awkward fumbling:** explore core Spanish grammar principles to avoid situations where you're left blank, not knowing what to say.

✓ **Improved recall:** Confidently express yourself in Spanish by learning high-frequency verbs & conjugations - taught through fun flashcards!